DATE DUE

DEMCO 38-296

THE HISTORY OF
SOUTHERN DRAMA

THE HISTORY OF
SOUTHERN DRAMA

CHARLES S. WATSON

THE UNIVERSITY PRESS OF KENTUCKY

Publication of this volume was made possible in part by a grant from the
National Endowment for the Humanities.

Scholarly publisher for the Commonwealth,
serving Bellarmine College, Berea College, Centre
College of Kentucky, Eastern Kentucky University,
The Filson Club Historical Society, Georgetown College,
Kentucky Historical Society, Kentucky State University,
Morehead State University, Murray State University,
Northern Kentucky University, Transylvania University,
University of Kentucky, University of Louisville,
and Western Kentucky University.

Editorial and Sales Offices: The University Press of Kentucky
663 South Limestone Street, Lexington, Kentucky 40508-4008

97 98 99 00 01   5 4 3 2 1

Library of Congress Cataloging-in-Publication Data
Watson, Charles S., 1931-
  The history of southern drama / Charles S. Watson.
     p.   cm.
  Includes bibliographical references (p.) and index.
  ISBN 0-8131-2030-6
  1. American drama—Southern States—History and criticism.
  2. Southern States—In literature.   I. Title.
  PS261.W356   1997
  812.009'975—dc21   97-19456

This book is printed on acid-free recycled paper
meeting the requirements of the American National Standard
for Permanence of Paper for Printed Library materials.

Manufactured in the United States of America

To my dear son and daughter,
WHITTEN SULLIVAN WATSON
and ELLEN CURRIE WATSON

Contents

Illustrations follow page 148

Preface

When the Carolina Playmakers sponsored the Southern Regional Theatre Festival in April 1940 at Chapel Hill, North Carolina, George R.
Coffman, chair of the University of North Carolina's English Department,
called for "a comprehensive history of drama in the South" from the
beginning to the present. At that time the plays of Tennessee Williams
had not yet added luster to the subject, nor had much scholarship on
pre-1900 drama been published. Since 1940, southern drama has reached
new heights, and valuable studies have appeared—but still no overall
account. Undeniably the time is ripe for the first history of southern
drama.

When I completed my chapter on southern drama to 1900 for *A
Bibliographical Guide to the Study of Southern Literature* (1969), I too recommended a comprehensive history of the subject. Yet drama was badly
neglected in the latest survey of southern literature as a whole, *The History of Southern Literature* (1985): in a volume of 605 pages, a chapter
entitled "The Old South, 1815-1840" devotes just one paragraph to pre-
1900 drama, and the chapter on "Modern Southern Drama" discusses
only Paul Green, Lillian Hellman, and Tennessee Williams—in seven
pages.

With this book I hope to rectify that neglect of southern drama, for
the history of southern literature is incomplete without attention to it.
Certainly Tennessee Williams and Lillian Hellman have become famous
for their widely performed works. But the numerous dramatic compositions that preceded and followed those have not been enumerated and
discussed in one published study. I present a sequential development,
from the plays of Robert Munford in the 1770s to those of current dramatists such as Horton Foote and Beth Henley. The early plays have much
to tell us about southern life by highlighting the political, social, and
moral concerns of the day. Playwrights of the modern period have reflected the durability of some of those concerns and the alteration of
others. Many—particularly African American dramatists such as
Randolph Edmonds—have lent their support to such causes as the civil
rights movement.

For any category of American literature to exist as a subject for study
and enlightenment, histories must first furnish an overview. This book

ix

proposes to make known the subject of southern drama and to establish it as a valuable body of knowledge. After this material has been tasted, digested, and assimilated, scholars can speak understandably of southern drama as a significant subject which has been surveyed in its entirety. Recent surveys of American drama as a whole have provided me with the foundation for a history of southern drama. I am particularly indebted to Walter Meserve's first two volumes of a new chronicle—*An Emerging Entertainment: The Drama of the American People to 1828* (1977), and *Heralds of Promise: The Drama of the American People during the Age of Jackson, 1828-1849* (1986)—plus his invaluable bibliography, *American Drama to 1900: A Guide to Information Sources* (1980). More recently, Gary Richardson has added to our knowledge of pre-twentieth-century drama by his *American Drama from the Colonial Period Through World War I: A Critical History* (1993).

For my own history I take the approach of a literary historian, which means that I am concerned with stages of development. Southern drama has undergone a sure, if erratic, progress marked by phases of greater and lesser activity. I take note of the historical context and recognize both political and cultural issues especially before 1900. To furnish information as well as to analyze the subject matter, I observe theatrical conditions (including the difficulty of developing drama outside New York), and examine not only the work of the dramatists but pertinent facts in their lives and careers. I have included ample summaries of rare or unpublished plays whose contents would not be known otherwise.

To do all this, I make use of plays, histories, biographies, criticism, and bibliographies. I have sought to locate enough plays to represent the full achievement of each dramatist, though this was a difficult task for the early writers and even for some in the twentieth century. Using all relevant materials available, I include data on the dramas and the dramatists for the reader seeking such knowledge in one volume—a task valuable in itself, since it may lead to future discoveries in the field. From the outset my intention has been to lay the groundwork for more intensive studies by providing an overall view and by including dramatists and plays ripe for further investigation. If my readers learn new names, I will be gratified.

For the early plays, my evaluative standard is historical significance—what the play tells us about the politics, culture, and society of the times—rather than literary merit. For this reason, I examine a substantial number of unperformed plays, many of which publicize important ideas for the first time and contain more interesting material than some staged but trivial works. For the twentieth-century plays, evaluation and analysis must expand to embrace artistic merit—vitality of character portrayal, thematic excellence, quality of ideas, dramaturgical skill—as well as historical significance.

In a volume covering such a quantity of disparate material, composed over two centuries by a long line of men and women, with varied perspectives and talents, generalizations are difficult and even risky. All the same, a clear trend emerges in the nature of southern drama, that is, what really identifies a play as "southern." I argue that southern drama has changed radically in its political orientation while remaining consistent in its cultural distinctiveness. That is to say, the southern play through the Civil War years is distinguished by sectional politics, especially regarding slavery, while concurrently reflecting the region's traditions, activities, and interests; from World War I to the present, the southern play rejects the sectional or predominantly southern stand in politics, especially with regard to the racial issue, while exploring with increasing success the rich cultural resources of the South. Ironically, the normative southern play of the twentieth century has repudiated the predominant political ideology of the South but has welcomed its distinctive cultural elements with open arms. When dramatists like Paul Green, Lillian Hellman, Tennessee Williams, and Horton Foote have composed such plays with artistry, they have lifted southern drama to new heights. Awareness of political and cultural features will furnish an illuminating framework within which to analyze the most noteworthy and interesting changes in southern drama.

Looking back on the making of this book, I am deeply conscious of support from many people. This project has been a collective undertaking in the fullest sense. I wish to acknowledge with gratitude the real contribution of Jackson Bryer, University of Maryland; Walter Meserve, formerly of the City University of New York; Horton Foote of Wharton, Texas; Lawrence G. Avery, University of North Carolina; Bill J. Harbin, Louisiana State University; and Philip Kolin, University of Southern Mississippi.

Among other academic colleagues who have given me encouragement and taken a warm interest in my work, I thank Robert F. Bell and Ralph Voss, University of Alabama; Bert Hitchcock, Auburn University; James H. Justus, formerly of Indiana University; M. Thomas Inge, Randolph-Macon College; and Robert L. Phillips, Mississippi State University.

At the University of Alabama, which has generously and loyally supported my work for many years, I thank my colleagues in the Department of English, Philip D. Beidler, Claudia Johnson, Neal Lester, Sara

Desaussure Davis (chair); my drama seminar students John McLaughlin and Eliot Kahlil Wilson; and Dean James Yarbrough, College of Arts and Sciences. Further, I would like to recognize helpful colleagues in the theater: the late Marian Gallaway, director of the University of Alabama Theatre; Edmond Williams, current director, who staged an excellent production of *The Trip to Bountiful*; and Paul K. Looney, artistic director, Theatre Tuscaloosa, who directed a fine performance of *Cat on a Hot Tin Roof.*

I also acknowledge the various archives that provided so much valuable material: Paul Green Collection, Southern Historical Collection; John Hill Hewitt Collection, Emory University Library; Horton Foote Collection, DeGolyer Library, Southern Methodist University; Missouri Historical Collection, St. Louis; South Carolina Historical Society, Charleston; and Espy Williams Collection, University of Southwestern Louisiana. My heartfelt thanks go especially to the staff of the University of Alabama Library.

On a personal note, I owe lasting gratitude to my aunt, the late Dorothy Sullivan Townsend, director of the Little Theatre, Anderson, South Carolina, 1933–45; she first introduced me to the marvels of the stage and inspired in me a love of plays. And I must not fail to thank some other contributors to my sustained work: my tennis partners in Tuscaloosa, Dr. William A. Hill, and my fellow members of Covenant Presbyterian Church. Finally, I owe an inestimable debt to my wife, Juanita Goodman Watson. All responsibility for the completed work is of course my own.

Prologue:
Definitions and Preliminaries

An unknown story waits to be told. For more than two hundred years, southern Americans both white and black have chosen the literary form immortalized by Shakespeare to tell about their region. In the course of that time the South has undergone drastic changes; southern literature has reached world-class status; and southern drama has revealed the impact of nationalism, sectionalism, modern realism, the artistic standards of the Southern Literary Renascence, and the civil rights movement.

From the early nineteenth century till the end of the Civil War, the theater was above all a political platform in the South, and the distinguishing feature of southern drama was its sectional argument. One may even say that some pieces performed during the Civil War were belligerently southern. After World War I, the representation of culture increasingly enables us to classify drama as southern.

I use "culture" as T. S. Eliot defines it in *Notes towards the Definition of Culture* (1949): "All the characteristic activities and interests of a people."[1] Culture, then, embraces the attitudes, customs, and traditions of a particular people living in a particular place. Eliot was thinking primarily of the British Isles, but his observations apply equally to southern culture within the larger framework of the United States. As an exponent of cultural variety, he contends that a dynamic national culture must be a constellation of cultures whose constituents, "benefiting each other, benefit the whole." He states further that a national culture profits from the friction of its parts: just as an individual is fortunate to have the right enemy at some time in his life, so is a national culture.[2] Because of its dissenting stance, the South has frequently produced friction in American culture and has been, so to speak, its enemy. Yet this friction has contributed to the dynamism of American thought and life. Above all, southerners have criticized the uncritical glorification of business. For example, the Agrarian philosophy that originated with Thomas Jefferson and its modern versions, expounded by the Nashville school in *I'll Take My Stand* (1930), have furnished an illuminating vantage point for disagreement with the dominant business culture.[3]

1

I have found guidance in studying the cultural nature of southern drama in the massive *Encyclopedia of Southern Culture* (1989), whose editors quote approvingly from Eliot's definition of culture as "not merely the sum of several activities, but *a way of life*."[4] The volume's table of contents lists components of southern culture—Black Life, Language, Politics, Religion, Violence, and Women's Life, to name the most heuristic—which identify leading topics in southern drama as well and have helped me identify the distinguishing traits of the southern play.

I use the phrase "southern drama" to mean drama that combines southern authorship *and* subject matter. I consider as southern dramatists only those individuals who were born in the South and/or have lived a substantial part of their productive years in the South. I accept the standard definition of the South as comprising the eleven states that formed the Confederacy plus the border states of Kentucky, Maryland, and Missouri, and I concentrate on plays that dramatize the life and people of those states. In short, the bulk of southern drama, as understood in this history, is composed of plays written by southerners about the South. Infrequently, I do cover plays set outside the South *if* they are by southern dramatists; I do not, however, cover those by northern dramatists who have written sometimes famous plays set in the South—such as Marc Connelly, author of *Green Pastures* (1930)—for including such authors would confuse the subject and make the study unmanageable. Further, I do not consider plays by those well-known southern writers—such as Thomas Wolfe, Stark Young, and Carson McCullers—who made their reputations primarily in nondramatic genres. The body of material studied, therefore, is large but not without limits.

What makes a play so distinctively southern that it may be spoken of as "a southern play"? What distinguishing traits must it exhibit? The characteristics of the southern play as I define them have emerged slowly over an extended period of time, from around 1776 to 1960, when Tennessee Williams finished his major plays set in the South. Obviously, no single work will display all these elements but to be legitimately designated as southern, a play should recognizably combine some of them.

First comes the presence of one or more distinctive social types. Having appeared with such frequency in popular and serious art, these types evoke strong emotions when they enter the consciousness of both southerners and nonsoutherners. The poor white provokes amusement or suspicion; the southern belle, immortalized by Scarlett O'Hara, suggests coquetry or delusions of grandeur. The antebellum South produced one shining female paradigm, the southern lady. She may be a stereotype but, skillfully handled, has much to reveal about the culture from which she derives. In theory, if not always in fact, she was virtuous, modest, pious, and submissive; as wife, she personified self-denial. Some southern ladies, however, protested their designated roles; plantation mistresses, for instance, resented the lack of control over their reproductive systems. Many of these resentments continued after the Civil War and surfaced in such modern plays as *The Little Foxes* (1939), in which the heroine chafes over woman's exclusion from the male-dominated world of business.

Southern dramatists must know their region's character types intimately, since drama relies heavily on types. The better plays will present variations, however, allowing us to meet interesting individuals with all their idiosyncrasies. Some of the best creations deserve to be called archetypes. I reserve that accolade for the premier realizations of a particular type, such as Blanche DuBois, archetype of the southern belle as fading coquette.

The evolution of the black character is also a major feature of southern drama. Appearing only comically in the early plays, he changes to a tragic figure in the persecuted educator of Paul Green's *In Abraham's Bosom* (1926). Green (in such plays as *Potter's Field* [1931]) and others strive for realistic characterization also, at the same time protesting racial injustice and advocating reform. (Although blacks appear in northern plays, to be sure, their personalities are not so intensely studied there.) More recently, black dramatists have assumed responsibility for truthful portrayals. However sympathetic the views of whites, black writers feel they can speak more authoritatively, and indeed they introduce persons from within the black community not previously encountered in drama, as in Ted Shine's plays.

An important cultural element in many southern plays is violence. Social scientists have blamed poverty and low educational levels for violence in society, but anthropologists emphasize cultural patterns conducive to high homicide rates. Indications of southern violence have appeared in the rise of the Ku Klux Klan and its repeated revivals, the passion for violent sports such as football, and greater admiration of the military. As further evidence, the South has tended to be more supportive than the North of capital punishment, gun ownership, and corporal discipline. Violence ties the early southern drama to the modern. Nineteenth-century plays dealt with dueling and frontier lawlessness. In the twentieth century, violence became chiefly racial: for example, lynchings are found in works of both black and white dramatists. Lurid passages in the plays of Tennessee Williams have impressed southern violence on the minds of audiences, although Williams himself regarded violence as rampant in modern life generally; he said in one typical statement that he

wrote "about violence in American life only because I am not so well acquainted with the society of other countries."[5] As becomes painfully clear
in his plays, however, he is most familiar with violence in the southern
part of the United States. Though not exclusively southern, of course, it
crystallizes some of the sharpest conflicts in the region and exposes them
to searching examination. Violence in modern plays has replaced the
sectional politics of slavery as the most deplorable trait of the South.

A third recurrent trait is dependence on southern legendry, which
again links the early with the modern period. Drama's fondness for heroes owes much to the possibilities in stage portrayals, and the legendary
figures who appear regularly in southern plays reinforce the assertion
that southerners are in love with the past. The South has idolized certain
personages, such as Andrew Jackson in the early drama and Jefferson and
Lee, two southern favorites, in more recent times. Black playwrights in
the 1920s celebrated their own heroes and heroines, such as Sojourner
Truth, thus enriching their work and filling the gaps left by white dramatists.

A fourth component of the southern play is fundamentalist religion,
whose palpable force in the South has persisted longer than in regions
such as New England, well known for its religious fervor in earlier times.
In southern plays of the 1920s such as Hatcher Hughes's *Hell-Bent for
Heaven* (1924) and in later ones such as Romulus Linney's *Holy Ghosts*
(1974), religious fundamentalism constitutes the central subject. The term
"fundamentalism" does not sufficiently cover the range of religion in the
South, however; for that reason, I also use the broader term "southern
Christianity" to indicate the vigorous piety of the region. Reynolds Price
has observed astutely that "southern Christianity" is unique, capable of
assuming either a comical or "transcendental" form.[6]

The South's religious life, authentically represented in plays by Paul
Green, is distinctive in ways that parallel the region's general distinctiveness. Four patterns stand out: the Bible serves as sole reference point;
believers claim direct access to God; Christian morality is defined in terms
of personal ethics; and worship may take spontaneous forms. These patterns appear particularly in Southern Baptist churches, by far the South's
largest and most influential denomination. Also important for understanding the nature of Christianity in southern plays is the unique dominance
of evangelicalism, which sets it off from religious practices in most other
parts of the United States. Of the two central rituals in Protestant churches,
evangelicals prefer baptism over communion. This preference under-
scores their focus on conversion to a new life, exemplified by the deci-
sions to "accept" Christ which climax the revivals of Billy Graham. The

new Christians experience the saving power of Jesus Christ very intimately, dividing their lives into two phases: before and after receiving the gift of salvation.

Fifth, not to be overlooked is a highly recognizable form of speech, in which rhythms and idioms mark the language as southern. The vitalizing effect of regional speech in southern plays may be compared to the impact of the Welsh language on the poet Dylan Thomas when he wrote in English (an inspiration praised by Eliot in his discussion of culture). Phonetically transcribed dialect, which began in the decade before the Civil War and continues unabated, is more important in drama than in other genres because the accent is heard in a performance, not merely read. It signals that the play is southern and prepares audiences for subjects they have come to associate with the South. The most noticeable cases of southern speech are humorous, as is the chatter of Jessie Mae in Horton Foote's *The Trip to Bountiful* (1953); southern dramatists who handle realistic dialogue expertly often provoke laughter.

Sixth, especially in plays of the Southern Renascence, 1920–60, dramatists provide a spirited injection of late local color: that is, the cultivation of picturesque settings and subjects. Local color flourished in southern fiction and poetry in the decades after the Civil War, and in plays about the Civil War by northerners, but did not appear in southern drama until later. DuBose Heyward's exotic settings in Charleston's black neighborhoods are good examples of the conscious employment of local color, which continues in plays by both white and black dramatists to the present.

Seventh, plays of the twentieth century often evince a love-hate attitude toward the South. Before the Civil War the prevailing mood was uncritical acceptance of southern society. But by the turn of the century the critical temper had galvanized trailblazing academic journals such as the *Sewanee Review*, founded in 1892 by William Peterfield Trent, who promised free inquiry into life and literature. In 1902, John Spencer Bassett of Trinity College, later to become Duke University, established the *South Atlantic Quarterly*, calling for real social reform in the South and denouncing appeals to racial hatred. This critical spirit gathered momentum with the social critics of the 1920s, such as Howard W. Odum, and inspired the reformist dramas of Paul Green. In southern plays after 1920 one finds again and again a protest, totally absent in earlier drama, against racial injustice. Along with protests, however, there is strong sympathy for the southern people; these playwrights recognized that the South had suffered from war and was still enduring economic deprivation.

Finally, one must emphasize the revisionist nature of many southern plays. Fascinated with the different culture in the South, northern dramatists presented the first and most famous depictions of this exotic region. Before the Civil War, George Aiken staged *Uncle Tom's Cabin*, a popular adaptation of Harriet Beecher Stowe's famous 1852 novel. Southern dramatists, disagreeing with what they considered false representations of slavery, countered by showing happy slaves who became miserable only after fleeing northward. Following the war, local color plays such as *Alabama* (1890), by nonsoutherner Augustus Thomas, not only revealed defective knowledge of southern topography but also exaggerated such types as the old Confederate who could not give up the Lost Cause. These plays created a moonlight-and-magnolia atmosphere, sometimes in a perfumed theater. The corrective to this romanticized picture of the South came decisively with the realistic dramas of Paul Green. In *The House of Connelly: A Play of the Old and the New South* (1931), Green attacked the moral corruption of the landed gentry, choosing as his hero and heroine two "New Southerners": the reformed scion of a plantation estate and a progressive, hard-working girl from the tenant class.

The revisionist spirit was not confined to white dramatists in the South; even before the Civil War the determination to gain freedom expressed in the slave narratives was echoed by other black writers, contradicting scenes of slaves refusing freedom in novels by William Gilmore Simms and others. William Wells Brown, from the slaveholding state of Missouri, dramatized in *The Escape: or, A Leap for Freedom* (1858) the desire for freedom he himself had felt before fleeing northward. Much later, as the number of black dramatists increased after World War I, a movement arose to correct the stereotype of the minstrel Negro by showing real individuals known to these writers. Willis Richardson chose to depict the urban rather than the more commonly portrayed rural black. Randolph Edmonds continued the effort to record black life realistically and replace the stereotypes; his *Bad Man*, a one-act collected in *Six Plays for a Negro Theatre* (1934), extols the noble qualities of a murderer. Wishing to reach black audiences with fresh characters based on real people, Edmonds, like the new realists, aimed to report the truth about life in the South. The power of many southern plays, featuring black as well as white characters, results from the determination to set right a popularized, inaccurate view.

Two examples of the genre will clarify further what I mean by "a southern play." Judged by the traits enumerated above, both are clearly southern—but in different ways. First, *A Streetcar Named Desire* (1947) features a provocative version of the southern belle, in this case a faded one; a well-known setting with some quaint local color; recognizably southern speech but not unadulterated dialect; and finally a prominent theme of the

South's literature, the glory of the Old South. Its graciousness and decay, personified in Blanche DuBois, accentuate the complexity and ambivalence of modern southern drama. Though this play is undeniably "southern," its emphasis on the power of sexual desire is universal. It is important to recognize that the best southern plays, however regional in their cultural distinctiveness, leave provinciality far behind through their profound universality.

The second example shows the variety found in southern plays. *In Abraham's Bosom* (1926), Paul Green's best Broadway play, focuses on the urgent need for black education in the South, at the same time highlighting the tragic conflict with hostile whites. The racial subject classifies the play as southern; the dialect and types further emphasize its regional quality. Though *In Abraham's Bosom* contains more of the principal components of a southern play, Williams's work surpasses it in artistic merit.

Beyond noting the distinguishing qualities of the southern play, a history of southern drama must examine its evolution, asking how the southern play has taken shape, been refined, and gone through periods of change. I will give my answer to that question below. The evolution of the southern play informs my consideration of southern dramatists, who not only have lived their formative years in the South, but have further identified themselves as southern by composing southern plays according to the preceding traits—to a greater or lesser degree. From a historical perspective it is evident that after murky beginnings, southern drama has become more and more identifiable in the twentieth century. It acquired and refined its most distinctive traits during the great period of the New York theater from 1920 to 1960 when dramatists such as Tennessee Williams produced their highest achievements, earning a place among the greatest dramatic artists. When they enriched their plays through inspiration from great southern fiction, the southern play reached its zenith, owing not a little to William Faulkner's far-reaching impact. (As Flannery O'Connor observed dryly but truthfully, southern writers must avoid being run over by his "Dixie Express.")

Up to the time of the sectional struggle between North and South, plays by southern dramatists—such as the pageants about Revolutionary War victories in South Carolina—glorified the state. A sense of the South as a distinct section did not arise in drama until the decade before the Civil War. That conflict is not the defining event in American drama as a whole that it is in southern drama. Although Arthur Hobson Quinn in his pioneering history of American drama uses the words "Civil War" to divide his chronicle, he devotes only six pages to northern plays and only one paragraph to a southern drama performed *during* the war.[7] Southern plays, however, received their first stamp as "southern" in works celebrating Confederate victories—such as *The Guerillas* (1862) by James Dabney McCabe—produced proudly while the Confederacy was waxing. From that time on, "southern" as a descriptive term would be widely applied to plays.

Peculiar to the evolution of southern drama has been its strained relationship with New York City, the country's theatrical capital. For the first decades of the nineteenth century, southern dramatists saw their plays produced, with a few exceptions, only in local theaters of the South. Rarely performed in New York, these pieces received little national exposure. After World War I, however, during the great days of the modern New York theater, Broadway success was the dream of all, and many playwrights from the South—DuBose Heyward, Lillian Hellman, Horton Foote, and above all Tennessee Williams—strove for hits there. Learning the hard lesson of what would sell in the theatrical marketplace, they preserved artistic standards as best they could.

The demands of critics and theatergoers further exacerbated this problematic relationship with the New York theater. Southern dramatists were expected to recycle stereotypes of the South. An adaptation of Erskine Caldwell's *Tobacco Road* (1933) enjoyed a phenomenal run by regaling audiences with its humiliating depiction of southern backwardness. The preconceptions of what "southern" drama should be powerfully influenced what playwrights could offer on the altars of America's dramatic temples. Ignorance, clownishness, and violence drew big crowds, as proved by Caldwell's bumpkins.

Over the course of a century, the relationship of southern dramatists to New York has varied from good to abysmal. Disillusioned with the commercial stage, Paul Green transferred his efforts to outdoor theaters far from New York. His remarkable success led the movement in the rest of the country to stage outdoor dramas, from Texas to Ohio. Since the 1960s the centrality of Broadway has declined with the growth of off-Broadway and regional theaters such as those of Louisville and Dallas. The present decentralization represents a return to the earlier nineteenth-century pattern, when regional theaters provided opportunities for new playwrights.

Readers should note that the first chapter headings of this history refer to localities, not dramatists. Since there are no major dramatists in the early period, classification by city is appropriate, particularly for Charleston and New Orleans, the two main theatrical centers of the early South. This organization makes it possible to study a succession of plays and to compare the dramatic material in different areas. As single names begin to appear, chapters are devoted to the most prominent ones individually, permitting examination and enabling us to see the emergence of important figures, a signal advancement in the progress of any literature.

Since southern drama evolved from dubious beginnings in the eighteenth century, the wonder is that it eventually flourished in the twentieth, paralleling the literary renascence led by William Faulkner. The first southern literary talents, finding little encouragement for plays, went into fiction and poetry. William Gilmore Simms, who set southern literature in motion with his popular novels, furnished a precedent for George Washington Cable, but no comparable figure did the same for dramatists. Before the twentieth century, southerners wrote only spasmodically for the stage. Because dramatic writing requires the support of urban populations, the South's overwhelmingly rural population presented a formidable obstacle until metropolitan centers began to develop after the 1920s. Even though theatrical energy permeated Charleston and New Orleans, that activity paled in contrast to the growth of theatrical art in Philadelphia and Boston, as well as New York. In the North, dramatists established a strong tradition, beginning with Royall Tyler's *The Contrast* (1787), and continuing vigorously with such playwrights as Anna Cora Mowatt, author of *Fashion* (1845), and Clyde Fitch, who wrote popular plays about modern city life in the early twentieth century. Eugene O'Neill realized the promise of these earlier dramatists with his first masterpieces, *The Emperor Jones* (1920) and *The Hairy Ape* (1922).

The record of playwriting by southerners lacks any such progression. Although I intend no disparagement of the early dramatists whose plays unquestionably sustained southern drama during its long gestation, none attained national acclaim until Paul Green won the Pulitzer Prize for *In Abraham's Bosom* in 1926, 150 years after Robert Munford of colonial Virginia composed the first southern play. The obstacles to the growth of southern drama had been almost overwhelming, but the early plays prepared the soil and planted the seeds of its modern efflorescence.

−1−

Nationalism and Native Culture in Virginia

Dramatic writing in the South began in Virginia, where there was far less Puritan prejudice against the theater than in New England. Theatrical activity there began early; the first recorded performance of a play in America was *Ye Bar and ye Cubb,* presented by three citizens of Accomac County at Cowle's Tavern in 1665. When English acting companies toured the new settlements, Virginia was often the first destination. Lewis Hallam's company performed *The Merchant of Venice* in Williamsburg on September 15, 1752, before moving on to other colonial towns. David Douglass's popular American Company toured Virginia from 1758 to 1761 and returned to Virginia and Maryland in 1770; George Washington saw its performance of Richard Cumberland's *The West Indian* in Annapolis on October 8, 1772.[1] Reflecting attitudes toward the theater in London, Washington and other prominent Virginians attended often and, continuing the English penchant for dramatic composition, gentleman farmers and lawyers wrote spirited plays for publication, even when there was little chance of production.

Although Virginia produced no professional dramatists during this early period, men like John Daly Burk and St. George Tucker who chose the dramatic form to express their political thought were all distinguished leaders, some with impressive intellectual powers. Their dramatic ventures link them to that other Virginian of multiple talents, Thomas Jefferson. The early plays of Virginia are above all noteworthy for their superior quality of political debate, which lends special interest to the drama written during the American Revolution and the War of 1812, when Virginia was supplying the principal leaders of the new republic. The state's first dramatist, Robert Munford, differed from Boston and Philadelphia dramatists of the Revolutionary War period, who wrote partisan propaganda supporting the patriot cause. Mercy Otis Warren of Massachusetts, for example, lampooned the Tories and the oppressive British of colonial Boston in her allegorical farce *The Group* (1776), whereas

Munford, despite his support of the American Revolution, depicted the two sides impartially in *The Patriots*.

Still, the foremost inspiration for the early drama of Virginia was nationalism. From 1776 to 1840 the new nation aimed first of all to achieve unity in the face of dangers, inside and outside its boundaries. Drama, poetry, and fiction—northern and southern—did their part in advancing this purpose, as is evident in the plays of William Dunlap, the poetry of Philip Freneau, and the novels of James Fenimore Cooper and William Gilmore Simms. In Virginia the spirit of nationalism produced plays defining true patriotism, celebrating Revolutionary victories, supporting the War of 1812, and recalling the first colonists of Virginia, the spiritual ancestors of living Americans. All these works joined in lauding the ideals of a new nation, betraying not a trace of the sectionalist bias that would soon transform southern drama.

Concurrent with their nationalism, there emerges in these plays, secondarily but consistently, a picture of Virginia culture revealing the state's characteristic interests and activities. Signs of cultural consciousness already appear in the works of Robert Munford and those of George Washington Parke Custis. The former describes local politics in Virginia; the latter commemorates the legends of Washington and Pocahontas, thereby preserving the history of early Virginia, the matrix of Southern culture.

Robert Munford (c. 1737-83)

Robert Munford was a colonial American who became an exemplary citizen of the United States. To public service he added the composition of dramatic comedies, in which he articulated independent political opinions. Born in Prince George County, Virginia, he went to England in 1750 but did not stay to continue his education at an English university, as did many young Virginians. When Mecklenburg County, a semifrontier area adjacent to the North Carolina line, was organized in 1765, Munford went there as an officer of the militia, a post he held until his death. Prospering on his farm, called Richland, he acquired ninety-one slaves, the largest number in the country. As a dedicated public servant, he belonged to Virginia's House of Delegates and fought in the French and Indian War. Abandoning support of the Crown, Colonel Munford eventually joined the Revolutionary movement and commanded two battalions of militia in the Yorktown campaign. The colonel's son William published *A Collection of Plays and Poems by Robert Munford* in 1798, thus assuring for his father the title of the South's first dramatist.[2] William Munford, who also tried dramatic composition, composed a Dryden-like play with an Oriental setting, *Almoran and Hamet,* which was published in his *Poems and Compositions in Prose on Several Occasions* (1798).

Robert Munford probably wrote his two plays, *The Candidates* and *The Patriots,* in the 1770s. Though never performed, they are skillfully written and are in fact more valuable to us than many that did reach the stage, since they comment intelligently on the times, expressing an enlightened viewpoint. William Munford states that his father's purpose in composing *The Candidates* was "to laugh to scorn the practice of corruption, and falsehood; of which too many are guilty in electioneering; to teach our countrymen to despise the arts of those who meanly attempt to influence their votes by anything but merit" (pp. v-vi). In this play's detailed depiction of a campaign for the House of Burgesses, Wou'dbe, an honest politician, is running against two corrupt men whose incriminating names, Sir John Toddy and Strutabout, show Munford's disapproval of some contemporary Virginia politicians. At a barbecue Strutabout makes extravagant promises he cannot keep; as one voter observes, this candidate would "bring the tide over the tops of the hills, for a vote" (1.3).

The Candidates contains a remarkable amount of local color for the time and in fact reveals an unmistakable southern flavor. It tells us as much of Virginia culture as it does of the local politics that was an integral part of the communal life. The voters assemble at two venues. The first is the barbecue, where there is much rowdiness and boisterous drunkenness; one voter named Guzzle hiccups continually, blaming his condition on gingerbread. The second meeting, on the day of the election, is a breakfast at the residence of the upstanding Wou'dbe, ally of the appropriately named Worthy, a former member of the House of Burgesses. At this decorous gathering a group of voters chat in neighborly fashion while enjoying a festive repast before going to cast their ballots. When Prize asks Wou'dbe about his "fishing places," the latter replies that they are "better than they've been known for some seasons." Mr. Julip allows that with regard to the harvest, "we crop it gloriously." Into this rural scene enter persons who give it a final southern touch: "several negroes" pass back and forth at the table serving drinks. Julip speaks to one of them in a form of address that has become too well known: "Boy, give me the spirit." The fittingly named Julip thinks that his chocolate beverage needs "a little lacing to make it admirable" (3.3).

Although having an alcoholic drink in the morning had become common in Virginia at this time, the gentility of the breakfast scene contrasts pointedly with the crude disorderliness at the barbecue, and the contrast of propriety with grossness expresses the political philosophy of the play.

In this election the voters of the county practice the honored, hierarchical custom of deference to their superiors by choosing the gentlemen planters Worthy and Wou'dbe over such disreputable incompetents as Strutabout and Smallhopes. Historians cite this account as convincing evidence of political deference in the colonial elections of Virginia.[3]

The play also evinces a keen sense of pride in being a Virginian, the beginning of the state loyalty that was to permeate the South. Its prologue, written later, pays tribute to "Virginia's first and only comic son," noting sadly that by the time of publication "the bard" is dead. After the election Wou'dbe does not forget to praise the people of Virginia for rejecting the unworthy candidates and selecting those capable of managing the affairs of the people. State pride shines forth in his words: the voters have shown good judgment, he declares, and "a spirit of independence becoming Virginians" (3.4).

Heavy drinking is a deplorable feature of elections in colonial Virginia according to Munford. At the barbecue Wou'dbe chides the comic John Guzzle for getting as drunk as "Chief Justice Cornelius," an allusion to Cornelius Carghill, senior magistrate of Lunenburg County.[4] The heavy consumption of alcohol in such campaigns was well documented by George Washington, who listed high expenses for alcohol at gatherings in Winchester, including the cost of twenty-eight gallons of rum.[5]

Such realistic details indicate that Munford's depiction is well grounded in actual colonial elections. In fact, some characters were modeled after living persons. The leading character of *The Candidates*, Wou'dbe, is based on Robert Munford himself, a well-to-do patrician from the Tidewater who was elected to the House of Burgesses in 1770. Worthy is likely modeled on Matthew Marable, Munford's colleague, who had previously been elected with him.[6]

Munford's comedies fit clearly into the tradition of political satire in America, initiated by Governor Robert Hunter of New York in *Androboros* (1714), which lampoons "the man-eater" of the title, General Francis Nicholson. As Royal Commissioner of Accounts, Nicholson had been sent to investigate Hunter's administration in New York. Like this satire and those of the English Restoration, Munford's comedies abound in allegorical names designed to attack his enemies and praise his friends.

The Patriots differs sharply from *The Candidates* in focusing on national politics rather than local customs. Munford's second play lacks a single reference to Virginia or Virginians, words that appear prolifically in his first. *The Patriots* is national not only in its concentration on tolerance of differing opinions during the American Revolution but also in its generalized setting. Already in these two differing works, American and southern viewpoints reflect the dual loyalties of Virginians.

In his introduction to this play, William Munford aptly characterizes *The Patriots* as "a picture of true and pretended patriots; by which the reader may perceive the difference between them, may learn to honour and reward the true, and to treat the false with infamy and contempt" (p. vi). The true patriot defends a fellow citizen's right to hold a different opinion, even if he opposes freedom from Great Britain, the dramatist argues. William denies charges of disloyalty on his father's part. If anyone should question Robert Munford's allegiance to his country, he writes, the record proves that he "boldly fought in her defense" (p. vi).

The play, set in the early days of the Revolution, was probably composed in 1779 when Munford, like the leading character Meanwell, was elected to the Virginia House of Delegates. Intolerance toward those who are cool to the Revolution arises at the outset as Meanwell and Trueman discuss the public's suspicion of certain men's patriotism. Both characters are likely based on Munford himself, who in 1777 was suspected of lacking zeal on behalf of his country. Munford probably suffered no personal examination by the local Committee of Observation, which was charged with prosecuting disloyalty to the republic, but his sympathy for the plight of his relatives the Beverleys, who were accused of being Tories, would have aroused suspicion. Like Munford, his character Meanwell says that above all he respects a man's right to hold his own opinion.

The high point of *The Patriots* comes when Tackabout, later exposed as a Tory himself, labels Trueman a Tory before the Committee of Observation. Speaking as a genuine patriot whose moderate position duplicates Munford's, Trueman declares: "I detest the opprobrious epithet of tory, as much as I do the inflammatory distinction of whig." When the conduct of neither Tory nor Whig is justifiable, he says, he is neither, yet when the "good principles of either correspond with the duties of a good citizen, I am both" (4.2). Like his great contemporary George Washington, Munford placed "the duties of a good citizen" above loyalty to a particular party.

Munford also defended the native Scotsmen who became notorious during the Revolution for their loyalty to the Crown. On April 14, 1777, Scottish merchants in Mecklenburg County were tried for disloyalty and expelled according to the resolution of 1776, which applied to all British merchants friendly to the Crown. In the play, three Scottish merchants suspected of disloyalty are brought before the Committee of Observation. When asked for proof of their disloyalty, one accuser retorts: "We suspect any Scotchman: suspicion is proof, sir."[7] Meanwell, on the other hand, defends the Scots against such intolerance, objecting that even those who have given no cause for offense have been persecuted.

Munford set a very high standard for political plays written in Virginia. He perceived the defects of Mecklenburg County, a backwoods area that stood in contrast to the Tidewater with its tradition of unselfish civil service and deference to seasoned leaders. Satirizing demagogic and unprincipled candidates for office, he ridiculed those who made promises, such as reducing taxes, that they could not fulfill. Wou'dbe, speaking for Munford, points out that a legislature will make the final decision, weighing private interest against public good.[8] With its droll scenes of politicking, *The Candidates* deftly catches the mood of a colonial election in Virginia. *The Patriots* censures the disparity between the proclaimed ideal of tolerating different opinions and the actual practice of punishing dissidents, which in a free society constitutes flagrant hypocrisy.

John Daly Burk (c. 1775-1808) and Others

John Daly Burk, known as a pioneer of American drama, did not settle in Virginia until late in his life, but he represents well the partisan politics that characterized drama there, especially the state's dominant Jeffersonian Republicanism. An advocate of Irish independence, Burk fled from his native country to the United States. He settled in 1796 in Boston, where he plunged into partisan journalism and where in 1797 his popular play *Bunker Hill; or, The Death of General Warren* was performed at the Republican-supported New Theatre. Innovative in featuring a spectacular battle scene as the finale, this pageant drama, like William Dunlap's *The Glory of Columbia* (1803), became a lasting success and earned Burk considerable fame. Dedicated to the Republican firebrand Aaron Burr, it is ardently nationalistic, anti-British, and anti-monarchy. At the funeral of General Warren in the final scene appear such slogans as "The Rights of Man," "Liberty and Equality," and "Hatred to Royalty."[9]

Burk next moved to New York, where his vigorously pro-French play *Female Patriotism; or, The Death of Joan of Arc* was performed in 1798. Written when Napoleon's armies were thought to be advancing the ideals of the French Revolution throughout Europe, this play supports that movement. One French soldier, while denouncing the British enemy, declares that he believes in "love and liberty."[10] Joan herself, a prototype of the nationalistic revolutionary, envisions a future free republic across the Atlantic Ocean.

While in New York, Burk antagonized the Federalists by accusing President John Adams of monarchic tendencies. He was defended by Burr, but because he was subject to the notorious Alien and Sedition Laws, this Republican journalist sought refuge in Southside Virginia, where he found a more congenial political climate.

Burk continued his spirited Republicanism but modified it to suit his new residency in Virginia. Settling first in Amelia County, he wrote Thomas Jefferson that he had moved there to become "principal of a college," and after seven years "of agitation and calamity" he was beginning to enjoy "the sweets of repose and independence."[11] Not long after writing this letter, Burk moved to Petersburg, which—although its mercantile interests fostered a Federalist minority—was predominantly Republican, like the surrounding plantation country. He became widely known and much admired for this three-volume *History of Virginia* (1804-07), the first of its kind after the Revolution and dedicated to Jefferson.

Petersburg's well-known fondness for the drama may have attracted Burk. E.A. Wyatt writes that "it was a nearly ideal place for a gentleman, who wrote plays and who was a Republican in politics."[12] Burk lost no time in associating himself with the theatrical life of Petersburg, which boasted a theater (built in 1796 by the manager Thomas Wade West) and a company of amateur actors called the Thespians. Burk joined the company and soon composed *Oberon; or, the Siege of Mexico,* which was performed at the Petersburg Theatre on December 4, 1802. It was repeated on December 7 for the benefit of the author, and thereafter played in Norfolk, Richmond, and New York. The *Republican and Petersburg Advertiser* pointed out some faults but approved the work as a whole.[13]

The play has not survived; the "Oberon" of the title was not Shakespeare's fairy king; he was rather the "champion of Mexico." And since Burk denounced the conquistadors on other occasions, the character Cortez must have been the main villain.[14] It is probable that *Oberon* indirectly supported a revolution in Mexico; we know that Aaron Burr and other Americans had long plotted to revolutionize Spanish America, taking their cue from the French expeditions in Europe.[15] Burk preserved his friendship with Burr even after the latter's fall from grace. When Burr passed through Petersburg in 1804, after killing Alexander Hamilton in a duel, Burk loyally took him to the theater and gave a dinner in his honor.[16]

Burk's last play, *Bethlem Gabor, Lord of Transylvania; or, The Man-Hating Palatine,* is the most significant of those he wrote in the South.[17] This Gothic melodrama was first performed in Petersburg in 1803 (the Richmond *Argus* for December 17 reported that the theater was crowded and general satisfaction was shown)[18] and published in 1807 by John Dickson, a member of the Republican Party. Burk, who was long remembered in

Petersburg for appearances on the local stage, wrote the play for the Thespians and played the title role himself.[19] The cast list in the published version, showing J.W. Green as Bethlem, indicates that it was later presented in Petersburg by the West and Bignall Company, which was headquartered in Richmond but performed in Petersburg as well (there is no record of its production in Richmond or elsewhere).[20]

• *Bethlem Gabor* is set in Hungary and again advocates revolution against tyrants, in this case the Austrians. Promulgating the same revolutionary ideology as Burk's previous plays, it is loosely based on the novel *St. Leon* (1799) by the English political radical William Godwin. In the novel Bethlem Gabor is a totally villainous secondary figure who dies in the end, but Burk makes him the hero and gives the play a happy ending: after defeating the Austrians and Turks, Gabor is reunited with his family.

In line with his political purpose, Burk shows Bethlem's transformation from resigned misanthrope to active opponent of Hungary's enemies, the Austrians and Turks. At first he laments the state of Hungary to St. Leon: "Alas for Hungary! Alas for humanity! In what bosom shall liberty and justice find residence?" (p. 3). When Bethlem (the common name for a madman) tries to imprison him, St. Leon asks why he behaves like a tyrant after suffering so much from tyranny himself. At the end Bethlem throws off his depression and leads the charge against the Austrians and Turks besieging his castle.

Burk again ends his play with a rowdy battle scene. Bethlem urges his men on in the most stirring speech of the drama: "Speak of the former glory of Hungary, and its present debasement—repeat [to the Hungarians] the bloody tyranny of the Austrians and Turks—breathe into their souls the flame of liberty. Liberty! Liberty or death!" (p. 47). These words, of course, recall not only lines from *Bunker Hill*'s battle scene but Patrick Henry's famous "Give me liberty, or give me death." Although the play is set in the sixteenth century, Gabor's exhortations applied as well to contemporary times, for Hungary was again suffering under the heel of an Austrian emperor. Experiencing a nationalistic revival of its language and literature, Hungary was ripe for an overthrow of tyrannical rule.

Burk's play adds to the revolutionary theme by satirizing a foppish valet who aspires to become an Austrian aristocrat. Frederick boasts to the maid, Nanette, that he is the son of the archduke and nephew of the Austrian emperor, who is "King of Hungary and Bohemia, and lord of the Holy Roman Empire." Born a count but replaced in the cradle by the nurse's son, says the valet, in these "levelling times of liberty and equality" he unfortunately cannot regain his rightful title (pp. 36-39). This topical allusion shows the author's wish to attack those opposing the egalitarian ideals of the French Revolution.

When Napoleon abandoned the ideals of the French Revolution and began to rule authoritatively himself, Burk and his fellow Virginians lost respect for him and the French nation. In a speech delivered in Petersburg on February 8, 1806, Burk denounced Napoleon's exchange of republican laurels for the power of a despot. He died in his thirties because he offended a Frenchman by disparaging France and was killed in the duel that followed. Showing their high esteem for him, Virginians honored Burk with burial on a plantation near Petersburg.[21]

Among other dramatists who successfully composed plays for presentation in Virginia theaters was Everhard Hall, a Newbern, North Carolina, lawyer, who wrote *Nolens Volens; or, the Biter Bit* (1809) for the Thespians of Petersburg.[22] The editor of the *Raleigh Star* called it "the first dramatic performance, composed in North Carolina."[23] Although set in England, this comedy contains observations on conditions in America. Repudiating the Jeffersonianism of Burk, Hall expressed Federalist sentiment by satirizing the French and the tyranny of the majority.

Two original plays given at the Richmond Theatre were *Oscar Fitz-James,* by an anonymous Virginian, in 1819; and *Nature and Philosophy,* by Gustavus Adolphus Myers (1801-69), in 1821. Myers, the son of a prominent Jewish family and a civic leader, also wrote *Felix,* an unpublished play performed on July 24, 1822.[24] The author of *Oscar Fitz-James* declares in his preface that Virginia should not let "her literary character" lag behind that of sister states.

It is not known whether David Darling was a Virginian, but his *Beaux without Belles* was performed at the Fredericksburg Theatre in 1820. The most interesting feature of this play is its rare expression of anti-slavery opinions.[25]

St. George Tucker (1752-1827)

In the first period of Virginia drama, some dramatists were unsuccessful in having their work staged. One of these was the distinguished jurist St. George Tucker, whose plays reflect the Federalist-Republican controversy and the nationalism inspired by the War of 1812. Born in Bermuda, Tucker served in the Revolutionary War, taught law at the College of William and Mary, and became federal judge of the District of Virginia. Besides poetry and other miscellaneous writings, he composed four plays from 1796 to about 1815.

The first two express Tucker's strong Republicanism, similar to Burk's.

Up and Ride; or, The Borough of Brooklyn: A Farce (1789) satirizes the Federalist John Adams in the character of a monarchist called Jonathan Goosequill. In the prologue to *The Wheel of Fortune,* written in 1796-97, the author deplores the lack of native drama, complaining that "our novels . . . and plays / Have been *imported.*" Since independence is now of age, "be pleased t'admit her, Sirs, upon the stage," he pleads.

Like Royall Tyler's popular *The Contrast* (1787), Tucker's play exploits the Anglophobia that followed the American Revolution. It attacks the vices of speculation, represented by a corrupt merchant who will not defend America's friends, the French, in their war with the English; he asserts, "I was bred an Englishman, and I will die an Englishman."[26] Because some of the characters resembled real citizens of Philadelphia, Thomas Wignell, an actor-manager, declined to stage it in that city.

Tucker's last two plays took a nationalistic stance regarding the War of 1812. *The Times; or, The Patriot Rous'd* (1811) presents a character named Trueman, who patriotically condemns impressment of American sailors into the British navy. *The Patriot Cool'd,* written sometime after the war, again presents Trueman, who has been wounded and can fight no more. The play ends happily as he celebrates Jackson's victory at the Battle of New Orleans, which ended the War of 1812.[27]

George Washington Parke Custis (1781-1857)

Virginia's early plays demonstrated little consciousness of the state's past until George Washington Parke Custis revived Virginia's colorful legendry and recorded that aspect of its culture in dramatic form.[28] His plays reflect the contemporary love of romantic history seen in the novels of Sir Walter Scott and James Fenimore Cooper.

Though assuredly an amateur, Custis became a prolific and popular dramatist, composing the first substantial body of plays by a Virginian. He also represents the changing political trends occurring in Virginia during his long life. As an impartial patriot concerned above all with the unity and strength of his country, Custis belongs in the tradition of his step-grandfather, George Washington. He was a Federalist for many years, but when that party dissolved, he became an admirer of Andrew Jackson, founder of the Democratic Party.

Orphaned by the early death of his father—George Washington's stepson—Custis was taken to live at Mount Vernon at the age of six months. The president felt his step-grandson was indolent and did not apply himself to his youthful duties, but Custis matured, served in the War of 1812, and became a highly respected citizen. Educated at Princeton and Annapolis, he lived at Mount Vernon until Martha Washington's death, at which time he built "Arlington" (also called the Custis-Lee Mansion). His daughter became the wife of Robert E. Lee and lived at Arlington till the beginning of the Civil War.

Washington Custis, as he was called, was always diligent in preserving the memory of the president. Every February 22 he contributed a recollection of his step-grandfather to the *National Intelligencer* of Washington.[29] His first play, *The Indian Prophecy*, was based on an incident in Washington's life, and in his amateur paintings he memorialized the Revolutionary general in "Battle of Princeton" and "Washington at Yorktown."

Custis gained renown as an orator in the area around Arlington, which included the national capital. He voiced his political opinions on frequent occasions; at sheep breeding fairs on his estate he not only encouraged the raising of a better breed for wool production but also attacked the Jeffersonians and Napoleon. In 1812 he praised the Federalists for defending freedom of the press. A strong exponent of national independence abroad, Custis delivered an oration in 1813 praising Russian victories over Napoleon. The Russian minister, condemning the French attempt to take away "our national independence," thanked Custis for his speech.[30] In 1826, Custis gave an address supporting Irish independence from Great Britain. Toasting "the Emerald Isle," he declared, "May she soon be relieved from the Lion's grasp, for the Lion is of a kind that fondles ere it kills."[31]

Custis was much more successful than previous dramatists of Virginia because by the time he began to compose plays, larger and more active theaters had arisen, undergirded by stronger acting companies. His proximity to theatrical centers, the demand for native plays, and not least the glamour of his name promoted success. Custis composed eight plays from 1827 to 1836, all of which were produced in major cities: Philadelphia, Baltimore, Washington, and New York. The following list includes place of first performance, if known, and date: *The Indian Prophecy* (Philadelphia, 1827); *The Eighth of January* (Park Theatre, New York; January 8, 1828); *The Railroad* (Baltimore, 1828); *Pocahontas* (Philadelphia, 1830); *The Pawnee Chief; or, Hero of the Prairie* (February 22, 1832, for the George Washington Centennial); *North Point; or, Baltimore Defended* (1833, celebrating the Battle of Fort McHenry in the War of 1812); *The Launch of the Columbia; or, American Blue Jackets Forever* (an operetta, 1836); and *Montgomerie* (Washington, 1836). All are set in America except the last, which takes place in Scotland. Only three—*The Indian Prophecy, Pocahontas,* and *Montgomerie*—are extant.

The Indian Prophecy is based on a little-known event in Washington's early life, which Custis set down in "A Memoir" preceding the text of the play.[32] Dr. James Craik had told him of the incident, which occurred in 1772 when Colonel Washington led a band of explorers into western Virginia. The Indian chief they met, having observed Washington's bravery at Braddock's Defeat, predicted that this great man could not die in battle and would found "a mighty Empire!!" (p. 6).

Custis wished not only to perpetuate the memory of Washington but also to preserve the legendary past of his state by dramatizing memorable events. Previous plays reflected state pride but no sense that Virginia possessed its own distinct history—although preservation of that history would appear soon in fiction with John Pendleton Kennedy's narration of stirring escapades of the Revolution in *Horse-Shoe Robinson* (1835). In Custis's play, the hunters place a Frenchman, Duquesne, in the forefront of their ranks where Washington should stand. But—like Joan of Arc, who could not mistake the Dauphin—the chief walks straight to Washington and speaks prophetically: "*The Great Spirit protects that man, and guides his destiny*" (2.3). After uttering his prophecy, Chief Kenawha says that he is ready to join his fathers and sinks into the arms of his attendant. In the remainder of the play Washington prophesies expansion to the West, American prowess in war despite European skepticism, and the happy future of a frontiersman's son, his namesake.

Custis's next play, *Pocahontas; or, The Settlers of Virginia, A National Drama*, achieved widespread success. It dramatized a topic already made on the stage by James Nelson Barker's drama *The Indian Princess; or, La Belle Sauvage*, performed at the Chestnut Street Theatre, Philadelphia, in 1810. Custis's colorful contribution to the genre opened at the Walnut Street Theatre in Philadelphia on January 16, 1830; it played at the Park Theatre, New York, that December and was also staged in Charleston, Washington, and Alexandria.[33] Clumsily written but vigorous, it is Custis's best play.

Although *Pocahontas* was rightly proclaimed a "national" drama, its main purpose was to celebrate the glorious past of Virginia as an examination of its main themes demonstrates. Custis praises the bravery and virtue of exemplary heroes like Captain John Smith and John Rolfe, and there are knowledgeable references to Smith's brave exploits in Transylvania, but the play dramatizes above all the grand conquest of Virginia. Smith leads his men against Powhatan's warriors daringly, taking for his war cry "Victory and Virginia!" (3.2)

The chivalric tradition of early Virginians is stressed repeatedly. Smith and others are addressed as "Sir Cavalier" (1.1). When fighting begins against the Indians, who protest that the English will occupy all their lands,

Smith refuses to abandon Pocahontas, a "distrest damsel," to the hostile enemy (3.1). In fact, the settlers can be viewed as Christian knights overcoming infidels, much like Crusaders battling Saracens. Pocahontas, who has gladly adopted Christianity, deserts her father, denouncing his bloody religion: he has offered up one hundred youths, on demand of the priest, in his effort to defeat the English.

Showing the romantic penchant for taking liberties with historical material, Custis presents a triangle involving Pocahontas, John Rolfe, and the hostile Indian Matacoran. Pocahontas, who falls in love with Rolfe at first sight, refuses to become the unwilling wife of the villainous Matacoran. The spotless heroine becomes "the friend of the English," in her words, and warns them of an imminent attack (3.1). Unlike other dramatists of his day, Custis placed the famous incident of Pocahontas's rescue of Captain Smith climactically at the end. When Powhatan starts to wave his fan as the signal to crush Smith's head, Pocahontas begs the executioner to kill her instead. The Manitou has inspired her "to a deed which future ages will admire," she declares (3.5).

In the last speech of the play, Chief Powhatan hopes that the descendants of Pocahontas and John Rolfe will be endowed with "the most exalted patriotism." He asks that future generations honor this birth of Virginia in plays and books, for by doing so they will be celebrating "the national story of Pocahontas, or the Settlers of Virginia." In short, the play commemorates the most famous legend of early Virginia, but Custis retains his national spirit by dubbing it a "national" drama (appropriately, it premiered in Philadelphia). At this juncture the synthesis of state and national feeling was still strong in southern drama.

Custis's last extant play, *Montgomerie; or, The Orphan of the Wreck,* was performed in Washington on April 11, 1836, although it had been composed six years earlier.[34] (On the title page Custis names himself as author of "Pocahontas, The Pawnee Chief, North Point, The Launch, etc. The Railroad.") Set in Scotland, the play depicts the restoration of the rightful earl of Montgomerie, allowing Custis to draw on material familiar to the readers of Sir Walter Scott. One of the characters, Ronald, is the hero of Scott's poem *Lord of the Isles,* and the time of the action is the fourteenth century, when Robert the Bruce fought for independence from England.[35]

Though set in a foreign land, *Montgomerie* presents a theme relevant to the era of Jacksonian democracy: the worth of the common man. Custis again asserts his nationalistic spirit by honoring a man who demonstrates his virtues by rising from humble status to a position of honored leadership. This was Andrew Jackson's democratic message, which by 1830 had become a national axiom. Custis had shown his admiration of Jackson before in *The Eighth of January* (1828), which celebrated Old Hickory's victory at the Battle of New Orleans. After Jackson took up residence in Washington as president in 1829, he and Custis became friends.

In this unintentionally ludicrous melodrama the young hero, Malcolm, becomes an orphan when his father, the rightful earl of Montgomerie, is killed on orders of the usurper Roderick. Malcolm remains in obscurity until he rescues Roderick's ward, Marion, from drowning. After learning his true identity from an old crone, Malcolm distinguishes himself at court as a swordsman and overcomes Ronald, Lord of the Isles, whom Roderick has chosen to marry Marion. Spurning Ronald, Marion declares that it is not necessary to be born noble to be noble. Roderick on the contrary insists that she should prefer the titled lord to this "peasant," an epithet repeatedly applied to the worthy Malcolm (pp. 14, 73).

The overthrow of tyranny, a popular topic of the times, is often seen in plays with foreign settings; for example, Robert Montgomery Bird's *The Gladiator* (1831) describes a slave uprising against Roman masters. In this melòdrama by Custis, who had previously shown his opposition to foreign tyranny by denouncing Napoleon's wars, the cruel tyrant Roderick is overcome by Malcolm and Kenneth the Pirate, a figure straight out of Gothic melodrama. The tyrant condemns himself in his final words: "Roderick, how have thy visions of power and greatness disappeared before the steel of the Pirate Kenneth" (p. 87).

The first plays of Virginia were written during a period of ardent nationalism, whose spirit permeated the drama as well as the politics of the whole nation but assumed a distinctive form in Virginia. Munford was a loyal supporter of the American Revolution but did not forget his responsibility to defend the minority. Burk and Tucker composed spirited nationalistic plays, always influenced by the republican ideology of Jefferson. Of particular interest, Custis expanded conventional nationalism to include the early history of Virginia, with its aristocratic chivalry, as a major part of the American legacy.

Although the dramatists covered in this chapter may be called southern because of birth and residence, their works lack one of the distinguishing traits of southern drama—until Custis, in whose compositions one can clearly recognize the love of state legendry that would become a hallmark of southern plays. It appears extensively in the fiction of William Gilmore Simms of South Carolina, but Custis chose the stage, where history could be viewed enjoyably, to remind his fellow Virginians of their splendid heritage. He celebrated the most famous legend of Virginia in

Pocahontas and preserved a little-known event from the life of the state's most illustrious son in *The Indian Prophecy.*

A small but significant number of these early Virginia plays may be considered southern in the cultural sense. Munford's *The Candidates* records both ugly and attractive scenes of colonial life: after learning of irresponsibility and dissipation at the barbecue, we eavesdrop on a convivial breakfast served by Virginia slaves. Later, as a devotee of colorful American history and an imitator of Scott's romantic tales, Custis made his special contribution to the formation of Virginia's aristocratic society by comparing Captain John Smith and John Rolfe to courteous knights: they not only fight courageously against barbarous Indians but receive the damsel Pocahontas with gentleness, speaking in the most polite manner. Thus does a play of Virginia history encourage chivalrous conduct in America—ironically favoring the ways of English nobility in a democratic society.

— 2 —
Prolific Playwriting in Charleston

Following its scattered beginnings in Virginia, southern drama took on a much clearer focus in Charleston, capital of the colony (and later of the state) of South Carolina, with the formation of a small but dynamic theatrical center. Although Richmond became the cultural as well as the political capital of Virginia when theatrical seasons began in 1784, it fostered no group of native dramatists. The Virginia playwrights had valuable comments to make on politics at local, national, and international levels, but they had no sense of belonging to a coherent movement. In Charleston, on the other hand, a vigorous tradition of playwriting for the local theater arose for the first time in the South.

As in Virginia, nationalism was the dominant political impulse. The state's first dramatist, William Ioor, bombastically celebrated the last Revolutionary War battle of South Carolina in *The Battle of Eutaw Springs* (1807). Like John Daly Burk and St. George Tucker, he took an anti-British view of contemporary evens, championing the ideals of Jefferson. He also provided a refreshing touch of local color in the first appearance of a famous southern type: the hospitable old gentleman.

Other early dramas of South Carolina, the mother state of the Deep South, offer glimpses of its distinctive culture. The first sectionalist speech defending the South's "peculiar institution"—which would become such an obsession that the state would eventually instigate secession from the Union—can be found in Maria Pinckney's significant though unperformed play *Young Carolinians in Algiers* (1818), in which a slave defends slavery humorously. The moral issues that most concerned the people, on the evidence of drama, seem to have been dueling and intemperance, as set forth respectively in John Blake White's *Modern Honor* (1812) and *The Forgers* (1829), another unperformed but illuminating work.

The Charleston Theater

The first theatrical season in Charleston began on January 18, 1735, with Thomas Otway's *The Orphan*, performed in the city courtroom. The next year, when a theater opened in Dock Street with George Farquhar's *The Recruiting Office*, drama had truly made its start in the city. Thereafter, leading eighteenth-century touring companies came to town, including Lewis Hallam's company in 1754. David Douglass's troupe arrived for three seasons, its 1773-74 season marking "the most brilliant" of colonial days in Charleston, according to theater historian Eola Willis.[1]

From 1793 to 1825 the theater in Charleston, supported by an able stock company, was a very popular place of entertainment for which a considerable amount of original writing was done by residents of the community. Furthermore, the stage was a vigorous political platform during this period of Federalist-Republican controversy. Here as elsewhere, political ideas made it a significant barometer of public opinion.

Theater in Charleston during these years can be best followed through its three most important managers: Thomas Wade West, Alexander Placide, and Charles Gilfert. West, an Englishman, established headquarters at Norfolk. This pro-British impresario initiated a "Southern Circuit" that included Richmond, Charleston, Savannah, and lesser towns and continued until 1825.[2]

West deserves much credit for strengthening the theater in the South. In 1793 he and James Hoban constructed a new theater in Charleston which, until 1833, was the stage for plays written by Charlestonians during the last decade of the eighteenth century and the first three of the nineteenth. Planned to serve the city's future needs, the building was unadorned brick on the outside, but elaborately decorated on the inside. Robert Mills, the architect of the Washington Monument and a former student of Hoban, described the Charleston Theatre as it looked around 1826 as a "large building, without any architectural display outwardly, which is a rather remarkable circumstance here, as the citizens of Charleston have always been patrons of the muse of poetry and song. . . . The interior of this building presents a great contrast to the present exterior. It is arranged with taste, and richly decorated; the tout ensemble produces a handsome effect."[3]

Alexander Placide (1750-1812) became sole manager of the Charleston Theatre on March 31, 1800, and held that position during the most flourishing period of the stage in Charleston. Born Alexandre-Placide Bussart in Paris, he never used his last name in America. Having enjoyed considerable success in France and Great Britain before coming to the United States, he was known best as a rope dancer and acrobat with the famous Nicolet troupe, but by 1772 he was composing and staging pantomimes.

After arriving in Charleston around 1794, Placide, an enthusiastic

Republican, became manager of the French Theatre and staged there a number of original productions glorifying the American and French Revolutions, which in the 1790s were ipso facto anti-British. On June 28, 1794, he announced a nationalistic spectacle, *Attack on Fort Moultrie*. The anniversary of this Revolutionary battle was already a patriotic holiday for the citizens of Charleston, where church bells are still rung on June 28. In this battle Sgt. William Jasper raised the flag at peril of his life, saying, "Let us not fight without a flag." Placide's spectacle, performed on July 1, 2, and 4 and August 4, 1794, was advertised as "a grand Military and Patriotic Pantomime in two acts, never performed here, called The 28th of June, 1776, or ATTACK ON FORT MOULTRIE," to be presented at the French Theatre in Church Street. It would end with an allegorical feast in honor of the "Brave American Heroes" at which Liberty was to be played by Madame Douvillier and America by Madame Val.[4]

After becoming manager of the Charleston Theatre, Placide continued to show his liking for nationalistic dramas, producing Burk's *The Battle of Bunker Hill* many times—though John B. Williamson, another Charleston theater manager, condemned this play in 1797 for appealing to "the prevailing Jacobin spirit in the lower ranks."[5] Placide also demonstrated his pro-Republican politics in productions of plays by the local dramatist William Ioor: *Independence* (1804 and 1806) and *The Battle of Eutaw Springs* (1807 and 1808). Consistent in making the theater a patriotic platform, he also offered *Liberty in Louisiana* (1804), celebrating the Louisiana Purchase; *Bombardment of Tripoli* (1805), in honor of the Americans fighting the Barbary pirates; and *Birthday of the Immortal Washington* (February 22, 1812).[6]

Journalist, playwright, and dramatic critic Isaac Harby offered Placide his harshest criticism. In his newspaper, the *Quiver*, Harby lauded a play by William Bulloch Maxwell of Savannah, "which Mr. Placide, the theatrical carver for the public taste in Charleston has *put off*, for the stuff of Dibdin, Cherry and O'Keefe—We are to be amused with harlequinades, Elephants, and Cinderellas, while the soft and sentimental efforts of Maxwell are hindered from their proper sphere of exhibition!"[7] Although Harby's comments indicate that Placide presented a great deal of frivolous, spectacular entertainment, he seems also to have increased the number of plays by the best English dramatists. Certainly, over a period of several years, a Charlestonian would have been able to see a variety of Shakespeare, the standard repertory pieces such as Otway's *Venice Preserved*, and works by influential contemporary writers—including those of August von Kotzebue and M.G. Lewis, which exposed the theatergoers to such movements as sentimentalism and Gothicism.

Charleston became the headquarters for the Southern Circuit under Placide's management, until he died in New York City in 1812, the year after his company suffered a disastrous fire at the Richmond Theatre on December 23, 1811.[8] He was subsequently described as a person of "most extraordinary accomplishments" whether considered as "a dancer on the tight rope, in which he had no rival, as a manager, or as a man of wonderful mind and resources."[9]

Charles Gilfert (1787-1829), who managed the Charleston Theatre from 1817 to 1825, resembled Placide in being a flamboyant figure who brought to the town's theatrical life a vitality that would be fondly remembered. Though Gilfert had periods of financial difficulty, he was working during a time when the Southern Circuit maintained a lively existence and before regional theatrical activity was reduced by centralization of the theater in New York. Of German descent, Gilfert was born in New York City, where he became a promising young musician. After marrying the daughter of Joseph George Holman, who managed the Charleston Theatre from 1815 to 1817, he accompanied his father-in-law to Charleston and directed the theater orchestra during Holman's management.[10] According to John Beaufain Irving, historian of the Old Charleston Theatre, Gilfert opened a "musical establishment," played in the Philharmonic Society Orchestra, and otherwise identified himself with the musical life of the city. He lived in a house dubbed "Brandenburg Castle," where he entertained theater patrons; the "choice spirits of the Day" met there, including Isaac Harby, himself the author of two produced plays. Known for his eccentric personality, Gilfert was caricatured in a performance of *Tom and Jerry* on March 1, 1824, when an actor imitated the manager by peering over his spectacles in a manner that convulsed the audience with laughter.[11]

When Gilfert assumed management of the theater in 1817, he had difficulty reviving interest in the stage, which had declined. One means he tried during the first season was the presentation of a local writer's work, Edwin C. Holland's version of Byron's *Corsair* (performed February 18, 20, and 21, 1818), for which he composed special music. Toward the end of this season the enterprising manager billed Thomas A. Cooper, an English actor popular in Charleston, who had a great success. The 1818-19 season, though, started badly, and Gilfert followed Placide's example of visiting Savannah for a few weeks. He and his troupe also toured Virginia from 1819 to 1823, and have been called "the most important company on the Richmond stage between 1819 and 1838."[12]

In March 1825, Lafayette visited Charleston and attended the theater as part of his tour of the nation, prompting Gilfert to offer for that

occasion Samuel Woodworth's *Lafayette; or, The Castle of Olmutz,* which recounted a South Carolinian's attempt to rescue the French hero from a
German prison. On March 16 a military ball was held at the theater in
Lafayette's honor, and shortly thereafter the company gave the first performance of *Fauntleroy,* written by one of its members, John Augustus Stone
(who later wrote *Metamora* [1829], the Indian play made famous by Edwin
Forrest).

The tributes paid Gilfert for his work in Charleston show that whatever his personal peccadilloes, he left behind many important accomplishments. Observing that a new era had started with Gilfert, Dr. Irving
praised him for engaging a strong company and holding it together. Visiting stars could rely on being well supported.[13] And his successful productions in Virginia and Georgia as well as South Carolina solidified the
southern theatrical circuit.

Besides vigorous theatrical management, Charleston boasted informed dramatic criticism in such newspapers as the *Courier,* the *City Gazette,* and the *Times.* The first important critic (though not the earliest)
was Stephen Cullen Carpenter, an Irishman who edited the *Courier* and
from March 30, 1803, to April 21, 1806, signed his reviews "Thespis."[14]
He was named first in Dr. Irving's list of local critics. In Charleston he
also published the *Monthly Register, Magazine, and Review of the United States,*
a national periodical, and later, in Philadelphia, the *Mirror of Taste and
Dramatic Censor.*

Carpenter's column for the *Courier,* expressing his philosophy of the
theater, displayed the spirit that would produce the plays of moral reform in Charleston. Agreeing with the predominant view of his time, he
held that parents and the public ought to compel theater managers to
make the stage "a school of morals and manners of the rising generation." Since the drama so interests the heart, he wrote, it must be "an
instrument of astonishing force in moulding, training, and perfecting
the dispositions of society" (March 30, 1803). Later, in the *Mirror of Taste
and Dramatic Censor,* Carpenter likewise described drama as a "powerful
moral agent" that should train us in our manners and deportment.[15]

Another principle Carpenter frequently mentioned was that besides
being a school of morals, drama should present characters that were true
to nature, an idea stressed by the eighteenth-century Scottish critics who
were influential in America. On March 15, 1804, "Thespis" wrote in answer to a letter, that for moral instruction to be effective, dramatic personages must be drawn so that we may reasonably suppose they exist. As
Falstaff believed, they should speak and act like folks of this world. Carpenter was particularly concerned with both the performances and the

personal conduct of local actors and was quick to censure their errors. On May 24, 1804, "Thespis" scolded the actors for neglecting to study their lines and for their lack of sobriety, adding that neighbors of the theater had complained to him about their conduct.

Carpenter made specific recommendations for improving the level of theatrical fare. On April 27, at the end of the 1802-3 season, he wrote that actors could make up for the deficiencies of contemporary playwrights by drawing on the "inspired pieces of Shakespeare, on the luminous wit of Congreve," and on other earlier writers. Thereafter, signs of improvement appeared at the Charleston Theatre: in the following season the number of evenings devoted to Shakespeare increased from three to seven; in 1805-6, the final season reviewed by Carpenter, Shakespearean plays were performed on fourteen evenings. Carpenter's growing satisfaction with the company at the Charleston Theatre makes evident that its professional quality was improving as well and that he must have felt responsible in some measure. On the opening night of the second season he reviewed (November 12, 1803), he praised a performance of M.G. Lewis's *Castle Spectre* and remarked that the manager (then Alexander Placide) had now gathered the best company yet to be seen on the Charleston boards. In his last season of reviewing, "Thespis" devoted an entire essay to the company, declaring the local troupe superior to any that he had seen in the best provincial theaters of England (November 20, 1805).

Following the early spectacles and pantomimes of the 1790s, the growing professionalism of Charleston actors was accompanied by an increase in original work performed and published in the city. The large number of plays written in Charleston from the end of the eighteenth century to 1825 shows the vitality of dramatic writing at this time. The first of these to survive in print is an anti-British piece by John Beete, an actor. It was performed on April 24, 1797, as a benefit for the author and published as *The Man of the Times: or A Scarcity of Cash. A Farce. As performed, with universal applause, at the Church-Street Theatre, Charleston. Written by Mr. Beete, Comedian.* Expressing his nationalistic feeling about dramatic writing in a statement "To the Public," Beete asked for support from those who wished "to encourage native dramatic literature, so that our stage may not always exhibit foreign productions."[16]

This play presents England as a land of instruction in chicanery and dishonesty, where Old Screwpenny has sent his son, Charles, to be educated in disreputable ways. But the latter has not adopted them. After soliloquizing that his son has returned with contempt for everything except "honesty, sincerity, philanthropy, and such stuff," Screwpenny asks where he learned such "nonsense," since he had given the boy letters to "noblemen." Charles replies that after seeing their "dissipation," he became sickened with "their follies and vices" (1.2).

James Workman's *Liberty in Louisiana,* celebrating the Louisiana Purchase of 1803, was performed at the Charleston Theatre on April 4 and 6 and May 21, 1804, and published the same year by its Federalist author.[17] Having come to Charleston before 1794, he had formed an association with the Federalist *Courier* and later moved to New Orleans, becoming judge of the County of Orleans from 1805 to 1807. As secretary for the Legislative Council of the Territory, he was responsible for much of the first legislation passed. In 1807 he was accused, but acquitted, of organizing an invasion of Mexico in connection with the notorious Burr Conspiracy. In a collection of his earlier writings, *Political Essays* (1801), he had proposed an invasion of Spanish America, a common scheme of the time, and had expressed many sentiments that were repeated in *Liberty in Louisiana.*

Widely seen and read, Workman's play was first performed at the Charleston Theatre in 1804, in New York and Philadelphia the same year, and in Savannah in 1805.[18] In Charleston, favorable responses appeared in the *Times* and the *Courier.* The former, on April 9, 1804, noted the laughter of the audience and reported that leading actor John Hodgkinson gave as "animated a picture of the character of O'Flinn" (a comic character) as the best performer on the British stage could offer. Carpenter reviewed the play in the *Courier* on April 4 and again on April 19, praising it highly but noting some grumblings from the audience because of the portrayals of an Irishman, a Scotsman, and a New Englander as "knaves." Believing that both knaves and honest men may be found in every country, he asserted that the object in view, "the commemoration of the introduction of the blessings of liberty into Louisiana," would cast respect upon "the piece, even if it had been what a few prejudicial critics have said of it."

This nationalistic play depicts conditions at the time of the Louisiana Purchase, expresses a widely held antagonism toward Spain, and presents a happy merging of the Franco-Spanish and American cultures. It serves as a particularly clear example of how the stage was used for political purposes in America at this time, since Workman's first objective was to denounce Spanish colonial rule, particularly the legal order, and thus to present the new American sovereignty as all the more glorious and desirable—a pressing need, because the inhabitants of Louisiana had objected to many changes, especially the new judicial system, brought by the Americans.

William Ioor (1780-1850)

William Ioor was the first native of South Carolina to compose and produce a play. Born on January 4, 1780, in St. George's Parish, near old Dorchester, South Carolina, he was married to a relative of the state's Revolutionary governor, John Mathews, and died in Greenville District on July 30, 1850.[19] According to family tradition, the Ioors were French Huguenots who fled to Holland, where they adopted the Dutch spelling of the name (pronounced "yore"). During the Revolutionary War, commemorated in Ioor's play *The Battle of Eutaw Springs*, his family name was well known, for William's uncle, Captain Joseph Ioor, had served on the *Randolph*, which went down in a fight with a British frigate in 1778.

Before he was twenty, Ioor received his diploma of medicine from the University of Pennsylvania, Philadelphia, and returned to South Carolina, where he was listed as a physician in the Dorchester area in 1805 and 1808. On the title page of his first play, *Independence* (1805), he gave his residence as "St. George, Dorchester, South-Carolina," the same as his birthplace. During the years when Ioor began to practice medicine, he was also much concerned with politics, serving as a member of the General Assembly from St. George, Dorchester, in the sessions of 1800-1 and 1802-3. This was the period of Jefferson's administration, the rise of the Republican Party in South Carolina, and the tension with Great Britain over America's neutral rights during the Napoleonic Wars. To argue his political beliefs, Ioor turned to the theater. According to his obituary (*Courier*, August 10, 1850), while "we were yet smarting" from wrongs committed by Great Britain, patriotism inspired him to write "his two plays, 'The Battle of Eutaw Springs' and 'Independence,' both of which were performed in Charleston."

Ioor's preface to *Independence* states that South Carolinians should "foster it, as it is the first play ever produced by a native of their state."[20] S.C. Carpenter, heading his review "The First Born of Carolina / Independence / A Comedy—by Dr. Joor," wrote in the *Courier* on April 1, 1806, that "the State has a right to be grateful to the author, who has afforded so fair an augury of their future drama."

Independence; or, Which Do You Like Best, the Peer, or the Farmer? was presented at the Charleston Theatre on March 30 and April 1, 1805, and February 26, 1806. It is set in England but indirectly praises the economic and intellectual independence of the American farmer, the mainstay of the Republican Party. Adapting *The Independent* by Andrew McDonald, Ioor altered this English novel to suit his political purpose, omitting numerous parts and adding passages of his own. With an American audience in mind, he had one character declare that "all Native Americans love the memory of their Washington" (5.3).

Ioor's most important accomplishment in *Independence* was to portray and focus attention on the life, ideas, and virtues of the small independent farmer, one of the most popular figures of the time. Jefferson himself stated: "Cultivators of the earth are the most virtuous and independent citizens."[21] Farmers were powerful in American politics and made up the rank and file of the Republican Party. Ioor's play is an early expression of Jeffersonian Agrarianism, a cornerstone of southern thought from Jefferson to the twentieth-century Nashville Agrarians.

Charles Woodville, the main character, is an independent farmer because he is free of indebtedness, the curse of many Americans in the post-Revolutionary period. In the first act, when Lord Fanfare, a caricature of the English aristocrat, boasts that he is a man of quality, Woodville retorts, "Quality is no word of conjuration with me, I assure you. I am an independent farmer, don't owe five guineas in the world" (1.2). Besides supplying his own food, Woodville resists the stratagems of Lord Fanfare and Lawyer Whittington to obtain his land. Talking with his sister, he says that though the large landowner covets his farm, it does not accord with his own "independent spirit to humor the peer" (2.1). Whittington recognizes that Woodville is known for "boasting of, his independence, and declaring, that an honest farmer knows of no dependence, except on heaven" (1.1). That reference recalls Jefferson's statement scorning those who depend on "the casualties and caprice of customers" instead of "looking up to heaven, to their own soil and industry, as does the husbandman."[22]

In Jeffersonian fashion Woodville favors the country over the city, confiding to his betrothed that in his youth he had associated with bad companions but has reformed, thanks to country life. Now, he tells his long-lost father, he leads the rural life in all its joys, "happy in my independence, and resolute to maintain it" (1.5). The pompous Lady Fanfare, showing urban disdain, remarks that it is a sin and a shame to rear a "decent female in the odious country!!!" (1.3).

Ioor's second play, *The Battle of Eutaw Springs*, advocates a defiant stand against Great Britain.[23] More widely performed than *Independence*, this spirited celebration of the Revolution was acted first at the Charleston Theatre on January 10 and 14 and February 23, 1807. On the title page appears this "Dedication": "To the Republicans of South Carolina in general; but to those in particular who honored the theatre with their presence, on the two first nights of its representation." The fervently nationalistic play was repeated the next season on May 9, 1808, and in

Richmond on September 27, 1811, by the Charleston Theatre company, then managed by Alexander Placide. On June 9, 1813, it was staged in Philadelphia by the troupe of William Twaits, formerly associated with the Charleston Theatre.[24]

Ioor's open declaration of party preference in 1807, possibly due to the increasing strength of the Republican Party in South Carolina, followed his indirect expression of Jeffersonian Republicanism in *Independence*. Produced during the period preceding the War of 1812, this second play had the specific political purpose of reviving the spirit that had previously motivated the new republic in its struggle with the mother country. Its advocation of a bold stand against Great Britain appears in speeches and in the anti-British nature of many scenes in the play. Foreseeing a second War of Independence, General Nathanael Greene refers in the first scene to the task of keeping the new nation "sacred and inviolable" and connects future Americans with a long roster of heroes: "Believe me, our posterity will, if we do not, complete the work which Warren, Washington, . . . the Pinckneys, and eke a thousand others have so resolutely begun." Making no secret of his political intent, Ioor stated in a letter to the *City Gazette* (published July 16, 1806) that the play's object was "to exalt the American character, and, possibly, depress that of the British government."

One anti-British segment appears in the subplot about a comic British soldier. Oliver Matthew Queerfish abhors having to fight Americans because they are "our own dear countrymen." He explains how he was recruited into the British army by force: after a successful performance at the circus in London, he had invited his friends to "kick up a row" by dressing as sailors and attending the theater, but on his way home a "press-gang" seized him "notwithstanding, I told them I was not the thing I seem'd; that I was no sailor, but Oliver Matthew Queerfish, esq. comedian" (1.2). After the Battle of Eutaw Springs, Queerfish decides that he will "go to Genral, get a discharge—become an AMERICAN CITIZEN" (5.1).

The role of Queerfish provides clear evidence that Charleston dramatists such as Ioor were well acquainted with local actors and conceived characters with certain performers in mind. Matthew Sully, a popular member of the company and father of the famous artist Thomas Sully, took the part of the comic soldier, whose name is partly derived from his own. Since Ioor knew this comedian could regale an audience, he shrewdly created for him the most amusing character in the play.

Contrasting with the dastardly Tories of this play are members of an admirable Whig family, Jonathan Slyboots and his son, both staunch patriots. The name "Jonathan" recalls Royall Tyler's true blue American in

The Contrast, which had previously played in Charleston. The curious name "Slyboots" is probably taken from a pro-Republican correspondent who used it as a pseudonym in writing to the Republican *City Gazette* in 1805, for Jonathan Slyboots exemplifies the best qualities of patriotic South Carolinians. In the first scene of act 2, Queerfish seeks refuge in the Slyboots cottage after being attacked by plunderers while on sentry duty. Following a conversation that reveals his humorous nature, Old Slyboots offers Queerfish a meal and listens sympathetically to the hardships of the former actor's life, proclaiming that every "child of sorrow" should be treated "by a native of the hospitable, and charitable state of South Carolina" as his brother.

At the end of the play, Old Slyboots indignantly refuses General Greene's reward for taking care of his fiancée, Emily Bloomfield (who is based on Greene's wife Catherine Littlefield); the "Washington of Rhode-Island," he says, does not know him or he would never have offered "that which keeps the miser awake." Having performed "a most important christian duty" by giving "succour to an unprotected, helpless female!" Slyboots wins the honor of giving Emily away in marriage and is labeled "Old Hospitality," making him the prototype of the humorous old gentleman character in many subsequent southern plays.

Drawing on the state's Revolutionary War legends, the play graphically depicts the strife between Tory and Whig, which was especially vicious in South Carolina. When General Greene arrived in the state, he attempted to reestablish civil peace, giving orders for the protection of both Whig and Tory families from outlaws of both parties. Ioor's play dramatizes these conditions in the beginning of Act 4 when Emily Bloomfield enters with a Tory in hot pursuit. In a highly melodramatic scene she implores Captain Manning to defend her. Manning kills the villain in a duel, but before dying, McGirt confesses his misdeeds, among which is dishonoring respectable women "before the eyes of their manacled husbands."

Emily then relates the tragedy of her family. While the men were at home on leave, McGirt and other "Tory plunderers" arrived and decided on "half hanging" her father to find out where his wealth was hidden. Her brother died opposing them; her mother was killed in a fall down the staircase; and the hanging of her father was completed. Finally, the plunderers set fire to "our elegant mansion," and while they tried "to inveigle away the negroes," she escaped.

The Battle of Eutaw Springs includes many of the elements found in Simms's Revolutionary romances of South Carolina: British avarice, the Whig-Tory conflict, cruel Tory plunderers, and the combination of historical and fictional persons. Both Ioor and Simms, like Robert Munford, present the Scots as Tories with names like "McGirt." Ioor's work may have influenced Simms, who owned a copy of Ioor's play and wrote that in South Carolina it was "among the first if not the very first, native dramas brought on the boards."[25]

Contemporary reaction to *The Battle of Eutaw Springs* is preserved in the two rival newspapers of Charleston: the Federalist *Courier* and the Republican *City Gazette*. Half a year before the play opened they carried on a journalistic debate about it. On July 2, 1806, Ioor wrote to the *City Gazette* under the pseudonym of "W.J. Youngschool" concerning proposals for printing his play. His brief description of the work and a short extract in verse were directed at potential subscribers. Six days later, in the *Courier* for July 8, 1806, "Oldschool" found fault with the play as described by "Youngschool," charging that the incidents to be dramatized were so recent that the audience would be "very naturally engaged in separating the fictitious from the true part of the story. Distraction will of course ensue, interest is out of the question." Furthermore, the verse did not "*chime*"—a criticism apparently heeded by the author, since the printed play is in prose.

Ioor sent a long, spirited rebuttal to the *City Gazette* on July 16, 1806, denouncing the *Courier* critic, whom he assumed to be Stephen Cullen Carpenter, and disparaging him as nothing more than the son of a Dublin box-office keeper. Declaring that this writer's purpose was in fact to prevent publication of the play, Ioor asserted that the American people would not let the opinion "of a foreigner carry any weight." Since his play was an original American production, it could not fail to earn the denunciation of a "*self-created Censor Morum,* whose predilection for every thing monarchical, every thing aristocratical has been notorious ever since he took up his residence amongst us."

On July 19, 1806, a cutting reply to "Youngschool" appeared in the *Courier,* signed "S.C. Carpenter." The critic stated that he had never seen the first letter from "Oldschool" before its publication, denied that he was the son of "a Dublin box-keeper," and dismissed the other insinuations, saying that they had been bandied about "a thousand times." Asserting that a play must have more to redeem it than patriotism, he concluded that if the author "had nothing but his pen to live upon, he would be as poor as his own soldiers of Eutaw."

After Ioor's play was performed, two laudatory letters appeared in the *City Gazette* for January 14, 1807. "A Republican and Whig of '76" expressed pride in seeing such a number of "republicans" at the play by "our countryman, Dr. Ioor" and appealed for local support: "Should we be found backward in encouraging the attempts at dramatic composition, by *our native citizens* we may look forward in vain for the time when authors of celebrity will be the growth of the state which gave us birth." State pride, seen in Virginia, appears in South Carolina also. This "Republican" called on the Society of Cincinnati and the Whigs of '76, two patriotic associations, not to allow the author "of a correct history of the Battle of Eutaw Springs" to lack support.

John Blake White (1781-1859)

Born in Berkeley County, South Carolina, on September 2, 1781, John Blake White, the state's first tragic dramatist, soon moved with his family to Charleston, where his father—a former Revolutionary soldier—was a builder. From 1801 to 1803 White studied painting in England with Benjamin West and met fellow South Carolinian and artist Washington Allston, whose sister, Elizabeth Allston, he later married. White tried painting in Charleston and Boston but found no encouragement for the depiction of historical subjects, his principal interest; nevertheless, four of his works, including his best known, *The Camp of Marion*, were eventually hung in the Capitol in Washington.

In Charleston he practiced law, became active in cultural affairs, opposed Nullification, was elected to the state legislature as a Democratic-Republican in 1818, and was later employed at the Charleston Customs House. He died on August 24, 1859.

Coming before Custis, White was the first dramatist in the South to write a substantial body of work, five plays in all. Three were performed at the Charleston Theatre. Presented on January 10 and 13 and February 24, 1806, *Foscari*, written in blank verse and set in Venice, was South Carolina's first tragic drama. Like the northern dramatist William Dunlap, who adapted *Fontainville Abbey* (1795) from a novel by Ann Radcliffe, White gratified the thirst for Gothic horrors with *The Mysteries of the Castle*, performed at the Charleston Theatre on December 26 and 29, 1806, and February 19, 1807. This Gothic melodrama condemns the villainous Fauresco's revenge.[26]

White is most significant as the first southern dramatist to compose plays advocating moral reform, the forerunners of social protest in the twentieth century. Although the reform movement never attained the success in the South that it did in the North, it did create great fervor among some southerners. Thomas S. Grimké, for instance, a close friend of White's in Charleston, supported modernization of the educational curriculum, popular education, and temperance. The reform movement in the South, however, was eventually extinguished by the sentiment against abolition, which linked all reformist proposals with the anti-slavery movement. White's plays condemning dueling and intemperance identified the vices that most disturbed southern audiences of his day. The diatribe against dueling in *Modern Honor* introduces violence as a subject identified with the South, as abundantly illustrated in Mark Twain's and William Faulkner's fiction. The violence of *Modern Honor* is more decorous but is the same in its defiance of the law.

Modern Honor was the first anti-dueling play in America.[27] Dueling had been attacked incidentally in *The Better Sort* (1798), an anonymous play in which a Yankee character says he considers the practice "anti-federal," but Josef Elfenbein finds that from 1782 to 1812 White's is the "only play of the period with the evils of dueling for a dominant thesis."[28] It was appropriate that it was written by a southerner, for in the early republic the custom of dueling was most prevalent in the South, especially in South Carolina and Georgia. Charleston, in fact, was conspicuous for the number of its duels from the Revolution to the decade after the Civil War. Any man wanting to be regarded a gentleman conformed to this "code of honor" or suffered contempt from high and low.

Despite laws and sermons showing opposition to dueling in the South, it continued vigorously. In 1809 Georgia passed a law against it, and in 1810 Virginia approved a similar ordinance—with no more effect than the Georgia law. South Carolina passed an ineffective act in December 1812—the year White's play was written—prescribing punishment and exclusion from the professions, trade, and public office for principals and seconds in a duel. General Charles Cotesworth Pinckney, a Charlestonian, was the best-known supporter of the anti-dueling movement in the early nineteenth century. He was so shocked by the death of Hamilton in 1804 that he used his great personal influence as president of the Society of Cincinnati to oppose the practice. Nevertheless, the custom persisted for a long time; prominent statesmen such as Henry Clay, John Randolph of Roanoke, and Andrew Jackson supported the code by precept and example.

White mentions dueling several times in his journal. On August 21, 1817, he lamented the death of a friend, Dennis O'Driscoll. He wrote that the condition of the bereaved wife and parents showed "the fatal effects of this hateful practice of Dueling."[29]

Modern Honor, first performed at the Charleston Theatre on March 6, 9, and 12, 1812, forcefully presents White's stand against dueling in the brief life of young Woodville, who has just returned from Europe, where he has learned the custom. In the first duel, enacted offstage,

Woodville kills Charles Devalmore, who had accused him of seducing his sister. In the second duel Woodville meets the villain Forsythe, his rival for the affections of Maria. Arguments *for* dueling are presented by the villains. Forsythe declares that the pistol has "more civilized the world / Than all the pratings of your grizly sages"; that in fact it brings peace by the severe penalty it imposes on him who "wages causeless strife." His henchman remarks that it is hardly necessary to argue in favor of dueling, since "the foremost characters in all our land" uphold its usefulness (2.1). Presenting the other side, Hanmer, Woodville's second, attacks "sanctioned murder" and in a soliloquy on the dueling grounds exclaims:

> Will no immortal patriot arise
> Inspired with legislative energy,
> To drive her from the land . . . [5.1]

Hanmer pleads with Woodville to replace so-called "modern honor" with true honor but cannot stop him from going to his death—which takes place on stage, thus forcing the audience to face the stark consequences of the duel.

One writer for the *Charleston Times,* commenting on *Modern Honor* and the influence of the theater (March 6, 1812), stated that since pulpit denunciations had been in vain, the best argument would be to show that dueling was not sanctioned "by magnanimity" or by "the opinions of the world," a goal that might be accomplished best in the theater. Yet although White noted that his play received "the utmost applause" on the first night, he was not satisfied with attendance at the next two performances.[30] Possibly the widespread support for dueling reduced ticket sales.

White's second play of moral reform confronts the vice of intemperance, another vexing problem of southern society, as demonstrated by the large number of associations advocating abstinence. According to Clement Eaton, temperance was the one reform movement that attained wide popularity in the antebellum South, because "it harmonized with the religious and puritanical feeling of many southern people."[31] In 1829 the South Carolina Temperance Society was formed, and the movement was supported in the following years by influential leaders such as Thomas S. Grimké and Robert Barnwell Rhett of Charleston. In 1836 Governor George McDuffie urged legislation to abolish liquor shops in Columbia because they corrupted college students, but he was so little heeded, Judge Belton O'Neal reported, that in 1857 there were sixty-four grog shops and only sixty-two temperance men in that city.[32]

As an inveterate reformer, White denounced drinking in *The Forgers,* which, though never performed, interestingly anticipates that successful temperance play *The Drunkard* and is worth studying for its social and political significance. Before *The Forgers* was published in the *Southern Literary Journal* (1837),[33] the American Temperance Union had given its sanction "to prose fiction and other 'light' literature as propaganda material for the movement." Short fiction supporting temperance appeared in great abundance during the late 1830s.[34] The best-known temperance plays, however, did not reach the stage until *The Drunkard* started its long run in 1844, and *Ten Nights in a Bar-Room* opened in 1858. White's *Forgers*, composed in 1829 and printed in 1837, thus stands as one of the first temperance plays.

On August 9, 1836, White's "Address Delivered at the Request of the Young Men's Temperance Society" advised that "'taste not, touch not,' is the only maxim of sound wisdom" and went on to urge legislative action: "The Legislature should at once declare Intemperance to be a crime, and define punishments due its demerits." White described "the frightful effects of mania a potu" (madness from lack of wine), causing the victim to be "perturbed with bad and disturbing dreams."[35]

The Forgers, a tragedy in blank verse first titled "Mordaunt; or, The Victim of Intemperance," dramatizes the sentiments expressed in that speech. It depicts the degradation of young Mordaunt, caused by numerous vices but most notably by intemperance. He is betrayed by Ridgeford, a false friend, who is in love with Laura, the betrothed of Mordaunt. Ridgeford persuades him to forge a check by signing the name of Laura's father and boasts of his power, declaring that it is he "Who tempts him, day by day, to drain the cup, / And add intemperance to his other crimes" (1.1).

In act 4, scene 2, Mordaunt "flushed with drink," accuses Laura of giving her love to another man, whom he attempts to murder. Ridgeford completes the murder with a dagger and both are imprisoned. Suffering from lack of liquor in prison, Mordaunt has hallucinations in a scene reminiscent of Poe. He sees forms that "revel in the flames / Hooting and shouting as they sweep along!" Ridgeford, in an adjoining cell, gives him a vial of poison; thinking it is liquor, he drinks it and dies, wracked with convulsions, in the presence of his father. The setting of this play is not named in the printed version, but the manuscript specifies "Scene, in any City of the United States, where Brandy, Whiskey, Wine, etc. etc. are freely drunk."[36]

White stated in a letter dated August 16, 1830, that he planned to submit this tragedy to the play contest of William Pelby, manager of the Tremont Theatre in Boston.[37] The play did not win the prize, but White's lengthy analysis in the letter reveals that he strove to follow high standards. Later the editor of the *Southern Literary Journal,* claiming originality for White's play, noted that intemperance had been treated "with levity" in most previous dramatic works, and the drunkard had often appeared as "one worthy of imitation rather than pity, abhorrence, or aversion." He concluded: "Indeed, this is the first time, we believe, that the Dramatic Poet has given the subject exclusively his attention and treated it after a grave and serious manner, although one most prolific of incident and capable of producing highly tragical effects."[38]

The Drunkard; or, The Fallen Saved, the most successful of the temperance plays, premiered in Boston in 1844, seven years after the publication of White's work, with which it displays a notable contrast. Turning to drink after marriage, Edward Middleton, like Mordaunt, commits forgery, considered an especially heinous offense in nineteenth-century America. Rather than being destroyed by an evil associate, however, this victim of drink is rescued by William, an abstemious Yankee who obtains a pledge of abstinence from Edward. The anonymous author was shrewd in attaching a happy ending to the story of a drunkard, thus ensuring popular success. White's more realistic tragic ending lacked audience appeal—though which approach actually converted inebriates to sobriety one can only conjecture.

White's commitment to moral reform led him to participate also in the campaign against capital punishment, which gained widespread support in the 1830s and 1840s. Before the Literary and Philosophical Society on July 14, 1834, he delivered "An essay on the Moral Effect and tendency of Capital Punishment, and upon the propriety of substituting punishments of a milder nature." A part of this essay titled "The Dungeon and the Gallows," graphically describing the execution of a man and woman, was later included in *The Charleston Book* (1845), edited by Simms. Requesting not that crimes go unpunished but that "milder punishments" should take the place of death, White contended that even the "vilest culprit" is a fellow being capable of repentance, which is impossible after death.[39]

The Triumph of Liberty; or Louisiana Preserved (1819) shows White employing the drama to argue a controversial political position.[40] Another unperformed but published play, it celebrates, first, Jackson's great victory in the War of 1812. The Battle of New Orleans and the idolization of Andrew Jackson were popular topics of dramatists in the South, as had been illustrated by C.E. Grice's *The Battle of New Orleans* (1815). The major purpose of *The Triumph of Liberty,* however, was to defend Jackson's actions during the Seminole War of 1818, after which Florida was ceded

to the United States. Following skirmishes between Americans and Indians along the Georgia-Florida border in 1817, Jackson led his Tennessee
Volunteers into the territory in March 1818. He captured two British col-
laborators with the Indians, Alexander Arbuthnot and Lt. Robert C.
Ambrister of the Royal Marines, whom he tried in a military court and
executed. In 1819 Jackson's proceedings were investigated by Congress
and denounced as exceeding the limits of military authority. The *Charleston Courier* joined the criticism of Jackson, but White defended him in his
play, published on May 3, 1819.

The scenes involving the Indians most significantly reveal the author's
interest in the Seminole War (act 1, scenes 2-5, and all of act 3). White
was not concerned with historical accuracy; he wished instead to confirm
the charge that Arbuthnot and Ambrister had incited the Seminoles
against the Americans, thus justifying Jackson's actions. The two Britons
promise the Indians that King George III will send forces to defeat the
Americans (1.2); at a subsequent council they supply weapons and urge
the Indians on, exclaiming "Exterminate!" (3.1). His praise of Jackson
also shows White's attachment to the Democratic-Republican Party and
pride that this national hero was a native of South Carolina (though North
Carolina also claimed him). A farmer from Tennessee tells his son: "South-
Carolina may be justly proud of such a hero. Behold in him, the gentleman and the scholar, the statesman, the patriot, the soldier, and the hero:
to make his character complete, the steady, stern, inflexible Republican"
(1.1).

Other Charleston Dramatists

The success of Ioor's and White's productions for the Charleston Theatre encouraged other dramatists and added to the prolific playwriting
in Charleston. As a friend of Charles Gilfert and a leading drama critic in
Charleston, the versatile Isaac Harby (1788-1828) is the best example of
the close link between dramatists and the local theater which distinguished
drama in Charleston during its flourishing years. School-teacher, journalist, dramatic critic, dramatist, and religious leader, he was well acquainted with the classics and Shakespeare and thus qualified to write
knowledgeable opinions of the drama.[41]

As a journalist, Harby began editing the weekly *Quiver* in 1807. He
next purchased the *Investigator*, changed its name to the *Southern Patriot*,
and edited it as an organ voicing strong Republican sentiments and support of James Madison's administration. Harby was also a leader of the
Jewish Reform Movement in America. Along with others in Charleston

favoring change, he formed a new congregation in 1824 called the Reformed Society of Israelites. His biographer, L.C. Moise, considers that in his work as a religious leader "lies the most important and the most abiding work of his useful life."[42] In June 1828 Harby moved to New York where he established a connection with the *Evening Post*, a position in which, according to Simms, he maintained his fidelity to the *litterateurs* and the press in Charleston.[43] He died in New York on December 14, 1828.

Harby's interest in the drama is well demonstrated by the fact that in addition to a considerable body of dramatic criticism, he wrote three plays of his own. Of his first play, "Alexander Severus," he wrote in 1806: "I was buoyed up in my laborious task . . . by the belief of its running the same chance of success that [White's] 'The Mysteries of the Castle,' [Ioor's] 'The Battle of Eutaw Springs,' [etc.] did."[44] The play was turned down by Placide, however, and never published. *The Gordian Knot*, written in 1807, was not produced on the Charleston stage until May 3 and 10, 1810. Harby's last play, *Alberti*, was presented by Gilfert on April 27 and 30, 1819. Though motivated by artistic goals, these works lack a significant connection with contemporary life.

A collection of Harby's writings contains examples of his dramatic criticism. "Defence of the Drama" emphasizes that it is as "a moral level that the statesman and philosopher should regard the stage." In "The Merchant of Venice" he made a rare attack on his idol, Shakespeare, who bowed "to the prejudices of his age" in characterizing Shylock, but Harby held that we can still enjoy "the brilliancy" of the greatest poet of any age despite various objections to this play.[45] Other essays in the volume deal with the work of famous actors in Charleston, including Thomas A. Cooper as Othello and Coriolanus, and Edmund Kean as Sir Giles Overreach and Lear.

Harby is most significant as a critic who applied dramatic theories to his own plays. The first principle that governed his dramaturgy was the rejection of the Gothic in favor of an imitation of nature. On this point, he agreed with other American critics who asked for an adherence to reality. Censuring Gothic melodrama in his preface to *The Gordian Knot*, Harby explained how he had dealt with the "horrors" in Wiliam Ireland's novel *The Abbess*, the source for his play. The novel had served as a warning to shun its "monstrosities," he wrote: "In pursuing NATURE, I found my road to be widely different from the path followed by Mr. Ireland."[46]

Harby's disapproval of Gothic melodrama shows his alertness to contemporary trends in Charleston. John Blake White had announced his taste for that style in *The Mysteries of the Castle*, a full-blown Gothic piece featuring scenes of horror and a malicious villain with designs on the pure wife of a count. When White's play was performed in 1807—the same year *The Gordian Knot* was composed—a debate over the Gothic, which exaggerated human emotions, broke out in the *Charleston Courier* (January 3 and 7, 1807). Harby, using the pseudonym "Stefanolf," objected to the violent emotions that erupted with no conceivable cause in *The Mysteries of the Castle* and censured the villain because he was a man abnormally different from other human beings.[47] "Philo-Fauresco" answered that anyone acquainted with the human heart should be able to account for the hatred of such a villainous character. According to William Charvat, however, many American critics of this time abhorred "wonders and miracles, and supernaturalism," preferring instead the "glow of humanity and the solidity of real people."[48] (Gothic's high-pitched emotion and grotesque figures were destined to reappear in twentieth-century southern drama with the plays of Tennessee Williams and Beth Henley, often provoking similar controversy.)

Alberti is an improvement over *The Gordian Knot;* the plot, though typically intricate, is better handled and the revenge theme developed more interestingly. The setting is approximately that of the preceding play, Florence in 1480 during the rule of Lorenzo de Medici. A military hero just returning from battle, Alberti relinquishes revenge. Like other contemporary plays with foreign settings, *Alberti* contains incidental sentiments applicable to American politics, such as Lorenzo de Midici's declaration that if tyranny were planted in Florence, he would cross the Atlantic to find "some wild retreat / And there court Independence" (5.1). That statement must have pleased President James Monroe, who was present at the second performance of *Alberti* on May 1, 1819.

The first native of Georgia to compose a play, William Bulloch Maxwell (1789-1814), published *The Mysterious Father* (1807) in Savannah, a play containing the egalitarian sentiment "Mankind were all by nature equal made" (4.2). In his history of the Savannah theater, J. Max Patrick mentions that Maxwell may have seen plays in Charleston; certainly he would have attended performances by the Charleston company in Savannah, which Placide regularly visited until 1805.[49] Reviewing the printed edition of *The Mysterious Father,* Harby indicated that Maxwell knew of playwriting in Charleston: he wrote in the *Quiver* that the support given to "our native productions, affords an opening prospect to future attempts. Encouraged by this anticipated view, a youth of Georgia has stepped forth on the stage."[50]

It was Edwin C. Holland (1794-1824)—a lawyer who became editor of the *Charleston Times* in 1818 and had demonstrated his poetic talent in

Odes, Naval Songs and Other Occasional Poems (1814)—who adapted Byron's *Corsair* for the Charleston Theatre. The *Corsair* was performed on February 18, 20, and 21, 1818. On February 20 a writer for the *City Gazette and Commercial Daily Advertiser* reported that the audience at the first performance was numerous and respectable, and the taste of the manager was well displayed in scenic effect and music. As for the author, this correspondent stated, Holland was well known, "and his literary talents have often come under public inspection"; the public will now decide if "native genius is to be encouraged or neglected."

Charles Gilfert must have felt honored that William Crafts (1787-1826) decided to write a dramatic work, *The Sea-Serpent*, for his company. Poet, essayist, and orator, Crafts was the most prominent literary figure of Charleston during this period and a fervent Federalist. William P. Trent comments that Crafts was for many years the "literary dictator of Charleston," had a particular interest in the theater during the "golden days" of drama in the city, and came to its defense in a witty essay noting how much revenue the city received from taxing this institution.[51] Born in Charleston, the son of a Boston merchant, Crafts graduated from Harvard in 1805 and returned to his native city to become a lawyer and a member of the legislature. In 1821 he became editor of the *Courier,* giving it a more literary tone.

The Sea-Serpent, a satirical drama written in heroic couplets, derides a contemporary event: the discovery in Massachusetts of a large fish first thought to be a sea serpent. The play satirizes the gullibility of those who speculated on the existence of a monster discovered by sailors near Gloucester. After the scientists of Boston express great interest in this news, the Justice of Gloucester declares proudly:

> Let Salem boast her museum, and her witches,
> Her statues Newb'ry, Marblehead her riches—
> We from them all the shining now will take,
> The snake and Glo'ster, Glo'ster and the snake! [1.4].

Local pride evaporates when the creature turns out to be laughably small. According to the stage directions, some men enter "bringing a Horse-Mackeral—or some fish as much like a snake as can conveniently be procured" (3.2).

The Sea-Serpent was given as an afterpiece on May 12, 1819, and again, following *Hamlet,* on May 2, 1821, at the Charleston Theatre. Writing in the *City Gazette* for May 12, 1819, that from the title "theatre-goers may expect something witty," "Dramaticus" requested citizens to patronize the play, for "it is written by a gentleman of this city." The short piece was also performed in Richmond on July 4, 1820, as a "satirical burlesque," by Gilfert's company, which was then visiting the Richmond Theatre.[52]

James Wright Simmons (c. 1790-1858), coeditor with Simms of the *Southern Literary Gazette*, composed four plays: *Manfredi* (1821), *Valdemar; or, The Castle of the Cliff* (1822), *The Master of Ravenswood*, and *De Montalt; or, The Abbey of St. Clair*. The first two were printed but not performed; the third and fourth were presented only on April 12, 1824, and February 2, 1843, respectively. The unperformed works furnish evidence of the penchant for printing plays in Charleston.

Maria Pinckney (d. May 13, 1836)—the daughter of General Charles Cotesworth Pinckney and a woman of unusual force of mind who wrote a defense of Nullification—published three plays in a collection titled *Essays, Religious, Moral, Dramatic and Poetical* (1818).[53] The first, *Young Carolinians; or, Americans in Algiers*, a nationalistic drama expressing sympathy for Americans imprisoned by Algerian pirates, is the most interesting. Since the Barbary Wars extended from 1785 to 1816, this play was probably written some years before its publication and belonged to a series initiated by Susanna Rowson's *Slaves in Algiers; or, A Struggle for Freedom* (1794). Its scenes alternate between settings abroad and at home, contrasting a lady of low-country high society with "Homespun," a man from the back country.

Though Pinckney's plays were never performed, *Young Carolinians* is notable for presenting the first black speaker and the first defense of slavery in a southern play. In authentic Gullah dialect, Cudjo prefers his own life to the poor buckra's (white's).

> To be sure I slave for true; but poor folks must work every where. Suppose me poor buckra; well, I serve some rich buckra, him pay me; but when Cudjo sick, or lame, or old too much for work, him turn me away; now misses give me too much nasty stuff for cure me— plenty sweet tea to wash em down;— bye and bye get well again, she look pon me with one kind eye, same like a dove—glad to see poor old Cudjo well. [4.3]

This speech anticipates passages—such as one in Simms's novel *Woodcraft* (1852), in which a slave refuses freedom—of a kind that became common in southern plays before and during the Civil War.

Of all the plays written by Charleston dramatists, Ioor's *The Battle of Eutaw Springs* best represents the southern play. It preserves the Revolutionary legends of South Carolina by its graphic account of vicious civil strife. It portrays for the first time a well-known social type in the humorous old gentleman "Jonathan Slyboots," whose name has both nationalistic and South Carolina connotations. In retrospect, "Old Hospitality" can be seen as the precursor of many hospitable gentlemen in southern drama, showing the high value placed on hospitality and thus adding to our understanding of early southern culture—as does White's play about dueling, a sign of contemporary and future violence in southern life.

Compared with the plays composed by Virginians, dramatic writing in Charleston demonstrates greater sophistication in significant ways. In this first theatrical center of the South, dramatists believed they were launching a tradition of playwriting. Direct contact with actors and managers greatly assisted the construction of plays, giving their writers a much better sense of what would succeed on stage than if they had worked in isolation. Connoisseurs of drama offered immediate evaluation (sometimes unfavorable) in the local press; after the premiere of a new play, there was spirited give and take in the newspapers. When White experimented with Gothicism, for example, one critic supported him enthusiastically, while the more traditional "Stephanolf" condemned the genre's untruthfulness.

The plays of Charleston, then, though not artistic achievements, did represent advancement over those of Virginia. Fruitful collaboration between native dramatists and the local companies made the plays produced at the Charleston Theatre more theatrical. It is possible to visualize the action and the personages more clearly even in reading a work like *The Battle of Eutaw Springs*. One is aware of an interchange between the dramatists and local critics, audiences, and actors, and there is a continuity in the succession of native plays seen in Charleston.

Virginia and Charleston both reveal the enthusiasm for playwriting in the Atlantic South. Now it is time to consider the Gulf South, less influenced by the mellifluous cadences of Shakespeare but more attuned to the extravagances of American life.

— 3 —

The Dramatist as Humorist
in New Orleans

As population moved westward, theatrical activities in the South expanded in that direction as well. With the French opera and numerous theaters, New Orleans became the second theatrical center in the nation after New York. In this polyglot city an English language theater ran concurrently with the French stage. Native drama accurately reflected western humor, frontier violence, and a political transition from nationalism to sectionalism in defense of slavery, the cultural institution that would shape southern plays irrevocably as well as the South itself.

In the Mississippi Valley the theater became a major civilizing force—even though it had its ruder side, to be sure, as described later by Mark Twain. A trio of managers constructed an imposing theatrical empire that extended from St. Louis to Mobile, with New Orleans as the center. James H. Caldwell, Noah Ludlow, and Solomon Smith attracted actors and playwrights from all over the country to their flourishing domain. This vigorous activity provided the milieu from some vital and interesting dramatic writing, led by the humorist Joseph M. Field, by far the most impressive dramatist to emerge from the colorful theatrical life of the southwestern frontier.

James H. Caldwell (1793-1863) was another Englishman who embarked upon a successful career as a theatrical manager. After coming to Charleston in 1817, he transferred to Virginia and set up a theatrical circuit, playing Richmond, Petersburg, and elsewhere in that state. Conceiving grander designs, Caldwell moved in 1820 to New Orleans, where he leased the St. Philip Street Theatre, organized an acting company, and became impresario of a far-flung circuit in the Mississippi Valley.[1]

In 1822, soon after coming to New Orleans, Caldwell constructed the Camp Street Theatre, which he continued to manage until 1833; for those eleven years he made it the finest theater in the South. Recognizing the opportunities outside of New Orleans, Caldwell also took his American Company to such towns as Natchez, Nashville, and Huntsville, and in 1829 he inaugurated theatrical performances in St. Louis. In that year Sol Smith, who became a famous actor and manager in the Southwest, joined his troupe. As New Orleans grew in reputation as a theatrical center, Caldwell engaged many outstanding actors, among them Edwin Forrest, who performed at the Camp Street Theatre in 1829, and Jane Placide, Alexander Placide's daughter, who was one of the most talented actresses in Caldwell's company.

By 1833 Caldwell had risen in New Orleans society and, having entered the business of supplying gaslight to the city, announced his retirement, leasing the Camp Street Theatre to Richard Russell and James Simon Rowe. Finding himself unwilling to give up his original career, however, Caldwell opened the splendid St. Charles Theatre in 1835 and began his second period of management in New Orleans. Turning his attention next to Mobile, he built the Royal Street Theatre there in 1841, assured that he had thereby triumphed over the two men who had become his rivals in the Mississippi Valley: Noah Ludlow and Sol Smith. His confidence proved to be short-lived: the St. Charles burned down on March 13, 1842, and with this disaster Caldwell announced his permanent retirement from management. Ludlow and Smith opened the New St. Charles Theatre on January 18, 1843, and for the next ten years succeeded him as the dominant theatrical force in the valley. Caldwell, who had ruled theatrical life for two decades, had been a dedicated supporter of legitimate drama, setting a high tone in the theater by his offerings. Though he was not above vying for attendance by playing to popular demand, he gave less support than his rivals and successors to the new brand of native productions that were lending a distinctive flavor to theaters on the frontier.

Unlike the English Caldwell, the other two theatrical pioneers in the Mississippi Valley were born in America: Noah Ludlow (1795-1886) in New York City, and Solomon Smith (1801-69) in rural Norwich, New York. Smith, the more colorful of the two and known for his low comedy roles, was an ardent Jacksonian and in later life opposed secession as a Unionist in St. Louis. Both managers have become well known through their theatrical memoirs: Ludlow's *Dramatic Life as I Found It* and Smith's *Theatrical Management in the West and South*.[2] Published in the Library of Humorous American Works, the latter's narrative of performances on the southern frontier abounds in funny anecdotes. According to Smith, who in fact ranks as a leading southwest humorist, theatrical humbugs were practiced on credulous audiences, and fundamentalist preachers often denounced performances.

A versatile writer, Smith contributed to the *St. Louis Reveille* and composed farces for the stage, one of which has survived. *A Scene before the Curtain; or, The Manager in Trouble* was presented in St. Louis, February 27, 1843, and, as *The Manager in Distress,* at the opening of the season in New Orleans, November 1, 1851. In this hilarious prelude to the evening's fare, several actors in the audience, disguised as spectators, protest loudly when the manager announces that Sol Smith cannot appear because of an accident.[3] The audience complains as well until Sol enters precipitously.

Because he often took elderly parts, Smith earned the sobriquet "Old Sol" and became a well-known character in tales of southwestern humorists, such as Field's "'Old Sol' in a Delicate Situation" collected in *The Drama in Pokerville, the Bench and Bar of Jurytown, and other Stories.* In "Ol' Sol. Once More" bedlam ensues after the actor fails to appear for a performance, as in "The Manager in Distress." In this tale signed by "Thunder," a carrot-headed youth who has come all the way from Copiah County, Mississippi, just to see the show, declares "he'd be durn if *he'd* be fooled out of his dollar in *that* are kind of a way!" To prove his threat of a fight, he mounts the stage, but pulls off his red wig and displays "the veritable phiz of 'old Sol,'" who is greeted by a shout that those present swear was "THUNDER!"[4]

After performing with strolling players throughout the Southwest—in Nashville, in Huntsville and other towns of Alabama, as well as New Orleans—Ludlow and Smith formed a partnership in 1835, based on a nexus of Mobile (where Ludlow lived) and St. Louis (Smith's home). Having been induced to join forces by the competition of Caldwell in Mobile, the two men continued their joint venture for eighteen years despite recurring disagreements. In 1837 the partners opened the first legitimate theater in St. Louis. Delivering the dedicatory address, Joseph M. Field, who had become a member of their company, proclaimed it the first theater in "the far, far West."[5] In the 1840-41 season, Ludlow and Smith opened the New American Theatre (formerly Camp Street) to compete with Caldwell in New Orleans. The popularity of the horse shows forced Caldwell, who had always tried to preserve the legitimate drama, to put on equestrian attractions as well. Then in March 1841 at the theater of Ludlow and Smith, Fanny Fitzwilliam (in *Foreign Airs and Native Graces*) burlesqued Fanny Elssler, the famous Austrian dancer appearing at Caldwell's theater. Competition between Caldwell and the partners was reaching a climax.

In January 1843 Ludlow and Smith achieved victory over their old competitor when they opened the New St. Charles Theatre, and thereafter until 1853 the two managers controlled the New Orleans-Mobile-St.

Louis circuit. They spent the winter season in Mobile and the summer and fall season in St. Louis; they shared management of the main season in New Orleans. (Contrasting the audiences at the St. Charles with those in the Mobile theater, Field wrote Sol Smith that the audience at the former was "too genteel by half after the halooing of the Mobilians.")[6] The managers suffered some dismal seasons but enjoyed prosperous ones as well. In 1845-46 they engaged such stars as Junius Brutus Booth, Charles Kean, Henry Placide, and James Hackett. The winter of 1852-53 marked their final season, after which these pioneer managers of the Southwest dissolved their partnership.[7]

Dramatic Writing

The first English-language plays printed in New Orleans reflect the same liking for battles and legendary figures as in the eastern South. In New Orleans the most popular event of the past was Andrew Jackson's victory over the British in the War of 1812, which C.E. Grice, a native of the city, celebrated in *The Battle of New Orleans,* featuring General Jackson as the central character. It was first performed in 1815 and printed in 1816. Sol Smith remarked slyly that it was "got up" by "Andrew Jackson Allen," who adopted a new name for the occasion.[8] This play became a nationalistic standby; it was given on Washington's birthday in 1828, and on January 8—the anniversary of the battle—in 1844 and 1845. In all, it was presented eight times in New Orleans before the Civil War.

Following the lead of the famous actor Edwin Forrest, Caldwell attempted to encourage the writing of native works with a prize-play contest. James H. Kennicott, a native of New Orleans, won $300 for *Irma; or, The Prediction,* a romantic tragedy in verse set in the early days of the Revolution. It was performed in New Orleans in April 1830, and repeated on February 15, 1831, when Jane Placide powerfully played the title role, according to a local newspaper review. An Indian play by the novelist Caroline Lee Hentz, *Lemorah; or, The Western Wild,* was presented at Caldwell's theater on January 1, 1833.[9] An interesting body of plays depicting the life of the western frontier corresponds to the fiction that also dealt with this fresh material, such as the border novels of Simms and Robert Montgomery Bird, some of which were adapted for the stage. These pieces were almost never published, but from various sources— chiefly newspapers—it is possible to gain a glimpse into their contents.

Native plays about the frontier received their first important support from another enterprising and innovative manager. Richard Russell, who leased the Camp Street Theatre from Caldwell in 1835 until his death on

May 19, 1838, competed successfully with the entrenched impresario of New Orleans. Differing from the policy of Caldwell, who favored dignified drama even when he sponsored native works, Russell appealed to popular tastes and thereby drew large audiences. Most significantly, he attracted a group of native dramatists to compose pieces for his theater.

James Rees, an ambitious dramatist and enthusiastic nationalist from the East—known later for his biographical volume, *The Dramatic Authors of America* (1845)—spent most of the 1830s in New Orleans. While there, he wrote *Washington at Valley Forge* for Caldwell's theater (1832) and preserved a legendary figure of western humor in *Mike Fink, The Last Boatman of the Mississippi* (this play is not extant, nor is its date of performance known). Rees also capitalized on the notoriety of a legendary Louisianian in *Lafitte*, depicting the former pirate Jean Lafitte, who became Jackson's famous ally during the War of 1812 and gave valuable support to the American forces. This play, given on nine nights between April 3 and 14, 1837, at the Camp Street Theatre, was highly successful.

Lafitte has not survived in print, but newspaper notices provide some information. The first performance was billed as the "Nautical Drama of Lafitte," indicating that boats would supply exciting stage effects. According to one editorial comment, the performance improved on the second night, when a Mr. Farren enacted a Yankee, "a whiskered Frenchman, and finally the inflexible Hero of New Orleans," whom he played "to the life" (*Picayune*, April 3 and 5, 1837). On the fourth night Mr. Abbott, who played Lafitte, was wounded by a musket shot in the wrist, making the performance more true to life than planned.

A competing work about Lafitte by Charlotte Barnes Conner, which had played in Mobile on March 13 with Sol Smith as General Jackson, was staged at Caldwell's St. Charles Theatre on April 15 and 17. It seems to have lacked the gusto of Rees's play, however, demonstrating once again Caldwell's attempt to keep his productions more dignified. *Lafitte—The Pirate of the Gulf* played only the two nights. According to the *Picayune*, the author, who was also well known as an accomplished actress, had dramatized the play from the novel of "Professor Ingraham."[10] After the second performance, the better attended one, the reviewer observed approvingly that the language of the play was "chaste" (April 18, 1837).

Nathaniel H. Bannister (1813-47), a talented and original actor-dramatist born in Baltimore, made his debut at the Front Street Theatre of that city as Young Norval in John Home's *Douglas* and appeared on the New York stage in 1831. He became best known for his equestrian drama *Putnam* (1844), set during the Revolution, in which a horseman thrilled audiences by descending a steep ramp on stage. After coming to New Orleans, Bannister showed his interest in western events by composing plays for Russell's theater, such as *Fall of San Antonio; or, Texas Victorious* given on January 1, 1836. It celebrated the recent defeat of the Mexicans which had led to the formation of the Texas Republic.

Bannister also dramatized the exploits of a famous southwestern desperado in *Murrell: The Great Western Land Pirate,* presented at the Camp Street Theatre on May 16 and 26, 1837. An account of John A. Murrell's activities in Alabama and Mississippi had been published in 1835,[11] and not long afterward Simms composed two border romances fictionalizing the legendary outlaw's exploits, *Richard Hurdis, A Tale of Alabama* (1839) and *Border Beagles, A Tale of Mississippi* (1840). Murrell was a former preacher who had recruited young wanderers into his criminal organization, which became notorious throughout the Mississippi Valley, causing enraged citizens to lynch members of the gang. After terrorizing citizens of Alabama and Mississippi for several years and reputedly instigating a slave rebellion, he was finally captured and put on trial in western Tennessee. Twain remembered hearing of him as a boy (*Life on the Mississippi,* Chapter 29). What little information remains on Bannister's play must be gleaned from the *Picayune,* which advertised "a new drama of thrilling interest" (May 16, 1837). Revealing the play's connection with the tall tale of southwestern humor, the cast featured one character named "Bob Steelborn, a Kentuckian, half horse, half alligator," played by a Mr. Foster and representing the frontiersman for New Orleans audiences.

George Washington Harby (1797-1862), like his brother Isaac Harby of Charleston, was an occasional dramatist. His first attempt, an Indian play, was performed at Caldwell's theater on February 22, 1835. *Tutoona; or, the Indian Girl* takes place during the Revolution, as indicated by the additional subtitle "The Battle of Saratoga." Like Bannister, Harby selected a popular western subject for his next play, given appropriately at Russell's theater. *Nick of the Woods* was based on Robert Montgomery Bird's novel of that name (1837), a tale of frontier violence about an Indian hater who takes revenge on those who killed his family. Its most popular character, however, was another Kentucky humorist; when Harby's play was given March 18, 19, and 23, 1838, "Ralph Stackpole," played by Mr. Parsons, headed the cast, showing the dramatist's wish to amuse the audience above all. According to the *Picayune* (March 18, 1838), the author had skillfully blended the language of the novel with his own, always a challenge for the dramatic adapter. This successful play was repeated often in the following years.[12]

Joseph M. Field

The most substantial dramatist to emerge from the theater of the Mississippi Valley was assuredly Joseph M. Field (1810-56). This versatile actor, journalist, manager, and dramatist had joined the flood of emigrants from the East in the 1830s and made his mark in the new states, where he lived until his death. The number and nature of Field's plays, which can be deduced from newspaper reports and such records as Ludlow's, indicate that he made a serious commitment to dramatic composition, one not adequately recognized.[13] It is difficult to assess Field as a dramatist because only one of his plays is extant, but numerous nondramatic writings have survived in print. A successful journalist, he contributed notably to the movement of southwestern humor.

In fact, what Field, Sol Smith, and other writers for the New Orleans stage contributed to southern drama was an irrepressible sense of humor, and their plays thus differ markedly from those of early Virginia and Charleston. Although there is comedy in the historical plays of Custis and Ioor, the dominant mood is typified by the tragedies and moral protest of John Blake White, whereas the purpose of Field and Smith in New Orleans, Mobile, and St. Louis, was to provoke laughter. The Southwest, with its greater appreciation of humor for its own sake, produced caricatures of living persons and satire of current folly. The comedy of character was honed to a fine edge in the self-caricature of Old Sol. Field, specializing in the ridicule of gullibility—so common on Twain's frontier, where con men preyed on the innocent dupes of backwater hamlets—expanded his humorous range with a burlesque of *Uncle Tom's Cabin*. Humor, which would become an indispensable part of the southern play, made a solid debut in his numerous farces.

Of Irish ancestry, Field was born in England, the son of a prominent Catholic. Perhaps because he arrived in the United States at the age of two, he shows clearly the traits of a native American, not a transplanted Englishman. After growing up in Baltimore and New York, he began his acting career at the Tremont Theatre of Boston in 1827. Around 1830 he went west, where he remained except to take sporadic acting jobs in New York and Boston and a summer abroad. As a member of the company of Ludlow and Smith from 1835 to 1844, Field lived the life of a strolling player, visiting the backwater towns so humorously described by Smith and Field himself in their writings. He made his St. Louis debut in 1835 as Richard III, and in 1837 he married the leading lady of the company, Eliza Riddle, whose relatives lived in Boston. Besides writing plays for her, he frequently shared the stage with his wife, and from all the evidence they enjoyed a happy marriage. The couple had one surviving child, Kate, who became a successful lecturer in the last half of the nineteenth century. As a leading actor in the company, Field tried many roles, such as Dazzle in Dion Boucicault's *London Assurance* (1841), but found his forte in the eccentric comedy that coincided with his penchant for writing humorous fiction, poetry, and drama. According to a Mobile memorialist, Field could do all kinds of things: act, write a play, compose a poem, edit a newspaper.[14]

Although Field's associates admired him as a man of many talents, some felt he spread himself too thin. Toward the end of his life he tried his hand at management, directing the Royal Street Theatre of Mobile with some success in 1850-52. Next, he opened Field's Varieties of St. Louis in 1852, but when that venture proved unprofitable, he resumed management of the theater in Mobile. He died there of consumption in 1856. According to a note dated April 18, 1856, the impecunious Field owed $1,147.69 at the time of his death.[15]

Concurrently with his career on the stage, Field followed a vocation in journalism for many years. His nondramatic writings—including *The Drama in Pokerville . . . and Other Stories* (1847), which collected many of his newspaper pieces—express his views and provide essential background for understanding his unpublished plays.[16] Field was first connected with the *Weekly Picayune* (to be distinguished from the *Picayune*, a daily) of New Orleans, and while acting at the theater of Ludlow and Smith in 1838-39, he wrote extensively for this widely distributed publication. Under the pen name "Straws" (signifying "trifles"), Field contributed scores of humorous poems, such as "Fanny's One Thousand Nightly" (reprinted in the *Picayune*, February 21, 1841), satirizing the exorbitant fees that Caldwell paid Fanny Elssler, the famous Austrian dancer. He was such a success on the *Weekly Picayune* that in 1840 he departed for Europe as its correspondent, sailing on June 19 for Liverpool and returning from Le Havre on September 1. By February 1841 he was back in New Orleans.[17] This voyage broadened his experience and must have improved his knowledge of French, since he later adapted plays from works in that language.

Field's journalistic writing in the *Weekly Picayune* accurately reflects his style as a dramatist. It contains much satire but—like William T. Porter's *Spirit of the Times*, the leading humorous weekly in those years—is nonpartisan in politics. Only in opposing abolition did Field's weekly pieces take an openly partisan stand. That opposition also marks a letter dated October 6, 1835, to Sol Smith, who opposed slavery; Field joked that since Sol's last letter was abolitionist, he should be glad that it was not intercepted.[18] Despite his disapproval of abolition, Field in one story deplored

the lynching of an abolitionist in "A Lyncher's Own Story," related by the
"Colonel" to a delighted audience on a steamboat.[19]

During his years in St. Louis he joined his brother Matthew C. Field,
another journalistic humorist, and Charles Keemle to found the *St. Louis
Reveille*. While editing this humorous weekly, Field indicated his literary
taste by defending Edgar Allan Poe, whom he had met, as "one of the
most original geniuses of the country."[20] The *Reveille*, which Field edited
from 1844 to 1850, attained a wide readership throughout the country.
Taking the pen name "Everpoint," he contributed humorous pieces whose
anecdotal quality and dialect reveal the southwestern style unmistakably.
Many of these tales were reprinted in the *Spirit of the Times* and afterward
in *The Bench and Bar in Jurytown and Other Sketches*, which became the second half of *The Drama in Pokerville*.

Although fictitious, *The Drama in Pokerville* is based on Field's experiences as a traveling actor in the Southwest. In this tale of a visit to a backwater village, Mr. Oscar Dust manages the Great Small Affair Company,
which comes to Pokerville for a season of two weeks. He opens with William Dunlap's adaptation of Kotzebue's *Pizarro* (1800), a theatrical standby
mentioned amusingly by Sol Smith as well. Mrs. Major Slope, descended
from the First Families of Virginia, invites the actors to an elaborate dinner at which company's singer, Mr. Fitzcarol, defends the actress Fanny
Wilkins from charges of immorality made by Mrs. Slope and Manager
Dust. Fanny is modeled after Fanny Fitzwilliam, the successful singer-co-
medienne of Ludlow and Smith's company. After Fitzcarol discredits
Fanny's critics, the manager leaves town in disgrace, being forced to dis-
miss the audience for his own benefit because it is so small. Sadly, he
must leave "his *foundation* in Pokerville to be built on by some more fortunate architect" (p. 87). In the sentimental ending, Fanny and Fitzcarol
marry, have a son, and are visited by "Mam'selle Nathalie," who is based
on Fanny Elssler.

Field's account of the dinner in Pokerville had a factual basis in his
own personal experience in 1835, when Sol Smith dispatched him to
Wetumpka, Alabama, to offer a two-week theatrical season in a converted
billiard room. Reporting his success to Old Sol, Field noted that the
Wetumpka citizens gave him a grand dinner, which was to be written up
in the *Wetumpka Times*: "What do you think—they have been giving me a
Dinner a dashing affair I tell ye and the first ever given at Wetumpka—we
had a delightful time." He recounted being toasted and, after getting
tipsy, enacting King Lear.[21]

According to Francis Hodge in his introduction to *Dramatic Life as I
Found It*, Field was recounting the story of Ludlow's itinerant company in

The Drama in Pokerville. Beneath the surface of his fiction lies Field's skepticism about the place of drama in the Mississippi Valley, evident in the vanity of the caricatured manager. Oscar Dust was probably based on Noah Ludlow, who lacked Sol Smith's levity and preferred to associate with important members of society. When a banquet in Mobile honored the inauguration of John Quincy Adams in March 1824, Ludlow was among those invited. In his theatrical history he describes the theater grandly as "the temple of the Drama."[22]

In Field's burlesque Manager Dust uses the same pompous language as his model. At Mrs. Major Slope's dinner he calls Mr. Wilson's store the town's "present temple" and grandly delivers a toast to "the Pokerville temple—the drama." The performance of *Pizarro* ends uproariously when Mrs. Slope becomes so distraught at the plight of the hero Rolla that she leaps onstage, proclaiming, "Hold, monsters!" Wryly, the author concludes that thus "the drama was founded in Pokerville!" (pp. 57, 58, 25, 27).

This short novel is a mixture of trivial burlesque (recalling the pen name "Straws") and serious satire after the manner of Twain. Field's fun with his portrait of Fanny Elssler is skillfully done but is only the lightest kind of froth. By contrast, he levels righteous indignation at some aspects of life on the southwestern frontier. A committed enemy of pretentiousness, he is unsparing in his ridicule of Manager Dust's premature claims. Like Twain, Field saw that culture was an imperiled commodity in frontier settlements, where the establishment of drama was likely to be short-lived. Further, he chastised the social airs and religious narrowmindedness of backwater towns by defending the good-hearted Fanny Wilkins against those who considered her a corrupter of their pure society.

The most significant body of Field's dramatic writing comprises his many farces, all unpublished but the delight of audiences, as can be ascertained from New Orleans newspaper accounts. In these humorous pieces, the equivalent of contemporary stories in collections like Williams T. Porter's, Field used the same mocking tone that pervades *The Drama in Pokerville.* His favorite target was the con-man, who exploited the naiveté of his victims. Like Mark Twain and Herman Melville in *The Confidence-Man* (1857) Field discovered con-men of every description in the Mississippi Valley. His satire of charlatans' dupes in the 1840s foreshadows Twain's writings, whose fiction like Field's drama owed much to southwestern humor.

Field believed that Americans were especially vulnerable to spiritual fads such as Millerism and Mesmerism, placing blind faith in what he considered outrageous humbugs. The Millerites were fair game for satirists. Their leader, William Miller, predicted the Second Coming in 1843;

when that did not come to pass, he named two more dates in the following year. The *Picayune* printed a notice mocking "an Arkansas Millerite" on April 21, 1843. In the *Reveille* of 1844, Matthew Field (Joseph's brother) published "The Second Advent," which relates a Millerite's prediction aboard a steamboat. This prophet uses the numbers in Revelation plus his own addition to arrive at "the year 1844 as clear as mud."[23]

To publicize his farce about the Millerites, Field write a poem called "The 23d—Final Preparations," in which "Straws" prepares for the end of the world: "I'm waitin' for the minute, Pic [short for "Picayune"] / One eye cocked up aloft." To be ready, he will get dressed up on April 20 "and go to Joe Field's benefit to-night!" (*Picayune*, April 20, 1843). That was the night *Twenty-third of April; or, Are You Ready?* was staged with Field heading the cast as Mr. Buz and Sol Smith as Judge Lynch. Also present at Judgment Day was "The Devil," as well as "Saints and Sinners by the Company."

Concurrently with Millerism, Mesmerism, originated by the Austrian physician Friedrich Mesmer, became the rage. The *Picayune* for April 18, 1843, for example, reported that "Mr. Moore, the mesmerizer" of Natchez was exhibiting "his wonders to the good people there." Matthew Field, alias "Phazma," wrote a poem satirizing Mesmerism along with flying machines and Mormonism (*Picayune*, March 9, 1843). "Everpoint" ridiculed this form of hypnotism in "Establishing the Science" (included in *The Drama in Pokerville*), stating that Mesmerists were charlatans claiming to restore health. In the sketch, a Wisconsin giant learns the art and heals a criminal, who pays with money he was stolen. The Mesmerist keeps the cash, boasting that he has now "*established the science*, by thunder" (p. 133).

Field's stage satire of Mesmerism or "magnetism" was called *Nervo Vitalics; or, The March of Science.* The *Picayune* (March 11, 1843) noted that since Field was already known as "a great Mesmerizer, upon principle," he should play the part of "Milky (phrenologist and magnetizer)" to perfection. The cast also included a medium named "Miss Clairvois," for Mesmerists claimed the power to communicate with departed spirits through a clairvoyant maiden—a practice castigated by Nathaniel Hawthorne in *The Blithedale Romance* (1852).

Field's *1943; or, New Orleans a Century Hence* also satirizes charlatanry: according to the *Picayune* (April 14, 1843), this farce doubted—sometimes wrongly—the "progress of steam, temperance, aerial navigation, Mesmerism, Millerism, &c." Poking fun at certain local citizens, this futuristic fantasy was "a hit" according to Ludlow. In an election for mayor, satirized in scene 3, "Judge Sally Jones" is "the candidate of the dames." "Men in petticoats; women in trousers" fill the stage, and "Mr. Beheard" conducts an auction of "old bachelors."[24] The *Picayune* (April 16, 1843) reported that this hodgepodge abounded in "local witticisms and humorous conceits."

Among unscrupulous exploiters of the public who became objects of Field's satire were theatrical stars who appeared throughout the country, charging exorbitant fees. One chronicler of the Mobile Theatre who decried the "Starring System" while Field was manager said stars received far too much money, the manager not enough.[25] Field's *G—A—G; or, The Starring System* was performed at the St. Charles Theatre February 20, 1841. In contemporary slang "gag" signified a deception of credulous theatergoers. This farce attacks the arrogance of traveling stars who perform at the expense of the stock company's earnings. Sol Smith says that the dramatist heaped ridicule on Fanny Elssler in this piece.[26] The newspaper notice called it an "antic, vocal, local sketch in verse" with Field heading the cast as "The Manager," assisted by "True-Taste" and "Shakespeare" (*Picayune*, February 20, 1841). In "The Gagging Scheme; or, West's Great Picture" Field contributed another "gag" to his collection of stories. Some impecunious actors on the frontier attract unsuspecting villagers to the exhibit of a painting claimed to be the work of the famous artist Benjamin West.

Among the charlatans competing with actors for the public's purse in 1843 was an astronomical lecturer named Dr. Dionysius Lardner, whose pseudoscientific lectures enjoyed great success in New Orleans.[27] The *Picayune* (April 16, 1843) noted on its editorial page that Dr. Lardner's lecture in Mobile had given much satisfaction. Field caricatured Dr. Lardner in *Dr. Heavy Bevy,* performed April 11, 1843, at Ludlow and Smith's theater. The advance notice in the *Picayune* announced that the professor in this piece would lecture on "Nebular and stellar clusters" and "Gagics!!!" (that is, topics exploiting the public's gullibility). Illustrations from "drawings by eminent observers" would be accompanied by "speculation upon cometary influence." Ludlow wrote that this burlesque of Dr. Lardner's astronomical lectures created a lot of merriment.[28]

Field also included foreign visitors among those charlatans taking advantage of American gullibility in his *Foreign and Native,* produced in St. Louis, June 21, 1845. According to the reviewer in that city, Americans have been fooled shamefully by foreign visitors, as evident in Field's farce, which ridicules the Flare Family. Like other "fashionables" infatuated by foreign noblemen and authors, they fall prey to "any crafty adventurer." The father wants his national vanity gratified; the mother desires "a *titled* husband" for her daughter. Noting that this play was a revision of Field's *Such as It Is,* given at the Park Theatre in New York, the reviewer praised the dramatist's character drawing but found deficiencies in plot construction.[29] In *Such as It Is* (first performed September 4, 1842) Field anticipated by three years Anna Cora Mowatt's brilliant satire in *Fashion* of Americans duped by bogus foreign noblemen.

Although Field was not primarily a political writer, he reacted to certain political issues when his satirical impulse was provoked. Written to support America's acquisitions in the Northwest, *Oregon; or, The Disputed Territory*—presented at the St. Charles Theatre on January 8, 11, and 14 and February 4, 1846, and in Mobile on January 26, 1846 was advertised as a new musical *jeu d'esprit* or burletta (*Picayune,* January 8, 1846). This was the time of the American slogan "54-40 or fight" in the dispute with Great Britain over the boundary between the United States and Canada; later in 1846, under President James Knox Polk, the United States compromised by accepting the 49th parallel. In Field's piece, John Bull relinquishes his demand for both Texas and Oregon after the American musicians give him a strong dose of "the Polk-a." Other allegorical characters include Oregon, Texas, Uncle Sam, the Goddess of Liberty, and "the staid and matronly Massachusetts," played by Mrs. Rowe.[30] Field probably wished to satirize Massachusetts by this solemn figure because that state, as the stronghold of abolitionism, opposed the acquisition of slaveholding Texas.

In November 1838, though he probably supported James Gordon Bennett's political aims, Field wrote three theatrical caricatures of the famous editor of the *New York Herald.* Showing the growing influence of Irish immigrants who read his paper, Bennett, a Scottish Catholic, branded Great Britain the international foe of republicanism, determined to keep the United States from achieving its proper place in the world. In 1838, Bennett advocated gaining all of the Oregon Territory in the dispute with Great Britain, a stand that would have pleased Field.[31]

Putting on his series about Bennett in New Orleans, Field took the leading role, as he customarily did in pieces composed for his benefits. On November 14, 1838, *Victoria; or, The Lion and the Kiss*—which was "a jumbled up mass, but contains many hits," according to the *Picayune* (November 16, 1838)—satirized Bennett's recent visit to England and showed the young Queen Victoria as afraid of committing herself to an unwise policy at the hands of this skillful diplomat.[32] Two nights later, in *The White House,* "Mr. Kinderhook" —President Martin Van Buren, a native of Kinderhook, New York—joined the cast with Bennett and Queen Victoria. Finally, on November 18, the satirical fantasy *Bennett in Texas; or, The Great Exile* revealed the editor to be an enthusiastic advocate of the admission of Texas, despite opposition in the free states. According to a theatrical notice in the *Picayune* (November 18, 1838), likely written by Field, Mr. Bennett wished it "distinctly understood that his exile in Texas is . . . solely induced by the faithlessness of the age and ingratitude of government"—a satiric way of backing Bennett's charge that Texas was being unfairly refused admission to the United States. As a pro-slavery man, Field would have supported annexation of Texas.

At the end of his career the pro-slavery Field initiated the theatrical rebuttals in New Orleans of *Uncle Tom's Cabin* (1852). Harriet Beecher Stowe's controversial indictment of slavery had brought the simmering sectional debate to a boil. Trained in the techniques of southwestern humor and theatrical farce, Field undertook to respond by another of his burlesques, relying on his experience as a satirist to counteract the moral suasion of Mrs. Stowe.

Uncle Tom's Cabin; or, Life in the South as It is, advertised as "a satirical, quizzical burlesque," opened on February 15, 1854, at the Southern Museum and ran for six successive nights. According to the *Picayune* (February 17, 1854), the play was "well got up and well acted," attracting full houses nightly. Uncle Tom was played by John Smith, a celebrated "delineator" of Negro life, backed by the whole company.[33] The burlesque blends comic scenes with melodrama and includes even more of Field's far-ranging satire than his futuristic fantasy *1943*. Advertised as written by "Mrs. Harriet Screecher Blow," the play opens with two scenes of "Mrs. Blow and Brother Crow" and a "World's convention of the Friends of everyone, opposed to every thing," indicating Field's wish to identify northern abolitionists with negativists of every description. In a third scene Negroes in Canada sing "Carry me back to Old Virginny." When the "Philanthropist," a common term for abolitionists, asks Uncle Tom if he wants a house or clothes, he answers, "No, Massa," but on hearing the strains of "Old Folks at Home," he exclaims, "Massa—*that's what I want!*" According to the *Daily Delta* this scene, which brought tears to the eyes of everyone, was considered "quite melodramatic and also exceedingly correct"—that is, truthful. As the curtain falls, a gang of Negroes performed the dance called "Juba."[34]

The importance to the development of southern drama of Field's and others' comic rebuttals of *Uncle Tom's Cabin* can hardly be overstated. In popular unmistakably southern dramatizations of distinctive material, politics and cultural combined in a new way. Strongly nationalist in preceding decades, southern drama now became militantly sectionalist in its pro-slavery argument. Ironically, the propagandistic purpose fostered a new cultural component: the inclusion of black life, seen vividly in dancing, singing, and humor that had appeared before only in minstrel shows.

Though distorted, the picture of southern life with its pairing of slave and master, the ridicule of northern abolitionists, and the sentimental return of slaves to the plantation proved a surefire formula for success. The reasons for the success of a new vehicle in the theater are not always admirable, nor is its rendering of life and personalities always accurate. The scenes of southern life in the comic rebuttals are exaggerated, superficial, and hardly comprehensive, but they embody the distinctive, biracial experience of the South, ideally suited for the stage with its appetite for exoticism and emotion. In short, the success of these comic pieces forecast an auspicious future for southern plays.

Field's one surviving play, like *The Drama in Pokerville* volume, attests to his skill as a writer. *Job and His Children*, a sentimental comedy with some interesting characters, is an example of the "Yankee play," which was widely popular in the 1840s and 1850s. James Hackett had made a comic Yankee (that is, a native New Englander) named "Job" popular in the farce *Job Fox; or, The Yankee Valet*, which played at the Park Theatre of New York, 1834-35.[35] After writing farces for many years, Field chose this new direction when he opened his St. Louis Varieties in 1852. W.H. Chippendale, a popular actor who took the title role, preserved a manuscript copy.[36] Upon seeing a performance, Kate Field called it "a beautiful piece."[37]

In this tightly plotted play, set in New England, the title character resembles the Biblical Job, first in the separation from his children and second in the recovery of his daughter. After Faith and her husband leave for the Far East against Job's wishes, the hypocritical son Hampden turns his old father out of the house, furnishing barely enough food to keep him from starving. Though loudly proclaiming his piety, Hampden demands an exorbitant rent from a clumsy fellow named Odebiah, who speaks in Yankee dialect. True to the rules of the genre, the supposedly dead couple return, to the father's joy. Tearing up the house deed bestowed upon his false son, Old Job pronounces the moral in good Puritan style: "Your desired last lesson, Hampden; though a deed do come from a dotard, never fail to have it recorded."[38]

The reviewer for the *Missouri Republican* stressed the religious significance, rather than the comedy, of the play. The writer, previously known only for farces and extravaganzas, had struck out in a new vein, he emphasized; those who had objections to the lightness of fare at Field's Varieties would find "edification" here. Chippendale, he wrote, was a "hit" in his role, and Mrs. Field as Faith brought tears to the eyes.[39]

This two-act comedy confirms Field's technical skill as a dramatist. Although it shows Field trying a different genre, like his farces it denounces hypocrisy and portrays an eccentric character of dry humor; it also repeats the sentimental ending of *The Drama in Pokerville*.

Overall, the dramatic writing of the western South surpassed in vigor that of the eastern South: the more sedate plays of Virginia and Charleston, composed under English influence. James Rees transposed the legend of Mike Fink, Mississippi raftsman; Nathaniel Bannister recognized the fascination of that colorful outlaw Murrell; and George Washington Harby adapted *Nick of the Woods*, featuring a half-man, half-alligator. Their stage pieces demonstrate that dramatists for the theaters of New Orleans could join in giving artistic form to new ways: the boisterous life of the frontier.

A good case can be made for calling Field a genuine forerunner of Mark Twain, another itinerant on the frontier. First, living in Missouri, a border state, gave them firsthand acquaintance with the customs of the Mississippi Valley but did not limit them to that region; Field's characters come from all points of the compass. Further, both writers saved their most indignant satire for the con-men who exploited frontiersmen's gullibility. If Twain portrayed a phony revivalist and Shakespearean actor in the King and Duke respectively, Field unleashed equal ridicule upon a Mesmerist and an astronomical lecturer named Dr. Dionysius Lardner, alias "Dr. Heavy Bevy."

The transfer of fictional humor into theatrical farces signals a fruitful connection between popular literature and drama. Field joined the literary movement of southwestern humor with his fictional writings but did not stop there. Always viewing American life critically, he kept up with the current fads, which provoked him to periodic outbursts. His satire of spiritual absurdities such as Millerism sounds a Swiftian note. His burlesque of *Uncle Tom's Cabin* again interweaves the threads of a literary work.

Joseph M. Field is a figure of considerable interest for those who want to understand the evolution of the American theater. Humorists of the Old Southwest who wrote tales (Longstreet) and novels (Twain) are widely familiar, but not one who composed plays. This actor-dramatist, like many of the humorists, moved from the North to the South, where he adopted its tastes and political opinions. His interests were eclectic, encompassing the popular fads, manners, and politics that became the topics of his theatrical satires, the products of a razor-sharp mind. Field possessed the same gift of humor that invigorated the new, democratic life of the frontier before the Civil War; when it spilled onto the stage, it transformed that medium into a more popular institution than ever before in America.

— 4 —
Drama Goes to War

In the next phase of southern drama, politics dominated the stage. Before the Civil War the argument over slavery sparked a raft of answers to *Uncle Tom's Cabin* and debates over such issues as the Free Soil controversy. Climactically, the war itself inspired the organization of an independent southern theater, complete with original plays celebrating Confederate victories and featuring heroines and heroes both fictional and real.

Rebuttals of Uncle Tom's Cabin

The most flagrant examples of sectionalism to appear on pre-Civil War stages were the dramatizations of *Uncle Tom's Cabin* (1852). Serious adaptations, which became popular in the North, were prohibited in the South—where copies of the novel were read only clandestinely—but this sensational and engrossing work provoked a large number of rebuttals from southerners, not only on the stage but in novels such as Simms's *Woodcraft* (1852) and Mary H. Eastman's *Aunt Phillis's Cabin; or, Southern Life as It Is* (1852).[1]

The northern dramatic versions of *Uncle Tom's Cabin* cover a wide spectrum. The best and most successful was by George L. Aiken, who was anti-slavery in his sentiments. Although the dramatic form required deletion of some parts and omission of the long argument over slavery between St. Clare and Miss Ophelia, such plays contained strong appeals for abolition, among them Uncle Tom's speech craving freedom. They were enthusiastically supported by abolitionists such as William Lloyd Garrison, editor of the *Liberator,* and won over the rowdy masses of New York, who had previously remained uncommitted to the anti-slavery crusade but were now persuaded by appeals to the higher law. H.J. Conway's adaptation, which was presented in November 1853 at P.T. Barnum's Museum in New York, offered a much milder version—in which harsh scenes like the slave auction were toned down, and Uncle Tom was rescued from the clutches of Simon Legree in the nick of time. Sam Sanford's so-called "Southern Version of *Uncle Tom's Cabin,*" which portrayed "Happy

Uncle Tom," a character who became common, opened in Philadelphia in 1853 and played widely until the Civil War. For northerners who wished to preserve the Union, a mild version of Stowe's novel seemed one method of reducing offense to southerners.[2]

Although the varied adaptations of *Uncle Tom's Cabin* contained elements indebted to the minstrels, such as the antics of Topsy and nostalgic singing, those treatments belong to a classification all their own. Minstrel shows, with comedians in blackface, had regaled audiences both northern and southern for many years, and their organizers seized on the Uncle Tom material quickly. The Christy Minstrels, highly popular in the North, did a takeoff on the novel in 1853 and a burlesque opera based on the story of Uncle Tom in the spring of 1854.

In these shows slavery was often humorously defended. George Kunkel's Nightingale Ethiopian Opera Troupe performed *Uncle Tom's Cabin; or, Freedom at the North and Service at the South,* in Richmond and at the Charleston Theatre in October 1853. According to the *Charleston Courier,* his production illustrated "the real history of a fugitive, who, weary of living *free to starve* among abolition bigots, returns voluntarily to slavery."[3] The subject of slavery in the South was so explosive, however, that the Charleston city council passed a resolution prohibiting blacks from attending Kunkel's minstrel show; the troupe was not allowed to perform at all in Savannah, and the remainder of its tour was canceled.

By contrast, New Orleans, the cosmopolitan and theatrical center of the South, reveled in refuting Stowe with many versions of *Uncle Tom's Cabin.* After Joseph M. Field's highly successful rebuttal on the New Orleans stage in February 1854, others followed in quick succession. On March 6, only a few days after Field's satire closed, William T. Leonard—a physician of New Orleans and one of the editors of the *Southern Ladies' Book*—answered Stowe's insulting treatment of his state in *Uncle Tom's Cabin in Louisiana.* This "new domestic drama" was composed expressly for Dan ("Jim Crow") Rice, who was enormously successful in various impersonations of Uncle Tom. He had acted the part to great applause in Conway's version at Barnum's Museum in New York on January 16, 1854, and in New Orleans was seeking another vehicle for Negro imitation at the Southern Museum (also called Dan Rice's Amphitheatre).[4]

In Dr. Leonard's play Rice delivered—as he had in New York—his popular ballad "Wait for the Wagon," in which Uncle Tom sings of his adventures in the northern states. Complaining that he is cold and starving because his hosts will give him no money, Uncle Tom pleads, "Gib me de plantation" and some mules and "we'll all take a ride."[5] Following Field's outline, Dr. Leonard's slaves reject freedom and return to the joys of slavery after having been transplanted to the North, where they were mistreated and homesick. The cast includes Uncle Tom, Aunt Tabby, and Eva as "Southern Characters" and, as "Northern Characters," "Mrs. Harriet Bleacher Straw, a Milliner Authoress," "Mr. Universal Freedom," and "Mrs. Convention Sympathy, a Higher Law Expounder and a Bloomer of First Class." Like Field, Dr. Leonard satirized the idealistic reformer, the butt of much mockery in the South.[6]

If Aiken's serious version of Stowe's novel enlisted the backing of the average audience in New York, Dr. Leonard's humorous version brought in the southern masses, not just the refined theatergoer of New Orleans. In both North and South the novel reached enormous audiences in its theatrical forms. The success of *Uncle Tom's Cabin in Louisiana* at the Southern Museum, enhanced to be sure by Dan Rice's singing, showed the desire of southerners to learn about this notorious novel even though, or perhaps because, it was censored in their states. Proclaimed "the most popular piece ever produced in New Orleans" (*Picayune*, April 1, 1854), it ran for an unprecedented twenty-three nights and the *Picayune* (May 21, 1854) observed that "thousands" who had seen it wished to see it again.[7]

The third rebuttal of *Uncle Tom's Cabin*, called *The Old Plantation; or, Uncle Tom as He Is*, which opened on April 6, 1854, and ran three more nights, attempted a serious refutation of the anti-slavery arguments.[8] George Jamieson, a native of New York who was considered one of the best Negro impersonators on the stage, composed this "new domestic drama" in three acts. Indicating the seriousness of this version, the advertisement lists no comic roles but rather "Robert," "Mr. Bradley," and "Virginia," personages who do not appear in the novel (*Picayune*, April 6, 1854). A rare comment in the *Picayune* (April 4, 1854) distinguishes Jamieson's drama from the facetious versions of *Uncle Tom's Cabin*. Stating that the humorous treatments had made little impression because they were of "a sketchy and ephemeral kind," the critic asserted that George Jamieson intended to do more than merely excite laughter. He had shown "the practical working of the mistaken philanthropy" of those who would interfere with southern institutions and social relations. He had drawn Uncle Tom truthfully and replaced "the transcendental heroine" (Little Eva) with a more representative character. Though this serious refutation of the accusations in *Uncle Tom's Cabin* did not have the immediate success of the comic version starring Dan Rice, it did receive substantial support at the box office. Revived in New Orleans in 1855 and 1861 and produced in New York in 1860, it also created a sensation in "several

Southern cities," according to the *Picayune* (December 9, 1855).[9]

The number and success of dramatic rebuttals to *Uncle Tom's Cabin* in New Orleans confirm the ideological primacy of that city. As headquarters for the principal business magazine of the South, *De Bow's Review*, New Orleans not only assumed commercial leadership but also led in the theatrical war. Unafraid to present the subject on stage, this city met the challenge presented to the South by *Uncle Tom's Cabin*. In the development of southern drama, the rebuttals of *Uncle Tom's Cabin* were particularly significant because for the first time a Negro took center stage as the leading character. That the presentation of black life delighted audiences by its contagious music and appealing characters opened possibilities for different, more complex treatments of the race question, stemming from this problematic debut.

Sectional Arguments

Besides answers to *Uncle Tom's Cabin*, southerners such as William Gilmore Simms composed original plays to argue the southern position. The foremost novelist of the antebellum South, Simms had also written numerous unperformed theater pieces, starting in 1825. As a friend and correspondent of Edwin Forrest, he invited the famous actor to visit his home in 1840 and wrote a play expressly for him. Even though Forrest accepted neither the invitation nor the plays, Simms continued his infatuation with the theater and his desire to compose drama.[10]

When the sectional controversy intensified in the 1840s, Simms entered the fray. In addition to articles, speeches, and fiction, he wrote two plays that expressed his southern partisanship. Campaigning for the state legislature in 1844, he advocated the admission of Texas as a slave state and to that end composed *Michael Bonham; or, The Fall of Bexar,* a play about the Battle of the Alamo. The hero was based on James B. Bonham, a native South Carolinian and Alabama lawyer who died at the Alamo. Though Simms did not succeed in getting this play produced before Texas was admitted to the Union in 1845, it was published in 1852 in the *Southern Literary Messenger,* bylined "by a Southron" (that is, an ardent southerner), and finally produced at the Charleston Theatre, March 26-28, 1855.[11] Still timely, it aroused sectionalist spirit, and helped raise money to erect the Calhoun Monument in Charleston. Simms's ode eulogizing Calhoun's defense of states' rights was delivered at the performance.[12]

The play supports the admission of Texas by showing the unity of Texans with the states from which they have emigrated and American

support in their struggle with Mexico. When the fighting against the
Mexicans begins, the titular hero tells his men:

> The old Thirteen, the great Southwest, the North,
> The Carolinas, Georgia, Tennessee, . . .
> Are looking at your actions, as their sons,—
> They must not be dishonored. [5.3]

The Texans are fighting in 1836 for independence from the Mexicans, still their enemies when they were seeking to become an American
state in 1845. Proclaiming their bravery in the battle against tyranny, Joe
Kennedy from Alabama sings that they have fought "old England" and
can "smite":

> We shall teach them that the bold
> Still inherit all the fruits.
> And their moustaches and gold
> We shall pluck up by the roots. [3.3]

A topical allusion to the congressional debate on slavery also emphasizes the political purpose of this play. When Michael Bonham reprimands
Davy Crockett for talking too much, Crockett answers that if Bonham
were "Quincy Adams now, you would lecture me in vain. He, poor fellow,
can't help his tongue" (1.1)—a reference to John Quincy Adams's continual speaking against the admission of Texas because of its slaveholding.

In 1847 Simms wrote one more play, *Norman Maurice; or, The Man of
the People*, dealing with the Free Soil controversy, which set the North and
South fatefully against each other. In 1846 the Wilmot Proviso enraged
the South by specifying that slavery would be prohibited in all the western territory gained in the Mexican War. This principle, adopted by the
Free Soil and Republican Parties, caused perpetual conflict between the
sections and led Simms to make his hero the advocate of slavery in the
West. This was the play designed for Forest, who probably declined it
because of its pro-slavery theme. Eventually, Simms published it in the
Southern Literary Messenger (April-August 1851) and included it in his volume of poems for the collected edition of his writings.[13]

Appropriately, this play takes place in Missouri, the gateway to the
West. The hero, like Calhoun, regards any restriction of slavery in the
West as a violation of the Constitution. At the public caucus for senator,
confident of speaking "the doctrine of Missouri," Norman Maurice would
have the Constitution "a ligament of fix'd, unchanging value, / Main-

tained by strict construction," which should not be "lopt" of its fair proportions by the ambitious demagogue who would "sacrifice the State" (5.6).

The "demagogue" is Maurice's disreputable opponent Colonel Ben, modeled after Thomas Hart Benton, who opposed Calhoun's defense of slavery in the West and was a candidate for reelection to the Senate at this time. (In this fictitious candidate Simms illustrates his opposition to the election of Benton.) After receiving the support of the caucus, Maurice is elected to the Senate by the legislative assembly of Missouri.

What lifts this play above the mere political tract is its reflection on a subject that has engaged dramatists from Shakespeare to Shaw: the qualifications of a good political leader. According to Simms, he should be a good counselor, able to follow his own wise counsel, which Maurice does. He shows his independent character by agreeing to become a senator but only on his terms. Responding to the popular demand, he explains that it "implies not / One effort of my own. You, sirs, may make me / A Senator, but not a Candidate" (3.3).

During the debate over the Compromise of 1850—the set of congressional resolutions that resolved the North-South dispute for a decade—L. (Louis) Placide Canonge (1822-93), the leading dramatist of French New Orleans, participated in the sectional struggle through a play advocating secession. Canonge received his education in France, from which he returned in 1839, full of the spirit of French Romanticism. When the Revolution of 1848 took place, he supported republicanism by defining the government of the United States in "Institutions americaines," published in the Parisian press. Ardent republicanism, typical of French Louisiana, would be the predominant ideology of his life.[14]

Like most Creoles (such as General P.G.T. Beauregard), Canonge supported the Confederacy. A passionate song he composed, "La Louisianaise," sung to the tune of "La Marseillaise" and bearing a quote from John C. Calhoun, was dedicated to the Louisiana Legion. Calling on southerners to take up arms against the North, it ends in the spirit of the French Revolution: "Marchons, / La Liberté nous montre le chemin! [March on, / Liberty shows us the way!]."[15] Continuing his support of the southern cause during Reconstruction, Canonge published a translation of H.R. Helper's violently anti-Negro tract, *Nojoque* (1867). His introduction to *Nojoque: Une grave question pour un continent* voices his determined opposition to postwar changes in the Negro's status and excoriates what he regarded as the Negrophile Congress of Reconstruction.[16]

Much of Canonge's writing was done for the newspapers and little magazines of New Orleans such as the *Courrier Français*. Nine plays composed between 1839 and 1856 include *France et Espagne; ou, La Louisiane en 1768 et 1769*, performed in June 1850 at the Theatre d'Orléans and published in New Orleans, and *Le Comte de Carmagnola*, which supports Italian independence, performed successfully and published in New Orleans in 1856.[17]

Canonge's most interesting and significant play is *France et Espagne*. Like his predecessors in New Orleans,[18] he celebrated the most honored event of French Louisiana, the stirring revolt of colonists against Spanish tyranny. Composed at a time when antagonism against the North was rising precipitously, *France et Espagne*—like other historical dramas of the period—indirectly supported the current issue: the secession of the South from the Union. An ardent believer in revolutions and a subsequent partisan of the Confederacy, Canonge recognized the historical parallel between the French rebellion against Spanish rule and the southern rebellion against what was regarded as northern tyranny. Conceived and produced as the sectional controversy was reaching a new peak because the Compromise of 1840 was opposed by extremists on both sides, *France et Espagne* was first performed on June 1, 1850, when the New Orleans newspapers were full of that debate. Only two days later the Southern Convention met in Nashville, loudly protesting Henry Clay's compromise.

By the 1850s the French population of New Orleans had adopted the outlook of their fellow southerners. Support for the sectional cause appears clearly in the stand taken by Pierre Soulé, whose viewpoint throws much light on Canonge's. This native of France, elected to the U.S. Senate in 1849, directed the states' rights Democrats, having received Calhoun's mantle when the southern leader died in 1850. Believing compromise with the North to be futile, he was one of the first to advocate secession as the only salvation of the South. Opposed to the Compromise of 1850, Soulé voted against the admission of California as a free state and called for "popular sovereignty" (that is, the approval of slavery by popular vote) in new western states.[19]

Canonge's play about the rebellion of French colonists stresses the parallel between past events and those of the present day. In *France et Espagne* Lafrenière, the ardent leader of the revolt, speaks with pointed relevance to an independent Louisiana, referring not to "Americans" but rather to "Louisianians." The French colonists will ask Louis XV to defend their rights against the Spaniards; if he refuses they will give a great example to the whole world by declaring themselves independent; "Nous ne serons ni Français, ni Espagnols, nous serons Louisianais, c'est à dire indépendants [We will be neither Frenchmen, nor Spaniards, we will be Louisianians, that is to say independent]." He and his men will fight for popular sovereignty (the rallying cry of belligerent southerners): "Nous ferons entendre ce mot sublime, magique; ce mot don't l'effect est sûr, et ne peut pas plus être empeché que notre fleuve dans sa course: Souveraineté du peuple! [We will make known that sublime, magical word; that word whose effect is sure and can no more be stopped than our river in its course: Popular sovereignty!]"[20] After being thrown into prison by the Spaniards, the young hero, Marquis, regrets the earlier attempts at compromise, using terms applicable to the Compromise of 1850: "Pactiser dans les revolutions, c'est se tuer [To make pacts during a revolution is to commit suicide]" (p. 39).

Sentenced to die, Lafrenière predicts Spain's eventual overthrow by her colonies in words that carry implications for the South's oppressor in 1850: "Espagne, un jour viendra où ceux que tu opprimes te demanderont compte du passé. Un jour viendra òu tes colonies, fatiguées enfin de ta domination, briseront ce cercle de fer lequel tu les comprimes! [Spain, the day will come when those you oppress will demand an account of the past. The day will come when your colonies, wearied finally of your domination, will break the circle of iron with which you oppress them!]" (pp. 52-53).

In the spirit of the French Revolution this play projects an anti-aristocratic tone, reflecting the sentiment of Canonge himself, and vilifies both French and Spanish monarchs. The French characters admire democracy: praising the spirit of liberty in the New World for elevating man, Lafrenière warns the French king that because Rousseau and Voltaire sowed the seeds of liberty far and wide, momentous events lie ahead. Contemptuously, he declares to Louis XV in his palace at Versailles that by ignoring the settlers of Louisiana, he is shunning his "meilleure noblesse [best nobility]" (p. 35). The Spaniards defend monarchy: the anti-democratic Spaniard Don José complains to his superior, "Comte O'Reilly," that the French leaders are fomenting revolution among the settlers by speaking the seditious word "Egalité" (p. 22).

Of particular significance in the French drama of New Orleans is the profound and continuing impact of the French Revolution. Canonge celebrated this epochal event rather than the American Revolution, which dramatists writing in English honored. The French Revolution inspired his abhorrence of the aristocracy in both *France et Espagne* and *Le Comte de Carmagnola*. Because the revolution of 1789 led to those of 1830 and 1848, revolutionary ardor continued to be strong in French New Orleans as well as in France and lent fiery form to what was considered another revolution against tyranny: the secession movement of the South, considered by many the Second American Revolution.

The sectionalist plays of Clifton W. Tayleure (1832-91), dramatist, actor, and Baltimore manager, reflect the middle course adopted by Maryland. A partisan of the South, he defended slavery and aroused sectionalist spirit but wished to preserve the Union. Tayleure was born in Charleston of Huguenot and Covenanter forebears. After attending New York theaters at an early age, he began his acting career in Richmond in 1850 and next moved to the Holliday Street Theatre of Baltimore, where he performed until 1856. From 1854 to 1859 he was manager of this theater and contributed nine plays to its offerings. In 1862 he joined the Confederate forces and was captured by federal troops but later released on parole. He then edited the *Baltimore Evening Transcript* until it was closed by military edict in 1864. After the war Tayleure managed the Bowery and Olympic Theatres of New York (1865-68), successfully adapted the popular novel *East Lynne* for the New York stage, and in the 1870s became manager for the actress Mrs. Frank Chanfrau, who was connected with the Varieties of New Orleans.[21]

Tayleure's first play was a rebuttal of *Uncle Tom's Cabin*, demonstrating the pro-southern stand and defense of slavery that also stamp his succeeding plays. He took the role of George Harris, a fugitive slave, in a production given in Detroit on October 2, 1852, and also played the part in Baltimore.[22]

In 1856, as the debate between North and South waxed hot, Tayleure encouraged sectionalist spirit and defended slavery in an adaptation of the novel *Horse-Shoe Robinson* (1835) by John Pendleton Kennedy, a fellow Baltimorean, who described the performance he attended as "amazingly noisy" but hugely popular with the gallery.[23] Adapted skillfully from Kennedy's colorful romance, this rollicking drama is among the best and most entertaining of the antebellum period. It was performed at the Richmond Theatre in September and October 1857 and at the New Bowery Theatre in New York, March 12-15, 1860.

Like Simms and Canonge, Tayleure compared the past with the present to argue a current stand: he used the American Revolution against Great Britain as the precedent for southern defiance of northern oppression. This was an analogy stressed repeatedly in speeches by politicians, novels by Simms, and plays about the Revolution. At the beginning of the Civil War, for example, when a piece recalling the Revolutionary general Francis Marion, the "Swamp Fox" of South Carolina, was offered at the St. Charles Theatre of New Orleans, the *Picayune* (March 3, 1861) observed that "we are to be treated to a new, original drama, under the taking title of 'Minute Men; or, Southerners on Guard,' which awakens associations of Marion and His Merry Men All, and suits well with the times we live in."

Tayleure's *Horse-Shoe Robinson* was another Revolutionary drama designed to strengthen southerners in their conflict with the North. The brave Maj. Arthur Butler of South Carolina, engaged in the struggle against the British (antecedents of modern northerners), is captured and about to be executed but is saved by his trusty comrade Horse-Shoe Robinson. At the end, the Americans all join to achieve victory at the glorious Battle of King's Mountain .

Tayleure's play employs the code word "rebel," as did Simms's novels, to link the opponents of British tyranny with the southern "rebels" of his day. In his Revolutionary novel *Katharine Walton* (1850), Simms relates how the "rebels" of South Carolina fought for independence, dubbing his heroine significantly "the Rebel of Dorchester."[24] The label occurs meaningfully in Tayleure's play when the villain Tyrrel says to Butler before he is to be executed: "Now, Sir Rebel, prepare to die."[25] Young Henry Lindsay of Virginia declares, "I go for the rebel cause heart and soul" (p. 777). Other remarks too betray a southern bias, which a partisan audience would have relished. As Horse-Shoe makes plans to attack some British soldiers, a young Carolinian promises not to desert: "That's not a Southern principle" (p. 800).

The most striking change from the novel to the play is Tayleure's insertion of a slave character to achieve his propagandistic purpose. "Steve" is a white woodsman of Virginia in the novel, but in the play he is Butler's slave and helps rescue his master from captivity.[26] Most significantly, he delivers a pro-slavery speech that has no counterpart in the novel. Following the practice in fictional rebuttals of *Uncle Tom's Cabin*, Tayleure places defense of slavery in the mouth of the slave himself. Steve insists that he is better off than a British soldier: "I'm a native American nigger but it am suxceptible of de strongest kind of proof dat I ain't no more a slave than you chaps, wot's got to do just as your ossifers tell you. If I disobeys massa, he larrups me—if you disobeys your ossifer—dat's *your* massa—he shoots you. I think I's a d'yam sight de best off of de two." The Briton suspects that there must be "some rebel spirit in this house" (p. 785).

Tayleure shows the dualistic view of Maryland in *The Boy Martyrs of Sept. 12, 1814,* which was performed at the Holliday Street Theatre in 1859.[27] Although strongly pro-South, this play must be seen as supportive of preserving the Union, a stance shared by many Marylanders, including John Pendleton Kennedy. The state generally defended slavery but—recalling its patriotic tradition deriving from the composition of "The Star Spangled Banner"—not secession.[28]

The play celebrates the Battle of Ft. McHenry, at which two boy soldiers are killed. In the last tableau they are wrapped in the American flag while "The Star Spangled Banner" is played, thus stressing Tayleure's support of the Union, but the enthusiastic praise of Maryland's fame as the cradle of civil liberty implies that the state should reject tyrannous demands for the abolition of slavery. The closeness of Maryland and South Carolina when Marylanders fought beside the Carolina regiment at the Battle of Camden will continue. Among those who supported the War of 1812 the patriotic heroine distinguishes "the pure and incorruptible Calhoun" of South Carolina (p. 8).

Tony, a comic slave, is a paragon of loyalty, whom slaves in the present should imitate. He serves his mistress faithfully, expresses no desire for freedom, and fights with the Americans against the enemy at the Battle of Ft. McHenry. Assaulting Lt. Stubbs, a fat Briton, he exults, "Lor, ain't dis fun?" (pp. 29-30).

The enthusiastic nationalist stand of early dramatists such as Tucker and Ioor made their plays much like other American plays in spirit. In the years of the sectional crisis before the Civil War, however, southern dramatists used some of the same history to present sectionalist arguments, directly opposed to those in the North. Politics rather than culture identified their works as above all southern plays. But the sectionalist spirit produced an incorporation of black life in a way not seen before and thus increased the racial diversity of southern drama—a feature that would continue visibly in Confederate plays, as blacks participated in the war.

Confederate Drama

During the years of the Confederacy, the demand for partisan drama reached its peak, eliciting a vigorous response. Professionals of the theater and press, along with amateur writers, composed a substantial number of plays that attracted enthusiastic audiences. The most fascinating figure to debut in these belligerent pieces is the heroine of Dixie, who combines bravery and charm in fighting for the South.

Theatrical activity reached new heights during the war years as southern theaters offered full seasons, and new circuits emerged. In a conscious effort to launch a separate southern drama, appeals were made to native dramatists and prizes offered. Two names stand out among the numerous, often anonymous, playwrights of the period: John Hill Hewitt, musical composer and author of many plays performed in Richmond and Augusta; and James Dabney McCabe, author of *The Guerillas,* the best-known play composed during the years of the Confederacy.

The Confederate theater passed through three distinct stages: the beginnings of new companies and theaters, 1861-62; the mature period of developed theatrical organizations accompanied by native plays, 1862-63; and the period of decline as the defeat of the Confederacy became unmistakable, 1864-65. As the principal places of urban entertainment, theaters flourished; regular seasons were extended into the summer without interruption; and tickets were hard to get for some plays. When Union troops occupied active theatrical centers such as New Orleans, adjustments were rapidly made: actors transferred to more secure locations such as middle Georgia. As new companies developed and southern "stars" began to rise in the theatrical firmament, Richmond, the capital of the new nation, became "the Broadway of the South." During the 1862-63 season the city had two theaters always open and sometimes four.[29] When the Richmond Theatre burned, the decision was made immediately to construct a replacement, and on February 9, 1863, a gala opened the New Richmond Theatre. On that occasion Henry Timrod's "Inaugural Poem," which won a prize of $300, preceded *As You Like It.*[30] According to the notice in the *Richmond Age* (March, 1864) the New Richmond Theatre was "second to none in the Confederacy."[31] Along with the Richmond Varieties (Franklin Hall) and the Metropolitan Hall, it offered a wide variety of entertainment, from panoramas to legitimate drama.

Theatrical seasons flourished in several other cities throughout the South as well. In New Orleans the actor-dramatist John Davis ran the Confederate Theatre and others until the city fell to General Benjamin F. ("Beast") Butler in 1862, then departed for Georgia. There were active theaters also in Montgomery, Mobile, Atlanta, Augusta, and Savannah. As the Union occupied more southern territory, Macon, Georgia, and Wilmington, North Carolina, became refuges for theatrical companies.

Despite sporadic complaints about theaters operating when men were dying on the battlefield, the newspapers were usually supportive, agreeing that the people required diversion. The *Richmond Punch* favored keeping the theaters open to prove that southern spirits were still high. When times were good and victories continued, plays were well patronized by the elite, but as Confederate fortunes fell, the quality of theatergoers did likewise; soldiers eager for diversion made up a large part of the audience, laughing and whooping at anything on stage.[32] In the waning months of the war, a decline accompanied soaring ticket prices, and conscript officers seized the casts of Richmond theaters to increase the manpower at Camp Lee.

Although John Hill Hewitt (1801-90) was first of all a musician, he is the most representative dramatist of the Confederacy because of the number and variety of the plays he composed throughout the war years. A man of recognized musical talent, some dramatic skill, and a thorough knowledge of wartime events and sentiments, he ardently supported the Confederacy in his dramatic compositions, and his numerous pieces were popular with audiences.

Hewitt was born in New York City, son of the composer James Hewitt.[33] After attending but not graduating from West Point, he joined his father in Augusta, Georgia, where they opened a theater in 1822. Beginning his career as an itinerant teacher of music in 1823, he taught flute, piano, and voice to families of wealthy planters and merchants in Augusta and directed singing societies and children's choruses as well. Always sensitive to social acceptance, Hewitt noted with appreciation the southern gentry's respect for teachers in contrast to its low opinion of mechanics.[34] Turning to musical composition, he won his greatest fame as a balladeer, becoming well known for songs like "The Minstrel's Return from the War" (1825) and "All Quiet along the Potomac Tonight" (composed during the Civil War).

In 1828 Hewitt moved to Baltimore, where he engaged in journalism. In his 1877 autobiography, *Shadows on the Wall or Glimpses of the Past,* he wrote that he had always considered Baltimore his home.[35] As editor of the *Baltimore Saturday Visitor* he offended the young Edgar Allan Poe in 1833: after awarding Poe the short story prize for "Ms. Found in a Bottle," the paper chose Hewitt's own poem, "The Song of the Wind," for the poetry prize, not wanting to give both to the same recipient. Angered by this decision, Poe harbored a lasting grudge against Hewitt.[36]

Besides composing music and poetry, Hewitt showed an early interest in writing for the stage. His first play, *Washington: An Allegorical Spectacle,* was performed in Baltimore in 1832; it was followed the next year by *Rip van Winkle. The Governess,* presented in Baltimore in 1853 and 1855, was considered a theatrical success.

Although Hewitt subsequently stated that he had been a strong Union man before the war, he evidently held southern sympathies: he composed a humorous song for Kunkel's Minstrels in 1853 ridiculing Harriet Beecher Stowe. In "Aunt Harriet Becha Stowe" a fugitive slave complains after arriving in New York City: "I couldn't get no work, I couldn't get no dinner, and den I wish dis Fugitive was back to ole Virginny."[37]

When the war began, Hewitt, then living in Richmond, threw in his lot with the South because he opposed Lincoln's calling out the army to enforce southern obedience. Though sixty years of age, Hewitt offered his services to Jefferson Davis, who reputedly denied him a commission because of his northern birth.[38] Hewitt's civilian talents, however, were very much in demand, because the theater could use a man not subject to conscription who had been writing and producing plays since 1832. Even though he lacked previous experience as a theater manager, he was prevailed upon to undertake management of the Richmond Theatre, the principal purveyor of legitimate drama in the Confederate capital. This respected teacher of music lost social standing thereby, he complained. Obliged to form a company from among disreputables, including prostitutes, he strove to maintain a decent atmosphere during his management.

On October 10, 1861, Hewitt announced the opening of the Richmond (or Broad Street) Theatre for the succeeding month, soon finding an opportunity to produce his own plays: *The Scouts, The Log Fort,* and *The Prisoner of Monterey.* It was on January 1, 1862, in the middle of the theatrical season, that the Richmond Theatre burned in the early hours of the morning, fortunately without loss of life. Hewitt left a vivid account of being suddenly awakened by the conflagration, his shock, and the flight of his associate R.D. Ogden, who later became manager of the New Richmond Theatre.[39] For the remainder of the season, he moved his operations to the Richmond Varieties.

The Scouts; or, The Plains of Manassas is important as Hewitt's first play about the war, though like his other theatrical productions it exists today only in the form of a prompt book.[40] Opening on November 18, 1861, it ran for six consecutive nights and was repeated throughout the season. A patriotic drama about guerilla fighters in Virginia, containing enough broad humor to win popularity, *The Scouts* relates how General Beauregard's horse was shot from under him at the First Battle of Manassas, July 21, 1861. (This battle, also regarded as a victory in the North, reached the New York stage as *Bull Run; or, The Sacking of Fairfax Courthouse,* a play by Charles Gayler performed at the New Bowery Theatre on August 15, 1861. In the North as well as the South, battles that were incontrovertible defeats never reached the stage.)

The Scouts also contains such surefire ingredients of the contemporary theater as young love—two brothers, Harry and Edward Ashwood, denoted "F.F.V.'s" (First Families of Virginia), both love their father's ward, Alice; in the battle Edward is killed, thus resolving the rivalry—and the heroism of southern women. Determined to show "the lords of creation" that women can fight also, some dress as Zouaves in order to capture a federal picket. Celebrating their victory, these southern heroines march to the strains of "Dixie," a song that sounded merrily on and off the stage during the war. Called "a rebel" by a Union officer, Kate Ashwood, Harry's bold sister, retorts that if opposing "canting hypocracy [sic]" be rebellion, she's proud of the label. Kate accepts a northerner's marriage proposal but declares that she'll take the vows only after the South has won. A comic love plot is provided by an Arkansas "free-fighter" who falls in love with Jeanette, another of the female soldiers. "Wildcat Pete" resembles the colorful frontiersman of southwestern humor. Not a regular soldier because of all the "marching and countermarching," he is full of "love and fight."

Betraying an influence from the minstrels, comments on slavery furnish broad satire. Uncle Abe wishes "dey'd christianed me wid anodder name." After capturing a New Englander, this loyal slave refuses the offer of "Comfort" to go north because there are too many "John Browns dar for dis nigger." When the northern prisoners are being led away in the end, "Wildcat Pete" says "Comfort" will be obliged to eat "fried tobacco" in Richmond, which is good enough for any abolitionist.

The most productive phase of Hewitt's career benefited from a close and apparently congenial association with the Queen Sisters company, which performed at the Richmond Theatre during his management. The only entirely new company to arise during the Confederacy, it was composed of the Waldron family: the father, Alfred, three sisters (hence the name), and three brothers whose youth exempted them from conscription. This popular troupe, which at first should be designated amateur, developed its abilities during the course of the war. Originating in the North, the Waldrons found themselves in Charleston at the beginning of the conflict. John Davis featured them at the Confederate Theatre of New Orleans in April 1862, where they sang "The Bonnie Blue Flag," "Maryland, My Maryland," and other pro-South songs. At the Academy of Music during that visit, they presented an original play portraying a southern martyr in New York City.

Moving to Augusta, the Waldrons opened in September 1862, at the Concert Hall, accompanied by the Palmetto Band. The Southern Field and Fireside (January 10, 1863) proclaimed their company's beginning "coeval with the Confederacy," forecasting "a better and purer day for the stage," to which the Waldrons would undoubtedly carry the "sterling qualities" of their private life. At the Augusta Concert Hall they were aided substantially by Hewitt, who comanaged it with them and whose plays and music began to fill their repertory during the 1862-63 season. Trying to encourage native drama after the fashion of Edwin Forrest, Alfred Waldron offered a prize of $300 for the best play on a southern theme, for which Hewitt competed, but whether or not he won is unknown.[41] During 1863 when Confederate fortunes rose highest, Hewitt produced no less than nine new plays at the Augusta Concert Hall.[42]

Hewitt's most successful play for the Queen Sisters, *The Vivandiere,* was performed in February 1863 and manifests the high spirits of the Confederacy at this stage of the war.[43] It was still possible to be lighthearted before such tragic defeats as the Battle of Vicksburg in the summer of 1863 changed the mood of the South. This romantic comedy, filled with songs and music, was based on the currently popular Donizetti opera *La Fille du Régiment,* but the text and music were entirely by Hewitt. In the opera the heroine, Marie, is also a *vivandiere*—literally, a girl who sells food and drink to soldiers, but in popular usage simply a female soldier. Providing a factual basis, such women appeared in Richmond, dressed in Turkish trousers and feathered hats after the French manner. With admiring men in their train, they strummed tunes on hotel pianos. *The Vivandiere* was presented five times at the Augusta Concert Hall with Laura Waldron in the title role and her young brothers in the parts of men. The *Augusta Daily Constitutionalist* (February 10, 1863) praised the performers but hoped to see work "of a higher order" from this well-known composer.[44]

The central figure is a heroine of Dixie, passionately devoted to the southern cause. Louise, a Louisiana beauty, feeling called to join the soldiers fighting near Manassas, sings: "At my country's call I come / With cheerful lips and eyes." She captures a federal soldier, who turns out to be her long-lost brother from New York, and converts him to "Southern Rights." Although Louise's morality is suspect because she carries a pistol and wears pantaloons, her purity is proven in the end. She is reunited with her sweetheart, and two female critics are reprimanded for doubting her virtue.

That the Dixie heroines of Hewitt's plays—his most appealing characters—had a firm basis in reality is shown in the diaries and journals of real women, whose blend of defiance and charm is striking. Judith McGuire of Alexandria, Virginia, wrote in May 1861 of her belief that the fighting men's hopes become "strong when they think of the justice of their cause. In that is *our* hope." She pauses to admire the beautiful flowers of spring before lamenting the northern invaders' appropriation of her sewing machine, which she had used to make soldiers' jackets. When she regains it, she vows to stitch "all the more vigorously for the wrongs it has suffered."[45] A famous live heroine with close similarities to Louise the Vivandiere was Augusta Evans Wilson, the leading female novelist of the Confederacy. After visiting her two brothers stationed at Norfolk, where she yearned to wave "a secession flag" in sight of Union cannoneers, she serenaded the Confederate troops at the Battle of Chicamauga with "Maryland, My Maryland."[46] The brave memoirs of southern heroines and the proclamations of those in Hewitt's plays confirm the common remark of friend and foe alike that the war lasted as long as it did because "the spirit of resistance flamed highest" in the women of the South.[47]

Also reflecting the high spirits of the Confederacy when the potent combination of Generals Jackson and Lee was riding high, Hewitt's *King Linkum, The First* was performed at the Augusta Concert Hall on February 23, 1863.[48] This satirical musical in iambic tetrameter, with lyrics set to popular tunes, featured young Alfred Waldron as "Linkum" and his sister Laura as "Queen Linkum." The *Southern Field and Fireside* (February 21, 1863) called it a "comical burletta on the Cabinet at Washington." (Farces similarly ridiculing Confederate leaders appeared in northern theaters, such as *A Supper in Dixie* by William C. Reynolds, in Chicago, 1865).[49]

King Linkum is one of the earliest dramatic treatments of Lincoln, illustrating that the northern president provoked more mockery than hatred from the southern side. Characterized as inept, henpecked, and given to inebriety, "Linkum" faces such problems as the Democratic victory in New York, monetary chaos, and the failure of his "On to Richmond" strategy. He sings a tipsy song of defeated generals: "McClellan, Napoleon the younger is he / But he couldn't outgeneral the rebel, Bob Lee" (p. 21). The emancipation proclamation of January 1, 1863, provokes a Negro orderly to lament: "Wha' for you free de nigger? —say— / Was it to let him die away?" (p. 25). The farce ends to the tune of "Yankee Doodle" as King and Queen Linkum sing comically of their failure to put the rebels down.

The Veteran; or, '76 and '62 (first performed in March 1863) is a patriotic play about five generations of Mayfields, a Georgia family.[50] The title indicating that a very old veteran of the American Revolution is supporting another revolutionary cause in 1862, emphasizes the ubiquitous interpretation of the South's war for independence as the Second American Revolution. This short comic piece focuses on a very real issue of the home front: the draft dodger, whom Hewitt puts to shame. Many men in fact paid for substitutes in the Confederate Army. When Hector Homespun tells Marion that he has not volunteered because his trigger finger is out of joint, she retorts: "It's your courage that's out of joint." She won't marry this young farmer until he volunteers. Captain Henry Mayfield, an active soldier, receives the plaudits of all by recounting how he and "the gallant sons of Georgia" fought at the Battle of Shiloh. Even little George gives "the hurra for Jeff Davis," while the Revolutionary veteran calls on all to "stand by the rights of the States."

James Dabney McCabe (1842-83) is noteworthy for having composed the most successful Confederate play. The Guerillas was performed first in Richmond on December 22, 1862, and staged widely thereafter.[51] Because, unlike Hewitt's pieces, it was published, it became generally available for use by theatrical companies. McCabe's play was not, however, the "first original drama" of the Confederacy, as claimed by both the author and a modern scholar.[52] Hewitt, John Davis, and others had written and produced plays earlier.

McCabe achieved some distinction as both journalist and author. Born in Richmond and educated at Virginia Military Institute, he started his career on a country newspaper at the age of fourteen. He edited the Magnolia Weekly (formerly the Magnolia) of Richmond from July 1863 to March 1864, and besides at least two plays about the war, he later counted among his "literary sins" a brochure against abolition (1860) and a sentimental novel: The Aid[sic]-de-Camp, serialized in the Magnolia Weekly (1863). Raising questions as to his southern loyalty, he ran the wartime blockade, moved to Brooklyn, and died in Pennsylvania. According to John Wood Davidson's Living Writers of the South (1869), however, his heart remained southern. After the war he published Life and Campaigns of General Robert E. Lee (1867) and some poems in William Gilmore Simms's War Poetry of the South (1866).[53]

Like Hewitt in his partnership with the Queen Sisters, McCabe formed a productive relationship with R.D. Ogden, the British-born manager of the New Richmond Theatre and the Richmond Varieties, where The Guerillas was first performed. In his "Editorial Introduction" to the play, McCabe thanked him for assisting its successful production and complimentarily named a Confederate lieutenant in the cast after him. Although Hewitt held a poor opinion of Ogden, the Magnolia Weekly (August 27, 1864) considered him more valuable in the theater than in the army, believing he had done more to encourage "Southern dramatic authorship" than any other prewar manager.[54]

The unusual quantity of newspaper commentary, both pro and con, that followed the premiere of The Guerillas demonstrates the vitality of theatrical criticism in Richmond. The Magnolia, noting that the large assembly approved loudly this "spirit stirring drama," praised Miss Katie Estelle, the heroine, as a fine representative of "the Southern woman," and Mr. Thorpe as the comic slave "Uncle Jerry."[55] The Examiner (December 27, 1862) liked the thread of love running through "the recital of blood, and wrong, and outrage." On Christmas Day the audience, according to this newspaper, yelled so exuberantly that they astounded the actors.[56]

The *Southern Illustrated News,* on the other hand, faulted all the actors, claiming that Walter Keeble as the young hero sounded as if he were reading blank verse from Shakespeare. Worse, the reviewer took the author to task for historical inaccuracy, which he found especially unfortunate because the "Southern people are *making history* now" and dramatists should be "faithful chroniclers." He conceded that "the play as a whole possesses some little merit" but objected that it was "full of 'blood and thunder.'"[57]

The Guerillas ran for a week at the Richmond Varieties and thereafter, among other places, was presented in Mobile (in June 1863); Macon (April 14 and 15 and September 3, 1864, and during the 1864-65 season); and Wilmington (July 1, 1864). It is a competently constructed melodrama of southern defenders opposing Yankee invaders during the period when prospects for the Confederacy still looked good. Set in the romantic mountains of western Virginia, where General Stonewall Jackson had pinned down General John C. Fremont in the spring of 1862, it includes vigorous depictions of southern bravery, northern villainy, and slave loyalty. Contrasting characters take on a symbolic dimension as representatives of South and North.

The play presents three generations of the patriotic Douglas family of Virginia. Grandfather Henry, who (like Hewitt's veteran) fought in the American Revolution, confuses the present "revolution" with the preceding one. He bestows the ancient sword of "Light-Horse Harry" Lee, father of Robert E. Lee, on his grandson Arthur, who escapes hanging to join "the glorious Jackson" winning "laurels in the valley" (pp. 9-11, 44). The heroine of Dixie stars in this play too. When Rose Maylie, Arthur's future wife, is charged with being a "rebel," this personification of defiance promises General Fremont that after killing all the men, "you will then have to meet the women" (pp. 29-30).

One of McCabe's principal aims was to condemn alleged northern brutality. In one bloody scene Colonel Bradley's Federals massacre the old grandfather and his son after burning the Douglas mansion; dipping his handkerchief in their blood, Arthur vows vengeance. Both Fremont and Bradley attempt to seduce Rose, who retaliates in the denouement by shooting the latter as, brandishing a pistol, she leads the guerilla attack.

The loyal slave, a stock comic character in Confederate plays as well as prewar dramas, also appears prominently in *The Guerillas.* (In fact, some slaves did serve loyally in hospitals and households, but Confederate dramatists ignored the fact that many joined the Union Army.) After Jerry saves Rose from the fate of the older Douglas men, Arthur offers him freedom, which he refuses, declaring. "You never gib me hard word in your life" (p. 25). Fremont does not execute the pro-Confederate Jerry after capturing him, because that would injure his reputation "as an abolitionist" (p. 31). But the loyal slave grasps the general's uniform so tightly in the end that he must flee without cap or coat.

Other dramatists of the Confederacy treated themes similar to those found in the plays of Hewitt and McCabe. The heroic *vivandiere* became a popular figure. Joseph Hodgson published *The Confederate Vivandiere* in 1862.[58] John Davis featured her in *The Roll of the Drum*, often given by companies he managed. It opened on November 4, 1861, at the New Orleans Academy of Music, where it played for a week and was performed in Atlanta on April 30, 1863, and seven nights thereafter; in Macon, April 11-13, 1864; and in Wilmington several times during August 1864. In this comedy the heroine is a northern maiden with southern sympathies who joins the Army of the Potomac and falls in love with a Confederate soldier fittingly named "John Davis."[59]

Among Confederate playwrights, James Dabney McCabe showed the most literary skill with *The Guerillas,* a clamorous tribute to southern bravery. John Hill Hewitt, who criticized the cowardice of draft-dodging, was a facile writer possessed of proven musical talent, some dramatic skill, and a sense of humor. His favorite character was the heroine of Dixie, who personified the defiance and charm of southern women. Both McCabe and Hewitt, with their noisy defense of "Southern rights," accurately reflected the attitudes of southerners during the Confederacy.

Although the concept of southern literature had its origin well before the Civil War, it took that climactic event to give birth to a firm idea of "southern" drama. During the optimistic years of the Confederacy, dramatists responded enthusiastically to the demand for plays that would be not merely South Carolinian or Virginian but consciously, even boastfully, southern. The South as an ideological force generated the drama of this era.

With the plays presented just before and during the Civil War, then, southern drama took on a much clearer character. New theatrical circuits developed within the South; a theatrical center emerged in Richmond, where new plays originated; a prize for the best play on a southern theme was offered in Augusta. Dramatists chose historical subjects through which they could comment on the sectional crisis. Simms's commemoration of the Battle of the Alamo cast a vote for the annexation of Texas, a slave state; Canonge's drama of the French revolt against Spanish tyranny in 1768 foresaw southern revolt against the North during the Compromise of 1850; Tayleure's play about the Revolution included a loyal slave who defended slavery, implying that one in the present would do the same.

The loyal slave, in fact, was among the noticeable southern types to come forward on the stage. Speaking a comical dialect, he was a southern response to Uncle Tom, who was humble and kindly but earnestly desired freedom; the southern Uncle Tom most decidedly did not but was happy down South, standing by his master and refusing freedom. Hewitt and McCabe gave large parts to Uncle Abe and Uncle Jerry, slaves who speak humorously and reject freedom vociferously.

The most significant and original figure to appear in the Confederate plays is assuredly the heroine of Dixie—exemplified by the *vivandiere* Louise of Louisiana and the female guerilla Rose Maylie—who impersonated on the stage the real women who sacrificed and served bravely in the Confederate cause, as Augusta Evans Wilson implored them to do. The immediacy of the theater gave such figures an iconic charisma, and the imaginative representations, even if stylized and hyperbolized, visibly concentrated the qualities of real models, catching the public's imagination. These southern heroines interestingly anticipate such women in modern novels, as Melanie of *Gone with the Wind* and Drusilla Sartoris of Faulkner's *The Unvanquished,* and such theatrical descendants as the spunky mothers Amanda Wingfield of *The Glass Menagerie* and Carrie Watts of *The Trip to Bountiful.* The heroines of Confederate drama are not unworthy ancestors of the heroines of modern southern drama, whose combination of steely tenacity and feminine grace has created powerful roles that actresses have rendered convincingly.

— 5 —

The Modern Drama
of Espy Williams

For a time after the traumatic end of the Civil War, playwriting in the South virtually disappeared except for stray amateur pieces. Some of these, with significant titles such as *The Tyrant of New York: A Drama by an Ex-Confederate Officer* (printed in Atlanta, 1873) reflected the political sectionalism that remained dominant in the South during Reconstruction.[1] Drama recovered much more slowly than fiction and poetry. George Washington Cable and Sidney Lanier led the resurgence of southern literature, and the sentiments of the Old South could still be expressed in tales by Thomas Nelson Page but not broadcast from a public stage.

Although many plays about the Civil War with southern settings— such as Bronson Howard's *Shenandoah* (1889) and William Gillette's *Secret Service* (1895)—attained great popularity and toured the South successfully, they were all written by northerners. Southerners were not disposed to dramatize their painful defeat, but they eventually ratified the interpretations of that conflict by northern dramatists. In fact, North and South took an encouraging step toward reconciliation by mutually applauding popular plays about the war that did not require southerners to disown their fallen heroes. At the end of one performance of *Shenandoah,* two veterans from North and South shared a warm and forgiving embrace.[2] These popular plays presented admirable virtues on both sides, such as loyalty to one's native soil, personal heroism, and woman's love prevailing over duty. To avoid southern displeasure, they did not emphasize slavery as a cause of the war and tactfully omitted harsh criticism of the South.

Eventually, professional dramatic writing resumed in the South. The first noteworthy postwar dramatist was Espy Williams (1852-1908) of New Orleans, a city that regained its central position in southern theater as it recovered from the economic disasters of the war. Williams joined northern dramatists like Bronson Howard in defending the profession against demands for commercial success at the expense of artistic integrity. His many plays, composed over an extended career, led the way to better playwriting in the South. His high artistic standards, admiration for modern dramatists such as Ibsen, and experiments with the problem play anticipated the serious American drama of ideas, which reached fruition in the United States with Eugene O'Neill and others in the twentieth century. Williams belonged to a new breed of southern dramatists: he was nonpartisan with respect to the sectional conflict, knowledgeable about current trends in drama, and liberal on the racial issue.[3] During his playwriting career, Espy Williams composed mainly serious, artistic works, but he also attempted popular plays for the commercial stage. He began as a serious writer, tried his luck later in the commercial theater, and returned to serious drama at the end of his life.

In the latter part of the nineteenth century, drama took on new life in Europe. Henrik Ibsen, whose plays are still an enduring part of the modern repertory, made the theater a great institution again, a platform of ideas. With innovative works such as *A Doll's House* (1879) and *Ghosts* (1881), incorporating the principles of realism, Ibsen signaled the beginnings of what we call modern drama. Soon playwrights such as August Strindberg and theaters such as André Antoine's Théâtre Libre in Paris added momentum to the movement. In England, George Bernard Shaw championed Ibsen in his essay "The Quintessence of Ibsenism" (1891) and launched the drama of ideas with such plays as *Arms and the Man* (1894) and *Caesar and Cleopatra* (1901).

Realism in the theater benefited further from the encouragement of William Dean Howells in his realistic dramas (as well as novels) and critical essays such as "The Ibsen Influence" (1895). This revolution in drama caught on slowly in the United States, however. James A. Herne argued its cause in his essay "Art for Truth's Sake in Drama" (1897) and in a series of realistic plays, including *Margaret Fleming* (1890) and *Shore Acres* (1892). Espy Williams became in time another practitioner of the modern style, a lonely but prophetic voice in the South. He took bold, unconventional stands on such issues as religious intolerance, political corruption, and marital infidelity.

Williams was born in Carrolton, Louisiana, an independent township near New Orleans. His father, an engineer and teacher, served as a guide to his son's early writing. Although they had come from the North, his parents remained in their adopted state during the Civil War but did not become political sectionalists, and Williams continued their impartiality. According to his daughter, "My father's loyalty to New Orleans was simply because he had been born there and he had a constitutional aversion to change of any sort."[4] Clearly, although Williams remained in New Orleans his entire life, he was never militantly southern.

Because of stringent family finances, Williams ended his formal education one semester short of graduation from a New Orleans high school in 1868. He then proceeded to combine business and drama in a double career, becoming a successful financier. At the time of his death he was chairman of the board of a New Orleans building and loan company. In 1896 he addressed the United States League of Local Building and Loan Associations in Philadelphia enunciating his conservative economic philosophy. He stated in "The Safeguard of American Finances" that soon the country's bonded debt would be held not by foreigners but by American citizens.[5] Yet although he earned his living in business, the theater became the compelling interest of Williams's life. He wrote more than thirty-five plays and at his death was pronounced by the New Orleans *Daily Picayune* (August 29, 1903) "the South's leading dramatist."

During his youth Williams developed high artistic ideals. As a young man of twenty-two he confided his cherished literary ambitions to his diary (1874-75), revealing a critical bent in lengthy commentaries on Shakespeare.[6] In Williams's view, the great dramatist strayed from historical facts in portrayals of Richard III, Lear, and Macbeth, and he found the plots of *The Tempest* and *A Midsummer Night's Dream* not only unnatural but incredible. After attending the performances of famous Shakespearean actors, Williams derided the ranting of some but considered Tomassino Salvini sublime in *Othello*. He labeled the last part of Hamlet "always a drag," since the interest no longer centers on the hero.[7]

Williams found the road to dramatic recognition long and arduous; for many years he gained little success. In 1874 he printed privately an adaptation for the stage of Bulwer-Lytton's novel *Eugene Aram.* According to his diary he sent it to H.H. Boyesen, a personal friend of "Lowell, Howells, Longfellow, Aldrich and others of the F.F.V. of Letters," a correspondent of George Washington Cable, and a Cornell professor. Boyesen was much taken with the play, which nevertheless remained unperformed.[8] Williams's other early pieces included *Morbid vs. Quick* (1873), a one-act about the New Orleans gallant; Queen Mary (1875); and *Witchcraft* (1886). Some of these early plays were produced in New Orleans.

Williams also composed verse, which he collected in *The Dream of Art and Other Poems* in 1892.[9] In his poetry, he paid tribute to both southern and northern leaders. In "Davis" he admonished those who tormented the Confederate leader to let death silence strife "and leave his fate to Time's impartial will" (p. 20). General Grant's work for peace was his "crown of fame" (p. 31). Recognizing the irony of a masterful slave, in

"The Grandissimes, Chapter XXIX" he hailed the struggle against slavery of Cable's Bras Coupé: "Thou King—though captive! human—though a slave" (p. 23). In "Dom Pedro" he lauded the Brazilian emperor who championed emancipation in the 1880s (p. 24).

Like James A. Herne and William Dean Howells, Williams clashed with the stars of the commercial theater while in pursuit of his artistic goals. Unequal conflict between art and commercialism marked this era of popular stars, epitomized by James O'Neill and Joseph Jefferson. For example, Charles Frohman, a producer who exploited the drawing power of Maude Adams, William Gillette, and others, believed that Americans preferred personalities to plays.

The first star whom Williams knew well was Lawrence Barrett, an actor respected for his noble character and intellectual stature who tried to improve the American theater by producing the works of native authors. He published a biography of Edwin Forrest and in 1883 successfully revived George Henry Boker's *Francesca da Rimini*. But even Barrett was bound by the exigencies of the commercial theater. In the 1870s and 1880s, traveling with Edwin Booth's company, he was obliged to accept second billing. This actor had appeared on the New Orleans stage soon after the war, and he met Williams there when he was engaged by David Bidwell, who managed the Grand Opera House, 1883-88.

Williams showed his *Eugene Aram* (1874) to Barrett and received some pointed advice from the theatrical star, who advised him to study "construction" saying that was far more important then literary merit. Williams confided to his diary that Barrett's remark showed a lack of literary "cultivation." Conceding that "construction" was necessary, he maintained that "if with the construction is combined literary merit certainly the work is enhanced; and if literary merit were made the *point* of excellence sought instead of merely construction the stage would be in much better condition in every way."[10] Williams later gained more appreciation for dramatic construction, however, expressing admiration for the "well-made play" in a lecture titled "Building a Play."[11]

At the end of his career Barrett was in dire need of a new acting vehicle. His arrangement with Booth had worn thin; New York critics had complained about their trading the main roles in *Othello* on successive nights. Turning to Williams, Barrett commissioned a play on a serious literary subject but did not live to perform in *Dante* (1893).[12] Williams wrote an elegy for Barrett, dated March 21, 1891, in which he spoke of the "Christian's soul."[13]

Williams fared better with another star of the day. Robert Mantell, originally from Scotland, made his New York debut in the enormously

popular *East Lynne* in 1879 and went on to act in Shakespeare, melodrama, and romantic plays in the large American cities, including New
Orleans. In 1886, he formed his own company, which was capably managed by Augustus Pitou.

Williams achieved his first theatrical success with Mantell's production of *Parrhasius*, a one-act classical tragedy in blank verse which he had
printed in 1879. It incorporates the highest artistic standards. After seeing a review of Williams's poetry collection *The Dream of Art and Other
Poems* in the *Boston Transcript* (1892) and reading *Parrhasius*, Mantell purchased the stage rights from Williams for $3,000 (according to the proud
report of the *New Orleans Daily Picayune* of June 14, 1892) and took it on
a nationwide tour. The *Memphis Appeal* exclaimed that "the play is the
best work of native origin that has been seen here in a decade."[14]

The troubled life of the artist became Williams's favorite dramatic
subject. *Parrhasius* bears the Shakespearean epigraph "Thriftless ambition!" and focuses on the tragic flaw of a great painter of ancient Greece.
(Williams had experienced such feelings himself, writing in his youthful
diary that he longed to "appease my craving ambition" by artistic success.)[15] The philosopher Theon begs Parrhasius to give up his ambition,
which will destroy respect for human life. This prediction comes true because the artist cuts out the tongue of his model for Prometheus in order
to silence protests. Ironically, the model turns out to be the father of
Parrhasius's wife, who falls dead on identifying his corpse. The tragic hero
now realizes the truth of Theon's prophecy that someday he would commit a murder: "Thus do the gods / Inflict our punishment with our own
hands, / And scourge us mortally with our own errors!"[16] Williams showed
artistic independence by choosing the form of Greek tragedy, which had
virtually disappeared from contemporary drama.

Like many writers since the age of Romanticism, Williams gave repeated attention to the life of the artist, a central theme in the contemporary theater: as seen in Ibsen's *Ghosts* (1881) and *The Master Builder*
(1892); Chekhov's *The Sea Gull* (1895); Rostand's *Cyrano de Bergerac* (1897);
and Shaw's *Candida* (1898). During his literary apprenticeship he had
taken a great interest in the artist's life. Always interested in how an artist
lives, what he believes, and how his greatness is achieved, he enjoyed Thomas Moore's *Life of Byron* and Edward Trelawny's *Last Days of Shelley and
Byron*. Pleased to discover that Byron was a man with human frailties, not
a god, he objected to critics' disapproval of Byron's morals, which the
poet was refreshingly honest in revealing.[17]

Williams's fascination with the artist's life was natural for a young man
who had recorded in his diary that he was "ambitious" for artistic fame

and would never relent "until this end shall be accomplished."[18] He contrasted the artist with other members of society in *The Dream of Art and Other Poems*. In "The Poet," "the World-Man" may chide the poet for wasting his time, but later buys his song and dies forgotten, while the verses live on (p. 94). Capable of seeing the humorous side, Williams jokes that if the poet finds himself at a loss for inspiration, a skirt may appear to remedy that deficiency. The critic in the poem of that name resembles the poet only in physical form but not in mind. He betrays his origin by "the smithy's soot and windy roar / And Vulcan's envy sadly sore" (p. 95).

The title poem of the collection presents the idea of art as a dream that can never be realized (a theme treated by Hawthorne in "The Artist of the Beautiful"). An impoverished sculptor finally makes the clay model of a statue he has envisioned all his life but ironically does not cast into bronze because he falls asleep and dies of the freezing cold: "Thus, dead beside the ruined clay, / The Sculptor dreamed life's dream away" (p. 4).

Williams also featured the artist's predicament in two works about famous figures of the Renaissance. In *Dante* (1893), which treats the conflict between Duty and Art, the great poet says that he will not shirk his obligation to Florence in her time of need. Would his friends have him "resign from the council, leave the state," and seek men's esteem only through the grace of Art? "Never—never!" he answers.[19] For Williams the practical businessman, art could not always take first place.

The one-act *A Statue's Tragedy* (published in *Fetter's Southern Magazine*, May 1893) examines the conflict between art and conventional morality. After Raphael has carved the nude statue of a count's wife, he is suspected of committing sexual immorality with her. Although no immorality has occurred, to satisfy propriety he must destroy the statue. Anachronistic in its rendition of Renaissance morality as prudish, the play engages in the battle against Victorian prudery, which was constantly waged by artists of the Mauve Decade.

Williams took up another favorite topic of modern dramatists by deploring intolerant religion. Ibsen ridiculed the narrow-minded pastor in *Ghosts;* Shaw condemned ecclesiastical censorship in *St. Joan*. Williams's antipathy to religious intolerance grew out of his own experience as a nonconformist. Although his wife was a strict Presbyterian (who frowned on her husband's Bohemian friends) and his daughters—whose church attendance he encouraged—married in the Episcopal Church, he never attended himself.

One of Williams's best-written dramas is *The Atheist* (1892), which denounces organized religion and defends the upright nonbeliever. Williams first dedicated this one-act masque in blank verse to Robert Ingersoll, the most famous atheist of his day, but the dedication was omitted when the play was published as the final part of *The Dream of Art and Other Poems.* A critic of the church and a free thinker, Ingersoll declared such doctrines as the divinity of Christ false. Much admired by Mark Twain, this foe of superstition wanted reason applied to religious dogma, holding that people should not allow the church to think for them. *The Atheist* is a tribute to the nonbeliever who is condemned by the church but fills his life with humanitarian deeds. Williams, the ironist, perceived the contradiction in condemning a good man who holds unconventional beliefs. Because the hero has been branded a heretic, his beloved has entered a convent, but she returns to him after hearing of the good deeds he has done for those in distress. Declaring that he has inspired in her "the faith to do," she throws off her religious garb. Confirming the rightness of her decision, a chorus of devils pronounces a final curse on the reunited pair: "May your hearts with fine pain / Be tortured in twain."[20]

Williams struck out in a new direction with a fantasy, *Ollamus: King of Utopiana,* set to music by a local composer and performed May 14-19, 1894, at the St. Charles Theatre in New Orleans.[21] Revised in 1901 as *A Royal Joke,* it was proudly hailed as "the birth of Southern opera."[22] *Ollamus* has a serious purpose since it effectively satirizes American democracy in the 1890s, the decade of the corrupt Tammany ring in New York, and opposes current imperialism plotted by American missionaries in Hawaii. Indebted to Gilbert and Sullivan's *Mikado,* this musical extravaganza stars Miss Liberty Equality Fraternity Jones, "a mugwump" (p. 94), who arrives by ship on a palm-shrouded island ruled by King Ollamus ("all of us" adore him) and his "counsellors" (pp. 105, 88). She tells Mike Dynamite, a Tammany wardheeler, not to worry about the cash until they take over the government "in the true American way" (p. 100): that is, in a fixed election making her the president and him the secretary of the treasury. Miss Jones opposes the marriage of her ward Perdita (the lost one) to Prince Chic because he is a prince; Ollamus objects because Perdita is a commoner. The prince saves the day by playing a phonograph record of the counsellors' plot to demote the king and vows to execute them all if he is not allowed to marry his beloved. Though Miss Jones, a feminist, opposes Perdita's marriage also because no man is good enough for a woman, she relents and even marries Ollamus herself. This farrago ends with the chorus singing in the style of Gilbert and Sullivan:

> Never tarry
> Let us marry

Woman's safest goal is man
Soon or later
Love will bait her
And he will mate her
If he can.   [p. 128]

Williams showed his affinity for Ibsen's modernism most noticeably by trying his hand at the problem play. This genre, often dealing with marital relations, was represented best in the United States by James A. Herne's *Margaret Fleming* (1890), in which the title character nurses her husband's child by another woman. Williams made a bid for popularity by adding some highly melodramatic elements. *The Husband: A Society Play* (1895) by "a member of the American Dramatists' Club" was produced at the Park Theatre of Philadelphia in 1895, with Robert Mantell in the leading role.[23] The introduction stated that this adaptation of a French play that had been translated into English as *Retribution* was for the most part original. Set in France, the plot involves two couples who suffer the consequences of marital infidelity. Both unfaithful spouses die.

As indicated by the title, the play gives most attention to the husband as victim of his wife's extramarital affair. Henri Lefevre, a naval officer who has been absent on a voyage in the South Seas, has remained faithful to his wife and longs for their reunion. He returns to find Therese, dead from consumption, clutching a miniature to her breast: "Blessing her for giving her last thoughts to me, I knelt beside and kissed those lips which for the first time failed in response to mine" (p. 43). When he looks more closely, however, he discovers that the miniature is the likeness of his rival, Gaston De Vigny.

The play also expresses Williams's ideas about a wife's response to a philandering husband (the subject of Herne's *Margaret Fleming*): if the man will not change his ways, the woman should leave him. After Heloise de Vigny sees her husband with the other woman, she tells him that he has destroyed her trust. Gaston, who will lose his wealth if they separate, threatens to ruin her reputation, boasting that a man may accomplish this easily despite a hundred witnesses to the wife's honesty. Asserting an Ibsenesque determination, Heloise defies his blackmail and refuses to return home with him. Henri kills Gaston in a duel, exclaiming in the last lines that he has carried out "Heaven's righteous judgment."

Williams includes the international subject, found in Bronson Howard's plays by a caustic comment on the American girl, who resembles Henry James's liberated Daisy Miller. Admiring the American girl's independence before marriage, an affianced Frenchwoman declares that she wishes to retain her freedom afterward as well. Colonel Rich of the United

States Army assures her that she can, since marriage does not change an American girl in the least (pp. 60-61). *The Husband,* like *Ollamus,* also includes satirical commentary on politics. According to Colonel Rich, Napoleon had predicted that the United States and Russia would be closely analogous in the twentieth century but did not specify in what respects. After the colonel conjectures that he meant freedom of the press and despotism of the politician, a witty Frenchwoman says that he has made a very "czar-castic" joke because the Russian ruler will permit neither, while the American people tolerate both (p. 30).

John Wentworth's Wife (written circa 1903), an unperformed piece, that Williams called "a modern play" on the title page, is another serious treatment of a marital problem.[24] Hilda Wentworth, recalling Ibsen's heroines, is honest, enlightened, and unconventional in behavior. After learning of her husband's infidelity, she faces his conduct directly. She holds no grudge against the other woman and reaches an understanding with her husband, whom she never expected to be faultless.

Tempted by the lure of popular success, Williams boldly entered the world of the commercial theater as a practicing playwright. Like Bronson Howard, who believed that any play worth its salt should reach the stage, Williams stated in a lecture that a play should not remain in the closet.[25] Yet this commendable stand created for him the dilemma faced by many serious playwrights: how to write for the commercial stage without sacrificing artistic integrity.

Williams's most successful play, and the only one to open in New York, (1898), was *A Cavalier of France,* which lacked any redeeming literary value, unashamedly catering to the popular taste for historical romance. First offered to Robert Mantell with the risqué title "The Queen's Garter," it was placed with Louis James—Barrett's supporting actor in New Orleans—who had declared that he would renounce tragedy and follow "the public demand for the romantic drama, which has during the last few seasons become so widespread."[26] Starring James, the play ran for a week in New York, then toured the country. It was staged in such cities as San Francisco, Philadelphia, Kansas City, and even Butte, Montana, and was still holding the boards in 1900, a year when no fewer than eight of Williams's plays were being produced. *A Cavalier of France* is a bombastic extravaganza of court intrigue during the reign of Henri III, enlivened with fencing encounters. Proved innocent of stealing the queen's garter, the hero boasts that it will be emblazoned on his coat of arms henceforth. According to the program note, this historical romance offered great opportunity for "handsome costuming and gorgeous effects."[27]

Williams's sensational *Unorna* (1902) reveals the worst effects of the star system. Minnie Brune, who resided for a time in New Orleans, took the title role of a hypnotist who performs a cobra dance. Colored pictures of "the American Bernhardt as Unorna" showed Brune in seductive poses. In order to enhance her own reputation, Brune wished to stress the play's connection with Francis Marion Crawford's popular novel *The Witch of Prague,* even boasting that she had inspired Crawford to create the mysterious Unorna, a woman accused of witchcraft. Although Williams had significantly altered the anti-Semitic novel, portraying the Jewish characters as courageous and compassionate in his adaptation, publicity linked the play to the famous novelist rather than to the little-known dramatist. Williams protested this injustice in a letter to Crawford, who replied graciously from Italy that the dramatist should indeed get "sole credit."[28]

Still, it was Williams's acquaintance with Minnie Brune that had led to her performance in the leading role; he had argued that the little-known actress was destined to become successful because of "a magnetic personality."[29] Brune hoped the play's successful tour of the South, which Williams joined, would lead to a New York opening. It did not, but theatergoers from Norfolk, Virginia, to New Orleans found the play "different" and "weird."[30]

The domineering influence of the star system is painfully evident in Williams's career, for deference to famous actors determined much of his writing for the stage. Minnie Brune's husband, Clarence Brune, corresponding from London, laid down his requirements for a new play and bought Williams's *The Emperor's Double* as a stage vehicle for himself. He never acted in it, however, because he decided that no British audience would attend a play with Napoleon as the hero.[31]

Although Williams bowed to the commercial stage in *Unorna,* he showed his professional commitment to playwriting by becoming a charter member of the American Dramatists' Club of New York, which Bronson Howard founded in 1891. Leading playwrights, among them Clyde Fitch and David Belasco, attended the inaugural luncheon. Howard worked diligently to establish the dramatist's profession in this country. Earlier playwrights such as Robert Montgomery Bird had failed financially, but when Howard proved the possibility of making a good living by his art, a new era began in American drama. During this age of rampant commercialism, Williams dedicated himself to the cause of serious drama. In "Modern Drama: Its Moral and Literary Value," a lecture delivered sometime after 1906, he called "the late Henrik Ibsen" the greatest of modern dramatists.[32] He showed discrimination by esteeming the work of Edmond Rostand, Gerhart Hauptmann, Henry Arthur Jones, Arthur Wing Pinero,

Bronson Howard, and Augustus Thomas. Supporting the realistic trend, he admired "truth to nature" when it appeared on the stage, in agreement with Herne's motto of "Art for Truth's sake." Believing that drama must change with the times, he called on contemporary playwrights to avoid the mistake of Ben Johnson, who had copied the classic form of an earlier age.[33]

Williams was expressing ideas also promulgated in an important book of the 1890s. Hamlin Garland in *Crumbling Idols* (1894), foreseeing a better day for American drama under Ibsen's influence, declared that the Norwegian innovator's "realism" might better be designated "modernism." He believed that modern dramatists should make their own comment on contemporary times because realism means not simply reproduction of "tanks and fire-engines" but the articulation of truth in an individual way, "irrespective of past models."[34]

Williams's most remarkable play is *The Clairvoyant: A Living Lie* (1899), an unperformed melodrama that has survived only in typescript.[35] Like Williams's other non-commercial works it examines seriously an interesting subject. This tightly plotted play in four acts, set before the Civil War, recounts the plight of a pitiful woman who believes herself to be a mulatto. In Paris, a corrupt fortuneteller informs her foster child, the beautiful Stella Perdue (meaning "lost"), that in America she would be by law a slave, since Negro blood ran in her mother's veins. Stella laughs bitterly, thinking of her "family tree" and what the future holds for her (p. 235). The villainous Paul Foscari has overheard this secret and plots to gain the beautiful woman for his mistress. The scene then shifts to New Orleans, where Stella takes the name Estelle Ruchard and, to earn money, leads a double life as Zenobia, the fortune-teller. Though Estelle rises in New Orleans society, being nominated as Queen of Mardi Gras, she is tormented by fear of exposure, which would doom her to slavery. Her anguish appears repeatedly in soliloquies, the best passages of the drama. On hearing from Zizi, her "'before the war' negro 'mammy,'" that purple spots under the fingernails are a sign of Negro blood, she vows to wear gloves thenceforth (p. 252). Alone, she thinks that if Zizi knew the truth she would despise her mixed blood and asks herself how she can get rid of this fear, crying out, "Oh why was I born?" (p. 255).

The remainder of the melodrama clears up some puzzles and ends with a sensational denouement. Estelle's faithful lover, significantly named Arthur Steadman, reveals that the tragic "mulatto" is in fact pure white; a spurned suitor of her mother took revenge by reporting that she was part Negro. Meanwhile, Estelle has swooned just before Paul Foscari, playfully acting the clairvoyant, can identify her as the mulatto Stella Perdue. Finally, he attempts to ruin Estelle's reputation by identifying her to Zenobia—who unmasks and burns the false record of her birth. Arthur enters, announces Estelle's white blood, and is knocked unconscious by the villain, whom Estelle stabs with a stiletto. The lurid scene ends when the room, lit by gas, bursts into flame as Estelle and Arthur escape.

This play is an excellent example of the unperformed but nevertheless significant work, one that went unperformed perhaps because of its sensitive subject matter. This study of the woman who allegedly has Negro blood, her problem not lessened by the fact that she is white, is far superior to Williams's commercial success, *A Cavalier of France*. Here he considers a real problem in American life, one treated by Dion Boucicault in his play *The Octoroon* (1859), George Washington Cable in *Madame Delphine* (1881), and Kate Chopin in "Desirée's Baby" (1893). Chopin tells of a woman who was banished by her husband for giving birth to a part-Negro child; ironically, it is he who transmitted the Negro blood. *The Clairvoyant* is also permeated with irony (characteristic of the currently popular Guy de Maupassant, who influenced Chopin), since the supposed mulatto suffers the agony of an actual mulatto. Williams writes with real feeling about this tormented woman's dilemma, a situation he may well have observed firsthand as a New Orleanian.

At the end of his life Williams combined his concerns regarding art and religion in a blank-verse drama about the artist's struggle against religious intolerance. In his words, he hoped to win "the blue ribbon" for literature with *Marlowe: The Buried Name*, written on his deathbed in 1908.[36] Speaking before a New Orleans literary group, Williams had previously reviewed a book arguing that Christopher Marlowe had written Shakespeare's plays. Declining to accept this theory in Wilbur Gleason Zeigler's *It Was Marlowe* completely, he still found a basis for questioning the authorship of Shakespeare's plays, which he transferred to his play about Marlowe. Further, Williams was particularly interested in the charge of atheism against Marlowe, which was fully attested by historical evidence.

In this unperformed play, whose clumsy construction betrays the writer's illness, Williams denounces those who accuse Marlowe of atheism. In accordance with historical facts a warrant demands the arrest of "Kit" Marlowe, who, calling the charge against him "the spume of canting hypocrites; / The witless superstition of the church," refuses to let his enemies "imprison thought" (p. 7). He defends himself before his beloved Jane as "player-dramatist, / Accused—falsely of being an atheist— / An infidel, a scoffer of religion / And on the testimony solely of my plays / Prejudged and precondemned to infamy" (p. 54). In a bizarre plot twist, Marlowe kills his rival for Jane in a duel and flees to France, leaving behind a corpse supposedly his own. In the end, Shakespeare presents Marlowe's plays at the Globe Theatre under his own name because the author warned him that "the pit" had branded him "an infidel" (p. 60). Ironically, the supposed atheist Marlowe can win acclaim for his plays only by concealing his authorship.

Williams also opposed religious intolerance in "The Union of the Church and the Stage." In this enlightened lecture, probably delivered in the latter part of his life, he implored priests and ministers not to censure the theater without learning first what goes on there. The clergy, properly informed, could promote "the victory of the good over the bad, the lifting of the moral plane of the audience into a higher and purer atmosphere."[37]

In the spasmodic, halting development of southern drama, Williams holds a unique place. Unlike many of his predecessors, he sustained an active career as a serious dramatist. Not writing primarily for a local theater, he composed works that toured the nation. Although his plays, written in the stilted language of the contemporary stage, lack dramatic distinction and rarely rise above mediocrity, they differ from the predominant thought of the South, enunciating a spirit not seen since Robert Munford's plea for political tolerance and John Blake White's indictment of dueling. This persistent critic of society adopted the dissenting voice of Mark Twain and of George Washington Cable, a fellow New Orleanian whom he admired. Cosmopolitan in outlook, he was free of sectional prejudice, preferring the tendency of the New South to cooperate with the North in a reunited nation. As a southern admirer of Ibsen, he fostered the new movement in drama, which would flourish in the works of Paul Green and Lillian Hellman.

Taking an enlightened stand in his lectures and eclectic writings, Williams joined new voices in the theater such as Ibsen and innovators of the American stage by exposing painful truths of modern society. He satirized political corruption and with Shavian candor discussed the anxiety of the mixed blood in New Orleans. Like Boucicault, he expressed sympathy for the disconsolate mulatto; like Clyde Fitch in *The City* (1909), he combined melodrama with realism to transcribe the stress of modern marriage; agreeing with James A. Herne, he deplored the double standard for husbands and wives. Selecting important subjects for the stage like his European contemporaries, he treated the artist's life and religious intolerance, thus anticipating another Williams based in New Orleans.

In short, the array of topics that Williams subjected to scrutiny is impressive. But who can say what views he was prevented from expressing by the demands of commercialism? In retrospect, he emerges as a lonely, frequently unheard voice in a theater dominated by a new force curbing the serious dramatist: commercialism was as inimical to free thought as social pressure.

— 6 —

The Leadership
of Paul Green

Scattered composition of local color plays filled the gap between the careers of Espy Williams and Paul Green. Contemporary with Williams was Lee Arthur (1870-1917), a Jewish playwright who was born in Shreveport, Louisiana, moved to New York in 1893, and wrote successfully for the commercial theater. His *We-Uns of Tennessee* (1899), advocating reconciliation of the North and South, ran for twenty-three performances in New York. In 1906 he wrote a one-act play, *The Last of the Hargroves,* which recounts a mountaineers' feud in Tennessee, but there is no record of its performance.[1] Dramatic pieces bristling with southern pride, copyrighted but not performed, include *Way Down South: Character Comedy in 4 Acts* (Mobile, Alabama, 1900) by Jonathan H. Lagman; *Dixie Doodle* (Anniston, Ala., 1907) by E.W. Fordyce; and *The Sweetest Girl in Dixie: A Comedy Drama in 4 Acts* (Monticello, Arkansas, 1907) by Freda Slemons.[2] After World War I, however, the South overflowed (comparatively speaking) with active dramatists who attained national recognition. Paul Green took the lead with sensitive and innovative folk plays that contributed to the progress of modern American drama.

The South of the 1920s was a place of continuing transition, where the old was passing away and the new was coming fast in a decade of great prosperity. For the first time, great fortunes were made by southerners: James Buchanan Duke in electricity, Robert J. Reynolds in cigarettes, Ernest Woodruff in Coca-Cola. Furthermore, this wealth remained at home to found impressive private universities such as Duke and Emory. Other enterprises in which the South was finally realizing its comparative advantage included lumber, oil, and textiles, with many economic spin-offs. Real estate flourished in Florida and elsewhere, making the South the equal of the Midwest in its boosterism and surpassing even some of Sinclair Lewis's examples. Seeing the proliferation of subdivisions, Thomas Wolfe wryly called Asheville, North Carolina "Boom Town, where everyone is full of Progress and Prosperity."[3]

Increased activity in industry and commerce had repercussions. It is no accident that the Southern Literary Renascence coincided with the awakening of the southern industrial giant in the 1920s. Southern writers, including dramatists, struggled to produce art that would not be outdistanced by material progress, for the highly touted new prosperity made them acutely aware of the South's backwardness in education, racial justice, and artistic achievement. When Thomas Wolfe ironically pronounced the slogan "Progress!" in 1923, he called for more "beauty and spirit" in the next breath.[4]

Signs of intellectual ferment also appeared in the long-somnolent South as a few first-rate universities—the University of North Carolina, Vanderbilt—nourished circles that published influential journals of sociology and poetry. Southern students were learning the advanced political, social, economic, and aesthetic theories of the Western world. During the recent war many had traveled to other parts of the country and Europe, making them the best educated and least provincial southerners since the Revolutionary generation of great Virginians.

Most significantly, the young southerners who molded the Southern Renascence possessed a different outlook from that of their elders. From firsthand experience they knew the older South, had a keen sense of the past, and were self-conscious southerners, but when they read indictments of backwardness such as H.L. Mencken's iconoclastic "Sahara of the Bozart" (1917), they nodded in agreement. As modern writers, they were eager to explore their own relations with southern society and to probe subjects long prohibited.

The signs of literary and intellectual vitality in the South after World War I were numerous and symptomatic. At Vanderbilt University a group of poets gathered to discuss literature and publish *The Fugitive* from 1922 to 1925. It was members of this group who composed a manifesto to confront the modern industrial world. In *I'll Take My Stand* (1930), John Crowe Ransom, Robert Penn Warren, Allen Tate, Donald Davidson, and other self-styled Agrarians protested the industrial gospel and reasserted the values of the traditional community. Forming a contrasting axis of intellectual activity, a group of sociologists at the University of North Carolina attacked the social and economic ills of the South. Howard W. Odum made the *Journal of Social Forces* the leading organ of southern self-examination in the 1920s.

In addition, new authors arose to give importance to southern literature. Ellen Glasgow, announcing that the South needed not magnolias and moonlight but blood and irony, produced novels such as *Barren Ground* (1925) and *Vein of Iron* (1935). Thomas Wolfe and William

Faulkner followed with works of great power and artistry. Dramatists, the stepchildren of southern literature, at long last began to produce plays of real literary merit.

A New Southerner

The leader of the new drama in the South was Paul Green (1894-1981). This versatile North Carolina writer, who enjoyed a long career as a professional dramatist, was from the beginning a man with a mission. He undertook to produce a drama that would depict southern life truly and critically.[5]

Though not the best dramatist of the region, Green is the central, indispensable figure in the development of southern drama because his work signals the decisive shift from the sectionalism of the earlier plays to the nonsectionalism, hinted at by Espy Williams, of the modern ones. Green encouraged reform of the existing racial system, working for social change in the state, region, and nation through his plays and public activities. Rare among the dramatists in this study, he became a public personality because of his engagement in political and social causes. He argued for abolition of the chain gang, integration of schools, and fair treatment in the courts irrespective of race; he advocated full access to education, jobs, and public institutions for blacks. Green may even be termed nonsouthern in the sense that he invariably opposed the political stand of most southerners. For the rest of the century that same dissent would distinguish southern plays, even as they remained more traditionally southern in a cultural sense.

Not only was Green a new voice for reform of the racial system, but he spearheaded the movement to represent the rich culture of the South in drama. Though differing with most southerners on racial matters, Green recorded their traditions, activities, and interests faithfully in dramatic works. From his folk plays of the 1920s to his historical outdoor dramas of the 1970s, Green exploited the rich material of the southern experience—such as the refusal of the Old South to surrender quietly—and thus gave definitive form to southern drama of the twentieth century, a synthesis of regional culture and enlightened racial views.

In his first series of plays, Green dramatized folk life, propelled by the folk drama movement in North Carolina and Ireland; and sustained an interest in the subcultures of blacks, tenant farmers, and Indians throughout his career. He brought to those works the liberating force of William Dean Howells's realism, then making its full impact on the American stage. He utilized native material, as the local colorists did, but was more interested in truth than nostalgia. Most notably, Green firmly rejected Negro stereotypes and presented blacks as individuals who grieved and hoped as strongly as whites. He not only transcribed the external realism of setting but rendered the inner realism of character as well.

Green's early life prepared him well for writing folk drama. Born in Lillington, Harnett County, in the Cape Fear River Valley of central North Carolina, he drew repeatedly on this "postage stamp" of territory for his dramatic saga. Descended from early Scottish and English landholding families, his grandfather had lost his plantation during the Civil War, but his father raised cotton on a large scale. During his youth, Green was a successful baseball player, a champion cotton picker, and a farm worker who knew both black and white tenants well. But his parents also instilled in him a love of books and music, and after graduating from Buie's Creek Academy, he served as principal of the country school in Olive Branch, North Carolina.

Following service overseas in World War I, Green returned to his home state where he graduated from the University of North Carolina in 1921 with a major in philosophy. After graduate study of philosophy at Cornell, he returned to his alma mater in 1922, married another devotee of the folk drama, Elizabeth Lay, and taught philosophy at the university until 1937 and dramatic arts until 1945.

In 1925 Green took over the editorship of the *Reviewer,* a little magazine started in 1920 by Emily Clark of Richmond, which strove to correct the lack of culture deplored by Mencken. When the magazine moved to Chapel Hill, Gerald Johnson, a crusading, liberal journalist, joined the board, along with Addison Hibbard, for whose *Literary Lantern* Green wrote book reviews. As editor of the *Reviewer,* Green protested the falseness and sentimentality of earlier writing in "A Plain Statement about Southern Literature."[6] The magazine concluded publication at the end of 1925, for Green suffered from unrelenting deadlines and the drain on his creative energy. Nevertheless, the experience was a valuable steppingstone to his leadership in southern literature.

As an undergraduate at Chapel Hill, with the University of North Carolina fast establishing itself as one of the intellectual centers of the South, Green had joined Jonathan Daniels, future liberal editor of the *Raleigh News and Observer,* and Thomas Wolfe as students under such stimulating professors as Norman Foerster, the literary critic, and Archibald Henderson, mathematician and biographer of Shaw. Most influential for Green's future plans was Frederick Koch, who had come from North Dakota in 1918 to teach playwriting. Green began writing plays under this pioneer of folk drama, heeding Koch's counsel to "write what you know around you, make use of the soil beneath your feet, of the tradition in your heart, of the struggle in your soul, of the breath of your hills."[7]

Moreover, Green found at Chapel Hill what all dramatists with serious aims sorely need: a receptive theatrical company. The Carolina Playmakers, founded by Professor Koch, had completed facilities for production by 1919. Since Koch encouraged young playwrights to draw on what they had observed since childhood, folk drama predominated at their theater. Thomas Wolfe, who first aspired to playwriting, saw his drama of mountain life, *The Return of Buck Gavin,* performed by the Playmakers in 1919.

The first of Green's pieces to be given by the Playmakers was *The Last of the Lowries* in 1920, which became a mainstay in the company's repertoire. Reflecting the influence of the Irish dramatist John Millington Synge, this tragic one-act features the Croatans, a mixed breed of Negroes and Indians inhabiting the coastal Carolina swamps. Like the old mother of Synge's *Riders to the Sea,* the aged Cumba grieves for the last of her outlaw sons: "But they're all gone, and what call hev I got to be livin' more."[8] Eight short plays produced at Chapel Hill from 1920 to 1925 gave Green his start as a professional dramatist; the Carolina Playmakers were as indispensable to his career as the Provincetown Players were for Eugene O'Neill.

The "folk" for Green were in effect the country people whom he had known so thoroughly during his youth. His essay "Drama and the Weather" expresses Agrarian attitudes toward country people, whose ways he much preferred to those of urbanites. Speaking in Hardyesque fashion, he called the folk "the people whose manners, ethics, religion and philosophical ideals" are not controlled "by the institutions of men in specialized society."[9] Green's folk plays first revealed the rich resources available to southern dramatists as he mined the little-known culture of rural blacks and poor whites, not hesitating to include superstition, bigoted religion, and violence. *The Last of the Lowries* takes us into remote swamps to meet a unique, if violent, people.

Green proved himself a comprehensive dramatist of southern life by portraying three major social types: the Negro, the poor white, and the aristocrat. The many one-act and full-length plays he wrote from 1920 to 1935 transformed the presentation of the South on the stage. Theatergoers could observe authentic scenes of southern life by a sensitive native, not secondhand treatments by northerners.

Green probed the life of the Negro in a series of one-acts, some of which served as sketches for later full-length plays. Barrett Clark wrote in the introduction to Green's *Lonesome Road* (1926) that the playwright had revealed "hidden corners of the soul and mind of the black man."[10] In this collection Green declared that his portraits were solidly based on personal observation. Acknowledging objections that these were not "representative" pictures of the Negro race, he answered that they were not meant to be; rather, they showed "the more tragic and uneasy side of negro life as it has exhibited itself to my notice on or near a single farm in the coastal plain of North Carolina."[11]

Many of Green's plays touched subjects that most southerners preferred not to contemplate. *White Dresses: A Tragedy in White and Black* (1920), his first play about blacks, confronts the poignant case of a young mulatto who loves a wealthy white man. When his father insists that Mary wed her black suitor, we hear her anguish. Mary's grandmother, after burning two white dresses given by white lovers to her daughter and granddaughter, warns, "I knows your feelings, child, but you's got to smother 'em in."[12] Because of the subject matter, this piece was not performed in Chapel Hill.

Wishing to show the liking for fantasy, he wrote *No 'Count Boy*, his first play to win national recognition; it played in little theaters of Chicago and Dallas before moving to New York, where it won the Belasco Cup in 1925. In this one-act, Pheelie dislikes her boyfriend's stolidity but enjoys the attentions of a young harmonica player, who describes the exotic places he has visited, until his mother reveals that he has never been there. Green examined wife abuse in *Hot Iron*, licentious religion in *The Prayer-Meeting* (both collected in *Lonesome Road*, 1926), and incest in *Supper for the Dead* (collected in *In the Valley*, 1928).

Hymn to the Rising Sun (1936), the best of Green's one-acts about the Negro, is a mordant protest against the chain gang (in the manner of Clifford Odets, whose *Waiting for Lefty* (1935) demanded a strike for higher wages). On the Fourth of July, ironically, the gang captain announces that the law expects him to turn prisoners into citizens by whatever means it takes. After confining Runt in a stifling box overnight, he scoffs that "Green" at the University has objected to such treatment of the Negro.[13] Runt dies but gets his wish to be buried beneath the railroad tracks, where he can always hear the sound of freedom from enslavement.

Green's most successful drama of the Negro was *In Abraham's Bosom*, which opened on December 30, 1926, at New York's Greenwich Village Theatre and then moved to Broadway under the auspices of the prestigious Theatre Guild. The play ran for nearly two hundred performances, garnered praise from *New York Times* critic Brooks Atkinson, and won the Pulitzer Prize in 1926, giving Green an esteemed place in the American theater. Although critics John Mason Brown and Stark Young found its dramatic construction faulty, Alan Downer in *Fifty Years of American Drama* concludes that it was the first play to capture "the inner spirit of the negro."[14]

Green choose the timely theme of black education to illustrate the struggles of the New Negro. Hoping to educate his people, Abe McCranie looks optimistically to the future when his white father, Colonel McCranie, gives him land to start a school. But Abe must combat both the opposition of whites and the resistance of blacks in his farming community. Some balk at schooling, even going to sleep in class. Soon the parents, dissatisfied with Abe, keep their children away. He must also fight the superstition of his old aunt, Muh Mack, who blames books for all the troubles in his family and, when Abe criticizes black preachers for taking the meager savings of their followers, predicts that God will punish those who utter such blasphemy. Finally, the white leaders, headed by Abe's half-brother Lonnie, flatly oppose Negro education and vote against continuation of the school.

Abe's flaw, his uncontrollable anger, makes this play a tragedy in the classic sense. His head or intelligence (which comes from the white part, according to the characters in the play) is in conflict with his heart or passion (which derives from the black). Abe himself and his black companions recognize the split. Furiously he strikes Lonnie, who has told him to forget about books, and loses his temper again with a schoolboy, whom he beats for taking a little girl's dinner. Eventually, Abe kills Lonnie and then hallucinates his own conception in a scene recalling those in O'Neill's *Emperor Jones*. Furiously he yells to phantoms of his father and mother: "Stop that, I tell you, that's me!"[15] Nor can Abe control his anger against his own son, whom he has named for Frederick Douglass, the mighty abolitionist. Douglass hates books, delights in the guitar, drinks, and fraternizes with crooks, causing his enraged father to banish him from home.

At the end, Abe is driven from the school by whites, dressed as Klansmen, whom Douglass has informed of his father's ambitions. Having exclaimed in a speech, "We got to be free, freedom of the mind and soul," he confronts the armed men with these words: "Yea, guns and killings is in vain" (p. 176). As the idealistic educator is killed by the mob, the wind sends the sparks in his house flying, signifying that the cause of Negro education will catch fire.

Potter's Field (1931) was Green's last major study of the Negro, the leading subject in the first phase of his career. Begun as the long one-act called *In the Valley* (1927), this little-studied play marks a thematic, if not an artistic, advance over *In Abraham's Bosom*. The earlier play focuses on an individual, as shown by the subtitle, "The Tragedy of a Negro Educator"; the later, appropriately subtitled "A Symphonic Drama of the Negro Race," embraces the whole black community.[16]

The road to performance of *Potter's Field* throws light on Green's tortuous relationship with the New York theater. After peddling the script unsuccessfully in New York, he finally found a producer in Margaret Hewes, who opened the play in April 1934 in Boston but postponed the New York production to allow time for a major revision. Green changed the title to *Roll, Sweet Chariot* and the place from "Potter's Field" to "Johnson's Hollow." Most important, he added a prologue showing the major characters working on the chain gang before coming to the boardinghouse, thus clarifying the subsequent action. Despite Green's efforts to improve the play, it did not appeal to New York audiences and closed after seven nights. In July 1936 it was performed in New Orleans by blacks as a project of the Federal Theatre.[17]

The critical response to *Roll, Sweet Chariot* expressed the mixed reaction Green met in New York, though some critics supported him strongly. Brooks Atkinson said that Green was a good man to have around when a strong, heroic play was needed; unfortunately, the succession of episodes, which might have "some obscure logic" in the dramatist's mind, baffled the theatergoer by the looseness of method. Bernard Sobel wrote glowingly of the production and thought it should return to the boards.[18] Edith Isaacs believed the play surpassed *In Abraham's Bosom* and particularly approved the synthesis of words and music, which she and others had long advocated. Lee Shubert nevertheless closed *Roll, Sweet Chariot* soon after its opening, telling Green, "Your play lacks entertainment."[19]

Green wrote bitterly about the failure of the play: on opening night the twenty-two choral voices lacked fire, and the audience erupted in laughter when the amplified voice of the law became garbled; seeking respite outside the theater, he ran into the critic Robert Benchley, whose irritation proved a bad omen. After the play closed, Margaret Hewes wrote Green that they had been the victims of some subtle politics in the theater.[20] Shubert's explanation to Green that the play lacked entertainment, however, is sufficiently candid.

Green did not hesitate to present the depths of Negro life in the appropriately named *Potter's Field*. The depiction of this anarchic, colorful slum owed much in content and idea to Maxim Gorky's famous panorama of Russian life, *The Lower Depths*. An admirer of Leo Tolstoy, Green was fascinated by Russian literature and, when he went to Europe in 1928-

29, found the contemporary theater of London sterile and trivial compared with the vital drama of Russia. In *The Lower Depths* Green saw a close resemblance to the misery of Negro life that he knew in the rural South. Reviewing Gorky's *The Judge* for the *Reviewer* (1925), Green said that this play lacked the greatness of *The Lower Depths*, which expressed the author's intense concern for the miserable outcasts of Russian society. Gorky's appalling scenes in that play were familiar to him, Green wrote, because within a mile of "a large Southern university" he had observed "a scene in a Negro's hut which outrivaled the misery, squalor, poverty, and debauchery of *The Lower Depths*."[21]

The picture of slum life in *Potter's Field* depicts such life graphically. As in Gorky's play, rivalry for a woman provokes murder when Sterling, the lover of Milly, kills Bantam, her little husband with the huge hands. Then, out of the depths of Negro degradation arises a charismatic leader, larger than life, like O'Neill's Emperor Jones; he also resembles Luka, the benevolent liar of Gorky's drama. John Henry is "a flimflam artist and escaped convict walking the earth as a preacher."[22] A paradoxical character, he profits from the sale of charms guaranteed to make the boarders rich, but he also preaches on Sunday morning.

As a university student, Green had been fascinated by the legend of John Henry and listened to all the phonograph records available of his folk ballad.[23] In the play, John Henry personifies both the physical and spiritual strength of the Negro people. When he returns to the chain gang, he chants words from the famous ballad: "Seas—rivers of bricks, mortar and iron—let it flow on—open the way," which is also the epigraph on the title page of *Roll, Sweet Chariot* (1935).[24] John Henry delivers the people of Potter's Field from despair after the deaths of Bantam and Sterling and leads the diggers of the chain gang in a gospel song as the slum dwellers fall obediently in line, singing of their heavenly reward. Enlisting the allegiance of other Negroes in a way that distinguishes him from the ostracized Abe McCranie, John Henry declares that the convicts have not lost hope: "Their arms are still strong."[25]

In the end, all members of this underclass come together, creating the sense of the whole that dominates this play, as it does Gorky's. As those uprooted by industrial society when the road invades the slum join others separated by the law, Richard Wright's ideal of solidarity and Faulkner's virtue of endurance take visible form. Facing the powerful convicts' advance, the white guards appear weak by contrast, according to Brooks Atkinson's review; the sheer force of bound Negro labor will drive the race on, he concludes.[26] The ending of this play predicts eventual triumph for those relegated to the bottom of society. In the midst of the Depression when the Negro's future looks bleak, the denizens of Potter's Field, a name truly defining their status in the larger world, possess a latent force prophetic of future victory.

In southern plays such as the *Uncle Tom's Cabin* rebuttals and the Confederate dramas, the Negro had appeared invariably as a comic stereotype, based on the hugely popular minstrels. After the Civil War, fiction writers like Cable and Twain drew varied black characters, presented sympathetically, and in the twentieth century important treatments of the Negro appeared onstage in O'Neill's *Emperor Jones* (1920) and DuBose Heyward's *Porgy* (1925). It was Green, however, who took the lead most forcefully in sustained portraiture of the negro, whom he often found tragic. Showing the social consciousness of the New South, he censured the chain gang, opposition to Negro education, and white men's callous disregard of Negro women.

Green wrote a second group of plays about the poor white, revealing the tenant farmer's inner life in several one-acts collected in *In the Valley* (1928) and in the long play *The Field God* (1927). The poor white had typically appeared as a comic figure, as in Twain's satirical portraits; Green too could show the lighter side, like the delight in music demonstrated in *Saturday Night,* but for the most part the playwright concentrated on the tragic. Most significantly, he analyzed the religion of poor whites. An inveterate, sometimes bitter, opponent, he considered narrow-minded fundamentalism a curse. (Two other North Carolina natives composed popular folk plays about fundamentalist religion which were performed on Broadway. Lula Vollmer knowingly portrayed a pious mountain mother in *Sun-Up* (1923), and Hatcher Hughes attacked a mountaineer's religious bigotry in *Hell-Bent for Heaven* (1924), which won a Pulitzer Prize.)

In Green's *The Lord's Will: A Tragedy of a Country Preacher* (1925), tenant farmer Lem Adams spends all his time preaching, not working for his family's betterment. When his daughter dies after he refuses to pay for a doctor, he attributes her death to the Lord's will. *Unto Such Glory* (collected in *In the Valley*) satirizes the hypocritical religion of Big Brother Simpkins, a sanctimonious preacher who seduces pretty women and tries to carry off one of his converts but is chased away by her little husband, who gains inspiration from an angel.

The Field God (1927), Green's full-length study of fundamentalist religion, was less successful on the New York stage than *In Abraham's Bosom.* Opening in April 1927 at the Greenwich Village Theatre, it ran for forty-five performances and thereafter had a short Broadway run at the Cort Theatre. It fared better in Chicago, where one critic observed in 1930:

"If *In Abraham's Bosom* . . . was worth a Pulitzer Prize, *The Field God* ought to have two."[27]

In this play, which affirms a humanistic faith, the strong farmer Hardy Gilchist, married to Etta, a narrow-minded fundamentalist, shocks her by denying that kissing and dancing are sinful. After her death Hardy marries Rhoda, the voluptuous niece of Etta, whose ghost (like the mother's in O'Neill's *Desire under the Elms*) haunts the premises. When Rhoda's son dies, the guilt-ridden Hardy believes that Etta's God has punished him for his remarriage. In the end, however, the couple reject Etta's life-denying deity and find God in themselves, prompting Hardy to declare his belief in "the God who is in us."[28]

In revising this play for his collection *Out of the South* (1939), Green made an even stronger attack on fundamentalism: Rhoda's return to the old religion provokes Hardy's suicide. Green defended the change in "Tragedy—Playwright to Professor" (1953). When a man who has fought for certain values in his life loses the struggle, let him refuse the insult of bowing to a God in whom he cannot believe, Green argued. Suicide becomes "his one defence against hypocrisy, even his own."[29]

For his play about aristocrats, *The House of Connelly* (1931), appropriately subtitled "A Drama of the Old South and the New," Green chose a theme that had obsessed southerners ever since the Civil War: the conflict between the Old and the New South.[30] Southerners such as Henry W. Grady and Ellen Glasgow had awarded the verdict to the new order. In this play, Agatha Adams remarks, Green grappled with the dream of lost grandeur which confronted every southerner of his generation, as did Thomas Wolfe in his unsuccessful play *Mannerhouse* (1920-23).[31]

The House of Connelly was the first production of the Group Theatre (the experimental company that later enjoyed success with plays by Clifford Odets) and ran for ninety-one performances at New York's Martin Beck Theatre to critical acclaim. Although Green appreciated the company's enthusiasm, he disliked the members' preoccupation with method acting and thought the performance showed a total ignorance of the South. Cotton hoers pounding a bare stage unnerved this erstwhile farmer.[32] Nevertheless, yielding to pressure from the liberal Group Theatre, Green changed the tragic ending to a happy one. Harold Clurman, its director, wrote that the company's faith in human perfectibility overcame Green's constitutional pessimism.[33] The dramatist did not agree with what he termed the automatic "yea-saying" of the Group actors but submitted to their pressure, having learned what was necessary to achieve New York production. Rationalizing his revision, he acknowledged that the rise of poor whites like the Dukes of Durham had given promise of a New South.[34]

Although one might surmise that victory over the old order expressed Green's final view, such was not the case. He published the happy ending in the first two editions of the play (1931 and 1939) but returned to the original tragic conclusion for the final edition in 1962.[35] In an essay published that year he remarked that he had been a bitter enemy of the Old South when he composed the play, and still was, but that the New South had fallen short of its high goals: because "much of the effort of the new South to be born out of the old South perished," the tragic conclusion was "for me the preferable ending."[36] This preference parallels the revision of *The Field God* to emphasize his disgust with narrow fundamentalism. It signified not Green's abandonment of the New South but rather his disappointment with the persistence of outmoded thinking. By rejecting happy endings for *The Field God* and *The House of Connelly*, Green showed his integrity, determined as he was to take a stand against narrow fundamentalism and the Old South mentality.

The House of Connelly treats schematically, if not always effectively, the battle between new and old. At first the former seems on the way to victory: Will, the Connelly scion, decides not to marry a Charleston aristocrat, the favorite of his mother and two maiden sisters. The Old South persists, however, in the stubbornness of the family matriarch, who will not sell the valuable boxwoods, as emblematic of ancestral pride as the cherry orchard in Anton Chekhov's play. The strong tenant daughter, Patsy Tate, who embodies the New South, falls in love with Will, who has until then found pleasure only with black women. Green had tried out the plot of the heir who can love only a Negro but eventually marries a white woman in *The Picnic*, one of three related one-acts (collected in *In the Valley*, 1928). From near-submission to the old sins of idleness and withdrawal, Will revives, thanks to Patsy's love. He supports her call for hard work and reclamation of the Connelly lands to benefit everyone. Here progressive farming symbolizes the New South, which is more often represented by business (as in Lillian Hellman's *The Little Foxes*, 1939).

In the tragic ending the long arm of the old society reaches out to dash the prospects of the new. Will believes that his mother is restless in her grave because he has chosen a tenant's daughter to be mistress of the ancestral plantation. Guilt-ridden, he rushes out, seeking to bring back his sisters, who have also condemned his marriage. While he is gone, two female retainers who represent the Negro guardians of the Old South, like the old servant in *The Cherry Orchard*, smother Patsy.[37] Although Green and others have recognized the close parallels between his play and Chekhov's, the American differs from the Russian by ending with the old order's victory.[38]

In writing full-length works for the legitimate theater, Green succeeded best with his plays of black life. Some portrayals rival famous heroes of modern drama and fiction: O'Neill's Emperor Jones; Richard Wright's Bigger Thomas; Faulkner's Lucas Beauchamp. Green did not create white characters comparable in power to Abe McCranie and John Henry. McCranie is a complex personality, overcome by his own rage as well as white prejudice. The charismatic figure of the legendary John Henry possesses the moral strength required to lead the impoverished denizens of Potter's Field; his call to unite in labor is rhetorically mesmerizing.

But Green's plays, even those that feature such compelling heroes, lack the impact of a tightly constructed plot. The progression of scenes is episodic, as in a novel: the dialogue is prolix; and the dramatic unities are nowhere to be seen (*In Abraham's Bosom*, for example, covers many years and settings). Too many characters bloat the casts: there are twenty speaking parts in *Potter's Field*. Failing to master concision in plotting, casting, and dialogue, Green himself admitted in 1957 that he had never "learned the art or skill of playwriting and I doubt I ever shall."[39]

Still, Paul Green holds a pivotal place in the development of southern drama. Knowing the South intimately, he wrote with the love of a native son but showed no signs of the defensiveness and pugnacious sectionalism that had marked southern writers from Simms to Thomas Nelson Page, as well as Bilboesque politicians. His was a large, humanitarian spirit. Stimulated by the political activism of Chapel Hill, he infused his work with the zeal of a Sinclair Lewis. In so doing, he attracted influential supporters such as Harold Clurman, Edith Isaacs, and Brooks Atkinson, who welcomed him as a brave spirit, committed to social progress.

Drama for the People

Green's limited success and consequent disenchantment with the New York theater, however, led him to search for a new dramatic vehicle, one that would combine music, dance, and pantomime with speech. Envisioning a form with an appeal broad enough to encompass his democratic philosophy, he found his model during a European sojourn in 1928. In Berlin he attended Alexis Granowsky's Moscow Jewish Theater, where the performances in Yiddish were unintelligible to Green but fascinated him with their combination of music and speech. From this imaginative kind of folk theater he fashioned his "symphonic drama," a blending of speech, music, and dance.

After the failure of his first experiment with such a synthesis in *Roll, Sweet Chariot* (1934), his thoughts turned to the potential of outdoor performance, which the Greeks and Elizabethans had attended in large numbers. In eloquent words Green argued that symphonic drama fit the dramatic needs of the American people, but their traditions, exuberant hearts, and even mechanical skill demanded a larger stage than the narrow conventional theater could offer. Percy MacKay (1875-1956), an earlier composer of civic pageants, already had staged outdoor shows successfully but did not inaugurate a movement. Green believed that attending a play outdoors would suit the American "mind and athletic muscle-power," and as automobiles became more common, Americans could easily reach any site that offered an interesting show.[40] Moreover, concerned with reaching the common people, Green proposed that his plays be acted and produced by and for the people, designed for their enrichment and enjoyment rather than for any special profit motive.[41] He felt strongly that the price of admission should remain low enough to make this "people's theatre," unlike the prohibitively expensive professional theater, available to all.[42]

As subject matter for his symphonic drama, Green turned to history, which—with one or two exceptions such as Maxwell Anderson—had not been a popular topic for serious dramatists of the 1930s. Why did Green choose history? In "Dramatizing Our Heritage," recalling that the Greeks dramatized and redramatized the lives of such heroes as Ulysses, he explained that Americans should also "seek to interpret and reinterpret" the heroes of the past, those who set forth our democratic ideals. Among others, he named Washington, Lincoln, and Woodrow Wilson. By contemplating our past, he believed, we could gain greater assurance for facing our future.[43]

From his previous works and explicit statements in essays, it is clear that in recreating history Green sought to see the past through the lens of social liberalism: that is, the values of Roosevelt's New Deal, which made the 1930s an exciting decade for intellectuals in America. His plays would consequently denounce selfish industrialism and extol the common people Green admired, sympathizing especially with the widespread loss of potential among the less fortunate of society, as did his adaptation of Richard Wright's *Native Son* (1941). Furthermore, his outdoor dramas would champion the ideals of freedom and social reform. Continuing his liberal stand on race questions, he would advocate nondiscrimination and civil rights for blacks. And as a passionate pacifist—shown in *Johnny Johnson* (1936) and many other writings—he would oppose war at every opportunity. In a reinterpretation of southern history (to which literary artists as well as historians have contributed), he would present a new view by a political liberal, not seen heretofore in southern drama. To balance this social teaching, his historical spectacles would gratify those southerners always fascinated by the deeds of their forebears, whether kin in truth or in imagination, and he would stage them near historical sites.

In earlier times, dramatists had celebrated historical events—a Revolutionary battle in Charleston, Andrew Jackson's victory in New Orleans— with pageantlike plays, the direct antecedents of Green's outdoor dramas. Prodding his state and region to exploit their rich history,[44] he took the lead in 1937 with *The Lost Colony*, the poignant story of Virginia Dare. Green's plays made full use of cultural material that audiences could relate to, but his outlook could never be called sectional or narrowly local. In fact it would be appreciated by spectators from across the nation who joined the communal experience in places like Bardstown, Kentucky, where Stephen Foster—according to legend—composed "My Old Kentucky Home."

In his first ten years of writing and producing outdoor dramas, Green was most successful with *The Lost Colony* (1937) and *The Common Glory* (1948), which treated the colonial and Revolutionary periods respectively. The former, Green's first and perhaps still his best, continues to be performed every summer on Roanoke Island, North Carolina, which has now become part of a large seaside resort, unlike the remote area it was when the play opened in 1937. Not only the attractiveness of the location but Green's appealing themes, embodied in effective characters, produce popular success.

Forecasting a better future for the common man is the life of John Borden, a poor tenant in love with wellborn Eleanor White, who marries well-to-do Ananias Dare. Borden becomes the leader of the colony after Eleanor's husband is killed by the Indians. Old Tom, who had been a ne'er-do-well in England, reforms and announces proudly at the end, "Roanoke, thou hast made a man of me."[45] Having taken on the duties of a sentinel, he defends the colony, serving responsibly and bravely. Another prominent topic of *The Lost Colony* is women's role in settling the new world. Eleanor proclaims their indispensability; the outspoken midwife hopes the first child born will be a girl and gets her wish. Even though the settlers disappear into oblivion at the end, John Borden still believes in Sir Walter Raleigh's inspiring dream of founding the first English colony: "And down the centuries that wait ahead there'll be some whis-per of our name—some mention and devotion to the dream that brought us here" (p. 571).

Thomas Jefferson, the central figure of *The Common Glory* (1948), had provoked differing appraisals before Green's portrayal. For the Vanderbilt Agrarians, Jefferson was not only the great commoner but also the spon-sor of those most able in society. John Gould Fletcher pointed out in "Education, Past and Present," an essay in *I'll Take My Stand,* that though Jefferson favored elementary education for all, he advocated higher edu-cation for only the most capable students. Exponents of the New Deal admired Jefferson as the founder of the Democratic Party and the de-fender of the people against special privilege, an estimate dramatized successfully by Sidney Kingsley in *The Patriots.* Kingsley's play honoring Jefferson opened in 1943, the year the resplendent memorial to the great Democrat was dedicated in Washington, D.C. It had a successful run in New York and moved to Washington for a command performance. Kingsley's work articulates the New Deal philosophy, extolling the com-mon man while advocating a better life for all.

Reflecting full sympathy with New Deal values, Green's play recog-nizes the indispensable contribution of common people to the Ameri-can Revolution. Jefferson converses often with Captain Hugh Taylor, son of a poor tenant farmer. Like John Borden, Taylor is prepared to give his life for his beliefs. Unhistorically, Taylor supplies Jefferson with the phrase "pursuit of happiness" for the Declaration of Independence, instead of "property," which the great men propose. Taylor says that his father as an indentured servant was never able to seek his own happiness freely.[46] Il-lustrating the worth of the common man humorously, Cephus, a shiftless chicken thief, reforms and takes up arms bravely, like Old Tom of *The Lost Colony.* In the finale of the play, the Jefferson Memorial shines in the background as the narrator quotes from the Declaration: "All men are created equal." Green wrote to a friend that he wanted "the ideal of de-mocracy" in *The Common Glory* to increase the crowds coming to see *The Lost Colony* on Roanoke Island, "where the spiritual birth of our nation took place." The voices of both John Borden and Thomas Jefferson "speak out, each in his different and dramatic way, this our American theme."[47]

The Common Glory repeats the great theme of the Jefferson Memo-rial, the freedom of the individual. In "American Theme—The Common Glory" Green named Jefferson as the chief spokesman for eighteenth-century political philosophy; he believed in "freedom of speech, of thought, of education, of opportunity, of religion and the right of revo-lution."[48] After the Declaration of Independence is signed, Jefferson explains at Williamsburg why Americans will fight against Great Britain: "We are fighting for a free earth," which means "the right to pass our own laws" and "to speak freely" (p. 130). Earlier in the play Jefferson had waged emancipation of slaves in the document, but Franklin advised him not to because, though right, it was impractical.

After focusing on colonization and the Revolution, Green directed his attention to the Civil War era in two significant works, *Wilderness Road* (1955) and *The Confederacy* (1958). Because they dramatized the critical event in the history of the South, these dramas lent themselves naturally to southern themes, figures, and indeed questions of current interest. The South's relationship to the whole nation was on the minds of audiences because of the school integration controversy, following the Supreme Court decision in 1954. In fact, *Wilderness Road,* which takes place during the Civil War, was composed in the midst of the integration crisis and subtitled "a parable for modern times."[49] It was produced at Berea College, Kentucky—which had always practiced a policy of non-segregation—and commemorates the founding and educational goals of that school.

The discussions that preceded its performance provide a very interesting look into how Green's drama for the people took shape in the context of his give-and-take with the public. Not just a theorist, this spokesman for the people practiced his democratic ideals in the composition of outdoor drama, receiving suggestions with unfailing cordiality, though always reserving the right to make up his own mind. Marshall E. Vaughn of Berea told him of a teacher, Mrs. Fairchild, who had taught a slave boy to read and write in 1858.[50] The hero of the play similarly helps a Negro boy learn to read. Some advisers, however, did not care for Green's anti-slavery emphasis. Dr. Elizabeth Peck, retired chair of the Berea History Department, wrote to President Francis S. Hutchins of Berea College that she did not want any "emoting" over slavery. Freedom of expression had been a more important issue than slavery to John G. Fee, founder of the college, she contended.[51] Green nevertheless retained slavery as a major subject, confirming later that he saw it as a way to comment on contemporary turmoil in the South.

Green also discussed the racial theme in extended correspondence with his friend W.D. Weatherford, vice-chairman of the Board of Trustees of Berea College. Weatherford echoed Dr. Peck: "We do not want a *Race Drama,"* he wrote; the college's main concern and goal of its founder was the education of Appalachian youth. To justify retaining slavery as a major subject, Green replied that the fictional educator of his drama, John Freeman, believes in the power of education but feels he must fight slavery, which is dividing the people. Finally he loses his life, Green continued, but the character of John G. Fee in the play admires the things he struggled for, which "are going to be struggled for by those he left behind."[52]

After the first successful summer run of *Wilderness Road* to audiences totaling 60,000, Weatherford wrote Green on October 25, 1955, that he did not know how integration would work out, especially in a state like Mississippi, but believed that we must find a solution if we would "ever grow into greatness." Although doubtful that the play's first great purpose of making the mountain people stand forth in all their dignity had been achieved, he praised Green's work, thanked the dramatist for dedicating the composition to him, and said he believed it would do great good.[53]

The story of *Wilderness Road* begins shortly before the Civil War in the border state of Kentucky, where John Freeman dreams of starting a mountain school based on the principles of freedom and equality. He looks ahead to education for blacks despite the opposition of pro-Confederate members of the community, including his brother Davie. Though he is a pacifist, Freeman finally joins the Union side and is killed at a bridge on Wilderness Road, the frontier entry to settlers of Kentucky. This battle, which is won by the Union forces, is the turningpoint of the war in Kentucky. John G. Fee eulogizes the dead hero, who believed in "the right to *teach*—to *speak* the truth," and announces to a crowd of both friends and former enemies of this farsighted educator that together they will all build his school.[54]

The play's passages about education for blacks were relevant to the integration crisis of 1955. When a free Negro requests a book to teach his son to read, Freeman gives it to him, adding that he will come by sometime to help. Informed of this visit, Davie, who has joined a gang of nightriders, denounces his brother for teaching "niggers to read—free niggers at that!" In lines resembling contemporary segregationists' words, he objects, "I tell you, John, things are going to bust loose in this country . . . and you are helping them to bust loose." Later the pro-Confederate leader of the community also condemns Freeman for giving the free Negro a book. "Surely a man has the right to teach his children to read," Freeman answers. One accuser angrily disagrees: "Not when he's a nigger."[55]

The public reaction to this drama demonstrated its connection to the raging crisis over school integration following the Supreme Court decision. John Popham, editor of the Chattanooga *Times*, was delighted with what he saw as Green's support of school integration. He wrote Ralph

McGill, liberal editor of the *Atlanta Constitution,* that *Wilderness Road* hits at such ugly things as "school bigots."[56] Popham also recommended the drama to Henry Lee Moon, public relations director for the National Association for the Advancement of Colored People (NAACP) and enthusiastically invited Thurgood Marshall and Roy Wilkins to attend the performance, which he assured them was integrated. According to Popham, the play was "a Godsend at this time" and should be continued "as long as we have the school issue before the nation." In his words "a great southern dramatist" has shown the only honest answer if things are to be worked out in Christian morality. If only many people would attend, their spirits would be "firmed up." See to it, he urged, that "Negro and white" go to the show.[57]

Others also believed that the play conveyed a strong religious message. Leon D. Sanborne, pastor of the Union Church in Berea, hailed its stand against segregation and praised its hero John Freeman for understanding "the problems of slavery and education, segregation and poverty."[58] The *Saturday Review* (August 4, 1956) concluded that the play reminded the mostly southern audience that compliance with the decision on segregation would put Christianity into practice. For this work, Green received the 1955 Freedom Foundation's George Washington Medal, an award established to promote better understanding of the American way of life.

Before Green worked out his characterization of Robert E. Lee in *The Confederacy* (1958), adulation of the famous general had risen steadily. In the 1920s he was regarded as a noble, tragic figure, admired above all for his character. Historians had examined his military strategy at length, asking, "What if?" What if Longstreet had carried out Lee's strategy at Gettysburg? What if Lee had continued guerrilla warfare in the mountains, which Jefferson Davis rejected. Donald Davidson in "Lee in the Mountains" versified his version of this proposal.[60] In the monumental biography *R.E. Lee* (1934-35) by Douglas Southall Freeman, Lee appears as a simple soul who had no inner conflicts in the course of his lifetime.[61] After this four-volume work appeared, his petrification as "the marble man" seemed final, and in the 1930s and 1940s he became a national hero. President Francis P. Gaines of the University of Virginia claimed that Lee was far ahead of his time because he supported a program of modern engineering education at Washington College. In his review after *The Confederacy* was produced, Lewis Funke acclaimed the general as a hero who belonged to the whole nation.[62] A southern dramatist had indeed performed a miracle when Robert E. Lee received praise in the *New York Times* as a national hero!

Among dramatized studies of famous southerners, Green's portrayal of Robert E. Lee is a rarity; he appears in no other significant play. But like most southerners, Green had grown up hearing about this towering figure, and chose to write a drama about Lee, he said, because the man's character fascinated him.[63]

Green did not simply second the growing idolization of Lee or engage in second guesses about his military strategy; nor is his Lee the marble man, devoid of contradictions and inner conflict. Judging him a man of peace but one who inspired fighting, Green remarked that Lee believed in the New Testament teachings of peace but that everywhere he walked, blood oozed. His Lee is a man tortured by the agony of disloyalty, constantly arguing with his fellow Confederates, and steadfastly opposing materialism in America. Green presents Lee agonizing over his decision to resign from the U.S. Army and accept command of the Confederate forces. At Arlington after visiting Washington, he hears that Virginia has seceded and cries, "She needs me"; he will not fight against his native Virginia and other states of the South.[64]

This Lee takes an enlightened stand on slavery: he has freed his slaves and asks other southerners to do the same. How will we win if we continue doing wrong by preserving slavery? he asks. (In fact Lee did free his few slaves and, near the end of the war, those inherited by his wife.)[65] He also argues for arming freed slaves, assured that they will fight, but Judah Benjamin and others will hear nothing of such a plan.

Green's most incisive contribution is Lee's critique of American business, which the playwright discussed with one sponsor of *The Confederacy* before it opened at Virginia Beach. When Henry Clay Hofheimer, a member of the Norfolk Chamber of Commerce and cochairman of the committee that produced the play, worried that it might be considered anti-business, Green sent him a telegram denying any cause for alarm about his "attitude toward American business."[66] In a later speech, however, Green did say that Lee had warned the South, whose ideals he considered superior to the North's, to lay less stress on material success and more on building human character.[67] And Richard M. Mansfield, writing on "Civil War Drama" in the *New York Times* (Sunday, June 8, 1958), quoted Green as saying that Lee sided with "the idealism he believed Virginia represented," which opposed the greedy commercialism of the North.

The Confederacy confirms the judgment of Stephen Vincent Benét in *John Brown's Body* (1928) that Lee and his southern troops were rustic antagonists of modern industrialism.[68] In the play Lee clearly articulates Green's criticism of American materialism, repeating the arguments of the antiindustrial Agrarians. Showing his antipathy to industrialization, he debates Judge William Barrett, a businessman from the new state of West Virginia who tries to dissuade him from remaining in the South. He accuses Judge Barrett of defending the Union to fill his pockets, saying that the greed of men like him is ruining the country. Barrett counters that the alleged "money-grubbing" Yankees are the real creators of the country, since they build the roads and towns while the South with its aristocracy and slaves creates nothing (pp. 13-14). After the war, Judge Barrett predicts the North will unite with "the new South" to form the mightiest nation on earth. The North has built bridges, dug mines—"power, strength, life! America!" He boasts, "I have created a big combine of financial power" (pp. 93-94). Like Green himself, Lee despises this glorification of money power and believes that Judge Barrett is describing a society without conscience.

By his portrayal of Lee, Green wished to promote national unity, not encourage sectionalism—a real danger during the South's resistance to integration in 1958. In answer to one correspondent's questions about how the Confederacy would be presented, Green wrote that he did not want to do anything "to plume up the Confederacy at the expense of the Union." The Civil War was simply one of "those crazy things" men indulge in.[69] According to the *Chapel Hill Weekly* (July 10, 1958), though the play stated lucidly why the South fought, it sounded "an urgent fanfare for greater national unity."

As the civil rights movement in the South gathered momentum, Green scheduled another outdoor drama, which is still running in St. Augustine, celebrating the four hundredth anniversary of that city. *Cross and Sword* (1965) tells of the founding of the first Spanish settlement in Florida by Pedro Menendez, a virtuous conquistador. During the previous year the city had undergone a prolonged period of racial strife. Consequently, on February 16, 1965, Lucille Plummer of the Southern Christian Leadership Conference solicited Green's help in communicating with whites. Green answered in a cordial letter that he wanted this anniversary to be a celebration for all.[70] Soon afterward the general manager of the event, Tom Rahner, seconded Green's statement by writing to assure Plummer that Green would not back any organization denying rights to Negroes; although the cast did not include blacks, since none had participated in the first settlement, the play supported the brotherhood and dignity of man. Rahner also stressed that the facilities would be "integrated."[71] And Green, corresponding with the music director, insisted that black singers be hired for the chorus.[72]

Green's reinterpretations of history contemplate some of the same material chosen by earlier southern dramatists. The difference resulted most noticeably from his democratic liberalism, which included admiration of the common man and racial tolerance. For example, both George Washington Parke Custis and Green dramatized the popular legend of Pocahontas and the founding of Virginia. In *Pocahontas: The Settlers of Virginia* (1830), Custis featured the chivalric Captain John Smith, who cries "Victory and Virginia!" in attacking the Indians but rescues the Indian damsel in distress. The democratic Green's *The Founders* (1957) differs by making John Rolfe the central figure, a common man who contributes moral and economic leadership. After studying the history of the settlement, Green concluded in "Jamestown—Thoughts for a Symphonic Drama" that the true hero of the first colony was John Rolfe.[73] He proves his tolerance by marrying the Indian maiden, whom Green believed was the first to suffer from racial prejudice on American soil. To foster peaceful trade, he offers tools to the Indians and lays a solid foundation for the colony by cultivating its most profitable commodity, tobacco. In fact, Green decided that Rolfe was "the main man in the final success of the venture" because he perceived that tobacco would save the settlement.[74]

Like L. Placide Canonge and other Francophone dramatists of nineteenth-century New Orleans, Green also dealt with the Franco-Spanish conflict in Louisiana. Unlike their plays, however, his does not favor the French at the expense of the Spaniards or end with the two sides at each other's throats. Initiating peace, the title character advocates cooperation in *Louisiana Cavalier: A Symphonic Drama Based on the Life and Times of Louis Juchereau de St. Denis,* first performed at the Grand Encore Amphitheatre, Natchitoches, Louisiana, on June 19, 1976.[75] Since Green's play was designed to commemorate Franco-Spanish reconciliation, it was appropriately staged near the former border between French and Spanish territories. In an unmailed letter to the director, Green repudiated a brochure that pictured a tomahawk-wielding Indian threatening an armed Frenchman and wrote pointedly in a letter he did mail that his play stressed "peace and good will—the trading of goods among peoples instead of the exchange of bullets and blows."[76] One historical character in both Canonge's *France et Espagne* (1850) and Green's *Louisiana Cavalier* illustrates their sharp differences. The latter's Nicholas Freniere is a soldier who follows the peace-loving St. Denis, but in the ardently pro-French play, Nicholas Lafrenière (Canonge's spelling of the name) fiercely opposes the Spaniards in Louisiana.

Paul Green's outdoor dramas, beginning in 1937 and still being performed, mark an important stage in the development of southern drama because their popularity gave a new vitality to regional theater. They have brought drama to a large cross-section of society, not merely the customary audience for legitimate theater. Besides expounding his liberal revision of southern history, Green's plays have confronted current issues such as school integration and honored the qualities of the common man, as seen in the brave leadership of John Borden, the racial tolerance of John Rolfe, and the educational idealism of John Freeman.

Because of its similarity to more superficial pageants, outdoor drama has never received much critical recognition; this is one reason Green's reputation as a dramatist is not high. He had the right talents for this particular genre, however, fortified by the ability to celebrate inspirational themes such as the common man's indispensability in America. He attempted to counter the objection that outdoor drama—given its very broad subjects—cannot probe individual character by studying Lee's puzzling personality.

It is hard to overestimate the leadership of Paul Green in giving direction to southern drama in the twentieth century. He discovered the right combination for its progress by blending cultural material such as the folk life of poor whites with political protests, particularly against racial injustice. Deserving his reputation as a man who broke new ground, he originated a folk drama movement in the South that inspired many others, and launched an ongoing movement in outdoor drama with *The Lost Colony*. Green gave southern drama wide national appeal, not penalized by the defense of racial inequality, and thus ensured its continued advancement.

— 7 —

DuBose Heyward's
Transmutation of Black Culture

The principal collaborator of Paul Green in fostering a renascence of southern drama after World War I was DuBose Heyward (1885-1940), the bearer of an old Charleston name. Lacking Green's intellectual training (he did not complete high school), he suffered a series of major illnesses from 1903 to 1917 and sold insurance before embarking on a literary career at the age of thirty-nine. Known primarily as the author of *Porgy* and the lyricist for Gershwin's great opera *Porgy and Bess,* he played a significant part in advancing southern drama in the 1920s and 1930s. Even more than Green, Heyward succeeded in transmuting black culture into art, both fictional and dramatic. His popularity was enhanced greatly by the addition of black singing to his plays, which are studded with tuneful music, both choral and solo. Combining scenes of black life and melodious songs proved a theatrical innovation that took New York by storm.[1]

In the first phase of his career Heyward joined the literary awakening that would become known as the Southern Renascence. As a dramatist he began by contributing to the folk drama movement led by Green. Striving for fresh portrayals, Heyward broke away from stereotypes of the comic plantation Negro to show individuals, such as the indigent urban black, based on his own observation. After exploiting the folk material of Charleston in the novel and play *Porgy,* Heyward turned to social criticism. First a skeptic about social advancement for blacks, he came to join reformers like Paul Green in condemning racial injustice in the South.

Heyward took the lead in Charleston to encourage southern literary artists. In response to H.L. Mencken's notorious essay "The Sahara of the Bozart," an indictment of the cultural barrenness of the South, he founded the Poetry Society of South Carolina in 1921. Under his direction this society published yearbooks from 1921 to 1925. In 1922, he and Hervey Allen put together a collection of local-color poems titled *Carolina Chansons.*

When Heyward first began writing poetry, he clashed with the social critics at the University of North Carolina. Gerald Johnson, his principal opponent (and editor of the *Greensboro Daily News*), adulated the university group at Chapel Hill, where he went to live in 1924. He unleashed a series of withering objections to the poetic creations of Heyward and his cohorts. In "The Congo, Mr. Mencken," Johnson admired the exotic variety of much southern writing but not what was "flashy" and "false." "At Charleston, away off to one side," he joked, DuBose Heyward and Hervey Allen were "trying out their 'cello and harp combination."[2]

Still, in the early 1920s, since southern writers like Johnson and Heyward were united in their goal of promoting a cultural revival, the chances for a beneficial exchange of ideas despite sharp differences were propitious. Both men contributed to the *Reviewer*, the principal organ of the new literature in the South. After each published an essay in 1923, the two corresponded directly. Johnson asked Heyward pointedly if he was offering only jewels, silks, and furs to "a pauperized section." Heyward defended himself with another question: Wasn't Johnson asking too much of a Poetry Society by requiring it to "*civilize* (to use a term of Mencken's) an entire section of the country?"[3] After this exchange, Johnson give a more favorable estimate of Heyward in the *Southwest Review* (April 1925). He wrote that although Heyward could carve "cherry-stones" exquisitely, he could also write realistically, as in the poem "Gamesters All" and the collection *Skylines and Horizons* (1924), which was no "bijouterie."[4] The yearbook of the Poetry Society for 1925 quoted these commendations at length.

At this stage of their relationship Heyward and the social critics also differed with regard to the Negro's condition. In "And Once More—The Negro" (*Reviewer*, October 1923), Heyward expressed skepticism about the social critics' advocacy of reforming the Negro; he wondered whether the Negro was eons ahead of or behind the white man. Of one thing he was sure, however: the reformers would have him eventually, and the Negro's instinctive feeling for happiness would be crushed. This admirer of primitivism, looking out the window, saw a stevedore who was about to be "saved" and wrote that such a man would in time be clad in a moral straitjacket and sacrificed to the machines.

Although Heyward's disagreement with the social critics was strong, he followed their prescription in his novel *Porgy* (1925) by portraying urban blacks with honest realism. His contention that there should be a turning away from the old comic stereotypes was seconded by others. Alain Locke in "The Drama of Negro Life" (1926) called for "the breaking down of the false stereotypes" with which the world saw the Negro.[5]

In the play *Porgy* (1927), coauthored with his wife, Dorothy Kuhns Heyward, Heyward added a fresh portrayal of the Negro to the American stage in the physically crippled but spiritually powerful title character. Like Green, he sought to plumb the Negro psyche. Women also earned new attention in the character of Bess, who resembles the conventional fallen wench but yearns for a better life with the unselfish Porgy.

Porgy may be regarded as a morality play. Good enters in the persons of Porgy and the kindly neighbor Serena, and the religious organization of Catfish Row calls for moral improvement with its slogan "Repent Ye Saith the Lord." The vicious Crown, who destroys Bess's attempt to start a virtuous life with Porgy, embodies evil, and the devil in the form of Sportin' Life with his "happy dust" takes Bess off to New York. But good triumphs in the end as Porgy leaves to rescue Bess. Like Green's *In Abraham's Bosom*, the play emphasizes the importance of religion in black life and its potential to save from despair.

The power of nature in the life of the characters links this play with Green's folk drama. The hurricane wreaks havoc in the black community and kills Bess's friend Clara, but the folk show their inner resources in the face of natural disaster, singing to calm their fear. Porgy and Bess step forward to adopt Clara's child, who has been orphaned by the storm. Nature intrudes also in the primitive impulses even of "good" characters such as Porgy, who kills Crown with savage glee. The influence of O'Neill is strong in this portrayal of the Negro as a primitive being.

The key to the success of *Porgy* on stage was the singing: the inhabitants of Catfish Row break into song whenever their emotions overflow. In an introduction to the play, Dorothy and DuBose Heyward commented that the characters turn to spirituals as they actually do in real life when ordinary speech is inadequate to express their emotions.[6] There is a full range of feeling in the songs, which are interspersed throughout almost every scene. Clara sings a lullaby to her baby (1.1); after Serena's husband dies, the fear of death almost overcomes his friends in the chorus "Deat' ain't yuh gots no shame!" (1.2); Bess, joined by all her neighbors, exults, "My soul's so happy dat I can't sit down" (4.2).

According to one reviewer the spirituals were worth the price of admission; another said no one could deny that "his eye, ear, and mind have been played on like so many instruments by the various hands of rhythm."[7] Heyward, who had a better ear for black music than Green, took advantage of the stage performance to let the audience hear actual singing that he could not transmit on the printed page of the novel. It is no wonder that George Gershwin recognized the potential for his great folk opera *Porgy and Bess* in this drama reverberating with song. Unquestionably, one of the cultural treasures of the South was black music, and Heyward succeeded better than anyone had before in transferring its infectious rhythm and melody to the stage.

Heyward achieved national success with this play, adapted successfully from his novel with the crucial assistance of his wife, who was trained in the craft of playwriting. He capitalized on the widespread interest in the Negro aroused by the waves of migration flowing north in the 1920s. Also portraying the Negro dramatically at this time, Thomas Wolfe attacked racial prejudice in his play *Welcome to Our City,* capturing some of the same humor and pathos dramatized by Heyward and his wife, who was one of Wolfe's classmates in George Pierce Baker's Harvard playwriting workshop of 1923.[8]

Although Heyward declined at first to take up the crusade for Negro advancement, he did read the writings of the social critics and eventually adopted their liberal approach to racial conditions in the South. By the time he published "And Once More—The Negro," new investigators were reporting the economic plight of blacks. In 1921 Howard Odum, a sociologist at the University of North Carolina, founded the *Journal of Social Forces,* a weighty periodical that gave special attention to the issue in such articles as "Multiplying Dollars for Negro Education" (1922) and "What Race Equality Means to the Negro" (1923). Gerald Johnson was an associate editor of this journal.

Heyward signaled a turning point in the development of his thought with "The New Note in Southern Literature," published in *Bookman* for April 1925, the same year as the novel *Porgy.* Noting that previous social critics of the South such as George Washington Cable had been ostracized for speaking out, he acclaimed the outspoken critics at Chapel Hill: Howard Odum and Gerald Johnson for their courageous and not invariably popular stands; Paul Green for plays condemning the evils of tenant farming and religious fanaticism. Heyward emphasized his new agreement with the social reformers in subsequent statements. In two succeeding articles for *Bookman* (1926) he complimented the *Reviewer,* then edited by Green. Noting that this journal was now "under the wing of an able group at the University of North Carolina," he singled out Addison Hibbard's essay "Literature South—1924" for praise. In that survey of contemporary writing Hibbard had issued a call for criticism of current life in the South, which Heyward would soon fulfill. Heyward quoted Hibbard's compliment that he portrayed mountaineers realistically in *Skylines and Horizons.*[9] Following a poor start, Heyward and the Chapel Hill critics were fast becoming a mutual admiration society. After attending the MacDowell Writers' Colony in New Hampshire in 1926, when he was dramatizing *Porgy* and Paul Green was finishing *In Abraham's Bosom,* Heyward did not miss the New York staging of Green's play in 1927. This advocacy of Negro education prompted him to write Green on February 2, 1927: "My hat is off to you for your bravery as well as your art."[10] Always insistent that the Negro be presented with literary art, he now esteemed "bravery" as well and combined them in his next works, thus continuing "the new note in Southern literature."

The University of North Carolina honored Heyward in 1928 with a D.Litt. degree. At Chapel Hill he was entertained by Dean of Arts and Sciences Addison Hibbard, author of the influential column "The Literary Lantern." Heyward recited his poem "Jasbo Brown" and told of his plans to finish *Mamba's Daughters,* a serialized novel then running in the *Woman's Home Companion.* Green, who attended the gathering and recorded his impressions of Heyward, read from his stories set in Bethel County.[11] Green and the social critics of Chapel Hill made a significant impact on Heyward's thinking over the next several years.

Heyward had moved toward more social criticism in *Angel* (1926), an unsuccessful novel censuring hypocritical fundamentalism among the North Carolina mountaineers (a subject previously treated in Hatcher Hughes's play *Hell-Bent for Heaven*). The full extent of the change in Heyward's writing did not become apparent, however, until *Mamba's Daughters* (1929), a highly successful novel that delivers a scathing condemnation of Negro exploitation in the phosphate mines and also describes with sociological precision the stratification of black society in Charleston. The indictment of economic injustice makes this novel significantly different from *Porgy.*

Mamba's Daughters provoked sharp disapproval. Heyward wrote to Hervey Allen on August 9, 1929: "Mamba's Daughters continues to sell, and to kick up much turmoil among my folks in and about S.C. But I rather expected the latter."[12] Writing for the *Saturday Review of Literature,* Hershel Brickell complained that the novel was "too much cluttered up with discussions of contemporary problems" and that the exposition of life in the phosphate mines was "frankly sociological."[13]

The most interesting objections to *Mamba's Daughters* came from Vanderbilt's Donald Davidson, a formidable defender of traditional southern ways who had taken up arms against the New Southerners of Chapel Hill and consistently castigated Johnson, Odum, and Green for their attempts to change southern life with social programs. Though Davidson believed that *Porgy* had been faithful to the earlier portrayal of the Negro by Thomas Nelson Page, he abruptly changed his opinion of Heyward with the publication of *Mamba's Daughters.* In "An Author Divided against

Himself," Davidson charged that Heyward had yielded to outside influences at the expense of his own artistic integrity, writing for New Yorkers
rather than for himself. Ceasing to be a local colorist, he had become "a
sociologist" in contrasting primitive with sophisticated Negroes. Davidson
praised the compelling story of the mother Hagar but deplored the social commentary. We observe, he wrote, "the unholy system" by which
workers at the phosphate mines are kept under the company's thumb
and endure more than a hint of "doctrinaire" attitudes. The success of
Hagar's daughter as a singer is "an unexplainably pat echo of the Harlem
school of rhapsody and propaganda, very surprising in Mr. Heyward."[14]
In his essay for I'll Take My Stand (1930), Davidson continued to denounce
the change in Heyward's writing, complaining that Heyward's and Green's
studies of Negro life were tinged with latter-day abolitionism. Later, in
"The Trend of Literature," included in William T. Couch's Culture in the
South (1934), Davidson lumped Heyward, Green, and social novelist T.S.
Stribling together for disapproval.

Unlike Davidson, the social critics responded to the new note in
Heyward's writings with praise. W.J. Cash, a close associate of Howard
Odum, singled out the author of Mamba's Daughters as an example of the
changing South: DuBose Heyward had abandoned the sweetness and light
formula "to cope with reality." Responding to the disfavor that the novel
had aroused among some southerners, Cash said he had heard it said
that the story "was both pointless and untrue to the Southern Negro, which
last was to say that Mr. Heyward's portrayals fit neither the Uncle Tom
formula nor that of the vaudeville buffoon."[15]

Gerald Johnson, who had earlier reprimanded Heyward for supercil-
ious writing, became another ardent admirer. In a review of southern
literature for the Virginia Quarterly Review (January 1935), he wrote that
Heyward and Green illustrated the new method of writing about the Negro. Heyward deserved special commendation for describing the urban
black. Johnson found "no keener eye, no more discerning mind than
his; there is no more honest and truthful writer."[16]

Three decades after Johnson penned this tribute, George B. Tindall,
professor of history at the University of North Carolina, recognized the
pronounced change that had taken place in Heyward's thinking. In The
Emergence of the New South, 1913-1945 (1967), he observed that Heyward,
after deploring social uplift in "And Once More—The Negro," had shifted
to encouragement of Negro aspirations in Mamba's Daughters and thereafter consistently composed works of social criticism: he censured prejudice against the mulatto in the play Brass Ankle (1931); the power of
conformity to stifle free thought in Peter Ashley (1932), a novel about se-

cession; and exploitation of the artist by the new plutocracy of the South in the novel *Lost Morning* (1936).

Brass Ankle treats the classic subject of the tragic mulatto, previously seen in Dion Boucicault's *The Octoroon* (1859) and Espy Williams's *The Clairvoyant* (1899). Green too had recognized the dramatic possibilities of the theme in early plays such as *White Dresses* (1920), which tells of a wellborn white man's love for a young mulatto and their separation. *Brass Ankle* portrays a woman unaware of her part-Negro ancestry—in the vocabulary of the region, a "brass ankle"— married to a poor white who becomes frantic after she gives birth to a dark son. Though Larry wrestles with this unforeseen development and tries to adjust, he cannot. Ruth saves her first child, a fair daughter, from ostracism by lying that she had the second child by a black man, provoking the husband to shoot her and the son.

This version of the tragic mulatto theme differs from others notably in that the white man comes not from the gentry but from the lower class. The play pleads for resolution of the racial dilemma through the advice of a Charleston aristocrat, with whose thinking Heyward clearly concurs. Dr. Wainwright, who comes to the bed of Ruth as she gives birth, has a thoughtful story to offer Larry. He tells of Ruth's part-Negro grandfather, John Chaldon, who had served in the Confederate Army; he was rewarded by the Wainwright family with a dinner in their home once a year, indicating acceptance in the white community rather than ostracism as a mixed breed.

But Larry finds these superior ways too strange for his liking. Despite the doctor's counsel to accept the son, move away, and remember Mendel's law that such births are the distinct exception, Larry cannot agree with the thinking of this broadminded man of the world; in Dr. Wainwright's words, he has "no philosophy" for such a case, only a few definitions and a code of honor.[17] Instead of finding guidance in the aristocrat's tolerance, he listens to the prejudiced teaching of his church by the Reverend Latterby, who tells racist jokes to a delighted group and, while Larry is groping for acceptance of his dark son, opposes receiving the children of another part-Negro family into the community school. To Larry's suggestion of accepting them in a Christian spirit, the preacher responds that "the matter has nothing to do with Christianity" and asserts that all must be relentless in ridding the community of mixed blood.[18] Unlike many other writers, Heyward here shows sympathy for the poor white mentality even as he recognizes the lack of intellectual resources available to Larry. What separates this play from mere melodrama is the plea for compassion, grounded in an enlightened philosophy. The blight-

ing influence of narrow-minded religion, however, ensures a violent denouement.

With the production of *Brass Ankle* Heyward made his main dramatic
contribution to the reformist movement led by the social critics of Chapel
Hill; he had truly joined the company of Paul Green, Addison Hibbard,
and Gerald Johnson. Yet despite its emotional power, the play had a dis-
appointing run in New York. Recognizing the need to satisfy the public,
Heyward was always on the lookout for some new way to attain theatrical
success. He discovered it in the operatic version of his tale of Porgy, *Porgy
and Bess.*

Heyward found collaboration with George Gershwin enormously
stimulating. Gershwin had read the novel *Porgy* in 1926 and discussed an
opera with Heyward. But he had to postpone the project because of other
commitments, and the two men went their separate ways for a time.
Unsurprisingly the stage version appealed to Gershwin with its songs and
music similar to the jazz that he composed. Then in 1932 Heyward noti-
fied the composer that Al Jolson wished to do a musical version of *Porgy.*
Gershwin was still not ready to undertake the opera, but Jolson never
went ahead with his plan. Finally, after Gershwin came to Charleston for
a month in 1934 to absorb the ambiance and talk with Heyward about
the opera, there was close collaboration; Heyward spent two weeks in
Gershwin's New York apartment working on the libretto. *Porgy and Bess*
was performed in 1935 to high praise (if not at first to financial success).
It ran for 124 performances and then left for a successful tour.

The evolution of Heyward's last play, a stage version of *Mamba's Daughters* (1939), demonstrates that he had learned to write successfully for the
New York theater. In 1935 the Heywards met the blues singer Ethel Waters at a cast party for *Porgy and Bess,* and Waters expressed her admiration for the novel *Mamba's Daughters.* She saw the mother, Hagar, as the
central character, representing all the lonely Negro women lost "in the
white man's antagonistic world."[19] At this encounter Dorothy Heyward
promised Waters that she would have first refusal of the role if her husband dramatized the novel. Later, Heyward showed sure theatrical knowledge when he and his wife refused to permit production of the play unless
Waters was the star.

In the production of *Mamba's Daughters,* Hagar became the dominant character, since the mother's sacrifice for her talented daughter runs
the entire length of the play—a design that gives unity to some previously disparate material. After Lissa sings on the radio, Hagar declares
that singing is the sole salvation of the Negro, a passionate belief permeating all the songs of the play. When a sorrowful Lissa vows never to sing

again, Hagar insists that the Negro's one advantage over white people is the comfort afforded by singing: "Dere ain't no trouble so big we can't sing about um."[20] The song "Lonesome Walls," with music by Jerome Kern, which Lissa repeats on the radio after a moving tribute to her mother recalls Hagar's years in prison:

> Stars is you still shinin' when evenin' falls
> While my heart's pinin' deep in dese lonesome walls?
> Lonesome walls, lonesome walls, deep in dese lonesome walls.
>
> [p. 115]

After Heyward's collaboration with Gershwin on *Porgy and Bess*, he added many songs to the dramatic version of *Mamba's Daughters*. Singing is more thematically essential in this play than in *Porgy* because in song both mother and daughter find their greatest fulfillment, and music is Hagar's most personal means of communicating love for her daughter. Worried about Lissa's getting hurt in Charleston without her protection, Hagar joins the choir of an adjacent church in singing "I'm a-leanin' on my Lord / Who died on Calvary" (p. 68). When the mother is banished from the city to a plantation for beating a man, she overcomes her longing to be with her daughter by singing and clapping to the triumphant spiritual "Come out de Wilderness":

> I do t'ank Gawd
> When I come out de wilderness
> A-leanin' on my Lord.
>
> [p. 69]

This scene recalls the exuberant singing in *Porgy* when Hagar breaks forth in pure Gullah while "shouting" (singing, the rhythmic stepping, and moving) with the congregation. At the opposite extreme of emotion, her close friend, old Vina, sings mournfully to end the play after Hagar has killed herself:

> Oh, my daughter
> Goin' to leabe yo' in de han'
> Ob de kin' Sab-yor.
>
> [p. 182]

Heyward captured the fascinating life of Charleston in his plays, but without the singing they would not have won the hearts of audiences.

This play is even more melodramatic than the novel, a difference that did not disturb the New York audience. Hagar's troubles reach a climax after Lissa is raped by the villain Gilly Bluton and gives birth to a child, who dies. Gilly subjects Hagar to blackmail, and to save her daughter from exposure the powerful mother strangles him and then commits suicide—first dictating a false confession that she killed Gilly because he abandoned her. Like Ruth of *Brass Ankle*, she lies to save the reputation of her daughter. Although melodramatic in the extreme, the denouement is made plausible by Hagar's determination to protect her adored daughter.

Awareness of what would play best on Broadway led to removal of the novel's social criticism, little of which remains in the stage version. White injustice is only implied in the hard sentence given to Hagar after she breaks the judge's order to stay away from Charleston. Corrupt politicians protect Gilly from the law, but his unmitigated villainy keeps white injustice far in the background. Proc Baggart, the poor white who exploits Negro workers at the phosphate mine in the novel, survives only as the sheriff whose bloodhounds pursue Hagar at the end. Since the plot focuses on the human drama of Hagar's self-sacrifice to save her daughter from ruin, the social criticism of the novel, stemming from the sociological protest of the Chapel Hill critics, disappears. Because of Heyward's decision to make Hagar the central character, the novel's depiction of Negro progress and celebration of the advancement of the New Negro are virtually absent as well. Making Lissa too much of a celebrity would have reduced interest in Hagar's fate.

Heyward proved that he had learned how to please the New York audience with *Mamba's Daughters*, whose engrossing elements added up to popular theater. The play ran for 162 performances in 1939 before going on a national tour, propelled by box office success, and returned to the Great White Way in March 1940 for a final run. It also established Ethel Waters as a dramatic actress as well as a singer. When Brooks Atkinson of the *New York Times* in January, 1939, found fault with her acting, nineteen theatrical figures ran an ad in that newspaper encouraging the public not to miss her performance.[21]

Having begun as a poet and novelist, Heyward later needed the assistance of a skillful playwright, whom he found in his wife. Paul Green, as a storytelling dramatist, also needed but did not find dramaturgical assistance in writing for the New York stage. Dorothy and DuBose Heyward combined the right ingredients in *Porgy* and *Mamba's Daughters*, supplying whatever was needed to publicize the southern play. Set in Charleston, that quintessential southern city, *Porgy* fused the local color of Catfish

Row and the Gullah dialect of low-country South Carolina to make a Broadway hit.

Heyward deserves much credit for breaking the Negro stereotype, for Porgy and Hagar are pathetic, not comic, and memorable for their strength of character. Though his novels and plays added another voice to the social protest rejected by the majority of southerners, his main accomplishment was to reveal on stage the emotional life of blacks—always transmuted into song. This sensitive artist understood how to let music fit the personalities of his characters, and his interweaving of black singing, as authentic and entertaining as in real life, was an extraordinary theatrical achievement. For the opera *Porgy and Bess* Heyward applied his knowledge and appreciation of black music, both religious and secular, to the libretto, which was indispensable to Gershwin in composing his superb melodies. Green had filled *In Abraham's Bosom* and *Potter's Field* with the same kind of spirituals and songs that Heyward included, but they were not as successful. Why? Perhaps the sheer verbiage of his plays stood in the way, or Green's lack of talent for creating excitement in melodramatic scenes perfectly suited to passionate lyrics. In any event, music did not elevate Green's plays to the heights that Heyward's reached. The latter's remarkable synthesis of song and dialogue verified the possibilities of black music in drama. Heyward, a white man, discovered—for the first time in plays—the richest, most distinctive cultural material that the South had to offer American audiences.

— 8 —

The Southern Marxism of
Lillian Hellman

Lillian Hellman (1905-84), the first important female dramatist of the South, stands out for her investigation of the New South from a Marxist perspective. Surpassing Paul Green's examination in *The House of Connelly*, which pits the Old against the New South, she composed two plays that trace the economic growth of the New South from its origin in the Civil War to its flourishing at the turn of the century. She perceived this historical event in human terms, grasping its transforming effect on the old society as well as on the new order of businessmen—represented chronologically in *Another Part of the Forest* (1946) and *The Little Foxes* (1939) by the Hubbard family, capitalists of the New South. What makes Hellman's indictment of capitalism most interesting is her application of Marxist dogma to southern society. In dramatizing dialectical materialism she included not only the aristocracy and the bourgeoisie, but also the proletariat. Since she admired the Communist regime of the Soviet Union, Hellman differed even more than Green from the political thinking of most southerners.

For her characterization of New Southerners and to a lesser extent Old Southerners, Hellman found rich, stimulating models in both her mother's and father's families, a fact fully substantiated by her several biographers. It is her mother's family, however, the Marx-Newhouse line, rather than the Hellmans of New Orleans, that provided most of her material. Though the families constitute special cases because they are Jewish, they closely resemble the leading southern social classes: the bourgeois capitalists and the feudalistic aristocrats. The setting for both plays is based on Demopolis, Alabama (called Bowden in *Another Part of the Forest*), which Hellman knew well from hearsay but never visited.[1]

The Marx-Newhouse branch represented the heartless capitalists of the South and elsewhere, who were driven by greed and ambition, though some had compunctions about their methods of making money. Emigrating from Germany about 1840, the Marx and Newhouse families steamed up the Tombigbee River to settle at Demopolis, which had a strategic location at the confluence of two major rivers. First settled by Napoleonic exiles, the little town considered itself sophisticated. Isaac Marx, Hellman's great-grandfather, was one of the first Jews to settle there. An itinerant peddler, he liked what he saw and sent word to family and friends to join him. Soon the Jewish population of Demopolis increased. The Temple B'nai Jeshuran was erected in 1858 and served as a place of worship for the congregation of 1860.[2] Marx rose to dry-goods merchant and profiteered during the Civil War. Stories of southerners who got their start in this dubious way have circulated widely in the South, but the Marxes, though typical businessmen, differed from other rich southern families in lacking an agricultural background and desiring to move north.

Isaac's son Jacob (or Jake) Marx was Hellman's great-uncle and a successful Demopolis banker who later moved to New York. The model for Ben and perhaps Leo (a future banker) in *The Little Foxes,* Jake impressed Hellman by his forcefulness and cynical estimate of people. When she told him about buying books by pawning the ring he had given her for $25, he repeated the phrase spoken by Regina to Alexandra at the end of *The Little Foxes:* "So you've got spirit after all. Most of the rest of them are made of sugar water."[3]

Lillian Hellman's grandmother, Sophie Marx, married Leonard Newhouse of Demopolis, a wholesale liquor dealer who died eight years before Hellman was born. She was a model for Regina, the would-be businesswoman of *The Little Foxes.* Sophie's brothers, including Jake, would gather at her house in Demopolis to scheme and talk of money. After her husband died in 1897, she moved to New York, where she bought a fine house admired by Hellman.

Julia Marx Newhouse, Hellman's mother, was gentle and innocent, the opposite of her materialistic maternal kin. She was the principal model for Birdie, a lady of the Old South in *The Little Foxes.* Long before Hellman was born, Julia's family had moved from Demopolis to Cincinnati and then to New Orleans in search of husbands for their three marriageable daughters. Julia married Max Hellman, an unsuccessful shoestore owner in New Orleans, who eventually moved to New York. According to her antibourgeois daughter, Julia was a middle-class woman who never rejected the middle class and would have been happier living with the Alabama blacks she had known in her childhood, men and women who had taught her the only religion she ever knew.[4] In this way she was also the model for the humble wife in *Another Part of the Forest* who identifies with the black lower class. For her, God could be found anywhere, Hellman realized, when she saw her mother mouthing words in a Baptist church, a Catholic cathedral, or less often a synagogue. Several times a week she and her mother would step into one of these houses of worship, where Julia always felt at home.

On Hellman's father's side, in sharp contrast, there was righteous indignation against unprincipled business. Lillian's adored father, Max Hellman, who was ridiculed by the Marxes because of his business failures, retaliated by denouncing his in-laws for their unethical operations, accusing them of cheating Negroes. Hellman records a conversation in which her father said the Marxes got rich by taking advantage of blacks who could not pay 50 percent interest on loans secured by their cotton crop.[5] This petty bourgeois sympathized in good Marxist fashion, with the proletariat, as his daughter would later.

Lillian's paternal grandfather, Bernard Hellman, who came from Germany before the Civil War, was the most singular of the Hellman line. Hellman preserved some of his traits in the cultured patriarch Marcus Hubbard of *Another Part of the Forest*, a character whom critics have praised highly. Bernard had spent a few years at Heidelberg University, and—like Marcus Hubbard—he served in the Confederate Army. In his memoirs, he narrated his service in Florida (which he liked because it was safe), and mocked his own comic attempts to become rich like the Bowmans, wealthy New Orleans Jews who were distant cousins. Bernard Hellman died before Lillian's birth, but she often contemplated his portrait over the fireplace in her aunt's New Orleans boardinghouse. Though he looked too serious and distinguished, she felt, he had permitted eccentricities in her father and aunts in an era that had little tolerance for them. At the age of sixteen Hellman discovered a cache of her grandfather's letters, asked her aunts for them, and copied out some of the letters for what she called her "writer's book," knowing that such "observation" was necessary for a would-be writer.[6] The aunts were pleased with her interest and recalled for her benefit Bernard's own "eccentricities" and "culture." When Hellman's aunts moved out of the boardinghouse, they could not find room for all their father's music and books.

Like most middle-class southerners of her time, Hellman encountered the working class primarily as black servants. In her memoirs blacks are a constant presence, as they were in the lives of all southerners of her generation, but the respect in which she held them was more unusual. The dramatist's closest contact was with her nurse and friend Sophronia Mason, an impressive woman, who probably served as the model for the cook Addie in *The Little Foxes*. Hellman noted that Sophronia and her family were well respected in New Orleans Negro circles.[7] "Sophronia

was the first and most certain love of my life," she wrote.[8] Lillian considered her the anchor of her youth and kept up the acquaintance. Two
redheaded boys Sophronia cared for aroused the girl's jealousy after the
Hellmans moved to New York.

Like William Faulkner and Robert Penn Warren, Hellman records
in her memoirs the wisdom and firm moral advice of strong black men
and women. Once, when Hellman broke her nose, Sophronia took the
child to the doctor but gave her this stern advice: "Don't go through life
making trouble for people."[9] In *The Little Foxes* Addie repeats such in-
junctions to Alexandra, who was partially based on Hellman herself—as
was Regina.

Not surprisingly, her memoirs provide valuable insights into Hellman's
mind and thought, including a love of the South and an acute awareness
of class differences. Although she stated that her family was entirely Jewish, and others have described her background as more Jewish-urban than
southern, her attachment to the South was real and long-lasting. She spent
the first six years of her life in New Orleans and thereafter divided the
year between that city and New York, where her parents had moved. Until she married at the age of twenty-two, she returned periodically to New
Orleans. After her divorce, and during her association with Dashiell
Hammett in Hollywood, she visited her Uncle Willy at his plantation house
in Louisiana. Much as she liked her farm in Pleasantville, New York, she
admitted that "there's nothing like the look of Southern land, or there's
no way for me to get over thinking so. It's home for me still."[10]

An interviewer once remarked to Hellman: "You've never dealt specifically in your writing with what it was like to be Jewish in the South."
Southern Jews, Hellman answered, particularly those of New Orleans, had
"different histories" from northern Jews. The larger society allowed them
to have their own community without ever accepting them in its own
circles. No Jew was admitted to the best Carnival balls, she observed, but
it never seemed to worry them.[11]

First among ideological influences on Hellman was Marxism, which
influenced her to oppose fascism in Spain and join the Communist Party
in the 1930s. Like many other American intellectuals and artists who rejected capitalism during the Great Depression, she adopted the doctrine
of Marx and was a member of the Communist Party from 1938 to 1940,
years that saw the composition of *The Little Foxes*.[12] Likewise, Clifford Odets
was a member of the Communist Party when he composed *Waiting for
Lefty* (1935), and John Henry Lawson also belonged to the party when he
wrote *Marching Song*, a play about the working class, for the 1936-37 theatrical season.

Hellman's Marxist ideology shaped her dramatic writing fundamentally. Revealing her sympathy for the proletariat in *Days to Come* (1936), which recounts a workers' strike against an Ohio company, she sides with the union as Odets did in *Waiting for Lefty*. During Hellman's membership in the Communist Party she certified her loyalty by refusing to permit a benefit performance for Finland after the Soviet Union's invasion, despite the protests of the anti-Communist star of the play, Tallulah Bankhead. Hellman made news in 1952 by defiantly informing the House Un-American Activities Committee that she would not cut her conscience to fit this year's fashions by naming former Communists. Yet her political opinions did change, for she eventually admitted in *Scoundrel Time* (1976) that she had remained blind to the sins of Stalinism too long.[13] Nonetheless, as *Another Part of the Forest* and *The Little Foxes* attest, she thought like a Marxist during the central period of her playwriting career.

The conflict between capitalists and workers, or the class struggle posited by Marx, plays a large but not fully recognized part in Hellman's two anticapitalist plays set in the South. Relevant to the saga of the capitalistic Hubbards are some principal tenets of dialectical materialism. According to this well-known theory, derived from Hegel, history is a process consisting of a thesis, followed by an antithesis, and finally a synthesis. Marx concentrated on the struggle between capital and labor, which the latter was to win once the dictatorship of the proletariat came to power, aided—according to the *Communist Manifesto*—by a coalition with the petty bourgeoisie. The revolutionary bourgeoisie would join and educate the proletariat, thereby assuring the transfer of power from the bourgeoisie to the revolutionary proletariat. Eventually, the classless society would become the synthesis.

The dialectics of thesis-antithesis lie behind *Another Part of the Forest*, which relates the struggle between the aristocratic Bagtrys and the capitalistic Hubbards, giving the decision to the latter inevitably. Hellman ended the play with a vision of the coming of the proletariat and gave a new twist to the coalition of petty bourgeoisie and proletariat by pairing the idealistic wife and her cook Coralee in starting a school for black children, providing a harbinger of the future.

The play handles subtly but effectively the lower-class origins of Lavinia, the conscientious wife of capitalist Marcus Hubbard: "Your people are my people," she tells Coralee. To atone for the sin of her husband's treachery against the Confederacy, she has written "the Reverend" of her "mission" to educate blacks in Altaloosa, "a mighty poor little village" and the place of her humble beginnings.[14] Lavinia further betrays her lower-class background by saying "ain't" (p. 311), singing a gospel hymn, and dressing shabbily like her forebears, to the embarrassment of her upper-class family. Coming from the proletariat, she rejoins them in the end.

Ironically, the humble Lavinia brings about the downfall of the capitalist in this play by revealing to her son Ben the secret of Marcus's treachery: he had informed the Union troops where twenty-seven Confederate soldiers could be found and killed. With this knowledge, Ben blackmails his father and acquires all his wealth. In return for Lavinia's information, Ben promises to fund her school. At the end, Lavinia asks, "I'll be hearing from you, Benjamin?" He replies, "You will, Mama. Every month, On time." As Lavinia departs with Coralee, she says, "Thank you, son. Thank you in the name of my colored children" (p. 393). In Marxist terms, these two women (for Hellman must work out her ideas in the lives of women) will educate a new class, the revolutionary proletariat. She envisions a union of blacks and whites in the South to form a new society or, if you will, a synthesis.

Viewing the Hubbard saga chronologically, one can trace Hellman's wholesale indictment of New South capitalism from its origins before the Civil War (in *Another Part of the Forest*) through its later flourishing (in *The Little Foxes*). Joseph Wood Krutch correctly calls *Another Part of the Forest* a Marxist play with a foregone conclusion because the decadent aristocrats will surely lose to the ruthless capitalists.[15] Set in 1880 but covering events of the Civil War, it studies the causes of the Hubbards' greed and ruthlessness.[16] Forerunners of New South capitalists, the family is scorned by the aristocrats because of its members' profiteering during the war and their refusal to support the Confederate cause. This ostracism by the landed gentry intensifies after the war as unscrupulous businessmen like the Hubbards become rich. The rejection of such businessmen, as Hellman dramatized it in *Another Part of the Forest*, fuels their ambition during the New South era, the time of *The Little Foxes*.

Hellman returned to an earlier period in *Another Part of the Forest* in order to reveal how the Hubbards became the way they are in *The Little Foxes* (which was written first). Marcus Hubbard, a capitalist contrabandist, becomes rich from selling salt at exorbitant prices. A lower-class girl who boasts of her father's death at Vicksburg says that Marcus stayed home during the war "bleeding the whole state of Alabama with money tricks" (p.344). Colonel Isham and John Bagtry, unreconstructed Confederates, disdain him because of his profiteering.

Hellman based this aspect of the play on historical truth. During the Civil War speculators did benefit from the turbulent economic situation: they bought up commodities that were in short supply and sold them at an outrageous markup. Salt was the first staple to become scarce and thus expensive. Although profiteering was widespread among southerners, Jews especially were charged with such operations. After the war got under way, some ran the blockade across land and engaged in lucrative speculation. In Alabama, they reportedly cornered two-thirds of the cotton crop.[17] Since Marcus Hubbard is representative of such southern profiteers, the townspeople shun the Hubbards. Regina's loneliness is a consequence of her father's sins.

To the tale of ill-gotten gains, the play adds the account of Marcus Hubbard's treason against the Confederacy. An early opponent of secession, he called southerners fools to believe they could ever win. Later, collaborating with Union troops in order to smuggle salt, he leads them to an encampment of Confederate trainees, where twenty-seven are massacred. After this incident the Ku Klux Klan threatens Marcus, who barely escapes the noose by purchasing a fraudulent paper from a Confederate officer to prove his absence at the time. The last days of the war spawned many such tales of betrayal, which Hellman had probably heard.[18]

After the war, Marcus and his sons continue their financial chicanery. The father cheats black workers who borrow from him. His son Ben buys up land from the impoverished gentry with money obtained from wartime profiteering and then, using his knowledge of Marcus's treachery, blackmails his father to gain control of the family finances; thus capitalistic intrigue divides a family. There is a historical basis for Hellman's depiction of these postwar practices as well. The Jewish peddlers who came to the South before the war and became prosperous storeowners like Marcus afterward would gain a lien on a Negro's crop and, after the white landowner had received his share of the cotton, take the rest. These merchants also obtained mortgages on the lands of Negroes, foreclosing when they could not repay the loans.[19]

Drawing on Marxist theory, Hellman composed a sharp critique of capitalism in her best play, *The Little Foxes*. She chose the South circa 1900 because it showed the economic exploitation she wished to indict and because it was a region "whose atmosphere I am personally familiar with as a Southerner."[20] A diligent researcher, however, she first read a great deal about southern economics. Before hiring an assistant to keep notebooks stocked with details, such as banking laws at the turn of the century, she made separate studies of the Negro, the cotton economy, and the industrial South.[21]

The dramatic force of *The Little Foxes* owes much to the theory of class struggle, which is evident in the overthrow of the aristocratic class by the capitalists. Critics invariably emphasize that this play is anticapitalist but neglect to add that proletarian discontent contributes much to its dramatic tension. The working class enters principally in the person of Addie, the black cook; it is she who attacks the Hubbards for cheating poor blacks. She tells Alexandra Giddens, revolutionary daughter of the bourgeoisie, "Well, there are people who eat the earth and eat all the people on it like in the Bible with the locusts. Then there are people who stand around and watch them eat it. Sometimes I think it ain't right to stand and watch them do it" (p. 205). Inspired by this working-class indignation, Alexandra determines to oppose the capitalists and in the last lines announces to her mother, Regina Giddens, that she will not stand by idly while her uncle Ben and others eat up the earth: "Tell him I'll be fighting as hard as he'll be fighting some place where people don't just stand around and watch" (p. 225). Ending the play, Addie, who has heard this ringing declaration, comes forward and presses Alexandra's arm.

The crooked businessmen of the Old South become the wealthy manufacturers of the New South, where capitalist profits increase geometrically. Horace Giddens says to Ben in *The Little Foxes* that his father made the thousands and now he will make the millions. The play condemns capitalist collusion which, in pursuit of profit, oppresses the proletariat of the New South. Outside capital, represented by Marshall and Company of Chicago, will invest in a cotton mill only if the Hubbards guarantee exorbitant profits; they in turn assure the northern investor that wages will be low, water power will be cheap, and meddling unions will be absent. In truth, the new factory will be harmful to the local community, setting blacks against poor whites and exploiting mill workers for the advantage of owners like the grasping Hubbards, who show no concern for the welfare of the disadvantaged. Both black and white workers will suffer, but racial division will prevent them from uniting for their best interests. Horace Giddens, Alexandra's father, realizing all too well what the consequences of the Hubbards' greed with be, refuses to underwrite their scheme.

Hellman repeatedly criticizes economic injustice toward blacks. The Hubbards' heartless cheating provokes the condemnation of Birdie, wife of Oscar Hubbard. Recollecting her life at Lionnet plantation, Birdie—who was one of the landed Bagtrys before marrying Oscar, a would-be capitalist—quotes her mother, who said she disapproved of the Hubbards not because they ran a store but because they made money cheating poor, defenseless blacks.

The Little Foxes presents the dark side of the New South. Ben Hubbard, a corrupt version of Henry Grady, feigns concern for the poor while setting whites against blacks. Equally despicable, Oscar Hubbard, an avid hunter himself, prohibits blacks from hunting on his property and proves the cruelty in his nature by spitefully striking his wife, Birdie. In *Another Part of the Forest*, forecasting his future character, Oscar is the little man who joins the Ku Klux Klan.

The postwar development of business ruins the Bagtry family, a decadent, if cultured band of land-poor aristocrats whose humiliation Hellman catches vividly. The aristocrats had looked down on the bourgeoisie, as shown in *Another Part of the Forest*, but now the latter retaliate. Utterly contemptuous, Ben scorns the Bagtrys, who cannot adjust to the new times, and ridicules their unbusinesslike habits. The lack of harmony between the agricultural and business classes is destroying the marriage of Birdie Bagtry and Oscar Hubbard, who married for money. Sharing no common language because of their different values, Birdie complains that Oscar does not allow blacks to hunt game on her former plantation, now owned by the Hubbards. Birdie wins our support as a charming lady of the Old South whose nostalgia is moving, but Hellman did not want audiences to sympathize with this impractical aristocrat.[22] Showing an unattractive side of her personality, Birdie escapes reality and responsibility by drinking too much.

The advancement of business in the New South had a major impact on the life of women, according to Hellman. In her characterization of the woman inclined toward business but frustrated by tradition, Hellman shows what she had learned from observing women like her grandmother, who schemed along with her brothers but could not join them fully in business ventures. Regina stands for those multitudes of ambitious women, from the turn of the century to World War II, who were eminently qualified but prohibited by society from becoming businesswomen. Such women worked behind the scenes while yearning for an exciting life in the big cities of Chicago and New York.

Rebellious and frustrated, Regina resorts to the most devious schemes to accumulate wealth. She is the New Woman who has been forced to do things against her will and must repress her natural inclinations in order to fit the role of a southern lady. Despite her villainy in hastening the death of her husband, Horace, Regina's positive side made her popular with audiences. Like Scarlett O'Hara, she is a strong woman who struggles against overbearing men and, in her unprincipled way, succeeds. Encouraging Alexandra to do what she wants in life, the mother admires her daughter for declaring that she will fight against the little foxes, those oppressors of the poor. At the end, she says (repeating Hellman's great-uncle's words to her): "Well, you have spirit, after all. I used to think you were all sugar water" (p. 225). Like her author, Alexandra will become a social activist.

Hellman reveals a keen insight into the particular nature of business in the South. Clifford Odets in *Awake and Sing* (1935) and Arthur Miller in *Death of a Salesman* (1949), among others, harshly indicted northern capitalism, yet before the production of *The Little Foxes* (1939) no play had treated this very important aspect of southern culture.[23] Lacking familiarity with business, Paul Green, for example, concentrated on farmers and country residents. Unlike many southern writers of her generation, Hellman came from a family of businessmen, and without her perceptive plays, firmly grounded in personal observation, there would be a glaring omission in the dramatic literature.

After *Gone with the Wind* (1936) became the most successful novel ever written about the Old South, no southern dramatist could escape its influence; it is doubtful that Hellman's plays about the South would have taken the same form or even have been conceived at all had it not appeared. (Green's *House of Connelly* lacked such a precedent and shows it.) In fact, one must ask to what extent *Gone with the Wind* inspired Hellman to write about the South after ignoring the subject in *The Children's Hour* (1934) and *Days to Come* (1936), her first two plays. Margaret Mitchell's celebrated novel presents some southern types that Hellman would have recognized; she knew them well and could present her own versions. Regina, like Scarlett, becomes the iron-willed woman involved in business.[24] And like Mitchell, Hellman perceived the economic vitality of the region after the war, but as a Marxist she made a significant addition to Mitchell's picture of the southern past by showing the class struggle and looking toward a better future for the black proletariat.

Influenced from abroad mainly by Ibsen and Chekhov, Hellman attempted to combine Ibsenite technique with Chekhovian mood in *Another Part of the Forest* and *The Little Foxes*. When the former play was presented in Russia, a reviewer observed that Birdie lost interest in life when the trees of the family estate were cut down, as did the characters of *The Cherry Orchard*.[25] There are also parallels between the Russian and American aristocracies in *The Little Foxes*, such as the poignant memories of Lyubov and Birdie. The former remembers her happy childhood home as she gazes out the window at the cherry orchard soon to be sold. Likewise, Birdie has a dream of restoring the plantation: "I could have a cutting garden. Just where Mama's used to be. Oh, I do think we could be happier there. Papa used to say that *nobody* had ever lost their temper at Lionnet, and *nobody* ever would" (p. 163). Supposedly, Chekhov forecast the Communist Revolution in Russia; for her part, Hellman foresaw a union of the enlightened bourgeoisie and the proletariat in the American South.

Although the parallels with Chekhov's *The Cherry Orchard* are unmistakable in the Hubbard saga, Ibsen's well-made and problem plays provided Hellman's crucial models. The Norwegian master's technique appealed to her logical mind and strongly realistic viewpoint, and she chose to follow the example of his well-made melodrama to convey her social criticism. As Ibsen deplores the fatal grip of old ideas on the new generation in *Ghosts,* Hellman ridicules the prolongation of military quixoticism after the Civil War in *Another Part of the Forest.* Regina is a brilliant version of Hedda Gabler—the vixen who detests the life of the docile frau—but is not merely a transplanted European. She is a fully convincing, rebellious woman of the New South, who makes *The Little Foxes* the excellent performance vehicle that it is. The role attracted the talents of such actresses as Tallulah Bankhead and Bette Davis because of its opportunities for virtuoso acting. The scene in which Regina refuses Horace his medicine and watches him crawl to the staircase holds audiences spellbound.

Hellman wrote only two plays about the Hubbard clan, but her saga of the South nevertheless provides a sense of historical evolution appropriate in Marxist analysis. The Hubbard saga not only covers three generations but embraces three major periods of the economic past: the protocapitalist days of the antebellum South, the illegal growth of capitalism during the war (seen in Marcus's smuggling), and the flourishing of immoral capitalism in the postbellum period, whether it is called the Gilded Age or the New South. Rooted in Marxist indignation, Hellman's work offsets Green's sympathetic analyses of the New South with its devastating indictment of the era's capitalist corruption.

When Marx described the class struggle, he did not have Russia in mind, much less the American South, but that is where Hellman saw an actualization of his theory. It erupts very credibly in the turn-of-the-century South between the landholding aristocrats (thesis) and the new capitalists (antithesis). With Marxist optimism, she did not stop there but foresaw a union of the humanitarian branch of the bourgeoisie with black workers, envisioning a better day for the black proletariat as Paul Green did in *Roll, Sweet Chariot.* Her original addition to the Marxist thinking of her Communist days is the vision of future black-white cooperation, exemplified by Coralee and Lavinia in *Another Part of the Forest* and Addie and Alexandra in *The Little Foxes.*

— 9 —
Black Drama:
Politics or Culture

From the outset the dramatic impulse has been strong among black southerners who found the stage a platform for protest and pride. From pre–Civil War times to the Second World War, three phases emerge: first, the era of early plays that denounce slavery but after the Civil War favor accommodation with whites; second, the literary renascence of the 1920s through the 1940s, in which folk plays and the shattering of stereotypes occur; and third, the celebration of black history. In the black drama of the twentieth century a constant tension has existed between politics and culture: between the effort to effect change and the urge to preserve the black experience. Sometimes these aims have separated; sometimes merged. The choice of emphasis also preoccupied white dramatists of the South such as Green, but it became even more problematic for black dramatists as they strove to decide what was proper and best for them.

Not surprisingly, black dramatists' perceptions of the South differ radically from those of white dramatists, at times becoming offensive to a white audience. Miscegenation, although present in plays by whites (as in Green's *White Dresses*), is ubiquitous in black drama, where it is regarded both sympathetically and bitterly but always ironically. A deeper, more knowing investigation of character goes further in replacing stereotypes. Moreover, there is inside criticism of faults in the black community.

Two strains in the early period stand out: protest and accommodation. The first, epitomized by W.E.B. Du Bois, insisted on full rights for the black immediately. The second, promulgated by Booker T. Washington, who has been discredited by most black leaders in the twentieth century, emphasized traditional values. After World War I, though not clearly falling into this second camp, many black southern dramatists continued to show some of its traits, especially in their indifference to politics.

Black drama made an auspicious beginning with William Wells Brown (c. 1816-1884), who was born near Lexington, Kentucky, the son of a white father and a mulatto mother. Dr. John Young, his mother's master, moved

144

to a farm ten miles north of St. Louis in 1827. In Brown's autobiography, *My Southern Home; or, The South and Its People* (1880), he gives a long description of life at "Poplar Farm." After being hired out by his master to work for Elijah P. Lovejoy's newspaper in St. Louis, he traveled on the Ohio and Mississippi with a riverboat captain as his master. Escaping to freedom in 1834, he later replaced Frederick Douglass as agent for the anti-slavery society of Massachusetts and became a successful speaker on the abolitionist circuit. In addition to plays, he wrote the first published novel by a black, *Clotel* (1853), the daring story of a beautiful mulatto who was reputedly the daughter of Thomas Jefferson.[1]

Brown recognized the potential of drama for conveying his message. Although neither of his two plays was ever staged, he gave them as dramatic readings with notable success. In 1856 Brown delivered *Experience; or, How to Give a Northern Man a Backbone* all over Massachusetts and subsequently in New York City, where audiences considered it not only amusing but a potent argument against slavery. At first, in this unpublished work, the minister of a Boston church condones slavery but reverses his stand after traveling to the South and being sold into slavery himself. Having undergone harsh treatment, he returns north a wiser man, thenceforth dedicated to abolition.[2]

Uncle Tom's Cabin and the slave narratives lie behind Brown's *The Escape; or, A Leap for Freedom* (1858).[3] This play, set in the Mississippi valley, progresses to full portrayals of black characters. Glen, like an abolitionist orator, enumerates the sins of slavery before striking the overseer and jumping out a window, announcing with good theatrical effect "a leap for freedom" (4.3). In Cato, a comic servant, Brown seemingly succumbs to the stage stereotype of white writers but transforms him with a song about going to Canada, where there are no whips like those in "this *Christian* country" (3.2).

The best writing in *The Escape* is Brown's satiric portrayal of whites. Based on his mistress in Missouri, Mrs. Gaines is a pious (if sometimes amusing) hypocrite; full of religious sentiments she is nevertheless a cruel person. When her servant Hannah asks the visiting Reverend Pinchen if he saw her old husband in his vision of paradise, Mrs. Gaines punishes her for asking such an impudent question but then requests the minister to continue with his "heavenly conversation" about the white souls he observed (1.4). The sanctimonious divine is revealed to be buying slaves in Natchez and selling them at a profit in New Orleans to pay his travel expenses.

Condemning the cruel South, Brown's play attacks whipping, separation of families, and the forced marriage of slaves, besides exposing

the master's seduction of a beautiful slave, the leading subject of *Clotel.*
Mrs. Gaines falsely denies that the light-skinned boy "Sampey," based on
Brown himself, could possibly be related to her husband, but she is determined to remove the slave Melinda from her premises because Dr.
Gaines has become infatuated with her. When Melinda returns to the big
house after being manhandled by the doctor, her sweetheart Glen
promptly marries her by moonlight in a ceremony presided over by Uncle
Joseph, an elderly slave. Like Harriet Beecher Stowe, Brown humanizes
the abolitionist argument with experiences of individual victims.

The years during and after the Civil War were for the most part devoid of dramatic writing by blacks until it was revived by the generation
growing up after emancipation.[4] Joseph Seamon Cotter (1861-1949), an
ardent disciple of Booker T. Washington, represents a widespread attitude among postbellum blacks. Unlike Brown, he was strongly accom-
modationist in his outlook. In an autobiographical sketch appearing in
Countee Cullen's *Caroling Dusk* (1927) Cotter stated that he was born in
Nelson County, Kentucky, and taken soon after his birth to Bardstown
(the birthplace of Stephen Foster). He gave all the credit for any success
to his mother, herself a poet, storyteller, and dramatist. The daughter of
free blacks (her grandfather, Daniel Stapp, having bought his freedom
in 1829), she became the common-law wife of a prominent Scotch-
Irishman of Louisville. Joseph's father Cotter reported that he grew up
the hard way, working as a teamster and a prizefighter. After completing
a high school degree in record time, he administered several schools in
Louisville. Becoming known in the city as a popular storyteller and a talented poet, he corresponded with the poet Paul Laurence Dunbar, whom
he introduced at a lecture in Louisville.[5] He was serving as principal of
the Colored Ward School at the time that his only play was printed: *Caleb,
the Degenerate: A Study of the Types, Customs, and Needs of the American Negro.*

Cotter revealed his traditional philosophy in two nondramatic pieces,
first espousing Booker T. Washington's emphasis on character building
in the poem "The Negro's Ten Commandments." One of these precepts
advises that if you have a mind to be industrious and honest, remain in
the South and you will reap your "character's worth."[6] Then, taking a
more critical look at the members of his race than Dunbar, Cotter versified an irresponsible life in "The Tragedy of Pete," which tells of a man
who drank and refused to work for small pay. After killing a man who
had driven off with his wife in a Ford, he welcomes execution.[7]

Cotter's *Caleb, the Degenerate*—published in 1903 with a preface by
the financial editor of the *Louisville Courier-Journal*—holds an interesting

place in the development of black drama.[8] This unperformed play is written in iambic pentameter, with stilted dialogue and unrealistic characters; moreover, it was belittled by critics for its crude craftsmanship and
unquestioning support of Booker T. Washington's doctrine.[9] Nevertheless, it deserves attention for confronting the significant issue of black
leadership. Pitting advocates of the work ethic (represented by the bishop
and his daughter who run the Industrial School) against those demanding the vote, academic education, and return to Africa, it dramatizes opposing forces among blacks at the turn of the century. Caleb, a member
of the second party, succumbs to the temptations of the false prophet
Rahab (the name of a dragon in Isaiah), smokes, takes cocaine, and dies
a miserable death.

During the time that blacks were being disenfranchised by the establishment of the white primary in the South, Booker T. Washington—in
his Atlanta address of 1895—advised them to avoid politics, prompting
many black editors to denounce him. William Monroe Trotter of the *Boston Guardian,* who asked what greater enemy of his race could be found
than a man who regarded disenfranchisement with equanimity, called
for a black Patrick Henry to overcome Washington's treason. In *The Souls
of Black Folk* (1903), Du Bois, the leading critic of Washington's influence,
blamed his spineless leadership for blacks' loss of the vote.[10] In a dramatic scene in Cotter's *Caleb* with direct relevance to that conflict, the
Booker T. Washington–like bishop debates the false counselor Rahab.
He compares Rahab to a conjurer of antebellum days who claimed to
cure all things with a magical bottle. "You are as simple as that conjurer.
/ You hold a vote is ample remedy / For all the ills a backward race may
have." According to the bishop, Rahab promises to obliterate the past by
declaring, "Voting is magical."[11]

Another response to white supremacy was the back-to-Africa movement led by Henry McNeal Turner, a preacher in the African Methodist
Episcopal Church, who recruited emigrants with assistance from the white
businessmen's International Migration Society. In 1896, many of the 325
who had left for Liberia died of malaria, and those surviving asked to
return home. (Turner was the ideological forerunner of Marcus Garvey,
who led the back-to-Africa movement in the 1920s.) In Cotter's play an
old man arrives at the Industrial School with his followers, intent on returning to Africa. Trying to dissuade them, the bishop declares that blacks
will leave behind a priceless heritage won on bloody fields, which should
not be abandoned. The old man refutes this claim: "Their heritage! A
little space to breathe— / A fruitless hour to feel one's loneliness— / A

country that is one ignoble grave."[12] Despite the bishop's repeated en-
treaties, the old man and his followers—dupes of bad leadership, in
Cotter's opinion—depart for Africa.

Beginning with the Harlem Renaissance of the 1920s, a separation
occurred in black drama between "propaganda or race" plays and "folk"
plays.[13] The differing purposes of these two schools of thought were stimulating to new dramatists but also divisive. Du Bois fostered the former
because of his crusade against racial injustice in the United States. The
propaganda play, political in character, protests such wrongs as lynching
and strives to effect social change. The leaders of folk drama operated
out of Howard University, the strategically located institution in Washington, D.C., to which southern Negroes gravitated. Howard professors
Montgomery T. Gregory and Alain Locke, admirers of Paul Green and
Frederick Koch, appealed for plays that would ignore racial tensions and
explore the undiscovered fields of black culture.

Associated with Howard University was a remarkable group of seven
women dramatists who helped launch the movement of "native" or folk
drama in the 1920s. Their plays have been collected by Kathy A. Perkins
in *Black Female Playwrights: An Anthology of Plays before 1950* (1989). Belonging to this group was Zora Neale Hurston (1890-1960), who eventually became a distinguished novelist and anthropologist. Born in the
all-black town of Eatonville, Florida, she had a long career as a writer and
highly original artist. Though her plays have received less attention than
such novels as *Their Eyes Were Watching God* (1937), which recounts the
liberation of a young black woman, she devoted considerable time and
energy to the dramatic form as well.

Hurston chose to write folk rather than propaganda plays. She wrote
to Langston Hughes in 1928, "The Negro's outstanding characteristic is
drama. That is why he appears so imitative. Drama is mimicry."[14] Her essay "How It Feels to Be Colored Like Me" stated categorically, "I do not
belong to the sobbing school of Negrohood."[15] Determined to write within
black culture and to resist the fashionable issues of racial tension, she
earned the disapproval of black men such as Richard Wright, who felt
she was not political enough and that she pandered to white audiences
by using minstrel technique and dialect humor.

Hurston knew Paul Green when she taught at North Carolina College for Negroes in Durham in 1939; she corresponded with him about
recording spirituals in Beaufort, South Carolina, and planned to coau-
thor (but did not) a play to be entitled "John de Conqueror."[16] An independent thinker, she felt that though white dramatists like O'Neill, Green,
and Heyward were well-meaning in portraying blacks, their plays were

From left to right: DuBose Heyward, Clifford Odets (the leading social dramatist of his day), Paul Green, Frederick Koch (founder of the Carolina Playmakers), and Barrett Clark (*New York Times* drama critic), at the Southern Regional Theatre Festival, held in Chapel Hill, April 1940. A call was issued then for a comprehensive history of drama in the South (Paul Green Foundation).

Above, the baptism of Virginia Dare in Paul Green's *The Lost Colony,* which launched outdoor drama in 1937 and still enthralls crowds at the Waterside Amphitheatre, Roanoke Island, North Carolina (Paul Green Foundation). Left, Horton Foote, the most significant southern dramatist to follow Tennessee Williams, in 1953, when he composed his best play, *The Trip to Bountiful* (DeGolyer Library, Southern Methodist University).

Above, Mrs. Carrie Watts, played by the accomplished actress Lillian Gish, implores the sheriff to allow just one more return to Bountiful before she dies (DeGolyer Library, Southern Methodist University). Right, Ossie Davis with his wife Ruby Dee in 1960, one year before his *Purlie Victorious* premiered. They costarred in this advocacy of civil rights, a genre chosen by numerous black dramatists of the South (Harry Ransom Research Center, University of Texas at Austin).

A deceptively demure Tallulah Bankhead, the most famous southern actress, as the scheming Regina Hubbard in Lillian Hellman's *The Little Foxes* (1939), an anticapitalist melodrama written when the author belonged to the Communist Party (Harvard Theatre Collection, The Houghton Library).

Southern drama reached its apex with Tennessee Williams, seen here in 1958, suave and triumphant (Harvard Theatre Collection, The Houghton Library).

Big Daddy, brought to life masterfully by Burl Ives, attempting to communicate with his son Brick, acted by Ben Gazzara, in *Cat on a Hot Tin Roof* (1955; Harry Ransom Humanities Research Center, University of Texas at Austin).

not as realistic as they should be. By her small but unique output of plays, Hurston sought to realize her ambitious conception of true Negro drama.

Color Struck (1925), a folk play of the recent past criticizing the prejudice against light-colored Negroes, is not political but rather pays attention to a part of black life overlooked by white dramatists.[17] In fluent, lively dialogue it recounts a cakewalk contest in St. Augustine, attended by participants from all over Florida. Because Emma, the dark-colored partner of John, unjustly suspects him of preferring the light-colored Effie, she refuses to dance in the finals. With unfounded jealousy she complains, "Oh the half-whites, they gets everything . . . the men, the jobs—everything! The whole world has got a sign on it. Wanted: Light colored. Us blacks was made for cobble stones" (p. 97). This tragicomedy ends consistently twenty years later when John, after his wife's death, visits Emma and finds her the unwed mother of a very light daughter. Worried that John will seduce her sick daughter, Emma foolishly delays fetching a doctor, who comes too late to save the daughter's life.

Hurston again examined color in *The First One* (1927), another tragicomedy. In a revision of Genesis, Noah curses Ham because the wives of Shem and Japheth—jealous of the father's favoritism—provoke him to do so. "Black!" Ham protests, but departs with his loving wife, prophesying: "Oh, remain with your flocks and fields and vineyards, to covet, to sweat, to die, and know no peace. I go to the sun" (pp. 87-88). He is heard in the distance singing happily and thrumming his harp. According to this fable, though the Negro's blackness is the unjust result of jealousy, it does not dishearten him.

Mule Bone: A Comedy of Negro Life, composed in 1930 by Hurston and Langston Hughes, is a full-length major play flawed by lack of finish but vital in its very crudeness. Though recently published and admired by some black critics, this amazing play has not received the attention or praise it deserves.[18] Hughes had high aims for the venture, which he considered "the first real Negro folk comedy."[19] Both authors felt that the arts of the Negro could achieve their best expression on the stage and that their play would offer audiences a new way of seeing black culture, so often caricatured by white dramatists. The work demonstrates convincingly the concern with folk expression of its authors, who hoped to inaugurate a pure Negro drama, going beyond dialect symbols to the authentic ones of communal life. As Henry Louis Gates has written, it was hoped that *Mule Bone* might accomplish in drama what Hurston herself would do for the novel, and Hughes for poetry.[20]

One reason *Mule Bone* is so little known is that a dispute between the authors prevented its production and ruined their close relationship.

Claiming sole authorship, Hurston attempted to copyright the play with no mention of Hughes's contribution. Gates concludes that Hurston probably did do most of the work on the play, which began as her story "The Bone of Contention," utilizing material drawn from her hometown of Eatonville.[21] Nevertheless, Hughes, a successful writer at the time, helped organize the material and provided some basic ideas. Notably, in developing the overriding metaphor of the mule bone, standing for contentiousness or the cause of a quarrel, the play acquired a depth and artistic quality lacking in the story. The metaphorical level likely appealed to Hughes as poet.

Mule Bone: A Comedy of Negro Life is a rich comedy with a happy ending, as its subtitle implies. Following the aim of folk drama, it depicts customs unknown to white dramatists and comments shrewdly on black life, making it provocative, important, and arresting. Mayor Joe Clarke's town, which is divided into warring Baptist and Methodist Church factions, highlights a characteristic of Negro life that can best be labeled "contentiousness." From the mayor and two preachers at the top down to the bothersome children (who significantly imitate the adults), the inhabitants quarrel constantly, each rival group or individual competing to best the opposing party. Such an existence would be intolerable were it not mollified just as constantly by well-tested devices of pacification: jokes, games (checkers on the front porch of the store), good-natured insults, and music (singing, dancing, and playing the banjo). The authors do not openly condemn quarrelsomeness but simply show it as it is, letting those interested change their ways if they choose.

Bones of contention are what give the play its dramatic tension. Foremost is the rivalry of Dave and Jim for the coquettish Daisy, who is "pretty as a speckled pup" (p. 85), recalling the Porgy-Crown argument over Bess. When they meet her at Joe Clarke's store, she flirts with both. A fight erupts when Daisy leaves the store with a red soda, bought by Dave, who accidentally steps on Jim's foot. Jim knocks Dave out cold with the hock bone of a mule and is found guilty of assault with a deadly weapon, since the farther back on a mule you go, the more dangerous he gets. Banished from town by the mayor, the best-realized character in the play, Jim retreats to the forest, where Dave and Daisy join him. After Daisy, expecting her future husband to bring home dollars, deserts both men because they decline to work as the white boss's yardman, Dave and Jim enjoy their music again and return to the town. The bone of contention, the enticing girl who nevertheless demands work of her future husband (like some other black women), vanishes from the scene.

Although quarreling erupts repeatedly, the resolution of disputes by the verbal interplay of humorous insults and jokes is a much admired skill, characteristic of Eatonville residents but not of white middle-class speakers influenced by the print medium. At the end, when Jim and Dave vie as to who loves Daisy the most, the contest of hyperbole defuses the violence implicit in their conflict so that aggression is channeled into mental rather than physical forms. Jim boasts to Daisy, "I love you like God loves Gabriel . . . and dat's his best angel"; Dave shoots back, "I love you harder than de thunder can bump a stump" (p. 144). Contentiousness threatens the men's comradeship, but verbal inventiveness restores it.[22]

Mule Bone did finally reach the stage in 1991, sixty years after its composition. Before it was performed, one hundred people, including Henry Louis Gates and the playwright Ed Bullins, attended a meeting at Lincoln Center to discuss the work. A Hurston scholar, Gates argued that the play aimed to undo a century of "racist representations of black people" but complained that some blacks today were afraid of showing each other unfavorably and that political correctness frustrated creativity (New York Times, February 10, 1991).

The play opened in February 1991, at the Ethel Barrymore Theater on Broadway, was performed by the Lincoln Center company for twenty-seven previews and sixty-seven performances, and closed April 11. Two critics for the New York Times panned the production. To Frank Rich in "A Difficult Birth for 'Mule Bone,'" it seemed like a rough draft, rarely offering a good scene from "a culture" shaped by the rich African heritage and "the oppression of American racism." Only in passages of the antagonistic Baptist and Methodist congregations and the final verbal duel of rivals, he said, did the work succeed with "linguistically fresh folk comedy." David Richards objected to "overly familiar types by now" such as domineering spouses. For him, the play checked in for two and a half hours when thirty minutes would have done just fine. Entirely missing in both reviews was any understanding of such larger meanings as the contentiousness symbolized by the mule bone (New York Times, February 15 and 24, 1991).

May Miller (1899-1995) joined Hurston in the writing of folk drama. Born in Washington, D.C., she was educated at Howard University and taught speech and dramatics at Frederick Douglass High School in Baltimore. Her interest in folk drama was encouraged by Frederick Koch, with whom she studied at Columbia University, and by Hurston, a close friend. Miller wrote of her own work, "We create from familiar elements, the possibilities of which are enhanced by imagination."[23]

Miller's Riding the Goat (1925) is a concise one-act stressing the importance of the lodge in the black community. Ruth, in love with Dr. Carter, dons a mask and impersonates him in the lodge parade. Bored by the lodge's rituals, the young doctor has decided to resign his post of grand master, despite Ruth's argument that he will lose patients thereby. "Riding the goat," which is what one woman was forced to do for spying on an initiation, means joining the lodge. Dr. Carter, however, will ride the goat only figuratively, as he decides that the right thing to do is to remain in the lodge and heal its members. Miller's *Stragglers in the Dust* (1930), which is almost a propaganda play, raises the question of who lies in the Tomb of the Unknown Soldier—also asked by John Dos Passos in "The Body of an American" in his *1919* (1932). Miller, while refuting the assumption that the unknown could only be white, notes ironically the disagreement between a poor black mother and a rich white father.[24]

Georgia Douglas Johnson (1886-1996) was the most prolific dramatist of the Washington circle. Born in Atlanta and educated at Atlanta University and the Oberlin Conservatory of Music in Ohio, she was the daughter of an Englishman whom Johnson knew very little. A teacher in Atlanta before moving in 1903 to Washington, she became the wife of Henry Lincoln Johnson, recorder of deeds for the District of Columbia. Besides working as commissioner of conciliation in the Department of Labor, she became known as a poet and published several books of verse. For many years her "S Street Salon" in Washington was a gathering place for such intellectuals as Langston Hughes, Alain Locke, Randolph Edmonds, May Miller, Owen Dodson, and Sterling Brown.

In the manner of Hurston and Miller, Johnson composed sensitive folk plays. *Plumes* (1927) is a one-act about the desire for fine funerals, but includes more polemical subjects as well. *A Sunday Morning in the South*, composed around 1925, protests the lynching of blacks, still a frequent practice at the time. Tom, Sue's grandson, awakens to hear that a white girl has accused a black youth of attacking her at 10:00 P.M., two hours after he had gone to bed following a hard day's work. Ironically, he is planning to study law to prevent lynchings provoked by such events. When a policeman enters with the girl, who is almost sure he is the man, the grandmother sends a message to the judge whose daughter employs her, imploring his intervention. While she listens to the words of the hymn being sung across the street, "Jesus will save me," news comes that Tom has been lynched.[25]

Johnson made miscegenation the theme of two one-act plays, showing the understanding of an insider. *Blue Blood* (1926) takes place in Atlanta not long after the Civil War. The vivacious May Bush is marrying John Temple because he is "light," rather than dark Randolph Strong, who is favored by her mother. When Mrs. Temple flaunts her social status, Mrs. Bush answers that May's father is none other than Captain Winfield McAllister, "that Peachtree Street blue blood."[26] Upon learning that John has the same father, Randolph Strong resolves the crisis by offering to marry May. John won't be told why his marriage is called off because black women must prevent their men from retaliating dangerously against whites, a policy practiced earlier by his mother. The problems arising from miscegenation must be met with resourcefulness, according to Johnson. Her *Blue-Eyed Black Boy* was composed for the Federal Theater Project, 1935-39, but not published until 1989. In this play a black mother saves her son from being lynched (because he brushed up against a white woman) by appealing to his white father, governor of the state, who orders the troops to intervene.[27]

Another female dramatist of Washington, D.C., Mary P. Burrill, wrote "propaganda" plays. Born and raised in the capital, she was educated at Emerson College in Boston, directed many dramatic productions in the Washington area, and attended Georgia Johnson's "S Street Salon." *Aftermath,* another post-World War I protest against lynching, was published in the *Liberator* (1919) and produced by the Krigwa Players of New York in 1928. Set in South Carolina, this tense play tells how John, a bemedaled soldier who has fought in France, returns home joyfully only to learn that a mob burned his father to death after he had disputed with a white man over the price of cotton. Armed with two pistols retained from his war service, John and his brother depart to punish Mr. Withrow. Burrill's other one-act, *They That Sit in Darkness* (1919), protests the prohibition against distributing birth control information to a poor black mother in a small southern town.[28]

Also treating the theme of miscegenation was the poet Langston Hughes (1902-67) in his best-known play, *Mulatto* (1935). Though considering Harlem his real home, he was born in Joplin, Missouri, and set several plays in the South, including *Scottsboro Limited* (1930), about the notorious trial of nine Negro youths for alleged rape; *When the Jack Hollers* (1936), a folk comedy written with poet Arna Bontemps; and *Mule Bone,* his collaboration with Hurston. Produced in 1935, *Mulatto* had the longest New York run of any play by a black up to that time—373 performances—and afterward went on a national tour but bypassed the South.

This powerful melodrama set in contemporary Georgia recounts Colonel Norwood's life with Cora, a black woman. Their capable, resentful son kills him in an argument and then takes his own life before a lynch mob can do so. Like Faulkner, Hughes presents the conflict between the racial code of the South, which demands that the white father disown his mixed offspring, and the human feelings that demand recognition. (A white man's rape of a black woman was added in the stage play, against Hughes's objections.) Unlike white dramatists, Hughes shows the life of the whole interracial family, not just the black part. Cora emerges as the dominant figure in her last soliloquy, remembering fondly how she loved the colonel and gladly gave birth to his children but finally how he died in her eyes when he beat their son. Maddened by the approach of the mob, she imagines that Colonel Norwood has revived to pursue his son as he did before. When the overseer slaps her in the last scene, Cora, preserving her dignity, does not move.

An important pioneer in black playwriting, Willis Richardson (1889-1977) was the first to compose a substantial body of plays and the first to edit a collection. He was born in Wilmington, North Carolina, but after a race riot in 1898 his family moved to Washington, where he graduated from high school and worked as a clerk at the United States Bureau of Engraving and Printing until his retirement in 1954. The author of more than thirty plays, he won the Spingarn Prize for Drama in 1925 and 1926, and the *Crisis* prize for *The Broken Banjo* in 1925. His play *Compromise* (1927) was published in the *Crisis*, the magazine of the NAACP. Working for many years in southern schools to encourage black drama, he wrote historical plays for children, striving to show the part blacks have played in building civilization. Several of these were published in *Plays and Pageants from the Life of the Negro* (1930), which he edited. He also collected plays of black history in *Negro History in Thirteen Plays* (1935), edited with May Miller.[29]

When Richardson began composing plays in the 1920s, fundamental debates were going on with regard to the nature of black drama. After seeing Angelina Grimké's *Rachel* (1916), which attacked whites, he decided to write not propaganda plays but dramas about the Negro's soul. He thus took the approach of Alain Locke, who chose plays about the black's inner life in editing *Plays of Negro Life*.[30] Though often considered folk drama in the style of Paul Green, Richardson's pieces differ significantly by depicting city life. Unlike Frederick Koch, who emphasized that folk drama was about simple, rural people in conflict with the forces of nature, Richardson tried to fathom the complexity of urban inhabitants. Like Sherwood Anderson, he was a psychological realist, seeking to discover the truth about the lives of humble people hitherto ignored. He made steady progress in counteracting the stereotypes of Negroes implanted by many white dramatists, revealing the inner reality of characters in his best one-acts.

After composing *The Deacon's Awakening* (published in the *Crisis*, November 1920), a play about the black bourgeoisie's objection to woman suffrage, Richardson turned to his most successful form, the realistic one-act depicting urban life (black dramatists have made the pungent one-act their most valuable artistic contribution to American drama). *The Chip Woman's Fortune* was first staged by the Ethiopian Art Players of Chicago and next moved to the Lafayette Theatre of Harlem on May 7, 1923, thus joining the literary outpouring of the Harlem Renaissance. Transferring eight days later to the Frazier Theatre, it was the first serious play by a black playwright to reach Broadway.

Like Richard Wright in *Black Boy* (1945), Richardson encouraged the solidarity of indigent blacks. In *The Chip Woman's Fortune*, Aunt Nancy's caring spirit holds together a disintegrating group. Living with the family of Silas Green, the old ragpicker has healed his wife with carefully chosen herbs. Catastrophe threatens when Silas is suspended from his store porter's job because he is behind on payments for a Victrola. He insists that Aunt Nancy supply the amount required from the hoard she has painstakingly buried in the yard. At this juncture the old woman's son, returning from prison, obtains the money for the Victrola from his mother's "fortune." The chip woman departs with her son, but he will return to see the Greens' daughter, thus predicting a future union.[31]

The Broken Banjo: A Folk Tragedy is another superior one-act. Performed in New York on August 1, 1925, by the Krigwa Players, it dramatizes the brokenness of the black community, symbolized by the broken banjo. Ill-tempered Matt Turner argues with his wife's brother, who pesters him by taking his food. Sam accidentally breaks Matt's banjo, which represents the centrality of music in the black's life (as in *Mule Bone* and *In Abraham's Bosom*). Recoiling from Matt's anger, Sam threatens to reveal his killing of an old white man who also broke a precious banjo. Despite Sam's promise not to tell, he returns with a policeman, an ever present figure in black drama. Preserving unity in the family, Matt takes his wife's advice not to kill the policeman but to go quietly, counting on eventual release because he had not acted intentionally. Although Matt has been a wayward husband, Richardson's play revises this stereotype by showing a gradual reformation.[32] *The Idle Head* (1929), a naturalistic one-act, was published in the *Carolina Magazine*, an organ of the Carolina Playmakers, confirming Richardson's link with the folk drama movement.[33]

Although black dramatists endeavored primarily to give their own version of contemporary life, their representation of the black experience in America would have been incomplete without dramatizations of past events. Consequently, a major development in black drama was the preservation of noteworthy figures in historical plays. Although the dramatists who wrote them came predominantly from the South, they chose not Andrew Jackson or Robert E. Lee to honor but rather Frederick Douglass and Harriet Tubman, who won the fight against slavery. They chose heroes and heroines celebrated by their own writers but overlooked by white dramatists, especially fugitive slaves whose experiences had been recounted in exciting narratives before the Civil War.

The focus on writing historical plays lasted around twenty years— from 1927, when Alain Locke and Montgomery Gregory collected *Plays of Negro Life,* until the climactic work of the genre was produced in 1947: Theodore Ward's play about Reconstruction, *Our Lan'.* The crucial anthology devoted to black history was Willis Richardson and May Miller's *Negro History in Thirteen Plays* (1935). Among Richardson's own contributions to the collection were *Attucks, the Martyr* (about Crispus Attucks, who was killed in the American Revolution) and *In Menelik's Court* (about Emperor Menelik of Abyssinia). According to one critic, Richardson wanted the dramatic picture of blacks in history to be more comprehensive than the one given by whites, and in these plays he captured the diversity and beauty of his race.[34] Plays of black history resemble folk more than propaganda plays. It should be noted that those in the principal collection were chosen by Richardson and Miller, both exponents of the folk drama.

In the introduction to *Negro History in Thirteen Plays,* Carter G. Woodson, to explain the purpose of this volume, tells of a play given by schoolchildren during "Negro History Week." "The Two Races" (included in Richardson's *Plays and Pageants from the Life of the Negro*) presents a black and white boy who are friends. Then they read a book that describes the accomplishments of all the races on earth except the Negro. This makes the black boy sad, and the two become estranged until the Muse of History reveals Negro achievement, motivating the black boy to do great deeds and the white boy to promise help. The aim of this collection is to inspire young blacks to be proud of their heritage and to emulate the deeds of the heroes and heroines of the past.[35] As Georgia Johnson wrote in "The Negro in Art," because widespread oppression makes it hard for the masses to rise, the successful individual deserves the highest praise.[36]

The first historical subject to attract black dramatists was the escape from slavery, told in slave narratives that had become well known but not previously enacted on the stage. Willis Richardson contributed *Flight of the Natives* to *Plays of Negro Life* and included four such plays by Georgia Johnson and May Miller in *Negro History in Thirteen Plays* (1935). Georgia Johnson's plays of escape emphasize resourcefulness and quickness of mind. In *Frederick Douglass* the title character finagles a pass from his future brother-in-law and catches the train to freedom. *William and Ellen Craft* relates the story of a couple who wrote a slave narrative after escaping. Disguised as a white man, Ellen takes William along as her servant on the train to Philadelphia. May Miller's contributions portray two famous black women. In *Harriet Tubman* the title character—who escaped but returned south to escort more than three hundred slaves to freedom—assists a young couple. Catherine is afraid to make the attempt because Sandy, a mulatto, is collaborating with the white master, who has offered a large reward for them. At Harriet's direction they stuff a rag in the informer's mouth and tie him up. By the time he gets loose, Harriet has reached the river with her fugitives. *Sojourner Truth* tells of the freed slavewoman who became famous for her abolitionist speeches. At an outdoor revival in Massachusetts she encounters a band of boys intent on burning the tents of the camp meeting. The sheriff allows her to speak after he learns that she has stopped the boys' plot. When one boy says the people will not attend to her any more than to the bite of a flea, she retorts, "The Lord willing, I'll keep them a-scratching."[37]

John Frederick Matheus, winner of many drama prizes, dramatized Negro migration to the North in *'Cruiter*, included in Locke and Gregory's *Plays of Negro Life*. Born in Keyser, West Virginia, Matheus became professor of modern foreign languages at Florida A&M State College (1911-22) and West Virginia State College (1922-53). His *Ti Yette*, a melodrama of miscegenation in antebellum New Orleans, was collected in Richardson's *Plays and Pageants from the Life of the Negro*. *'Cruiter* (1926), recalling narratives of escaped slaves, recounts the surreptitious departure of a young couple from Master Bob's place in lower Georgia at the beckoning of a Detroit recruiter. Generational conflict, which often accompanied such migration, arises in the reluctance of the grandmother, born in slavery, to leave. She remains behind when the recruiter refuses to allow her dog on the train.

The most impressive drama of Negro history from this period is Theodore Ward's *Our Lan'*, a full-length work about ownership of land during Reconstruction which combines folk and propaganda elements. Born in Thibodaux, Louisiana, Ward grew up in that state and Missouri, was educated at the Universities of Utah and Wisconsin, and became a playwright, teacher, and actor. For the Federal Theater Project in Chicago he composed *Big White Fog* (1938), named for the term used by blacks for the bewildering white society they encountered in the North. This play protests the living conditions of blacks in the United States.

After organizing the Negro Playwrights' Company in Harlem with Langston Hughes, Paul Robeson, and Richard Wright, Ward finished *Our*

Lan' in 1946, aided by a Theatre Guild scholarship. It was the first play of
black history to reach Broadway, where it ran for forty-one performances
in 1947. Ward set this moving melodrama about the blacks' desire to own
property in the time of Reconstruction because he wanted to recapture
the period in which blacks, first realizing the reality of their situation in
America, recognized what was necessary for salvation: ownership of land.[38]
Set on a Georgia coastal island, this episodic play tells how a band of
freedmen raise cotton on land granted them by the federal government
but lose the property when Union troops restore the plantation to the
white owner. Ward also sympathetically portrays poor whites (who are
usually vilified by black dramatists): redneck Confederate veterans protest that like the freedmen, they have acquired no land from the greedy
planters, whom they curse.

Dominating the play, the aptly named leader, Joshua, determines tragically to hold the land. His solemnity contrasts with the vivacity of the beautiful mulatto Delphine, whom he allows to stay in the community even
after she becomes pregnant by a Savannah youth. To the villainous former
owner who attempts to repossess the property, Joshua declares: "This is
ouah lan'. We done wukked 'n paid for it. Not only here but all over this
cruel South. De graves . . . over yonder is mah witness." Northern collusion, the play implies, seals the doom of the freedmen when Union troops
reclaim the land by force. Joshua dies in the battle as Delphine sings,
"Deep river, my home is over Jordan."[39]

Black drama after World War I belongs to the Southern Literary Renascence as much as to the Harlem Renaissance. Gaining direction from
Paul Green and Frederick Koch, a dynamic group in Washington, D.C.,
mined black culture to create the folk drama that filled the anthologies
of Willis Richardson and Alain Locke. Playwrights such as Zora Neale
Hurston, May Miller, and Willis Richardson, who preferred to explore
black life rather than voice social protest, adopted the moderate approach
toward race relations that would distinguish the work of some black
southerners. Climaxing many one-acts performed in the 1920s, the full-
length *Mule Bone* composed in 1930 by two leaders of black literature,
Hurston and Hughes, sought to initiate a distinctive art by blacks. This
work, whose status as dramatic literature remains undecided, is in my judgment the single most fascinating work of black drama before World War
II and the one most in need of further attention.

Contrasting sharply with the folk play, the propaganda or political
play solicited by W.E.B. Du Bois, the implacable opponent of Booker T.
Washington, gained momentum as the pressure increased for an end to
the intolerable racial situation in the United States, heightened by blacks'

sacrifice in World War I and the continuation of lynchings. Langston Hughes, who had first written folk drama, turned to protest in *Mulatto* (1935). And after the proud but subdued commemoration of black history in *Thirteen Plays of Negro History* was published in 1935, Theodore Ward added righteous indignation to folklore in *Our Lan'*, a protest against the loss of property promised freedmen during Reconstruction. After World War II, when the civil rights movement began, black dramatists would intensify their political commitments, not forgetting their obligation to black culture but assigning it second place.

—10—
Randolph Edmonds
and Civil Rights

The civil rights movement, beginning with the Supreme Court decision against segregated schools in 1954 and culminating with Martin Luther King's "I Have a Dream" speech in August 1963, produced two major changes in the black drama of the South. First, the political aim to achieve civil rights supplanted folk life as the primary concern. Second, overt but nonviolent efforts, such as sit-ins and bus boycotts, to end segregation in the South gave dramatists causes to be *for,* whereas before they had had only injustices to be *against.* This change made the plays more positive in tone. Previously the emphasis had been on protest against racial oppression, seen in antilynching plays such as Georgia Johnson's ironic *A Sunday Morning in the South.* Now, on the basis of personal experience, black playwrights dramatized the confrontations between advocates of integration and their white adversaries. Such events provided the material for highly charged political plays that made the stage a powerful instrument in the fight to achieve the full freedom blacks had sought since the time of slavery. Though the civil rights plays are often lacking in art, they compensate by commitment to a high cause. Significantly, most of the plays depicting the struggle originated with southern, not northern, black dramatists.

The successor to Willis Richardson in black educational institutions was Randolph Edmonds (1900-1983), who carried further the cultivation of drama in black colleges of the South. A tireless supporter of theatrical associations on college campuses, he was the foremost of several dramatists who coupled playwriting with teaching. At the end of his career he joined those composing plays to promote the civil rights crusade, which galvanized black playwrights as no political movement had before. Edmonds' shift from folk to civil rights drama typifies black playwriting after World War II.

Born in Lawrenceville, Virginia, where he graduated from St. Paul's

Normal and Industrial School, Edmonds subsequently received a degree from Oberlin College, acquired an M.A. from Columbia University in 1932, and did further postgraduate study at Yale. During his long academic career he taught from 1929 to 1934 at Morgan College, Baltimore, where he organized the Negro Inter-Collegiate Drama Association in 1930. Next, teaching at Dillard University in New Orleans from 1935 to 1947, he established the first drama department at a black college (1935) and founded the Southern Association of Drama and Speech Arts, later named the National Association of Drama and Speech Arts (1936). Finally, he chaired the Theatre Arts Department at Florida A & M University in Tallahassee from 1947 to 1969.

Edmonds worked tirelessly to encourage theater in black colleges, believing that dramatists must have stages of their own to create a vital drama. Author of essays on drama and forty-seven plays, editor of collections of his own works, he is the central figure in the development of contemporary black drama in the South. In honor of his contributions to drama departments in predominantly black colleges of the southern United States, Edmonds was named "Dean of Black Academic Theatre" in 1970 by the National Association of Dramatic and Speech Arts.

Edmonds is important too as a theorist of black drama. His preface to *Six Plays for a Negro Theatre* (1934) states that although the dramas were written for the black stage, he hopes they will be performed elsewhere as well, since really worthwhile works by black dramatists should contain "universal elements."[1] Frederick Koch's foreword to this collection stresses the author's affinity with the folk drama movement, naming Paul Green's *Lonesome Road* (1926) as the inspiration for Edmonds's folk plays performed at black colleges.[2] To promote playwriting by blacks, Edmonds published two other collections of his own plays: *Shades and Shadows* (1930) and *The Land of Cotton and Other Plays* (1942), which includes socially relevant and historical subjects.

Edmonds forcefully expressed his ideas about the nature of black drama in the preface to *Six Plays*. Observing that Negroes were alienated not so much by dialect as by "the repelling atmosphere" and "the psychology of the inferior" found in "peasant plays," he said he would attempt to meet these objections by four additions: "worthwhile themes, sharply drawn conflict, positive characters, and a melodramatic plot." Edmonds wished to find encouragement in troubled but admirable characters and to reach audiences not yet ready for starkly serious drama. He hoped that the results would be tragedies neither too revolting in theme nor too subtle and psychological, featuring personages with "character and conviction" who "fight heroically in their losing struggles."[3] Later, though remarking that Green had presented black life truly, Edmonds objected to his hopelessness and lack of sympathy for oppressed characters.[4] Like Hurston, he admired but had reservations about the white dramatist's black characters.

At the Southern Regional Theatre Festival, "Drama in the South," held in Chapel Hill, North Carolina, on April 5, 1940—also attended by Green and Heyward—Edmonds laid down a plan for the development of black drama. Speaking after Zora Neale Hurston, he recommended an organizational rather than what he called "the individualistic" approach. The latter term referred to several short-lived little theater groups all named the Krigwa Players, which W.E.B. Du Bois had established in New York, Washington, Baltimore, and elsewhere in 1926. Negro drama, he contended, must develop in the South, where most Negroes reside, not in highly publicized "northern centers like Harlem." The center of such activity must be the college theater, not amateur groups.[5]

Edmonds went on to report on the success of his efforts to build a foundation for Negro drama. The Inter-Collegiate Drama Association had emerged from a March 7, 1930, meeting held at Morgan College, Baltimore, where he was then teaching, joined by Hampton Institute, Virginia State College, Howard University, and Virginia Union University. After four years, 204 plays had been produced by thirteen white and four black directors. In 1936 Edmonds had also organized the Southern Association of Drama and Speech Arts, and he announced that thanks to these associations, presidents of colleges were hiring drama instructors, and audiences had improved because the plays presented "real Negro People" rather than blackface stereotypes. Looking ahead optimistically, he hoped that what was then only the daybreak of Negro drama would turn into "a brilliant sunrise."[6]

In the same speech Edmonds expressed gratitude to Frederick Koch and the Carolina Playmakers for indicating "the true path to travel."[7] Koch, Paul Green, and others had attended meetings of the Southern Association of Drama and Speech Arts, he reported. Implying a further similarity to Green, Edmonds composed *Whatever the Battle Be: A Symphonic Drama*, first produced in Tallahassee's Lee Auditorium on November 3, 1950.

Although in retrospect it cannot be claimed that Edmonds's vision produced nationally acclaimed black dramatists, his aims were sound and well-considered. Theater did in fact become stronger in black colleges, providing a receptive atmosphere for apprentice dramatists. Ted Shine, Thomas Pawley, and others followed Edmonds's lead in composing plays while remaining in the academic profession.

Edmonds's *Six Plays for a Negro Theatre* is the best collection by a black dramatist before the decade of the 1960s. Characters are believable, themes are interesting, and emotions run from rage to pity. Some characters resemble stereotypes but exhibit individual traits as well. The six plays may be divided historically. First, *Nat Turner* and *Breeders* take place in slavery times. Next, *Bleeding Hearts, Bad Man,* and *The New Window* are set in the Reconstruction period, showing the dire living conditions of blacks during that era. Finally, *Old Man Pete* recounts the migration to Harlem.[8]

When Edmonds wrote his play about Nat Turner, the subject was much more obscure than it is today. Since then, William Styron's celebrated *The Confessions of Nat Turner* (1967) and black critics' objections to that novel have made Turner much better known. Edmonds was daring in the 1930s to choose this notorious insurrectionist as the subject of his contribution to Richardson's *Thirteen Plays of Negro History* (1935). Like Styron (who did not know the play), he considered Turner a complex personality tortured by doubts but one who remained true to his own feelings. Edmonds differed from T.R. Gray, Turner's contemporary interviewer and transcriber of "The Confession"; in "A Notice to the Public" (part of which Styron reprinted), Gray termed the revolt only "the offspring of gloomy fanaticism."[9]

Edmonds's portrait of Nat Turner is a pioneering study of this complex figure, delineating a mysterious, charismatic leader, smarter than the other slaves, who respect his ability to read and write. Considered an upright man and inspired by God, he is addressed as "Prophet Nat" (p. 193). Earning their awe, Nat relates his vision of Christ, who commanded him to take up his yoke and "fight de serpents": that is, slavery (p. 206). This dramatic character repeats—in dialect—the words of Turner's printed "Confession," thereby verifying Edmonds's knowledge of that document. On the evening of Sunday, August 21, 1831, the title character exhorts his listeners to join him in fighting for freedom so their children will not remain in slavery. Though slaves like Job are skeptical, others join the eager Will in cheering him on when he drills them as "General Nat." As they march off to fight for freedom at the end of Scene 1, we hear the sounds of killing and lamentation, and the glee of the slaves.

Scene 2 presents a totally different atmosphere on an ominous evening, the following Wednesday. A haggard Nat admits that many of his followers fled from the white enemy and that his most trusted lieutenant, Hark, has failed to join him to renew the offensive. Jesse, fatally wounded, enters and dies; his sweetheart, Lucinda, denounces Nat as "a beast" and predicts that the whites, whom she will inform, will hang him (p. 215). Full of doubts, the once confident leader now falters. He begs the Lord to send him a vision as He did before the rebellion. At the end of this one-act, Nat regains his determination, saying that he wants to fight "some mo' fuh freedom" so that all "de black slaves" will be free. Rushing out, he shouts, "Show me how to git hit, Lawd! . . . Sperit of Gawd! Show me de way!" (p. 216). Though Edmonds describes a tormented soul, he admires Nat's strength in the face of defeat, thus reinforcing the tragic heroism of this enigmatic, powerful rebel.

Breeders tells of Ruth, a sensitive, attractive girl, who is designated by her master for alliance with a black stud to produce strong offspring. Breaking the stereotype, Ruth is not loose sexually and refuses to go with Salem, preferring her weak lover, David. The latter is killed defending Ruth, and she takes poison. Questioning God's plan, Ruth's mother does not want to doubt His justice but asks how long He will let His "chilluns be sold down de river lak horses an' cows"? (p. 101). Breeders was presented at the Southern Regional Theatre Festival in 1940, by a cast from Dillard University.

When Frederick Koch saw a performance in Richmond of Edmonds's Bad Man by the Negro Inter-Collegiate Dramatic Association, he was much impressed by its freshness and enthusiasm.[10] A corrective to the stereotype of the Brute Beast, the principal character, who is named Thea, is "the bad man" of an Alabama sawmill camp, a milieu Edmonds knew from experience. Although Thea has murdered several men, he nevertheless possesses a noble character. Maybelle, who is visiting her boyfriend, believes he has a good streak not yet revealed. Touched by her faith, Thea refrains from killing a dishonest card player. When a mob of poor whites arrives demanding the murderer of an old man, Thea, representing the older generation, sacrifices himself for Maybelle's future husband.[11]

Bleeding Hearts describes the callousness of whites in the face of black suffering and the outcry over the tragedy of life allowed by God. A white plantation owner wants the daughter of Miranda, who is dying of pneumonia, to resume work at his house. While Sis' Jenny attempts to care for Miranda, the preacher and friends pray and sing with her, demonstrating how singing strengthens the griefstricken. Dying, Miranda sings "Free at last," but her farm-worker husband, Joggison, protests to God over his loss. Again Edmonds shows the black's questioning of God's justice when Joggison decides he must leave this place so that he won't turn against the Lord: "Maybe den ah'll be free," he says as others stare at him incredulously (p. 127). Having to endure white callousness and unanswered prayers, while the world is falling around him, the black finds it hard to keep faith.

In *The New Window,* an overly sensational melodrama, Bulloch Williams is a bootlegger who abuses his wife Lizzie and stepdaughter Hester, and has killed the brother of one Simon Turner in the course of his operations. Simon, who believes he has been sent on a mission of God like another "Turner," challenges Bulloch to a duel. Because Hester has blunted the firing pin of Bulloch's pistol, Simon succeeds in killing him. Lizzie had predicted that doom would come to someone in the house after her husband built a new window to spy on unwanted visitors.

Old Man Pete takes black life forward to a modern dilemma, the problem of older people from the South who move to Harlem. Pete and Mandy come from Virginia to stay with their children, who are embarrassed by their parents' old-fashioned ways. After reprimanding Vivian, his son's wife, for drinking and smoking, Pete attempts to return home but freezes on a park bench. Up here in this God-forsaken city, he tells his wife, no one cares if you live or die.

Among Edmonds's later works, *Earth and Stars* is a significant response to the civil rights movement. Put into its final form when Edmonds was sixty-one, this full-length play was first produced at the Dillard University Little Theatre on February 13, 1946. Revised in 1961—obviously altered in response to the civil rights movement—and published in 1971, it has been performed more than a hundred times, making it the most frequently staged work by a black dramatist in black colleges and community theaters of the South.[12] Like Paul Green, however, Edmonds did not compose the kind of play that would succeed on Broadway.

This work offers Edmonds's solution to the racial conflict confronting America. It is the same as Dr. Martin Luther King's: nonviolence. The play's leading figure, Rev. Joshua Judson, advocates love, not hate, despite the loss of his son, a radical whom he disarmed. His wife begs him to withdraw from the struggle, but he departs to preach brotherhood, noting that many blacks have died as martyrs, though none willingly. Acknowledging that he has faced death with dignity, Judson's opponents finally acclaim him "a real martyr" (p. 461).

Although Edmonds remains true to his aim of writing melodrama in this exciting play filled with violence and villains, he reaches for tragic effect, for the Reverend Judson is a hero who falls because of his conscience. Unlike his wife, he is not deterred when his only son, who has joined the Freedom Riders, is assassinated; he goes forward, single-mindedly believing that the just cause will prevail. Edmonds views religion not as an opiate but as the cause of hard dilemmas. Over and over, his characters question God's will because of harrowing events. The minister keeps his faith despite the tragedy of his son's death, which he sees as part of God's plan to extend brotherly love to all, but his wife demands to know why.

This play might well be compared with a Shavian drama of too many ideas, which inevitably reduce some of its tragic power. The South is dissected severely in the microcosmic setting of "Southern City" (p. 399). First, Judson takes moderate whites to task for wanting to go slowly. They are represented by the weak-kneed Herbert Martin, who wants Judson to call off the sit-ins and speaks condescendingly of the "boys" who work in the union (p. 433). After Judson lectures him for abandoning the South to the bigoted minority, its representative "Reb" Smith enters the minister's home and forces him to pray on his knees, "Now I lay me down to sleep" (p. 436).

Through his character's story, Edmonds's play frankly and forcefully articulates dissatisfaction with some blacks. It censures the pillars of the church for impeding the Reverend Judson's social program. The bishop's representative opposes day care for children and youth recreation; Sister Cora cares only about honoring her deceased husband with a stained glass window. The exasperated minister says that he must fight three classes in the black community: "the Uncle Toms, the good-time addicts, and the miseducated intellectuals" (p. 426). Probing the recurrent issue of black leadership, Judson explains that teachers don't make good leaders because they deal with ideas, not things themselves, and are dependent on the establishment for their jobs. He considers that better choices are editors, labor organizers, and ministers. The last, if they are modern ministers, suit the times best. Joshua Judson, named after the courageous man who led the Children of Israel into the Promised Land, leaves "a courageous example," says his daughter in the closing lines of the play (p. 463). Although showing Christian love, he aggressively backed activist measures like the sit-ins. By supporting his son in radical demonstrations, he united the older with the younger generation.

As to literary merit, it must be said that this play is overloaded with plots. Showing the effect of having originated before the civil rights movement took place, it includes the reactionary-liberal struggle in the black church as well as labor disputes, a subject Edmonds had presented earlier, as in *The Land of Cotton* (1942). Other writers' plays about the civil rights movement—Ossie Davis's *Purlie Victorious* and James Baldwin's *Blues for Mr. Charlie*—achieve a clearer focus. Yet, despite its chaotic structure, *Earth and Sky* aims high, throws light on many important issues, and climaxes Edmonds's career as a leader in black drama.

The work of Edmonds and others demonstrates that southern blacks contributed most heavily to the drama of civil rights. Northern dramatists, far removed from southern locales, were less involved—except for James Baldwin, whose stirring *Blues for Mr. Charlie* (1964) is based on Emmett Till's murder (significantly, Baldwin had visited Mississippi soon after the incident to meet Medgar Evers, whose assassination in 1963 inspired him to compose his play). In the North, during the peak of demonstrations in the South, LeRoi Jones anatomized the rage of black intellectuals against white liberals in *Dutchman* (1964); Ed Bullins offered such plays as *In the Wine Time* (1968) about the joys and troubles of black youth; and Charles Gordone composed the Pulitzer Prize-winning *No Place to Be Somebody* (1969) about "Charlie fever," the hatred of whites. But none of these plays, set in the North, directly supported the struggle for civil rights led by Martin Luther King. By contrast, southern black dramatists, sharing the experiences of their fellow blacks in Birmingham and Selma, joined the effort to gain civil rights with all their dramatic energy.

Writing in Edmonds's spirit of nonviolence is Loften Mitchell (1919-). Though he has spent most of his life in the North, he was born in Columbus, North Carolina, and graduated from Talladega College in Alabama. His memorable play about the civil rights struggle in the South, *A Land beyond the River* (first performed in 1957), dramatizes the life of Rev. Dr. Joseph DeLaine, who protested in court against the lack of bus transportation for black students in rural Clarendon County, South Carolina.[13] Taken to the Supreme Court, the case influenced the 1954 decision to outlaw segregation in public schools. In the play, "the Rev. Layne" progresses from attempts to repair a rundown school to a court case. He obtains a ruling from the state court that the schools of blacks and whites must be equal, but does not stop there; he carries his fight for integrated schools to the highest court in the land. In the process, he counters the wish of his parishioners to meet the violence of whites with like violence by declaring that only love will accomplish their goal. Mitchell paid further tribute to Joseph DeLaine in his dramatic history of blacks in America, *Tell Pharaoh* (1967).[14]

The civil rights movement of the 1960s produced two main styles of black playwriting: the serious and the comic. Edmonds wrote effectively in the former manner; Ossie Davie and Douglas Turner Ward chose the latter, using the rich lore of race jokes as the cultural underpinning for their political convictions.

Born in Cogdell, Georgia, on December 18, 1917, Ossie Davis attended Central High School in Waycross, Georgia, and graduated from Howard University. He has become one of the best-known black actors and a popular speaker at historically black southern colleges. Starting his career in 1941, he took roles in *Green Pastures, A Raisin in the Sun,* and *Anna Lucasta.* His play *Purlie Victorious,* which opened in 1961 with the author and his wife, Ruby Dee, in the leading roles, advocates nonviolence to achieve integration. Set in rural Georgia during the time of the civil rights movement, this farce presents the struggle of a black preacher to acquire a church building inherited by a young black woman. Though unsuccessful financially, the play was made into the film *Gone Are the Days* and the highly successful musical *Purlie!* It was also performed successfully in 1964 on a tour of southern states by the Free Southern Theater, headquartered in New Orleans, which promoted integrated audiences in the South. Well known as a civil rights activist, Davis was master of ceremonies when Martin Luther King spoke to participants in the March on Washington. He has stated that what King tried to do with love, "I am trying to do with laughter."[15]

Purlie Victorious uses bald humor to laugh the old order of segregation out of court. Ridiculing southern whites in a manner going back to William Wells Brown, it focuses on a defender of the old order, Cap'n Stonewall Jackson Cotchipee, whose son integrates the new church. When the astonished captain loses possession of the church building to the Reverend Purlie Judson, he becomes the first man to die standing up and is buried with the Confederate flag draped around him. Blacks too come in for ridicule, among them Gitlow, the captain's "Deputy-for-the-Colored."[16] Gitlow, however, undergoes a conversion and supports the overthrow of segregation, singing with new meaning "Gone are the days" (p. 182). The Reverend Purlie, strengthening a young woman's pride in her color, asks if her mistress's white skin is so precious, "why does she spend half her life at the beach trying to get a sun tan?" (p. 142). At the end, duplicating the style of Jesse Jackson, Purlie appeals to all: "Let us, therefore, stifle the rifle of conflict, shatter the scatter of discord, . . . and grapple the apple of peace" (p. 185).

Douglas Turner Ward was born in Burnside, Louisiana, in 1931. He grew up in New Orleans, made his New York debut in O'Neill's *The Iceman Cometh,* and acted the leading role in the national tour of Lorraine Hansberry's *Raisin in the Sun.* Ward attempted to stage his two one-acts about civil rights in 1960 but did not succeed until 1965. He won an Obie (off-Broadway) award for his acting in *Happy Days* and *Day of Absence,* set in Harlem and the South respectively. Paul Green, reading these two plays in 1968, pronounced them "terrific."[17] In 1968, Ward founded the Negro Ensemble Company and became its artistic director.

Subtitled "a satirical fantasy" and called by its author "a reverse minstrel show done in white-face," *Day of Absence* underlines whites' dependence on blacks in a southern town.[18] One day all the blacks suddenly disappear. In the home of a frantic white couple the maid is not present to care for the bawling infant, and Mayor Henry R.E. Lee is helpless without Mandy, who alone can straighten his desk. Reports arrive that the elderly are dying without their black nurses, the local factory cannot function without black workers, and a policeman goes insane because he cannot meet his quota of two blacks arrested per day. In an expressionistic scene recalling the reductio ad absurdum of Eugène Ionesco, all activity in the city comes to a standstill. The next day, when the blacks return to work, one worried white asks another if things will ever be the same. The unspoken answer is that blacks have discovered their power and will use it in the future.

Initiated by Randolph Edmonds, the tradition of playwriting in the black college continued in the works of Thomas D. Pawley and Ted Shine, academic colleagues who cooperated closely in the advancement of black drama. The college theater was particularly appealing to black teachers of drama living in the South, far removed from the Great White Way. Their attempt to design plays for black audiences followed the example of black theaters in New York and Chicago, which insisted with Du Bois that black dramatists should compose plays of, about, and for blacks, free of whites' expectations.

Born in Jackson, Mississippi, Thomas D. Pawley Jr. (1917-) received his A.B. from Virginia State College, and his M.A. and Ph.D. from the University of Iowa—where, in 1937, he knew Tennessee Williams.[19] Pawley taught at Prairie View State College, Texas, and has held various visiting professorships, mostly in the Midwest. He was for many years professor of speech and drama at Lincoln University in Jefferson City, Missouri. Pawley has published *Jedgement Day,* a dramatic satire of black religion, in *The Negro Caravan* (1938); won first prize for the best play of Virginia history, *Messiah* (1954), awarded by the Jamestown Corporation; and written numerous essays on black drama. As evidenced in his coeditorship of *The Black Teacher and the Dramatic Arts: A Dialogue, Bibliography, and Anthology,* he has striven to improve the quality of drama in black colleges. This volume grew out of an Institute in Black Repertory Theatre held at the University of California–Santa Barbara, June 17 to August 2, 1968.[20]

Pawley's principal play, *The Tumult and the Shouting,* first produced at the Lincoln University Institute of Dramatic Arts in 1969, is most interesting for its knowing picture of life at a black southern college, a culture little known to whites. In this realistic chronicle David Sheldon, a professor of English transplanted from Mississippi to Virginia, struggles to maintain academic standards and raise a family properly. Constantly worried by inadequate funds, a situation worsened by the Depression, he must also bear the indignities of white merchants who call him "boy." The older generation, we learn, must make heavy sacrifices so that some may advance, like Sheldon's son, who earns a Ph.D. His children, growing up in a sheltered atmosphere, discover what it is like to be black only when they leave their campus residence. Although this play lacks genuinely dramatic scenes, it offers a unique glimpse of life at a black college, where, as in real life, whites ordinarily know only one individual—the president.[21]

A more important and prolific teacher-dramatist is Ted Shine, professor at Prairie View State College, Texas. Born in Baton Rouge, Louisiana, on April 26, 1936, he was educated in the public schools of Dallas, graduated from Howard University, and received his M.A. from the State University of Iowa and Ph.D. from the University of California-Santa Barbara. Shine composed twenty-four plays from 1960 to 1971, several of which have been performed at Howard University and Lincoln University, and by the Negro Ensemble Company of New York.

Actively involved in college dramatics as well as playwriting, Shine has stated that he considers himself primarily a teacher. As a Texan, he feels an obligation to the people of his state, especially black youth, "to seek out, encourage, and develop that talent which will one day make us *all* proud."[22] Shine has spent most of his time in the academic milieu, but he did write a television series, *Our Street*, intended to turn youth away from harmful behavior. He resembles his academic predecessor Randolph Edmonds but has had more success in the professional theater. He not only protests white injustice but censures blacks as well, including prostitutes in *Flora's Kisses* (1969) and an overly religious mother in *Herbert III* (1974). Always interested in a youth's development, Shine deplores the gullibility and materialism of adolescents. In this respect he may be compared with Ed Bullins, who depicted a troubled youth's life in *In the Wine Time* (1968).

Morning, Noon, and Night, Shine's first important play, was composed in 1964 but not performed until 1968 at the University of California—Santa Barbara. A trenchant study of religious fanaticism—like James Baldwin's *Amen Corner* (1965)—this work, set in Earth, Texas, with acts divided into morning, noon, and night, asks the audience to consider some universal themes. The central and most memorable character is the vigorous grandmother, Gussie Black from Forney, Texas. Full of vitality despite her seventy-two years, she is a comic personification of evil. Burning her grandson's books with antiintellectual fervor, suspicious of men in general, and incorrigibly lazy, she is a colossal hypocrite for good measure. Though opposed to smoking and drinking, she enjoys a ciga-rette after yet another show of repentance, and she drinks apricot brandy because being reborn enables her to backslide a little. Gussie is hardly the stereotypical grandmother; she has not only poisoned her white em-ployers but disposes of unwanted kin such as her daughter-in-law's sister Ida Ray, who dies slowly from ingesting roach killer put in the stew. Like Flannery O'Connor's self-proclaimed Christians, Gussie is a grotesque, with her wooden leg of pure Georgia pine which she must continually repaint white. Her own leg, crushed by the cornerstone of a church, has been replaced by "something religious," symbolizing her hard soul.[23] This outrageous hypocrite plans to start her own profitable Gussie Black and Grandson Tabernacle.

The innocent youth of this play, a hard-to-believe eleven-year-old, undergoes an initiation as he encounters evil in the person of his grand-mother. Ben could benefit from the influence of a Harvard professor who encourages his reading and of his aunt, Ida Ray, who stands for Truth as she refutes his claim to be a prophet. Instead he succumbs to the tempta-tion of religious fanaticism, represented by Sister Sue, a visiting evange-list who lusts for him in the style of an Erskine Caldwell vamp. After envisioning Gussie's previous killings in a trance, Ben leaves his grand-mother to burn, literally, as she undoubtedly deserves. Not as free as he claims, however, he foolishly joins Sister Sue, who is preaching in the inauspiciously named town of Muleshoe.

Herbert III, included in *Black Theater, U.S.A.* (1974), is a thoroughly up-to-date, affirmative one-act of family life, showing the influence of Shine's writing for television. Margarette, an anxious mother worrying over one son's absence at 3:00 A.M. and the plights of her other sons—one of whom is in prison and the other in Canada to avoid the Vietnam War—finally persuades her husband to trace Herbert III. Contradicting the stereotype of irresponsibility, this father locates his son in a bowling alley but lets him remain. The black male who accepts his son as a man is indispensable in the family, according to Shine.

Shine's most important dramatic work is a trio of one-acts, published under the title *Contributions.*[24] *Plantation, Shoes,* and *Contribution,* per-formed at Tambellini's Gate Theatre in New York on March 9, 1970, dis-cuss three very topical subjects in an original style.

Plantation is an angry satire that denounces opposition to integra-tion. Papa Joe Vesquelles, a Louisianian, resists integration with such vio-lent measures that although a bishop of his state sympathizes with him, he is excommunicated by a Yankee cardinal. Not realizing that his own mother was black, Papa Joe is thunderstruck when his wife gives birth to a black son. Having willed everything to his heir, Papa Joe stabs himself, leaving the son to a black couple, who hail him as a second Jesus.

Shoes confronts such contemporary problems as deterioration of the family, the conflict of generations, and youthful materialism. Three teenagers who work at a country club outside Dallas discuss fine clothes, especially shoes, in expertly rendered dialect. Speaking for traditional values, Mr. Mack advises them not to spend so much money on clothes, and Mr. Wisely refuses to give Smokey, whom he has helped raise, the $150 saved for him. Influenced by his alcoholic mother, who says that all you can do in life is get money and spend it on yourself, Smokey almost shoots Mr. Wisely in order to buy the clothes he wants. After Mr. Wisely hands over the money, Mr. Mack urges Smokey to join his friends, who, he remarks, are only in his pocket or on his back. In this play the surrogate fathers fail to overcome the all-consuming materialism of the younger generation.

Contribution, written for black audiences, was first performed by the Negro Ensemble Company, directed by Douglas Taylor Ward, in 1969. In this comic treatment of sit-ins, the black rage of LeRoi Jones takes a ludicrous turn. Mrs. Grace Love, another untypical grandmother, tells her grandson about her "contribution" to the civil rights movement: she loved white people as long as she could, but when the doctor let her husband die, she poisoned him and his family. Now this apparently harmless grandmother who pretends to know her place has sent poisoned cornbread to the sheriff, who is prevented thereby from stopping her grandson's sit-in. Hearing that demonstrators are meeting armed resistance in Mississippi, she departs to cook for the governor of that state.

The evening of three one-acts brought Shine his largest critical response. Martin Gottfried in *Women's Wear Daily* (March 10, 1970) said that *Shoes* showed the compensation for poverty sought by boys like Smokey; James Davis in the *Daily News* (March 10, 1970) commended Shine for trying to turn young people away from materialism; and Walter Kerr of the *New York Times* lauded *Contribution.*[25]

If there had ever been any doubts about who could best argue for black causes, the authors of civil rights plays removed them. Playwrights such as Paul Green had previously assumed much of the responsibility for condemning racial injustice, and when the civil rights movement began in the 1950s, white southerners such as Tennessee Williams offered support. The protracted struggle for civil rights as reflected in drama, however, enlisted primarily the efforts of black dramatists from the South in plays advocating integration by means of nonviolence, such as Davis's *Purlie Victorious* and Edmonds's *Earth and Sky*.

Another interesting contribution to the civil rights play, a distinctive genre shaped by southern blacks, was the burlesque of stereotypes, both blacks and whites. Because of their polemic purposes, these dramatists exploited rather than avoided stereotypical characters, branding segregationist types as the worst enemies. From condemnation of the bigoted poor white in *Earth and Stars*, they proceeded to outrageous caricatures. Ossie Davis ridiculed the overbearing southern colonel without neglecting the obsequious Uncle Tom; Douglas Turner Ward parodied the southern politician and clubwoman to underline whites' total dependence on blacks; Ted Shine portrayed the "kindly" black grandmother as surreptitious civil rights advocate.

It is important to note that even as black drama became dominated by the political objective of desegregating the South, its representation of a culture that only black dramatists knew continued fruitfully. Their pictures of modern urban life—replacing quaint times of the legendary past, as in Hurston's works—were usually confined to a black community devoid of whites. Edmonds reported critically on the inner workings of the church, which remained the central institution of black society in the South. Pawley wrote sensitively of realities in the black college. Shine illuminated the generational differences, fragmentation of the family, and problems of adolescents. They thus offered fresh views of genuine problems and conditions that otherwise would have remained unknown to a larger public.

—11—
The Cultural Imagination of Tennessee Williams

Southern drama had been advancing steadily and impressively with the works of Green, Heyward, and Hellman, but reached its apex in Tennessee Williams (1911-83). The southern play attained its highest sustained expression in Williams's work from 1945 to 1960. This ambitious, gifted dramatist, who attained the goals sought by many of his southern predecessors, became a Broadway success with a national audience, thus surpassing Green, who could never learn how to satisfy the New York critics. At the same time, he treated major themes of the South and created individual characters who incorporate universal qualities that are the stuff of major drama. Following Hellman especially, Williams took up the theme of the Old versus the New South and gave it his own distinctive slant. Moreover, he dealt frankly with sex in the southern family.

Williams's career may be divided into the first phase, when he looked back nostalgically toward the Old South, and the second, when he joined others in condemning racial injustice in his native region, depicting the South and southerners much more harshly. As with Hellman, it is illuminating to draw on biographical information showing that even though Williams left the South at an early age and spent much of his career elsewhere in the nation and abroad, his seminal experiences in the South, periodic residence there, and continual contact with southerners informed his plays. Such material throws light on their southern quality.

Williams's interest in the culture of the Old South demonstrates a comprehensive view, for he looks at the total culture and responds imaginatively in an original way. Throughout his works, this international dramatist manifests an interest in foreign cultures as well, signified by his inclusion of foreign languages, like Italian. He analyzes whole cultures in his plays, especially the Latin, in numerous works. Seeing contradictions, dichotomies, and bifurcations as the key to understanding, he takes as his guiding principle "the logic of contradictions," an intriguing phrase

174

he uses for the music-loving Germans of *The Night of the Iguana* because they sing gloriously while celebrating the bombing of London.[1] The culture of *The Rose Tattoo,* realized in the sensual but devout Serafina and her husband—the victim of a Mafia-like attack on his banana truck—reflects the duality of spirituality and corruption in Italian immigrant life. The French culture in the New Orleans of *A Streetcar Named Desire* implies sensuality contradicted by romanticism and overrefinement (epitomized elsewhere by Camille, a Williams favorite). The Hispanic in *Summer and Smoke* contrasts spirituality with sensuality (exemplified by the passionate Rosa Gonzales). Williams does not resolve these contradictions but tries to understand the riddle of a culture by recognizing them.

The culture that most absorbs Williams, however, is a southern subculture (since the South comprises several cultures, including the black, his selection must be granted him): that of middle- and upper-class, composed of native whites in the Deep South, looking back to the plantation; it has dominated the entire South and with justification may be spoken of as constituting the main southern culture. Williams is ambivalent about it but leans toward reproof rather than approval. Its essential dichotomy is between gentility and violence. The first element is attractively portrayed in Amanda Wingfield of *The Glass Menagerie* and Blanche DuBois of *A Streetcar Named Desire.* The second, evident in such villains as Jabe Torrence of *Orpheus Descending* and Boss Finley of *Sweet Bird of Youth,* threatens the chivalric order of courtesy and kindness. The plays present the two elements in eternal conflict rather than reconciliation, thereby implying the divided nature of southern culture.

Williams's imaginative understanding of the dualistic southern culture comprehends its division not only into country and town, men and women, old and new, but into gentry and poor whites as well. His presentation of the last group (also present in the works of Erskine Caldwell and Flannery O'Connor) indicates that he shares the outlook of the gentry, evident in the Episcopalian ladies of *Orpheus Descending,* who describe the xenophobic men of Two River County as "the poorest kind of white trash."[2] Attributing to this clearly defined class such faults as bigotry toward blacks and foreigners, Williams condemns the prejudice of poor whites; by contrast he admires the chivalric values of the gentry.

T.S. Eliot says that "to understand the culture is to understand the people, and this means an imaginative understanding," not merely knowledge of particular manifestations such as economics.[3] Williams's imaginative understanding of the South is not spelled out discursively but implied symbolically. Like Faulkner, for example, he is very conscious of symbolic houses; his most comprehensive symbol of the South is the house, usually Victorian Gothic, rather than the familiar southern colonial. It has not been sufficiently noticed that Williams's settings center on a house of that style in *Summer and Smoke, Cat on a Hot Tin Roof, Suddenly Last Summer,* and *Sweet Bird of Youth,* thus linking his plays to the southern Gothic tradition. (Faulkner's story "A Rose for Emily" includes a similarly forbidding residence with symbolic overtones.)[4] Like Belle Reve, the lost plantation mansion in *A Streetcar Named Desire* and a patent reminder of the decadent Old South, the Victorian Gothic house reveals certain truths of southern life. The Victorian style suggests emotional repression.

Williams's house supplements Ibsen's concept of ghosts, for above all, the gabled, fantastically carved, secluded Gothic house connotes the ghosts of the ominous past. Secrets are kept hidden so that all seems well but is not. In the Gothic rectory of *Summer and Smoke* Mrs. Winemiller, the wife of the Episcopal rector, has regressed to infantilism. Southern Gothic has become known for implying eccentric personalities, mental abnormality, and the sexual repression caused by Puritanical or Victorian Christianity—all traits that arise in the Victorian Gothic houses of Williams's plays.

In this symbolism Williams is saying something about the class of people who *are* "the South" for him. The families are as doomed as the house in *This Property Is Condemned.* We must still ask why. The Victorian style of many houses suggests sexual prudery, repression caused by life-denying religion, particularly evident in the rectory of *Summer and Smoke:* Alma suppresses her natural sexuality and turns finally to license as compensation. Jacob H. Adler is mistaken in arguing that Alma makes a successful resolution of the conflict between body and soul; that she must still swallow tranquilizers to find sexual gratification indicates that Williams blames southern Victorianism for producing psychological misfits.[5] The blighting effect of strict religion is a root cause of southern decadence in his view, which he suggests in the style of his houses.

Williams's awareness of and liking for southern writers confirms that he was well acquainted with some leading literary analysts of southern culture. In 1939 he attended a performance of Lillian Hellman's *The Little Foxes.* That the play dramatized the conflict between the Old and the New South, and that it was written by a southern playwright and starred Tallulah Bankhead, a member of a prominent southern family impressed him greatly.[6] Not long afterward, in 1941, Williams expressed ardent admiration of several southern authors who had much to contribute to his understanding of the South. He wrote his literary agent, Audrey Wood, "Thanks for the clipping about Eudora Welty. She and Carson McCullers and Wm. Faulkner and Katherine Anne Porter have practically got a deep southern corner on the best imaginative writing in America."[7]

Williams's first and greatest plays such as *The Glass Menagerie* (1945) draw on one of the strongest traditions of southern culture: Agrarianism. It may seem unlikely that the cosmopolitan bohemian should uphold the conservative heritage, but that is surely the case. Williams's fondest memories of his early life came from his stay in Clarksdale, Mississippi, in the heart of the Delta, where his maternal grandparents, the Dakins, lived for many years. He spent considerable time with them, once even staying for a full year during a childhood sickness.[8] Yet here too he saw contradiction: Williams appreciated the fields and lush vegetation that surrounded the country town, while despising the ugly streets of its business district. In his mind, one side of the Sunflower River offered natural beauty; on the other, human vices proliferated.[9] His reaction to this setting and to St. Louis, which he detested, repeats the view of the Nashville Agrarians who published *I'll Take My Stand*. Not to be forgotten is the outlook of his ancestor, Sidney Lanier, an Agrarian who deplored the heartlessness of business in poems like "The Symphony." Williams acknowledged their kinship and cited two of Lanier's poems in an interview.[10]

The strong Agrarian bias in Williams's plays gives them much of their distinct southern flavor and undergirds the elegiac tone of Amanda and Blanche as they remember the plantation society of yore. *The Glass Menagerie,* the first long work in which Williams made full use of his southern experience, is his most Agrarian play. The Agrarian sentiment appears clearly in the description of the ugly urban surroundings of the Wingfield family. The tenement "is flanked on both sides by dark, narrow alleys which run into murky canyons of tangled clotheslines, garbage cans, and the sinister lattice-work of neighboring fire-escapes."[11] Amanda complains that a fire escape is no substitute for a front porch, and Tom hates the "celotex interior" and fluorescent tubes of the shoe warehouse (p. 290). In sharp contrast, Amanda recalls the blooming of jonquils in the Delta. She had planned to marry a planter and live on a large estate, but instead married a telephone salesman who "fell in love with long distances" (p. 278). In gratitude for the hospitality shown him, Jim O'Connor, the gentleman caller, toasts "the old South"—to Amanda's pleasure.[12] We must conclude that Williams shared her feeling.

In the introduction to *I'll Take My Stand,* John Crowe Ransom writes that the amenities of life, such as manners, suffer in a business-dominated society.[13] Williams often regrets the loss of good manners in the city. Amanda complains about the rudeness of northern Episcopalians at her church, and Jim's manners undergo a decided improvement under her tutelage.[14] Blanche DuBois, in *Streetcar*, distinguishes Mitch from Stanley because his manners make him "superior."[15]

A relentless satirist of capitalism, as shown later in the caricature of Lord Mulligan in *Camino Real* (1953), Williams ridicules the brashness of American business in *The Glass Menagerie*. Jim tells Laura how he will rise to the top, bragging "Knowledge—Zzzzp! Money—Zzzzp! Power!" (p. 329). Because Jim's dream—like Willy Loman's in *Death of a Salesman*—is business success, the anticapitalist Agrarian Williams can only recoil with scorn.

The Agrarian sentiment also pervades Williams's other plays with southern settings. In *A Streetcar Named Desire* Blanche misses the refined way of life at Belle Reve plantation; the crude atmosphere of Stanley's apartment provokes an uncomplimentary contrast between the Agrarian life of her family and the cramped urban existence of her sister. Implicitly contrasting the DuBois mansion with the Kowalskis' dilapidated quarters, Blanche asks her sister, "What are you doing in a place like this?" and then answers with disbelief: "Never, never, never in my worst dreams could I picture—Only Poe! Only Mr. Edgar Allan Poe!—could do it justice! Out there I suppose is the ghoul-haunted woodland of Weir!" (p. 20).

In *Summer and Smoke* (1948), which takes place in a Delta town based on Clarksdale, the beautiful sky and park differ from the depressing views of the dingy alley in *The Glass Menagerie*. The only play actually set in the country, however, is *Cat on a Hot Tin Roof* (1955), in which Big Daddy, proprietor of a plantation, dislikes the citified ways of his lawyer son, who is employed by a Memphis bank. In the country, he observes to his younger son, Brick, intolerant ideas do not spread as they do in the city. "One thing you can grow on a big place more important than cotton!—is *tolerance!*—I grown it."[16] Whether or not Big Daddy's implication that tolerance of homosexuality can grow in a rural environment is true, Williams pays a compliment to the country by having Big Daddy make it.

Big Daddy, who is crucial to an understanding of Williams's use of southern culture, embodies another vital tradition. Despite the lack of evidence that Williams read the humorists of the Old Southwest, Big Daddy surely emerged from the same milieu that produced Sut Lovingood, created by the Tennessee humorist George Washington Harris. Sut and Big Daddy have the same talent for exaggerated comparisons. Describing a youth who cannot wait to take a wife, Sut says he is "hot and es restless es a cockroach in a hot skillit."[17] When the hospital informed Big Daddy that his test for cancer was negative, he "breathed a sigh of relief about as powerful as the Vicksburg tornado" (p. 75). Like a "ring-tailed roarer" of Tennessee, Big Daddy boasts that his property is "the richest land this side of the valley Nile" (p. 82). In the revised last act of *Cat on a Hot Tin Roof,* his joke about a zoo elephant aroused by a neighboring female recalls the racy humor of Sut Lovingood. In short, Big Daddy continues the style of southwestern humor that has been a hallmark of writers from the state of Mississippi, such as Faulkner.

Although Williams hated his father in childhood and suffered greatly from C.C. Williams's ridicule of his effeminacy, he modeled characters after him and came to think better of him in later life.[18] He clearly recognized the dramatic possibilities of his colorful father. In *The Last of My Solid Gold Watches,* a one-act play composed around 1943, Mister Charlie Colton, like C.C. Williams, is a noted salesman of the Delta. Reaching the end of his career, this old-fashioned shoe salesman bemoans the new stress on smartness and the concomitant decline of quality. He laments the loss of that fine tradition of the South, good manners. What is more, he says, the cotton now growing in the Delta is not worth picking off the ground.[19]

Williams acknowledged that Big Daddy was modeled partly after his father, who had a great gift for such phrases as "nervous as a cat on a hot tin roof."[20] This gargantuan character showed that Williams could successfully portray a country man of the Old South, which for him was the era of his parents' youth—about the turn of the century. A poor white who succeeded in large-scale farming by his initiative and drive, Big Daddy seeks to perpetuate the Agrarian tradition through his favorite son Brick—not through Gooper, an unscrupulous lawyer from Memphis.[21]

Williams found another model for Big Daddy in Jordan Massee Sr., the father of his friend Jordan Massee Jr. He met this huge man clad in a white linen suit—whom his granddaughter had dubbed "Big Daddy"—on Sea Island, Georgia, in the summer of 1941. An enthralling raconteur, Massee delighted Williams with colorful expressions and anecdotes of plantation life "on the richest land this side of the Nile."[22] Here was rich material for the future dramatist to use when he developed the dominant figure in *Cat on a Hot Tin Roof.*

In addition to the Agrarian tradition originating with the country people, one must not forget Williams's imaginative re-creation of the small town, for that gets to the heart of his feeling about the South. The country-town division has been another southern dichotomy, as shown in *The Little Foxes,* and many of Williams's main characters—Blanche, Amanda, Alma, Maggie—are townspeople, having more in common with Faulkner's Compsons than his McCaslins. They exhibit their neuroses in town, like Welty's customers at the beauty parlor. What preoccupies Williams's townspeople, most conspicuously women, is personal anxiety, especially the old maid's terror. What will happen to the unpopular Laura, the nomadic Blanche, the painfully genteel Alma? This worry maddens Williams's women who, after a sheltered upbringing, live out their lives in small-town hells or reappear in big cities with the same psychological complexes, intensified by the demands of respectability and the model held before them of the conventional wife.

Not by accident, Williams's best icons of the South are women (who have often symbolized a whole culture, as did Joan of Arc and Marianne of France). Beginning with the heroines of Dixie, for a long time Woman symbolized the South, Man the North. Williams, who identified imaginatively with women, drew on this mythology. Women authors have imagined the best personifications of the South—Scarlett O'Hara and Hellman's Birdie Bagtry Hubbard—except for Tennessee Williams, the male author who, even better than Faulkner, recreated the glamorous but pathetic belle. His women are neurotic but always spunky, even heroic. There is magic in the sybillic words when Amanda, looking at the slipper of a new moon, tells her daughter to wish for "Happiness! Good fortune!" (p. 307).

Williams makes his most singular contribution to the development of southern drama by analyzing sexual maladjustment in the family. Paul Green had taken up sexual problems frankly, and Lillian Hellman treated a daughter's near incestuous relationship with her father in *Another Part of the Forest*, but it remained for Williams to bring the unspoken subject of sex out of the Victorian closet and to analyze in depth the origin of sexual problems and their ramifications. By doing so he pointed to a major cause of decadence not only among descendants of the Old South aristocracy but also among members of the New South class.

Williams's investigation into the sexual life of his characters must begin with the mother, for he indicts this towering figure of southern culture as the cause of much of the trouble. The prototypical figure is Amanda Wingfield, a lady of the Old South who, though transplanted to St. Louis, has deep roots in Blue Mountain, Mississippi. D.H. Lawrence's novels, which glorify sex, horrify this prudish Episcopalian; it is a subject that Christian adults don't discuss, she would say. Amanda, by sweeping sexuality under the rug, represents the response of the typical southern lady, which causes Williams to stress obsessively the power of sex.

The mother's repressive influence on the son becomes clear in the person of Big Mama, a formidable mother indeed, in *Cat on a Hot Tin Roof*. A typical southern mother with her bossy ways and attachment to her second and favorite son, in whom we see good evidence of the Oedipus complex, Big Mama pours out her affection on Brick after Big Daddy loses interest in her. Happily remembering the sight of him undressed, with near-incestuous love she smothers him with kisses, which he rejects. Brick's repressed homosexuality can be attributed to a possessive mother as much as to an uncommunicative father—a destructive combination. The Pollitts are decidedly not from the gentry, as the parents' grammar and the father's past as an overseer show, but in their parent-child relationship Williams discovers the same sexual maladjustments as among well-born southerners.

Violet Venable of *Suddenly Last Summer* (1958), yet another possessive southern mother, is a wealthy resident of New Orleans, the center of sophistication. Though urbane and seemingly not bothered by Amanda's Victorian strictness, Mrs. Venable will not recognize the homosexuality of her son. Having catered to Sebastian's every wish and caring nothing for her rich husband, she has spoiled this Oedipal son, indulged his desires, and even become his procuress of homosexual partners without ever admitting the truth; her sophistication only masks the old prudishness. Violet's refusal to face the reality of her son's homosexuality influences Sebastian's view of himself.

Along with the influence of parents on children, the impact of the southern background on the parents should be recognized. The Old South tradition accentuates the mother's gentility and idealism, which prevent a realistic view of sexual impulses. Williams loves the grace of the Old South and its manners, but he and others knew that many southern ladies, idealizing the past, withdrew into illusion and refused to face sexual realities.

That the prudish mother who is incompatible with the aggressive father generates the Oedipus complex—that is, the son's inordinate attachment to the mother and hatred of the father—stands out in Williams's treatments of the family. As his psychoanalyst said, the most important experiences of his patient's life occurred in childhood.[23] Williams's mother's possessiveness and his prolonged dependence on her during childhood illness gave him special insight into the Oedipus complex. Given his fondness for that favorite pastime of introspective southerners, family analysis, he ruminated on this experience in plays. Another variation of it can be seen in Mitch, the mama's boy of *A Streetcar Named Desire*.

Williams's hatred of his father influenced his seductive male characters, producing hostility but also a strong attraction. The longing to identify with the virile father produces such dark, sexually aggressive figures as Stanley Kowalski and Alvaro of *The Rose Tattoo* (1951). Like the characters of D.H. Lawrence, a major influence on Williams, these male figures

are sexually vigorous if intellectually deficient.[24] The ambivalent dramatist portrays them as physically attractive but also repellent. Often he makes
these characters nonsouthern, probably out of a belief that they are more
attractively seen as foreigners, different from his father and yet possessing some of the same masculine traits.

C.C. Williams's attitude toward his younger son, Dakin, throws light
on his unhappy relationship with the elder. Whereas the father rejected
Tom (Tennessee's family name) as effeminate, he accepted the second
son warmly. For C.C., Dakin was *his* son; Tom, the mama's boy. He took
the former to St. Louis Cardinal baseball games and slept in his room.[25]
Significantly, Dakin developed into a heterosexual male; his brother did
not. At the root of the tragic relationship between Tennessee Williams
and his father was the paternal refusal to accept and love him. On the
basis of such evidence, it is my conclusion that Williams's sexual orientation resulted primarily from this deep-seated conflict with his father.

Williams's most important relationship, next to that with his mother,
was with his sister Rose, a shy but highly sexed girl. The daughter of a
Victorian mother, she could not discipline her strong sexual feelings and
eventually suffered a mental breakdown. She is the model for many of
Williams's daughter characters. In Blanche, he epitomized the daughter
of an Old South family with its Victorian mores and refinement. She cannot forget the ideals of a lady but has the passions of an oversexed woman.
Guilt-ridden, she eventually becomes deranged, unable to reconcile the
demand of ladylike conduct with her actual behavior. Alma, in *Summer
and Smoke,* is a similar type, viewing sex only in spiritual terms as a result
of her strongly religious temperament and upbringing; it is no wonder
that John cannot turn to her for sexual pleasure. Unable to resolve her
inner conflict, Alma finally chooses sexual promiscuity.

In all these characterizations, Williams is saying something interesting about the southern family. He finds a common figure in the mother
who is Victorian in her attitude toward sex, refined in manners, and unrealistic regarding the past and present. Likewise, he typically portrays a
father who is uncompromisingly masculine in his tastes and uncommunicative with his son. Such couples produce a fateful division of personality in son and daughter. Although most certainly universalized, this
condition is reinforced by the legacy of the Old South, which is distinguished by feminine gentility and masculine roughness. The consequence
of these parental and social influences can be female frigidity or nym-
phomania and male homosexuality.

Williams's concentration on sexual behavior that diverges from the
social norm undoubtedly increased his popularity, but at the same time

it distorted southern life. His picture of the South as a land of sexual marvels or casualties provoked the same cries of foul as Erskine Caldwell's exposure of backwardness. Yet despite the deviant behavior found in *A Streetcar Named Desire, Suddenly Last Summer,* and *Sweet Bird of Youth,* audiences can relate to the characters because they share common emotions.[26] By portraying tormented, lonely souls barely surviving on the margins of society, Williams touches audiences at a deep emotional level, arousing their sympathy.

Coming at the end of World War II, *The Glass Menagerie* changed the direction of the American theater. In the preceding decade, documentary realism and the social protest of Odets had reigned, but Williams realized that he could initiate a different kind of drama. In a prophetic letter to Horton Foote in 1943 Williams observed that "a new theatre is coming after the war with a completely new criticism, thank God." With himself in mind, he wrote that "the singular figures always stand a good chance when there are sweeping changes."[27] In writing a new kind of play that focused on inner emotional drama, as seen in Blanche's struggle to keep her footing in a disintegrating life, he opened the way for that new theater—realized also by William Inge and Edward Albee, both admirers of Williams and analysts of the psyche.

Tennessee Williams's treatment of the South, underwent a marked change between his first plays and those of the 1950s. His view was ambivalent in the former, deploring the retreat from reality but admiring gallantry in the face of disappointment, as shown by Willie (a young version of Blanche) in *This Property is Condemned* (1946), an excellent one-act. His view of the South became much harsher in the late 1950s because of his reaction to the racial violence that followed the Supreme Court decision against segregated schools in 1954. Thereafter, in plays such as *Orpheus Descending* (1957), he presented a South riddled with racial prejudice. The political issue, southern resistance to racial change, increasingly consumed Williams's attention.

The decisive experience that precipitated his altered presentation of the South was his visit to Mississippi in late 1955 for Elia Kazan's filming of the screen play *Baby Doll* (1956). This Caldwellian depiction of bigoted poor whites who turn against an Italian intruder anticipates the finale of *Orpheus Descending.* Williams had at first told Kazan that he would not return to Mississippi because the South had ostracized him: "I left the South because of their attitude towards me. They don't approve of homosexuals, and I don't want to be insulted. I don't want my feelings hurt."[28] Nevertheless, he did go and observed the filming of his screen play in Benoit, near Clarksdale in the Delta.[29] At this time he was already working on *Orpheus Descending* and *Sweet Bird of Youth,* which both reveal his reaction to the racial crisis.

As part of the racial conflict that had erupted following the Supreme Court decision of 1954, massive resistance was organized in the Mississippi legislature, and White Citizens' Councils were practicing intimidation. Several killings occurred in 1955, the most notorious of which was the murder of Emmett Till, a black youth from Chicago, who proposed a date to a storeowner's wife in Money, Mississippi. After his mutilated body was found in the Tallahatchie River, an all-white jury in Sumner, Mississippi, acquitted Roy Bryant, husband of the woman, and another man on September 23, 1955. Despite a storm of protest led by the NAACP, the U.S. Department of Justice refused to enter the case, but later worldwide furor led the attorney general to draft the legislation that became the Civil Rights Act of 1957.[30] *Baby Doll* parallels details of the case, since the Italian's "wolf-whistle" at Baby Doll bears the same label as Emmett Till's whistle.[31]

Baby Doll, released as a film in 1956, is the first work by Williams to show clearly his changing view of the South. The main target of his criticism is prejudice against foreigners, specifically Italians, which reflect the author's interest in this nationality during the years when *A Rose Tattoo* was written and when he was touring Italy with his companion Frank Merlo. Originally, the movie was based on *27 Wagons Full of Cotton,* first published in 1946; in that comic one-act set in the Delta, strong prejudice exists against Vaccaro, the Italian, but the main conflict is between private farmers and the Syndicate Cotton Gin, a farmers' cooperative, reflecting Williams's previous support of New Deal experiments. In the film as released, however, the cuckolded husband Archie Lee has become older; material from another one-act called *The Unsatisfactory Supper* (1946) has been added, principally its appealing old maid, Aunt Rose Comfort; and prejudice rather than anticapitalism is the main subject. Because Archie Lee, a mechanic who aspires to aristocracy, wants no such foreigner as Vaccaro, manager of the Syndicate, intruding on his business, he torches its competing gin. In this revision of the earlier play, the Italian becomes a more sympathetic character. He again wins the affection of Baby Doll, Archie's immature wife, but is not sadistic and is especially kind to Aunt Rose Comfort, inviting her to come live in his house after Archie Lee banishes her. In short, *Baby Doll* shows Williams's shift from Democratic liberalism to outrage over the antiforeigner and racist atmosphere of the South.

The setting for *Orpheus Descending* (1957) is Two River County, a hotbed of racial violence. It is based on Clarksdale in Coahoma County, the residence for many years of Williams's beloved grandfather, the Episcopal rector Reverend Walter Edwin Dakin. The author uses this locale also for *Summer and Smoke, Cat on a Hot Tin Roof,* and *Kingdom of Earth* (1968), and his use of recurring characters, places, and incidents make it Williams's equivalent of Faulkner's Yoknapatawpha County. Appropriately named, Two River County, like Coahoma County, contains the Sunflower and Tallahatchie Rivers. The town of Glorious Hill, where *Summer and Smoke* takes place, is referred to repeatedly, and Moon Lake is a well-known landmark. Such characters as Dr. Buchanan, the Cutreres, and the Reverend Tooker are familiar personages, appearing in more than one play. In this microcosm of the Deep South, where Williams's sense of place is strongest, he is thoroughly familiar with its best and worst faces.

As can be shown by comparison with its first version, *Battle of Angels* (performed in 1940, published in 1945), subsequent events clearly influenced *Orpheus Descending;* Williams noted that 75 percent of the writing was new.[32] Additions to the later version include the prejudice against foreigners heard in anti-Semitic slurs, and references to such racial incidents as Bessie Smith's death outside a segregated hospital in Memphis and the execution of Willie McGee for allegedly raping a white woman in 1951 (a punishment Faulkner condemned in a public letter).[33] The Emmett Till case reemerges in the theme of sex envy, which James Baldwin considered the leading motive for the murder in his version of the Till case, *Blues for Mr. Charlie* (1964). In *Orpheus Descending* the envious husbands immolate Val because of his appeal to their sex-starved wives. Citing a county where the sun is not allowed to set on a Negro, Sheriff Talbott informs Val, who had admired his wife's painting, that he must be gone by sunup—but he is not allotted that much time. The hellishness of the racist South is conveyed by infernal imagery at the end as the blue flames of blowtorches illuminate the faces of Val's lynchers.

The other play that shows increasing condemnation of the South is *Sweet Bird of Youth,* which Williams worked on from 1955 until its New York production in 1959—writing, in all, eight versions.[34] This play about an aging actress develops further his picture of the South as an earthly hell and adds to his thinking on sex-envy as the underlying cause of racial tension. Set in the immediate present, it contains direct allusions to the integration crisis, incorporating the issue in the person of a segregationist politician. Boss Finley did not appear in the tryout of this play in Coral Gables, Florida, in 1956, and the demagogic comments against desegregation that filled the Boss's lines in the New York production were missing.[35] Probably the worsening situation caused Williams to add the racist politician and the issue of integration to the final version of the play.

Though some have rightly compared Boss Finley to Huey Long, who inspired Robert Penn Warren's Willie Stark of *All the King's Men*, the resemblance to Orval Faubus suggests a more contemporary model.[36] This well-known governor of Arkansas was the most prominent opponent of integration while Williams was composing the play; he appeared on television in September 1957, to oppose integration at Central High School in Little Rock. Like Faubus, who was born in the Ozarks and titled his autobiography *Down from the Hills* (1980), Boss Finley descended from the hills as a youth to enter politics, and he too denounces desegregation on television.[37] Boss Finley is also another character partly based on Williams's father, manifesting examples of the southwestern humor noted in Big Daddy. This time, however, the humor is cruel, reflecting one conspicuous strain of that style. Upon learning that his mistress has written on the mirror of the lady's restroom, "Boss Finley is too old to cut the mustard" (p. 68), this practical joker presents her with a diamond brooch in a fine case; when Miss Lucy reaches for the jewelry, he shuts the lid hard, leaving her fingers black and blue. His sadistic humor adds to the ugly portrayal of the southern politician.

Carrying further the analysis of sex-envy, Chance Wayne, former lover of Boss Finley's daughter, claims that those who have not enjoyed sexual pleasure have a "sick envy" of those who have (p. 54). When he hears of the castration performed on a Negro because he accosted a white woman, he dubs it "sex-envy" (p. 90), adding that he has been the victim of that envy himself. Finally, Chance is himself castrated by order of Boss Finley, who had announced earlier that the operation on "the unfortunate colored gentlemen" was done to protect the chastity of white women (p. 108).

Receiving their share of condemnation in the play are signs of religious faith which, Williams shows, are merely superficial. The town is named St. Cloud; "the Voice of God" has called Boss Finley to save the white women of the state; his daughter is named "Heavenly"; and the action takes place on Easter Sunday, yet no spiritual revival will occur as long as racial hatred prevails.[38] Only the aging actress, whose stay in St. Cloud has been nothing less than "hell," enjoys a temporary rebirth because of the success of her latest movie (p. 119).

The Night of the Iguana (1961), Williams's last great play, focuses on the religion of his region, which he knew from personal experience. Growing up as the grandson of an Episcopal rector in Columbus, Mississippi, Williams attended the Reverend Dakin's services regularly. He heard and probably read some of his grandfather's sermons;[39] accompanied his grandfather when he called on parishioners in Clarksdale; and was deeply concerned with religious questions all his life, converting to Roman Catholicism in 1969 at the urging of his brother, Dakin.

Many southern authors have expressed their usually heretical thoughts about religion in their works. Mark Twain satirized the Protestant Christianity of his day, attacking hypocrisy and emotional religion in *Huckleberry Finn*. In the twentieth century—despite Flannery O'Connor's southern advocacy of Christian faith—the prevalent approach to religion has remained critical, often censorious. Faulkner, no admirer of fundamentalist Christianity, denounces rigid Presbyterianism in *Light in August*, in which the hero, Joe Christmas, repudiates the rigid and life-denying creed of his foster father. The leading southern authors of Williams's era, not to mention such other American authors as Hemingway and O'Neill, have roundly satirized and often denounced Christianity.

Williams, likewise, had earlier satirized representatives of the organized church: the Reverend Winemiller of *Summer and Smoke*, who suppresses the natural desires of his wife and daughter; the Reverend Tooker of *Cat on a Hot Tin Roof*, whose primary goal is to obtain contributions for stained glass windows in his church. In *The Night of the Iguana* Williams ridicules a group of teetotaling, querulous teachers from a Baptist Female College in Texas, whose overbearing leader, Miss Fellowes, attempts to preserve the virginity of one young woman.

The imaginative depiction of religion in Williams's South is relentlessly negative and grows harsher. Professing Christians among his characters are on the whole repulsive—with a few notable exceptions such as Vee Talbot, the devout wife of the sheriff in *Orpheus Descending*, who reprimands the immoral women of Two River County, and the lovable Aunt Rose Comfort, who sings "Rock of Ages" at the end of *Baby Doll*. In *Suddenly Last Summer* (1959) the central character, Sebastian Venable, searches for answers to his religious questions. He wishes to discover God and believes he has done so on his voyage to the Encantadas: when he observes a flock of predatory birds that swoop down on hatched sea turtles and devour them before they can reach the water, Sebastian announces: "Well, now I've seen Him!" His mother adds, in unequivocal words, "and he meant God."[40] Thus Williams repudiates the traditional image of a God of Love by picturing a cruel, annihilating deity, preparing the way for a similar vision of God in *The Night of the Iguana*—which goes on to replace traditional Christian doctrine with a humanistic ethic. In short, Williams finally rejects the traditional Christianity that was his legacy as a small-town southerner reared in the church.

The author makes religious belief the central theme of *The Night of the Iguana* and gives his clearest answer to the classic query of theologians: "What is the nature of God?" Before being dismissed from his pastorate, T. Lawrence Shannon, who holds a Doctor of Divinity degree from the University of the South (also the Reverend Dakin's alma mater), delivered a fiery sermon to the Episcopal parishioners of Pleasant Valley, Virginia, in which he told them they were wrong to believe that God was a "senile delinquent" who petulantly punished human beings "for his own faults in construction" (p. 60). This defrocked priest, one of Williams's best male characters, believes in a "God of Lightning and Thunder, . . . His oblivious majesty," who ignores the suffering of earthly creatures. Consequently, Shannon feels that it is incumbent on him to do God's work himself. He extricates himself from the ropes wrapped around him, freeing himself from the tortures of his self-imposed guilt, and goes on to cut the rope holding the suffering iguana. He explains to Hannah that he will "cut the damn lizard loose," since "God won't do it and we are going to play God here." Because God shows himself in the lightning and thunder but not in rescuing the suffering creatures of the earth, "we'll play God tonight like kids play house with old broken crates and boxes" (p. 123). After this decisive action Shannon stops persecuting himself, decides not to take the long swim to China, and commences a new life with his willing partner, the voluptuous Widow Faulk.

In the process of replacing traditional Christianity with a secular morality, Shannon listens gladly to Hannah Jelkes and her saintly father, whose beliefs will constitute his philosophy of life, or new religion. Hannah sympathizes with Shannon's suffering at the hands of his "spook," which she likens to her "blue-devil" (that is, the cause of depression, or blues), and tells him that the way to overcome it is just to endure its attacks with the help of poppyseed tea or other "tricks that panicky people use to outwit and outlast their panic" (p. 167). Realizing that Shannon sorely needs something to hold on to, she tells him, "I've discovered something to believe in." It is not God but "broken gates between people so they can reach each other, even if it's just for one night only." In "communication" between two people like herself and Shannon, "on a verandah outside their . . . separate cubicles," there will be "a little understanding. exchanged between them, a wanting to help each other through nights like this" (p. 107).

Shannon also receives welcome guidance from the old poet Nonno, Hannah's ninety-seven-year-old father, who is based on Williams's kindly grandfather. Delivering his last poem just before he dies, Nonno apostrophizes the human but very precious virtue of courage, a quality that Shannon badly needs to fortify his shattered life:

> O Courage could you not as well
> Select a second place to dwell,
> Not only in that golden tree,
> But in the frightened heart of me?
>
> [p. 124]

Shannon, the spokesman for Williams, having abandoned the Christian doctrine he has found insufficient, constructs in its stead a wholly humanistic ethic.

It is interesting to speculate why Williams enjoyed so much more success in the New York theater than most other southern dramatists. One striking difference is his continuing collaboration with key people in the theatrical world. Williams was particularly fortunate early on to work with Elia Kazan, who directed *A Streetcar Named Desire, Sweet Bird of Youth,* and *Cat on a Hot Tin Roof.* For the last, this shrewd critic persuaded Williams to compose a new ending that made the play more successful. By contrast, Paul Green, who argued with Harold Clurman about *The House of Connelly* and accepted an optimistic ending very reluctantly, never formed a lasting bond with a theatrical mentor. Williams's sustained collaboration with a perceptive director gave him an edge, on Broadway and abroad.

Williams also benefited from the performances of stage stars who fit the parts remarkably and brought his characters to life—Laurette Taylor as Amanda, Marlon Brando as Stanley, Jessica Tandy as Blanche, Burl Ives as Big Daddy—and screen stars who expanded the fame of his characters: Vivien Leigh as Blanche, and Anna Magnani as Rosa Delle Rose in *The Rose Tattoo.* The cast for the film of *The Night of the Iguana* was especially outstanding. Richard Burton displayed his brilliant talents in Shannon's tormented howlings; Ava Gardner, as the Widow Faulk, found a perfect vehicle for her vampish kindness; and Deborah Kerr was superb as Hannah, the serene survivor of a tortuous life. When she presents Shannon the soothing poppyseed tea, we can indeed believe that her grace will calm that savage beast.

It is generally agreed that Amanda and Blanche, archetypes of the southern belle in unique form, are Williams's best creations. Big Daddy has not received comparable acclaim, even though he looms solitary, like Faulkner's bear, and dominates his play as much as Amanda and Blanche do theirs. I would argue that Williams's supreme male creation is Big Daddy, who possesses the raw power of the playwright's living father; with this character Williams put the seal of artistic genius on the southern play once again. Modernizing the archetype of the southwestern humorist—thereby recalling Sut Lovingood and, yes, Mark Twain—he carved a colossus. Big Daddy's language (country southern to the core) and his contrasting traits (cruelty balanced by kindness) make him endlessly interesting. Transmuting the rich lode of southwestern humor, Williams constructed a character equal to the best in American drama and gave an imaginative glimpse into the man's world of southern culture, complementing the portrait of the genteel, feminine side of southern life for which he is justly famous.

Big Daddy's colorful language finds its best expression in remarks about his wife, Big Mama, who, like Falstaff, is the cause of much jocularity. His outbursts occur sometimes in her presence, sometimes in her absence. When Big Mama pulls the Reverend Tooker into her lap, Big Daddy roars, "Big Mama, will you quit horsin'? You're too old an' too fat fo' that sort of crazy kid stuff" (p. 51). He rebukes his wife for taking over the household because he is presumably dying: "Didn't you have an idea I was dying of cancer and now you could take control of this place and everything on it? I got that impression, I seemed to get that impression. Your loud voice everywhere, your fat ol' body butting in here and there!" (p. 57). He laughs the eldritch laugh for which his creator was famous when Big Mama exits: "Why when Big Mama goes out of a room, I can't remember what that woman looks like, but when that woman comes back into the room, boy, then I see what she looks like and I wish I didn't" (p. 70).

Though Big Mama's genuine love for her husband is made even more moving by Big Daddy's satiety, one cannot help laughing at the following exchange. Big Mama asks, "Sweetheart? Big Daddy? You didn't mean those awful things you said to me?" After she departs with a sob in her voice, Big Daddy says to Brick: "All I ask of that woman is that she leave me alone. But she can't admit to herself that she makes me sick. That comes of having slept with her too many years. Should of quit much sooner but that old woman she never got enough of it" (p. 72). And again, "I haven't been able to stand the sight, sound, or smell of that woman for forty years now!—even when I *laid* her!—regular as a piston" (p. 80). His diatribes are outrageous but ludicrous, accentuating the pungency of his bombast.

How do southern elements contribute to Williams's achievement as a dramatist? In what way does it matter that he came from the South? Above all, it matters because this feisty man's quarrel with the South produced much of the nervous tension in his plays. If Melville, who fascinated Williams, had a quarrel with God that never ended, Williams had one with the place of his birth for as long a time. Without doubt, Williams loved but also hated the South—as Quentin did in Faulkner's *Absalom, Absalom!*— while protesting petulantly that he did not. This ambivalence stimulated his cultural imagination, leading him to express in southern characters and houses his indignation at southern sexual, religious, and racial narrowness.

Williams's quarrel with the South during the first part of his career consists of complaints about the inner qualities of southerners. He lambasts its ladies' Victorianism and flight to the past, traits seen best in Amanda. Such women wreck the lives of their children, not to mention their own. Blanche and Alma have divided personalities: they are drawn to sexual promiscuity but stunted by the southern lady's code of propriety. In faulting these wellbred southerners, Williams undercuts the favorable impression they may have made on the audience. The resulting ambivalence prevents close identification and increases Bertolt Brecht's "alienation effect."

In the second half of his series of southern plays, Williams's quarrel with the South turns outward. Rightly considered a dramatist of inner character conflict, Williams is not at his best in judging the larger society. All the same, his indignant tone of protest from the mid-fifties on galvanized his later plays. Having known ostracism in the South himself, he could speak from personal experience as well as social consciousness. Now he quarreled with the prejudice against foreigners and intensified the manifestations of violence in his plays—the burning of the "Wop's" orchard in *Orpheus Descending* and the castration of Chance Wayne in *Sweet Bird of Youth* are only two—thus earning a reputation for sensationalism. It is true that when Williams's indictment of the South reached fever pitch, character subtlety suffered, as can be seen in the bigoted and one-dimensional husbands and wives of *Orpheus Descending*. Unlike his mildly critical portrait of Big Daddy, his depiction of a father from the later period reveals no worthy qualities whatsoever. Boss Finley, based on well-known personalities in the racial conflict, is a stereotypically demagogic politician; Williams lets him convict himself when he excuses castration of a black man.

Without this unceasing quarrel with the South, nevertheless, Williams's plays would lack their durable passion and drive. Perhaps the last stage of his quarrel got out of hand, but that too is the Tennessee Williams the world keeps watching.

—12—
Past and Present Cultures in Recent Drama

The emergence of important dramatists in the years following the success of Tennessee Williams attests to the continuing vitality of southern drama. Horton Foote, Beth Henley, Marsha Norman, Preston Jones, and Romulus Linney have composed a substantial number of plays, carved out distinct places for themselves in the American theater, and added to the achievement of southern dramatists. All of them reveal the impact of the great writers of the Southern Literary Renascence, especially Faulkner, Williams, Welty, and O'Connor.

After the great plays of Williams and the vigorous civil rights drama written by blacks in the 1960s, southern drama entered a different phase. The former conflicts of blacks versus whites, Old versus New South, and gentry versus poor whites which had given southern drama much of its power had dissipated. Political issues attracted dramatists less, because with civil rights legislation the racial issue lost immediacy. Beginning with the works of Tennessee Williams, it became evident that southern drama was paying less attention to race questions and more to inner emotions. The southern play, no longer distinguished by its protest against racial injustice (as it had been since the plays of Paul Green), shifted its focus to cultural subjects: the transition from country to urban life, generational disagreements—real questions troubling modern southerners.

In plays of the post–Tennessee Williams or postmodern era, then, one finds incisive views of both past and present cultures. For a long time southerners have looked to the past in order to understand the present, and southern dramatists are still doing so. Reinterpretations of the past accompany assessments of change in the contemporary South.

Covering past as well as present cultures, Horton Foote (1916-) is the most significant dramatist to follow Tennessee Williams. Representative of the western South, he hails from Gulf Coast Texas, the area around Houston, where a little known subculture suffers from oil fever—unknown

192

in the eastern South. Foote was born and grew up in Wharton, Texas, which he calls "Harrison" in all his plays. He studied in Hollywood and acted in New York, then turned to playwriting. After gaining financial security with the film script of *To Kill a Mockingbird* (1962) and other movies, he withdrew to the woods of New Hampshire from 1974 to 1977 and there completed his most ambitious undertaking: *The Orphans' Home Cycle,* a saga of nine plays. During his long career Foote has continually returned to Wharton, where he may often be found at the cemetery, according to one friend. Foote agrees, joking that he knows "more people [there] than I know alive."[1] Foote has a highly developed sense of place, even for a southern writer. Virtually all his plays are set in "Harrison, Texas," his counterpart of the county created by Faulkner, whom he admires.

Born on March 14, 1916, the son of Albert Horton and Hallie Brooks Foote, Horton graduated from high school in 1932. He studied acting at the Pasadena Playhouse School Theater in California, 1933-35, and at the Tamara Daykarhanova School Theater in New York City, 1937-39; he performed in New York, 1936-42, and began to write plays, many of which have been produced by the Herbert Berghoff Foundation of New York. In 1945 Foote married Lillian Vallish, who died in 1992. One daughter, Hallie, has acted in several of her father's plays.[2] Foote won the Pulitzer Prize for drama in 1995 for his intriguing *The Young Man from Atlanta,* premiered in New York in 1955 by the Signature Theatre Company and performed in Chicago and on Broadway in 1997. His latest plays include a modern parallel to Greek tragedy, *The Habitation of Dragons,* first performed in 1988 and shown on Turner Network Television on September 8, 1992.[3]

Formative in Foote's development as a dramatist was his association with the American Actors Company from 1938 to 1944 in New York. This vigorous organization worked to exploit the geographical diversity of the country by dramatizing the culture of particular regions, a purpose with strong appeal for Foote. Besides plays by Foote, the company performed new works by Paul Green, Thornton Wilder, Tennessee Williams, and Lynn Riggs (author of *Green Grow the Lilacs,* set in the western plains). Calling the company "a rare, stimulating group," Curtis Pepper recognized its central objective in the *New York World-Telegram:* "They breathe American in appearance. . . . The actors have scored again in frankly presenting a play of the American scene with force and charm."[4]

Foote has frequently expressed opinions that reveal his southern background and throw light on the themes of his plays. He once objected to deleting the southern accent from a Dallas radio announcer's pronunciation.[5] Discussing his movie about a country music star, *Tender Mercies*

(1983), he acknowledged that like most of his fellow Texans he is a fan of country music; the film captures the popularity of this sound, which launched a new life-style in the South. Commenting on cemeteries in New York City, he has deplored their impersonality; when someone dies in Wharton, he says, people recall personal experiences connected with the deceased.[6]

Foote's frequent and important contacts with other southern authors have provided a firm basis for their influence on his work. He currently belongs to the Fellowship of Southern Writers and regularly attends its biennial meetings in Chattanooga, Tennessee. In 1944 Tennessee Williams allowed him to direct the last section of *The Glass Menagerie*, titled "The Gentleman Caller," at the Neighborhood Playhouse in New York before the play's premiere in Chicago.[7] Foote adapted Faulkner's short story "Tomorrow," which was produced by the Herbert Berghoff Foundation in 1968, and wrote television adaptations of O'Connor's "The Displaced Person" (1977) and Faulkner's "Barn Burning" (1980) for the Public Broadcasting System. His movie adaptation of Harper Lee's *To Kill a Mockingbird* (1962) won the Academy Award, and his musical version of *Gone with the Wind* was staged in London in 1971. Foote was a good friend of Stark Young, a Mississippi-born theater critic who encouraged him to compose *The Orphans' Home Cycle* and wrote the foreword to *The Traveling Lady* (1955).

As Foote has indicated in interviews, he is indebted to Eudora Welty, Katherine Anne Porter, and Chekhov, a recurring influence on southern dramatists.[8] He is the first dramatist in this study to show a consistent awareness of the southern literary tradition, including the work of dramatists, signifying the maturity of southern drama. He admires and clearly borrows from Faulkner, Porter, Welty, O'Connor, Reynolds Price, Peter Taylor, Erskine Caldwell, and Tennessee Williams. Discussing dialogue, Foote says that his "sense of music" is close to that of Welty, Porter, and O'Connor.[9] Of Tennessee Williams's works, his choice is *The Glass Menagerie*.[10]

Foote's affinity with Katherine Anne Porter, a fellow Texan, is particularly important. He began reading Porter just as he was concluding that Paul Green was such a regionalist that it limited his style; Green's quaint plays in the vernacular seemed to be saying, "Look how different we are." Foote's clear link with Thornton Wilder's picture of the American small town gives his plays an all-American quality, lacking in Green's very localized settings in North Carolina. Choosing not to be a regionalist like Green, Foote decided to go in Porter's direction.[11] Presumably he found Porter more American and her writings free of distracting local color (in fact her fiction of Central Texas is only intermittently southern).

Porter's extensive Miranda series in *The Leaning Tower and Other Stories* (1944) and *Pale Horse, Pale Rider* (1949) forms a striking parallel to Foote's saga in *The Orphans' Home Cycle.* Porter begins with the grandmother of Miranda before the Civil War. Next she comes to Miranda's childhood, showing her discovery of and initiation into the world. In "The Grave," Miranda as a girl learns existentially that everyone is doomed to death, but not only that: it is important how one thinks of the inevitable event. In his cycle, Foote too presents characters, such as Horace Robedaux, who come to terms with death. In 1918, a play about the flu epidemic of World War I (the subject of Porter's *Pale Horse, Pale Rider*), Horace endures his daughter's death with the support of his wife's love. Porter's short novel follows Miranda through the death of her first love. Although Foote's series is less autobiographical (the leading character, Horace, is based on his father, rather than himself), both trace the history of a family. The nine plays of *The Orphans' Home Cycle* may be divided under the labels "Youth," the first four plays, about Horace's early years: *Roots in a Parched Ground, Convicts, Lily Dale, The Widow Claire;* "Marriage," three plays about Horace's subsequent life: *Courtship, Valentine's Day, 1918;* and "Death," two plays about Horace's many kinfolks and the death of his maternal grandfather, a leading citizen of Harrison: *Cousins, The Death of Papa.*

Porter's philosophy of writing also throws light on Foote's outlook. Discussing the reason for her writing, she noted that though we seem to find order in the universe—in the movement of stars, even in the cycle of human life—we do not find it in the midst of living: we do not know what will happen to us, or why. The single value of the artist is to put the disparate elements of life "in a frame to give them some kind of shape and meaning."[12] Foote has stated similarly that what interests him about life in Wharton—and his family has been there for seven generations—is trying to bring "order out of disorder," seeing "the patterns in people."[13] In other words he is fascinated by "the twists and turns of life."[14] Wondering why some people survive and others do not, he concludes that the fortifying qualities include courage, love between husband and wife, and the creation of a lasting, happy home.

A reading of Foote's plays brings to mind many writers of the southern literary tradition and shows their pervasive influence. The one-act *Blind Date* (1982) may be read as a hilarious takeoff on *The Glass Menagerie.* The genteel aunt instructs her un-Laura-like niece Sarah Nancy in how to be gracious and a good conversationalist when Felix, son of a woman known to the girl's mother, arrives. Totally frank, Sarah Nancy tells him he cannot sing a note, and the evening seems ruined until Felix speaks with equal frankness about her plain looks. Thereafter, the two sit comfortably reading old yearbooks. In its recurring characters *The Orphans' Home Cycle* echoes Faulkner's saga of Yoknapatawpha County. India, the bitter spinster of the one-act *Road to the Graveyard* (1985) is reminiscent of Sister in Welty's "Why I Live at the P.O." The contrast between those who survive the toils of life and those who succumb anticipates Robert Drake's West Tennesseeans in *Survivors and Others* (1987). The talk of Bertie Dee and Lenora in Foote's *The Land of the Astronauts* (1983) is similar to Lee Smith's dialogue in the stories of *Cakewalk* (collected in 1983).[15]

Foote's best play is *The Trip to Bountiful*, which captures imaginatively the universal desire to return home. First produced on the Philco Television Playhouse in 1953, it transferred the same year to Broadway with Lillian Gish in the leading role. In 1985 Geraldine Page won the Academy Award for best actress as Mrs. Watts in the excellent film version. Emerging from the Golden Age of television, when rising playwrights such as Paddy Chayefsky dramatized the ordinary situations of life realistically on the small screen, Foote's play goes beyond the "small" television play by taking up larger themes that give it universality: the desire to return to one's childhood home and the harrowing move from country to city in modern times. It is arguably the best play to have made the transition from television to the stage.[16]

The Trip to Bountiful, set in the present, sharply contrasts a way of life in the past with a much less attractive existence in the modern world. The central character, Mrs. Carrie Watts, finds in her abandoned country home the strength missing in the big city of Houston. Returning to the fields where she did farm work, seeing the birds and smelling the Gulf, she regains her strength. "It's so eternally quiet. I had forgotten the peace. The quiet. And it's given me strength once more," she tells her son. "To go on and do what I have to do. I've found my dignity and strength" (p. 64). The satisfaction of belonging—to a house, family, a town—is what she has missed in the big city.

In a relevant article titled "The Trip to Paradise," Foote gives a clue to the larger meaning of the abandoned town of Bountiful: as a boy, visiting the ghost towns of Texas with his grandparents, he always questioned why one town declined and another flourished. He recalls Frost's poem "Directive," in which a modern traveler discovers the values of an earlier time in "a town that is no more a town."[17] He is glad to have seen a photograph collection preserving views of forgotten towns with names like

"Sublime" and "Paradise." Bountiful, which grants blessings bountifully, is also a paradise for Mrs. Watts.

Though possessing little education and having done physical labor all her life, Carrie Watts is a lady through and through. She is not the southern lady of the Delta, like Amanda, who reenacts the old-time belle entertaining a gentleman caller, but rather a hymn-singing country lady who is genuinely kind to all. Back in Bountiful she assumes the teacher's role—as Shaw's Candida does for Marchbanks—with her troubled son Ludie, one of Foote's defeated men who regains his moral strength as Mrs. Watts recalls the example of his grandfather. Observing the tragic lives of men who failed to make the change from agrarian to urban life in the South, Foote featured them in many plays.[18]

Providing the indispensable comic relief to the serious themes is Ludie's shrewish but unconsciously humorous wife, whose grating voice sounds shrilly throughout. Jessie Mae is a version of the silly, gabby southern woman seen in the beauty parlor customers of Welty's story "The Petrified Man," speaking authentic "Southernese." Foote remarks that Jessie Mae has been done many times in southern fiction, "but you have to cut through all of that somehow." Such a type "endures."[19] She may with justice be called the archetypal southern woman as flibbertigibbet; she epitomizes the idle wife whose most important decision of the day is which of two movies she will attend. Her shallow, rootless existence brings neither her nor her long-suffering husband contentment. Indeed, her constant thirst for Coca-Cola is symptomatic of the infinite desires of her life which cannot be sated, thus leaving her nervously unfulfilled. Impatient to leave Bountiful, she cannot wait to stop by the drugstore in Harrison: "I'm so thirsty I could drink ten Coca-Colas" (p. 67). Preoccupied with having enough money to satisfy her own selfish wishes, Jessie Mae keeps her mother-in-law in the cramped city apartment for one reason: her monthly pension check. Ludie and Mrs. Watts do everything to satisfy her personal demands, but to no avail. In Bountiful this confirmed urbanite finds none of the spiritual nourishment so precious to Mrs. Watts and her son.

The Trip to Bountiful movingly expresses the sentiment of Agrarianism, which links Foote to a temperamental bent widely shared among southerners and perhaps most familiar in the essays and poems of the Nashville Agrarians. Foote, however, does not present an attack on heartless industry such as Robert E. Lee's diatribe in Paul Green's *The Confederacy*. His complaint is more akin to Tennessee Williams's disapproval of the ugly city in *The Glass Menagerie:* the Watts family too occupies a cramped apartment with cars screeching outside. The climax of the play is the return to the country dwelling of Carrie Watts, where she regains her moral strength.

With this play, Foote clearly aligned himself with those American writers who find their greatest values in the past. In that respect he belongs with Thornton Wilder, Frost, and Faulkner, rather than with authors like Hemingway. Foote, who abhors such aspects of modernity as rootlessness, finds answers not in radical revolt from former behavior, as Tennessee Williams does, but rather in a revival of traditional beliefs. By adopting this frame of values, Foote alienates those who favor discontinuity with the past, as do many New York theater critics.

The Orphans' Home Cycle the sequence of nine plays, that Foote wrote from 1974 to 1978, is held together by the life of Horace Robedaux of Harrison, Texas, and based on Foote's own father's life in Wharton. Ignoring the demands of the commercial media, Foote wrote in the tradition of O'Neill's massive trilogy, *Mourning Becomes Electra*. The middle three plays of the cycle have been produced as a television movie, "Story of a Marriage." The first, *Courtship*, with its self-contained plot and anti-patriarchal outlook, seems best suited for one evening's performance today.

The Orphans' Home Cycle is the best and fullest recreation of the southern past by a recent dramatist. Foote's chronicle reaches from the turn of the century to 1926, but the memories of its characters go back to pre-Civil War times in Texas. Foote offers an original perspective on the traumatic change from agricultural to town life that the South experienced, since he pictures that transition in Gulf Coast Texas, the part of the state most like the plantation South.

The second play, *Convicts*, offers a notably different interpretation of the Old South in the characterization of Soll Gauthier, owner of a plantation worked by black convicts who seem little different from slaves. Foote shows skill in creating original characters; he invented this old man, from whole cloth.[20] Emblematic of the Confederate South and showing its losing grip, Soll holds on to the former ways doggedly if ludicrously. He keeps his plantation going only by the use of forced labor, but having killed a convict, this solitary old man lives in constant fear that the convict is in the closet preparing to kill him. Climbing into his coffin at the end, the old Confederate dies and thus finally releases his grip, both literally and figuratively, on Horace, the young hero, whose friendship with one of the convicts forecasts a better day.

With the self-centered Lily Dale, Horace's sister, Foote comes closest to his predecessor Tennessee Williams in the sensitive probing of a neurotic woman. We understand her fully by the end of the cycle, for besides seeing her as a character in *Roots in a Parched Ground, Lily Dale*, and *Cous-*

ins, we get occasional information about her in the other plays. Lily Dale, unlike her brother, is given all the advantages needed to ensure happiness; her stepfather dotes on her to the total neglect of Horace. Yet ironically, Horace achieves a fulfilling life that contrasts with the spiritual death of his immature sister, who suffers from Victorian prudery and dependence on her mother. Horace experiences the consequences of parental neglect but rises above them; his sister is virtually smothered with support but finds no happiness.

In the play *Lily Dale,* Horace remembers the bad as well as the good in his family's past and learns from facing that truth. Lily Dale prefers to remember only the good times and reprimands her brother: "I want my children to know about happy times, pleasant things. I don't want to tell them about drunkards and dying and not having enough to eat. And I want you to quit talking to me about it. Every time I feel the least bit good you begin on all that."[21] Lily Dale's refusal to face the dark side of the past forecasts accurately her unrealistic flight from whatever painful realities may occur in the future.

In *Cousins,* which takes place after World War I, Foote satirizes the highly vaunted but vanishing southern traditions of close kinship. Cousin Lewis shows no manners toward his kin, and Cousins Lola and Marty backbite their relatives. But Foote offers hope in the humaneness of his hero, Horace Robedaux, a southerner who will practice kindness to others, whether black or white.

Foote returns to his procession of defeated men begun in earlier plays in the last part of the cycle. Henry Vaughn, the petulant brother of Horace's wife, appears in *Valentine's Day, 1918,* and *The Death of Papa.* Failing to succeed like his father, "Brother"—played strikingly by Matthew Broderick in the television "Story of a Marriage"—illustrates the classic family conflict of authoritarian father and son which ends unhappily. In *1918* the father, a prominent businessman of Harrison, reprimands Brother for his bad habits of drinking and gambling. When he hears that Brother has flunked out of Texas A & M, Mr. Vaughn says in the presence of his son and others, "His record in school is a record of failure."[22] Wanting to make a lot of money, Brother is a young man sorely disappointed with himself. In *The Death of Papa* he mismanages his inheritance and looks to oil, not cotton, as the panacea—a fatal sign, to Foote's way of thinking.

In studying the etiology of failed lives, Foote does not underestimate the essential of character. Horace tells his mother-in-law, Mrs. Vaughn, how he overcame his bad habit of gambling—as Brother has not—saying, "I just did. I loved Elizabeth and I did" (p. 191). The contrast between Brother and Horace is illuminating. Brother suffers from the lack of a fortifying individual, like Elizabeth in Horace's life, and his father intensifies his inferiority complex. His mother, instead of letting him suffer the consequences of his mistakes, bails him out of one business failure after another. Foote's full-length portrayal of Brother shows a signal case of a nonsurvivor in the small town. Here as elsewhere in the cycle, his vision is desolate when the realities of past life foreshadow a bleak continuation of the present. *The Death of Papa* concludes this saga of the South with the passing of Horace's grandfather, a New South businessman of civic spirit; the commercial South that will begin the next year, in 1927, is heralded by the coming of talking pictures—the announcement of modern times in Harrison, Texas.

Following his composition of *The Orphans' Home Cycle*, Foote entered another stage of playwriting. His one-acts of the 1980s were produced in small theaters such as the Loft Studio in Los Angeles and off-off Broadway venues such as the Ensemble Studio Theatre in New York. That none has transferred to television or the movies may indicate Foote's commitment to serious rather than commercial drama. Reinforcing this trend, he began the shift to independent production of his own plays in 1985 with the filming of the antiwar *1918*.

In the plays of the 1980s Foote's deteriorating heroes reach their lowest point. Pervaded by a sense of the absurd, these one-acts dramatize chaotic lives with little or no hope for peace and order (significantly, Foote admires the plays of those morose existentialists Samuel Beckett and Jean-Paul Sartre, especially the latter's *No Exit*).[23] Two of them, *The Man Who Climbed the Pecan Trees* (1982) and *The Road to the Graveyard* (1985), present defeated men whose possessive mothers frustrate their attempts to mature. A mood of anxiety and dread hangs over these plays, both of which take place appropriately on the eve of World War II, with its air of impending doom. In reviews, critics use the terms "Southern Gothic" and "Texas Gothic" to describe the haunting settings and hysterical characters.[24]

The Road to the Graveyard, presented at the Ensemble Studio Theatre in New York, earned the enthusiastic praise of Frank Rich, influential critic of the *New York Times,* who wrote four very favorable reviews of plays by Foote in 1985 and 1986. This perceptive reviewer is not put off by the depictions of small-town life (as was Brooks Atkinson, an early admirer of Foote but one whose dismissive judgments in the 1950s are in need of correction). Calling this play "overpowering," Rich writes that on the surface it seems like vintage *Saturday Evening Post,* but beneath there is an "unbearable turbulence." Although Foote has been writing about a changing Texas for decades, this "may be among the finest distillations of his concerns." The dramatist looks back at a world whose "idyllic glow belies all manner of unacknowledged neuroses and sexual and economic injustices."[25] Rich later singled out this play as a sign of the vibrancy of the theater in 1985, declaring that it created "a magnetic field of anxiety" almost "suffocating in its intensity."[26] Here to be sure is a retort to the charge made by Brooks Atkinson that Foote's plays lack dramatic force (*New York Times*, 4 November 1953).

Foote's most perceptive analysis of contemporary culture brings his defeated men up to the present in *The Land of the Astronauts*, a long one-act produced at the Ensemble Studio Theatre in 1988. In this amusing view of life in the Space Age, the dramatist portrays a would-be astronaut living in the year 1983. Phil Massey has become fascinated with the astronauts, especially Alan Shepard, who said "Hi" to him on one occasion. In order to fulfill his desire to fly off into space, he finishes his high school education, quits his café job, and goes to Houston, leaving his wife and daughter in their motel room. He seeks paradise in the faraway, neglecting the more realistic chance for happiness near at hand. Phil is another of Foote's displaced young men, a casualty of changing times. Like Ludie Watts, who also moved to Houston, his life is aimless and unfulfilling. When Phil disappears into the city, he sends a postcard signed significantly "Guess Who?" He has no firm idea about who he is or who he may become. On his return to Harrison he complains bitterly to his wife that he is thirty-five years old and nothing has happened to him. "I am tired of reading about things happening to other men. I want something to happen to me."[27]

Striking out in a new vein as he abandoned the restraints of television and cinema, Foote wrote uncompromisingly for the serious theater in his later works. The change is especially noticeable in his sustained portrayal of defeated men, implicitly contradicting the popular image of success. Foote's plays dissect various manifestations of the type and plumb the depths of unhappy lives, discovering the parental causes and dramatizing the human ruins. In his gallery of defeated men, he writes plays like Arthur Miller's about modern tragic heroes.

Representing a new generation of southern playwrights, Beth Henley contributes a striking picture of contemporary life in the South. She has established herself as a new voice in American drama with her successful *Crimes of the Heart,* which won both the Pulitzer Prize and the Drama Critics' Circle Best Play Award of 1981. Premiered at the Actors Theatre of

Louisville, this play benefited from the encouragement offered a new dramatist of the South by regional theater. It played successfully on Broadway and was made into a film (1986).

Born in Jackson, Mississippi, in 1952, Henley is the daughter of Charles Henley, a state senator, and Lydy Henley, a very influential figure in her life. After receiving a Bachelor of Fine Arts degree in 1974 from Southern Methodist University, where she took playwriting classes, she did postgraduate work at the University of Illinois in 1975-76 and acted at the Dallas Minority Repertory Theater. In Los Angeles, failing to obtain good roles, she turned to playwriting and composed *Crimes of the Heart* in 1976. Though she returns to Mississippi on visits, she now lives in Los Angeles.[28]

Growing up after the Southern Literary Renascence, Henley nevertheless reveals its impact. She resembles Foote in her concentration on small-town life, though she writes less in the manner of Thornton Wilder than of Tennessee Williams, whose influence Henley has acknowledged. She acted in *Summer and Smoke* in the fifth grade and stated in a recent interview that she thinks he is "great."[29] The most striking parallel between the two dramatists is Henley's fondness for the losers of life epitomized by Blanche DuBois, whom Henley's women often resemble. Her characters are the ostracized, the defeated, the spiritually and physically maimed. Yet like Williams's orphaned girl in *This Property Is Condemned* (1946), they are gallant fighters who by the end of the play have acquired strength that gives them hope for a better life. Significantly, Henley has observed: "I do feel that all my plays are extremely optimistic."[30]

As for literary models in general, Henley has named Chekhov as her foremost influence, because he does not judge and presents both the comic and tragic sides of life, moving the audience deeply. After the offbeat characters of *Crimes of the Heart* were likened to Flannery O'Connor's grotesques, Henley read that writer for the first time and rated her excellent.[31] She likes split images, the innocent combined with "the grotesque," such as a child walking with a cane. Southerners bring out the grisly details in any event, she observes, because they are fascinated "with the stages of decay people can live in on the earth—the imperfections."[32] Because of this penchant for decadence and macabre scenes, Henley, like Williams and Foote, has been called a "Southern Gothic" writer.[33]

Henley keeps up with changes in the modern South, examining both conventional and unconventional life-styles in her zany manner. *Crimes of the Heart,* her first performed and best play, is skillfully constructed and densely filled with striking themes. The title indicates the excusable— not heartless—crimes committed by all three Magrath sisters, "excusable" because they are done out of a desperate longing for love. Meg, the middle sister, selfishly refuses to leave a beach cottage during Hurricane Camille, causing her boyfriend, Doc Porter, to be injured. Lenny, the oldest and most conscientious sister, who has taken responsibility for Old Grandaddy, as long last attacks Chick, her harassing cousin next door, who calls "Police" as Lenny drives her up a tree. The lonely Babe shoots her husband Zackery because he has met her search for love with verbal and physical abuse. In contrast to the sisters, Zackery is guilty of heartless offenses such as wife abuse and fraud. A conflict of generations arises in the relations between the sisters and their domineering grandfather, who forced Babe into a marriage with Zackery to achieve social status. On hearing that Old Grandaddy has gone into a coma, the sisters cannot help laughing, indicating their liberation from his domination.

A special family occasion, a birthday, signals a new day for the troubled characters of this play—and shows Henley's recurring emphasis on the centrality of food in modern life. Whereas food divided the family when Meg provoked Lenny to tears by eating her birthday candy, it unites them when Lenny receives her cake (one day late). In making her wish before blowing out the candles, she has a vision of the three of them laughing together—about what, she cannot say. The traditional birthday party takes on new life for these modern women as they enjoy the cake and Lenny's sisters celebrate their own rebirths along with hers. They need not be like their distraught mother, who killed the cat when she committed suicide because she could not bear to die alone. Closeness of the family unit overcomes loneliness, giving promise of a happier life.

Three subsequent plays show that Henley is a dramatist with the resources to make progress in her art.[34] They repeat some themes from *Crimes of the Heart*—such as family solidarity to weather the storms of life—while venturing further into the absurdity of modern existence. The fragmentation and rootlessness of the characters' lives continue the picture of contemporary life one sees in Foote's more subdued but similarly chaotic *The Land of the Astronauts.*

Each play involves a traditional holiday. *The Miss Firecracker Contest* (first performed at the Manhattan Theatre Club in 1984) takes place on the Fourth of July. Wishing to leave the town in a blaze of glory, Carnelle has entered the Miss Firecracker contest. At its end the crowd, no longer mocking her sexual promiscuity by yelling "Miss Hot Tamale," applauds her tap dance to "The Star Spangled Banner." All the same, she comes in last and is devastated. But Mac Sam, the balloon man, says there is always "eternal grace" and admires her ability to take it on the chin (p. 68). Her loyal brother Delmount, who had beaten Ronnie Wayne's head into the ground for insulting Carnelle, consoles her, as does her beautiful but unhappily married sister, who had won the contest several years before. In the last scene Carnelle joins her brother and his popeyed girlfriend atop a carnival tent to watch the fireworks, remarking that it is a nice night after all. "As nice as they come," brother Delmount agrees (p. 71).

The Wake of Jamey Foster (1983) takes place at Eastertime, when the characters eat chocolate bunnies. Jamey, like the deceased Sebastian of Tennessee Williams's *Suddenly Last Summer*, exists only in memory, but his repugnant personality becomes abundantly clear. When Marshael refuses to attend the funeral of her husband, from whom she suffered drunken abuse, an earthly resurrection begins. As the family assembles at the wake, Marshael gains support from her sister Collard, demonstrating once again the value of female bonding. Seeking "redemption," Marshael finds one of sorts with the middle-aged bum Brocker, who sings to her (p. 61).

The Lucky Spot (first performed at the Manhattan Theatre Club in 1987), a violent play set in a Victorian farmhouse converted to a dance hall west of New Orleans, ends on Christmas morning with the observance of holiday customs: kissing under the mistletoe, and a happy exchange of gifts by people who are poor in the goods of this world. After a toast to "dumb luck" proprietor Reed Hooker tosses oranges to everyone, including Sue Jack, his estranged wife, just released from the penitentiary (p. 67). Then with current (1930s) music playing on the nickelodeon, they all dance with one another: women with women, men with men, and women with men. Like one big happy family, they join in making it a joyous Christmas celebration.

Against the meaninglessness of modern life, then, the antidote advocated in Henley's plays is the reinvigoration of traditional celebrations. On these occasions a support group made up of kin and friends rallies around the lost soul, giving each play an affirmative, upbeat ending.

Often linked with Henley, Marsha Norman falls on the borderline of southern drama, in both geography and identity. Nevertheless, her career throws light on recent southern drama. Lisa J. McDonnell discusses Norman's southern qualities—her "bizarre Gothic humor," her gift for storytelling, and her similarities with Eudora Welty and Flannery O'Connor—in an article comparing her with Beth Henley.[35] In the dramatist's *'Night, Mother,* a witty passage recalls the mother and daughter in O'Connor's "The Life You Save May Be Your Own": Jessie Cates jokes that her mother enticed a carpenter to build an unneeded porch for their country home because she wanted a son-in-law. All Norman's plays are set in the present except for *Loving Daniel Boone* (first performed at the Actors Theatre of Louisville on February 26, 1992), an original fantasy about an aimless modern man whose meeting with Daniel Boone on the dangerous frontier of the past renews his life in the present.[36]

Born in 1947 in Louisville, Kentucky, where she grew up as the precocious, musical daughter of rigidly fundamentalist parents, Norman received a scholarship and graduated from Agnes Scott College in Atlanta with a degree in philosophy. After working with disturbed adolescents at the Kentucky Central State Hospital, she drew on this experience to compose her first play, *Getting Out,* which won an award at the Louisville Actors' Theatre in 1977. She has long been an admirer of Lillian Hellman, who served as a guide for Norman's playwriting when she was seeking a female model.[37]

Getting Out is the engrossing drama of a schizophrenic young woman who strives to integrate her divided personality. In this technically experimental play that presents two time lines alternately, Arlie is getting out of a correctional institute in Alabama, where she served a sentence for killing a cab driver. While there she began rehabilitation after the prison chaplain gave her a picture of Jesus and called her "Arlene." Returning to Louisville, she insists on being called "Arlene," rejects the importunings of two exploitive boyfriends, and takes a female ex-convict's advice to choose dishwashing over prostitution. Proving that "Arlene" has supplanted "Arlie" at the end, she refrains from assaulting an abusive male, explaining "I ain't Arlie. She coulda killed you."[38]

Norman's most successful play, *'Night, Mother,* ran for ten months on Broadway, won the Pulitzer Prize, and was produced as a film in 1986. This controversial, dense drama of a woman's decision to take her own life, an act that is carried out at the end of the performance, is a gripping work packed with a woman's pitiless self-examination. In a no-holds-barred talk with her mother, Jessie explains that she has not realized the potential her life promised, nor will she in the future; she has lost "who I tried to be and never got there. Somebody I waited for who never came. And never will."[39] In her own eyes, her decision is a victory because herself is choosing what to do with her life. Mama, who continues maternal dominance by insisting on marshmallows in Jessie's last cup of cocoa, fails to stop her daughter, whose determination she can no longer stifle with food—a classic mother-daughter syndrome, according to Norman.

In this unlocalized play, which could take place anywhere in the United States, Norman took pains to omit southern details. "When you are even remotely from the South," she has remarked, "there is always this judgment": people from the South talk funny and are not smart. Wanting to give her characters "a real chance at getting through to the audience," she purposely eliminated "locale, accents, dialect"; "heavy accents" were to be avoided because they would "distance the audience" from the characters.[40] Nevertheless, Douglas Watt named the South as the setting on the basis of "speech patterns and the author's Louisville background."[41] As another clue, the leading part was played by Kathy Bates, a well-known actress from Memphis (who later appeared in the film *Fried Green Tomatoes,* set unmistakably in Alabama).

Even if Norman would not wish to be called "a southern dramatist," there is a good argument for recognizing her southern roots in order to understand their influence on her work.[42] The value of religion, for example, is a persistent subject among southerners—including dramatists—reared by strong believers. Norman's attitude toward southern Christianity is ambivalent, like Paul Green's: she rebelled against the religious fundamentalism of her family but later found herself coming back and "wanting there to be things to believe in."[43] With *Traveler in the Dark* (1988), her analysis of religion became more theologically sophisticated and substantial, showing the influence of her philosophical study. In it the inquisitive descendant of a nonbelieving surgeon and evangelist grandfather wants to know all about Job and the Bible. Seemingly, religious faith may skip a generation only to resurface in the next.

Preston Jones (1936-79) is another recent dramatist who is considered southern by many who have seen his widely performed *Texas Trilogy,* but again the inclusion requires qualification. In these farces he parodies southern traits in superficial though sometimes hilarious fashion. Mark Busby, who has written a critical monograph analyzing Jones's work, considers him a western writer. According to Busby, Jones concentrates on themes central to much western literature, such as ambivalence toward the values of the mythic West and the heroic images it produced.[44] Born and reared in Albuquerque, Jones graduated from the University of New Mexico in 1958 and set his last three plays in New Mexico. After receiving his master's degree from Trinity University, San Antonio, in 1966, Jones continued his association with the Dallas Theater Center, where he had acted in an adaptation of Faulkner's *As I Lay Dying.* His *Texas Trilogy* was performed there in 1973-74 before moving to New York, where it lasted only three nights, but it ran again for five weeks in 1976 to mixed reviews. Jones's one-act *Juneteenth,* the holiday commemorating slave emancipation in Texas, was performed by the Actors Theatre of Louisville in 1979.

A Texas Trilogy demonstrates the extensive influence that southern culture has exerted on writers of nearby regions. The chronological series comprises *The Last Meeting of the Knights of the White Magnolia, Lu Ann Hampton Laverty Oberlander,* and *The Oldest Living Graduate.* They concentrate in Faulknerian fashion on recurring characters from one town, Bradleyville, West Texas. Unlike other recent dramatists, Jones takes up the racial issue again, though only superficially.

Colonel J.C. Kincaid, the most popular character in the trilogy, is based on Jones's South Carolina father. An outrageous caricature of the southern colonel, Kincaid has a World War I military background, belongs to the racist Knights of the White Magnolia, and speaks ludicrous dialect, his favorite phrase being, "Betcha didn't know that, did you?"[45] *The Oldest Living Graduate* recalls Tennessee Williams's *Cat on a Hot Tin Roof* at several points, for the colonel resembles Big Daddy in relating outrageous anecdotes of his travels and preferring his football-playing son over another. The fact that his death is imminent also recalls Big Daddy. Although *The Last Meeting* takes place during the crisis over integration in 1962, its allusions are brief and insubstantial. The Knights pledge to uphold "the principles of White Magnolia-ism." One member, a bartender, declares, "Let 'em all squawk about lunchrooms and schools all they want. In mah place ah simply reserve the right to refuse service to anybody" (pp. 34, 113). Following decades of original variations, the southern play in Jones's hands reaches a reductio ad absurdum.

Still, Preston Jones has much in common with the black dramatists of the civil rights movement who ridiculed the defenders of segregation. Ossie Davis, Douglas Taylor Ward, and Ted Shine, in the same spirit as Jones, resorted to farce in denouncing opponents of civil rights. Jones's Colonel Kincaid, a personification of the reactionary South, passes out at the end of *The Last Meeting*, recalling the finale of Davis's *Purlie Victorious* (1961) in which Cap'n Stonewall Jackson Catchipee—another comic representative of the Old South—dies standing up and is buried with the Confederate flag wrapped around him. Jones and the black dramatists caricature racist whites repeatedly.

Romulus Zachariah Linney (1930-), the fifth to bear that name, is a novelist as well as a dramatist but is best known for plays about the southern folk and historical figures. Though born in Philadelphia, he is descended from people of western North Carolina and spent his childhood—which he credits for much material used in his plays—in Charlotte and Boone, North Carolina, and in Madison, Tennessee (near Nashville), with summers in the mountains.[46]

Linney has maintained a close relationship with the academy. After two years in the army, he graduated from Oberlin College in 1953 and received his M.F.A. from the Yale School of Drama in 1958. Among many academic appointments, he was visiting professor at the University of North Carolina in 1961, then director of fine arts at North Carolina State

University. Later he taught at the University of Pennsylvania and Columbia University, and received fellowships at Yaddo and the MacDowell
Colony. He now lives in New York City. Linney has worked in television,
has been stage manager for the Actors Studio, New York, and has acted
in summer stock. Twice married, he has two daughters. Acclaimed a major talent in the theater and winner of an Obie award (for best off-Broadway play), Linney has produced numerous one-act and full-length plays,
including an interesting study of Frederick the Great titled *The Sorrows of
Frederick* (1968).[47] He inscribed a copy of this play to Paul Green, writing,
"There is a great deal of you and *The Lost Colony* in its bones."[48]

Like Foote and Henley, Linney has often produced his plays elsewhere than Broadway. All three have staged their serious, noncommer-
cial works at the Louisville Actors Theatre, as has Marsha Norman. Linney's
The Death of King Philip (based on the life of an Indian chief in colonial
Massachusetts) and *Holy Ghosts* were presented there in 1983. In New York,
Linney and Foote have found a welcome at the Herbert Berghoff Foundation and the Ensemble Studio Theatre. For their innovative works of
the 1980s, both necessarily sought out such experimental theaters, determined as they were to write according to their own highest artistic standards. Linney, Foote, and Norman appeared together on a panel of the
Eighth Biennial Conference on Southern Literature, held at the University of Tennessee at Chattanooga, April 7, 1995.

As a post-Renascence writer, Linney has benefited from the insight-
ful approaches to southern life initiated by his predecessors. When he
was learning to write, he remarks, Faulkner took the place of a psycholo-
gist, explaining his childhood to him and letting him know "these things"
were not just in his head. Linney has commented further on the influence of specific writers: "I always loved Katherine Porter, Flannery
O'Connor, and the Southerners."[49] The inclusion of grotesques in
Linney's plays strongly suggests O'Connor's influence. His attitude toward the South, however, is profoundly ambivalent (like Tennessee
Williams's). When Paul Green advised him to return to North Carolina,
he responded, "I love the land and I hate the people and I'm not coming
back." The South may have an almost physical hold on him, but he feels
alien there: "I love to go back to the Southern beaches, but the values of
the South are not mine."[50]

Though recognized for the variety of his subjects, Linney has been
faulted for the failure to concentrate his efforts. Most distinctive, however, are his plays about fundamentalist southern religion. Unlike Green
and Heyward, he does not condemn its narrowmindedness, for he discovers positive values among believers. As a boy in the South, he noticed

that when evangelists came to town, they provided a support that people direly needed. His religious plays draw on this background, leading him to remark, "Religion and the South just go together in my mind."[51] Linney's nondramatic writings about religion include *Jesus Tales* (1987), a collection of amusing apocryphal stories which repeat some of the material in his play *Old Man Joseph and His Family* (1978).

Holy Ghosts (1974), which, Linney notes, is of all his plays the one "done the most," is a sympathetic, dramatically successful treatment of fundamentalism.[52] This gripping drama shows how a snake-handling cult gives real support to its members during a worship service. Testifying, the worshipers recall O'Connor's grotesques with their bizarre case histories. Carl is inconsolable over the loss of his hunting dog, which consumed ground glass in its meat, and Bonnie has pulled up her dress willingly for "any good Christian boy" in one church after another. As the unbitten worshipers handle the rattlers ecstatically in the climax, the sworn enemy of the cult, a husband come to rescue his wife, undergoes conversion. He too grabs a snake, believing that the Holy Ghost has made him sufficiently pure, while the congregation sings "There's a wideness in God's mercy."[53] It is this sort of play that has prompted the critic Mel Gussow to call Linney's work "mountain Gothic."[54]

Also receiving high acclaim from Gussow, Linney's main and most knowledgeable supporter in New York, was Linney's other major play focusing on religion, the original and well-conceived *Heathen Valley*. Whereas *Holy Ghosts* looks at fundamentalism in the present, this play returns to an earlier time. Written first as a novel in 1962, *Heathen Valley* effectively dramatizes the story of an Episcopal bishop's meeting with pagan mountaineers. First performed at the Philadelphia Theatre Festival in 1987, the play was staged the next year in New York and in Boone, North Carolina, near its historical setting.

Despite its harrowing depiction of primitive mountain life in the 1840s, based on a true account, this work presents conflict between life-denying religion (treated by Paul Green) and life-affirming Christian faith. The orphan Billy recalls the bishop's arrival at Valle Cruce, an isolated valley plagued by superstition, incest, and murder. The real savior turns out to be a reformed drunken killer named Starns, whom the bishop appoints as deacon to the mountain denizens. Using folk wisdom and deep understanding of the natives ("Poor folks have poor ways"), Starns rehabilitates the mountain community, performs the wedding of the violent youth Harlan, and builds a school.[55] The play ends tragically, however, as the bishop reinstates the formal ceremonies, opposed by Starns, who dies a martyr.

Linney depicts religion in the South critically but sympathetically. Recognizing the grip of inherited beliefs and superstitions, he supports the application of homely wisdom and common sense. Since Harlan is afraid of a church with square corners because they harbor witches, Starns constructs an octagonal building. In Starns's ministry Linney portrays and acclaims the beneficial and indeed civilizing results of Christian love.

Linney draws on his tale-telling skill in humorous pieces that recall the southwestern tradition. In *Tennessee* (1980), an old woman tells of being carried off by her husband because she insisted she would marry no one but a man who would take her from North Carolina to Tennessee. After he dies at the age of eighty-nine, she returns to her mountain birthplace, only to discover that she had never left North Carolina after all. She will now go "back to Tennessee. Where else?"[56]

Besides writing in the storytelling tradition, Linney proves he can compose in the style of modern southern humor, exemplified particularly by Eudora Welty and Flannery O'Connor. In *Good-bye, Howard*, three elderly ladies—recalling those writers' earlier creations—become hilariously confused at Duke University Medical Center when they telephone the news of their brother's death, then learn that they had gone to the wrong room, and Howard is not dead. In *F.M.*, a young redneck reads beautiful Faulknerian sentences to a creative writing class of astonished women, including one outraged feminist, at an Alabama college near Birmingham. These plays have been performed, along with *Tennessee*, under the general title *Laughing Stock* (1984).[57]

The Captivity of Pixie Shedman (1981), although considered southern gothic of the worst kind by critic Frank Rich, provides insight into Linney's love-hate attitude toward his southern heritage.[58] Written with his usual verve, this experimental play revives the ghost of the eponymous character (based on the dramatist's grandmother), who was abducted by a Confederate veteran of North Carolina before marrying his drunken son. When questioned about the comparison of her autobiography to stories of Indian captivity, Pixie replies tartly, "The truth is in the poetry! Dumbbell!"[59] The lesson for the struggling grandson is to learn from the past but "shed" it.

The dramatists considered in this chapter have all shown flexibility in adapting to a changing theatrical situation after 1960. Whether or not the decline in Broadway's dominance will be to their advantage remains to be seen. Repeating previous fluctuations in the American theater, Broadway has been supplemented by off- and off-off-Broadway as well as regional theaters. Some southern dramatists have made the change very successfully, such as Henley and Norman, who have joined the new roster of women writing for the stage.

Recent southern drama deserves recognition for its "maturity," the right term to denote a sequence of playwriting arising out of a solid tradition. The current dramatists benefit greatly from the legacy of the Southern Literary Renascence, which had measurable impact on succeeding literature, including drama. The most influential writers in order of importance are Faulkner, Williams, Welty, and O'Connor, whose works provide a ready frame of reference for analyzing such superior works as *The Trip to Bountiful* and *Crimes of the Heart*. Critics repeatedly apply the term "southern gothic," meaning bizarre humor and grotesque characters, to indicate a likeness to Faulkner, O'Connor, or Williams. Since drama demands a heightened tone to express the disturbed sensibility of modern life, "Gothicism" is especially effective in plays by Foote, Henley, and Norman.

Many recent plays, in cultivating the distinguishing traits of the southern play, increase their richness. Betraying the influence of Welty, Foote transcribed southern speech with new success in the comic monologues of Jessie Mae, and Jones has caricatured such types as the southern colonel: parody is the sign of a long, self-conscious tradition. Showing the continued importance of religion in the contemporary South, southern Christianity abides: Linney's *Holy Ghosts* and Norman's *Getting Out* take a sympathetic view of the long-maligned fundamentalism. If the racial issue is no longer the indispensable feature, the exploration of southern cultures past and present still identifies a play as southern: Henley surveys the counterculture as it exists in the contemporary South; Foote presents times past that are familiarly southern but nevertheless emphatically Texan. In sum, as southern drama matures, it remains recognizably southern.

Epilogue:
Politics, Culture, and the Rise of
Southern Drama

The choice between the political or the cultural play, faced by black dramatists of the 1920s, is the same one facing southern dramatists from the beginning to the present. Most often confronting the racial crisis, the southern political play has changed from defense of the status quo to advocacy of full change: that is, equality and justice for blacks. At first, dramatists such as Simms and McCabe sided with the majority, defending slavery to a man. In the modern period, southern dramatists joined the dissident minority in condemning lynchings, disenfranchisement, and segregation. Without exception, though with differing intensity, white dramatists such as Green, Hellman, and Williams have confronted these injustices honestly and unflinchingly. If southern dramatists had not rejected the segregationist position of most southerners, modern southern drama would not have gained the moral force that impelled it. As was to be expected, southern black dramatists such as Edmonds and Davis denounced racial inequality and strongly supported the civil rights movement.

Coincident with the political theme has been the cultural, often present in the same work. Either separately or together, the two have identified the southern play. Southern dramatists' fascination with the rich culture of the South began with Robert Munford. In the early period it inspired the iconography of Dixie heroines—such as Louise the *vivandiere*—who perpetuated the Confederacy. In the modern period Heyward invigorated his plays of black culture with passionate singing. More than elsewhere in the United States, folk drama thrived in the South, especially in the works of Hurston (who captured black life uniquely in *Mule Bone*) and Green. Tennessee Williams castigated the sexual primness of southern ladies, symbolized by the Victorian houses of his sets. The cultural possibilities for southern drama seem inexhaustible. Just when they seemed to have reached the point of diminishing returns, along came

Horton Foote, approving some Victorian ways in Gulf Coast Texas but detesting oil fever.

From the amateurish beginnings in Charleston and Richmond to the masterpieces of Tennessee Williams is a quantum leap, to be sure. Seen in retrospect, southern drama has been formed sometimes consciously, as during the Civil War and by the trailblazer Paul Green, but more often without plan. Thus, one must recognize its rise inferentially, after the fact.

Turningpoints stand out. To the instigating date of the Civil War, when southern drama was first proclaimed as such, two later events should be added. First, the Southern Literary Renascence of 1920 to 1960 bestowed prestige on all southern literature and encouraged the composition of artistically superior plays that analyzed the South critically.

Second, the civil rights movement inspired an outpouring of plays by African American dramatists such as Randolph Edmonds. The achievement of racial integration during the explosive 1960s initiated a new era: plays composed thereafter do not focus on segregation and its many ramifications. Southern drama since 1970, taking integration for granted, has turned to new interests, as in the plays of Beth Henley and Romulus Linney.

Although playwrights of the South have faulted the New York theater for ignoring their best efforts, the flourishing of southern drama did in fact coincide with Broadway's greatest era. From 1920 when O'Neill's plays ruled till 1960 when Tennessee Williams's plays culminated, southern drama reached its widest acceptance and greatest artistic heights. Paul Green, DuBose Heyward, Lillian Hellman, and Horton Foote all saw their works performed creditably in New York and sometimes loudly acclaimed. Needless to say, Williams attained the greatest success with an impressive series of plays that were performed all over the world. *A Streetcar Named Desire* and *Cat on a Hot Tin Roof,* with their authentic southern settings, put the definitive stamp on the southern play in the minds of audiences and critics in New York and well beyond.

The decline of Broadway has led to the inauguration of regional theaters in the South (as elsewhere) but not to the emergence of a real theatrical center, comprising many theaters, a community of critics, and a large, knowledgeable audience. Thus it is uncertain if the current upsurge of regional activity will produce better southern drama.

In spite of everything, a distinctive southern drama has emerged over the course of some two hundred years. No, there have not been many native theater managers (though we could mention Margo Jones of Texas) and not many great actors (though we could name Tallulah Bankhead of

Alabama). Most notably, no real theatrical center has arisen in the South, despite the early activity in cities like Charleston and New Orleans. From the 1890s to the present southern dramatists have had to run the gauntlet of New York, with its defensive lines of directors and often unsympathetic reviewers. Continually present, however, have been talented people with an urge to write. Southerners have shown from an early date that they are cursed or blessed with the *cacoëthes scribendi,* and where writing is a major artistic urge, one is likely to find composition of drama, which after all must begin with the written word.

Drawing on southern history, the particular culture of the South, and the Southern Renascence, led by Faulkner, southern dramatists have made distinctive achievements. Of course, dialogue is the meat and potatoes of drama, and fortunately for southern dramatists this is their forte, as liberal quotations from Williams, Foote, and others have illustrated. The rhythm of southern women's talk (as captured in the popular play *Steel Magnolias* [1986] by Robert Harling, and the stories of Eudora Welty, Flannery O'Connor, and Lee Smith) is a specialty; expertly rendered it perhaps above all stamps a play as undeniably southern. And because it is actually heard, not just read, the "southernese" of actresses enables us to appreciate the sound as well as the (non)sense. Tennessee Williams is the first master of this unmistakable speech, which we find not only in Amanda's chatter but also in Big Mama's gushing and the wives' jabber of *Orpheus Descending.* Black dramatists show first-rate talent in the humorous dialogue they assign to both men and women, as in Ted Shine's hilarious lines for Gussie Black and Ossie Davis's for the Reverend Purlie.

Like the historically oriented novelists, Faulkner and Robert Penn Warren, southern dramatists have also shown a keen sense of their region's history. C. Vann Woodward has praised this historical consciousness in *The Burden of Southern History* (1960). Paul Green favors North Carolina or historical figures he knows well as a southerner, such as Robert E. Lee. Following the novelists, Green finds meaning for the present in events of the past. A sense of place (as recognized in Eudora Welty's essay "Place in Fiction," 1956) is another common element, permeating such works as those of DuBose Heyward (Charleston's Catfish Row) and Horton Foote (Wharton, Texas).

Theorists of American drama—Cooper, Poe, Howells—have often pondered the question of creating a distinctive American drama. Southern drama finally produced its theorist in Paul Green, who formulated the most proposals for the composition of drama in the South. When he was following Frederick Koch's guidance by writing folk drama, he emphasized his preference for rural folk over urban in an essay collected in

The Hawthorn Tree (1943). His example encouraged many apprentice dramatists in the South to exploit the folk material of their states.

Green's most lasting influence was his creation of a new dramatic form, outdoor drama. In essays collected in *Dramatic Heritage* (1953) he argued for the establishment of outdoor theaters, pointing to the glorious precedent in Greece and urging that American plays too should extol the virtues of heroes, such as Jefferson. Green's lasting effect on drama in the South is evident today in the continuing production of outdoor dramas by others in such locales as the North Carolina mountains. The Institute of Outdoor Drama, a resource center, is located fittingly at his alma mater, the University of North Carolina in Chapel Hill.

Lending further distinctiveness to southern drama is the character of the South's foremost theatrical city. New Orleans can claim that title historically, by virtue of its theaters, personalities, and other intangibles, though such cities as Atlanta, Memphis, and Houston would contend for the current honor. After Charleston arose as the leading theatrical center from 1800 to 1825, New Orleans took the lead when Caldwell, Ludlow, and Smith directed flourishing theaters there in the 1840s and '50s, and Field wrote and acted in his spicy burlesques. In the twentieth century, New Orleans continued to stand out. Its free, artistic atmosphere that attracted Faulkner and Sherwood Anderson—different from the academic climate that nourished the poets of Nashville—may have been a factor. It is also significant that leading modern dramatists have been closely associated with the city. Lillian Hellman was the greatest playwright to be born in New Orleans. From 1934 to 1947 Randolph Edmonds taught there at Dillard University, where he organized the first drama department at a black college and founded the Southern Association of Drama and Speech Arts. Finally, New Orleans was the favorite destination and inspiration of Tennessee Williams, who used its background for *Suddenly Last Summer* and *A Streetcar Named Desire*, the best play set in that theatrical city, with its gaudy panache.

Of the many dramatic responses to the civil rights movement, particularly outstanding are plays advocating Martin Luther King's doctrine of nonviolence. Loften Mitchell's *A Land Beyond the River* (1957) recounts the drive for equal schools in South Carolina, led by a black minister who pleads with his followers to love not hate. In Randolph Edmonds's play about sit-ins, *Earth and Stars*, the Reverend Joshua Judson loses his life while practicing nonviolence. Ossie Davis's *Purlie Victorious* uses laughter to appeal for nonviolence.

Led by Paul Green and Tennessee Williams, the southern play received its definitive form in the years of the Southern Literary Renascence.

Green made the fullest dramatic use of the raw material that others had begun to exploit in novels, stories, and poems. By the volume of his writing, he placed the southern play on a broad and enlightened foundation. In his folk one-acts and full-length dramas the social types of the Negro, the poor white, and the aristocrat took on individual outlines; their depth and plausibility as dramatic characters increased. It remained for Hellman and Tennessee Williams to add the crowning touch of artistic genius.

The vitality of the southern play is attested to by the kinds of changes that have occurred during its evolution. Some formerly characteristic elements have disappeared, such as the loyal slave; others have continued but taken new forms, such as the southern belle. New styles have arisen: the outdoor drama and southern Gothic. Southern speech, especially the comic variety à la Welty, continues to be popular with new dramatists such as Henley. As proof of its longevity, southern Christianity persists in works as recent as Linney's *Holy Ghosts.*

With regard to literary artistry, I have throughout this history offered critical evaluation as well as a sequence of figures and phases, but some general comments may be in order. Among names and plays most meriting critical recognition, of course, Tennessee Williams is the leading figure; perhaps only his plays can justly be compared in literary quality and cultural originality with the novels of Faulkner, that giant of the Southern Literary Renascence. But one can liken plays to other superior works and find further signs of comparable excellence. For example, in the *Orphans' Home Cycle* Foote features characters fully equal to the creations of Katherine Anne Porter in psychological interest. Horace Robedaux faces the trauma of death in *1918* with the same sort of endurance that Miranda displays in *Pale Horse, Pale Rider.* And with the southerner's gift for humor, Foote makes an original advance over Welty's comic women in "The Petrified Man" with Jessie Mae, a prisoner of big-city compulsiveness in *The Trip to Bountiful.*

Further, from the array of authors and their plays come some underappreciated names and titles. Joseph M. Field was an exceptional satirical dramatist for the early New Orleans theater. In the era of Kate Chopin, Espy Williams composed a sensitive though unperformed play examining the prohibited subject of a putative mulatto: *The Clairvoyant* (1899). Anticipating William Styron by thirty years in his one-act about Nat Turner, Randolph Edmonds probed the mind of this early rebel against slavery. Zora Neale Hurston, aided by Langston Hughes, attempted a full-length play (recently revived) of black folk life, with original characterization and symbolism.

If the number of performances is an index of artistic quality, as it certainly is of popularity, then Tennessee Williams's plays again take first place; even his lesser-known works such as *Orpheus Descending* have been revived in New York. Of plays by blacks, *Purlie Victorious* has enjoyed the most sustained runs, showing that Ossie Davis could succeed with jokes about both blacks and whites. Though Paul Green's plays for the legitimate theater have disappeared from the repertory, his outdoor drama *The Lost Colony*, with its democratic theme of opportunity for all in America, sets the record for the longest run. Hellman's *The Little Foxes* continues to be performed by college actors and theatrical companies throughout the nation.

Drama possesses the unique power of giving life to imaginative creations through the talent of actors, and southern plays boast an imposing list of characters that have attracted gifted interpreters. Successive productions discover an unforeseen Amanda or Big Daddy; an original Regina or Birdie; a new Carrie or Jessie Mae Watts. If a theatergoer says of a successful reinterpretation, "That was a superb Blanche," we visualize immediately that fragile but defiant intruder. Such dramatic creations forecast success for southern drama in the future—always profiting from the cultural wealth of the South.

Notes

Prologue

1. T.S. Eliot, *Notes towards the Definition of Culture* (New York: Harcourt, Brace, 1949), p. 30.

2. Ibid., p. 58.

3. Twelve Southerners, *I'll Take My Stand: The South and the Agrarian Tradition* (1930; rpt. New York: Harper, 1962).

4. Charles Reagan Wilson and William Ferris, *Encyclopedia of Southern Culture* (Chapel Hill: Univ. of North Carolina Press, 1989), p. xvi. For interesting explorations of the topic, see also the new journal *Southern Cultures* (1993-).

5. Tennessee Williams, foreword to *Sweet Bird of Youth*, in *Three by Tennessee* (New York: New American Library, 1976), p. xi.

6. Susan Ketchin, "Narrative Hunger and Silent Witness: An Interview with Reynolds Price," *Georgia Review* 47 (Fall 1993):536.

7. Arthur Hobson Quinn, *A History of the American Drama from the Civil War to the Present* (New York: Harper, 1927), pp. 6-7.

1. Nationalism and Native Culture in Virginia

1. Hugh S. Rankin, *The Theater in Colonial America* (Chapel Hill: Univ. of North Carolina Press, 1965), pp. 10, 11, 47-50, 168; Arthur Hobson Quinn, *A History of the American Drama from the Beginning to the Civil War* (1923; rpt. New York: Appleton-Century-Crofts, 1943), pp. 47-50.

2. Robert Munford, *A Collection of Plays and Poems* (Petersburg, Va.: William Prentis, 1798). Page references in the text cite this edition. For a biographical sketch of Robert Munford, see Jay B. Hubbell, *The South in American Literature* (Durham, N.C.: Duke Univ. Press, 1954).

3. See Richard R. Beeman, "Deference, Republicanism, and the Emergence of Popular Politics in Eighteenth Century America," *William and Mary Quarterly* 49 (July 1992): 401-30.

4. Rodney M. Baine, *Robert Munford: America's First Comic Dramatist* (Athens: Univ. of Georgia Press, 1967), p. 60.

5. Ibid., p. 67.

6. Ibid., p. 60.

7. Quote in ibid., p. 73.

8. For an illuminating analysis of Munford's dislike of the unruly politics in his frontier county because it lacked the Tidewater's respect for traditional

values, see Richard R. Beeman, "Robert Munford and the Political Culture of Frontier Virginia," *Journal of American Studies* 12 (Aug. 1978): 68-83.

9. Joseph I. Shulim, "John Daly Burk: Irish Revolutionist and American Patriot," *Transactions of the American Philosophical Society*, n.s. 54, pt. 6 (1964): 9-11.

10. Ibid., pp. 20-21.

11. Quoted in Edward A. Wyatt, *John Daly Burk: Patriot-Playwright-Historian* (Charlottesville, Va.: Historical Publishing, 1936), p. 10.

12. Ibid., p. 11.

13. Shulim, "John Daly Burk," p. 40.

14. Ibid.

15. Milton Lomask, *Aaron Burr: The Conspiracy and Years of Exile, 1805-1836* (New York: Farrar, Strauss & Giroux, 1982), pp. 6-7.

16. Shulim, "John Daly Burk," p. 42.

17. John Daly Burk, *Bethlem Gabor* (Petersburg, Va.: John Dickson, 1807). References in the text cite this edition.

18. Martin Staples Shockley, *The Richmond Stage, 1784-1812* (Charlottesville: Univ. Press of Virginia, 1977), p. 170.

19. Wyatt, *John Daly Burk*, pp. 94-95.

20. Shockley, *Richmond Stage*, p. 171.

21. Shulim, "John Daly Burk," pp. 47, 51.

22. Everard Hall, *Nolens Volens; or, The Biter Bit* (New Bern, N.C.: John S. Pasteur, 1809).

23. Richard Walser, ed., *North Carolina Plays* (Richmond, Va.: Garnett & Massie, 1956), p. 5.

24. *Oscar Fitz-James* (Richmond, Va.: William A. Bartow, 1819); Gustavus Adolphus Myers, *Nature and Philosophy* (New York: R. Hobbs, 1830). *The Richmond Compiler* (July 24, 1822) credits "Felix" to the author of *Nature and Philosophy*.

25. David Darling, *Beaux without Belles; or, Ladies We Can Do Without You* (Charlottesville, Va.: C.P. and J.H. M'Kennie, 1820).

26. Hal Laughlin, "A Critical Edition of St. George Tucker's *The Wheel of Fortune*" (master's thesis, College of William and Mary, 1960), pp. 1, 4.

27. For information on Tucker and his plays, see Meta Robinson Braymer, "Trying to Walk: An Introduction to the Plays of St. George Tucker," in *No Fairer Land: Studies in Southern Literature Before 1900*, ed. J. Lesley Dameron and James W. Mathews (Troy, N.Y.: Whitson, 1986), pp. 87-100.

28. For information on Custis and his plays, see Murray H. Nelligan, "American Nationalism on the Stage: The Plays of George Washington Parke Custis (1781-1857)," *Virginia Magazine of History and Biography* 58 (1950): 299-324; Walter Meserve, *Heralds of Promise: The Drama of the American People during the Age of Jackson, 1828-1849* (Westport, Conn.: Greenwood, 1986), pp. 166-168; George Washington Parke Custis, *Recollections and Private Memoir of Washington*, with "A Memoir of the Author" by his daughter (New York: Derby & Jackson, 1860).

29. E.T. Crowson, "George Washington Parke Custis: The Child of Mount Vernon," *Virginia Cavalcade* 22 (Winter 1973): 37-47.

30. Custis, *Recollections*, p. 66.

31. In *Proceedings of a Meeting of the Friends of Civil and Religious Liberty, Residing in the District of Columbia . . . arranged and published by John Boyle* (Washington, D.C.: Peter Force, 1826).

32. Custis, *The Indian Prophecy* (Georgetown, D.C.: James Thomas, 1828). All references cite this edition.

33. Custis, *Pocahontas; or, The Settlers of Virginia* (1830); in *Representative American Plays*, ed. Arthur Hobson Quinn (New York: Appleton-Century-Crofts, 1953).

34. Nelligan, "American Nationalism on the Stage," p. 321.

35. All references are to a manuscript copy of Custis, *Montgomerie*, held by the Huntington Library, San Marino, Calif.

2. Prolific Playwriting in Charleston

1. Eola Willis, *The Charleston Stage in the XVIII Century* (Columbia, S.C.: The State, 1924), p. 59.

2. For information on West, see Susanne K. Sherman, "Thomas Wade West, Theatrical Impresario, 1790-1799," *William and Mary Quarterly*, 3d ser. 9 (Jan. 1952):10-28.

3. Robert Mills, *Statistics of South Carolina* (Charleston, S.C., 1826), p. 423, cited in Julia Curtis, "The Architecture and Appearance of the Charleston Theatre, 1793-1833," *Educational Theatre Journal* 23 (1971): 10.

4. *City Gazette and Daily Advertiser,* March 20, 1795, cited in Julia Curtis, "The Early Charleston Stage, 1703-1798" (Ph.D. diss., Indiana Univ., 1968), pp. 265-66.

5. Quoted in William Dunlap, *History of the American Theatre*, 2 vols. (1832; rpt. New York: Burt Franklin, 1963), 1: 312-13.

6. W. Stanley Hoole, *The Ante-bellum Charleston Theatre* (Tuscaloosa: Univ. of Alabama Press, 1946), pp. 69-73. Dates of all theatrical performances in Charleston after 1800 have been checked in this source or in the *Charleston Courier.*

7. Quoted in William Bulloch Maxwell, *The Mysterious Father*, ed. Gerald Kahan (Athens: Univ. of Georgia Press, 1965), app. 2, p. 56.

8. *Richmond Enquirer,* Dec. 28, 1811; Sylvie Chevalley, "The Death of Alexander Placide," *South Carolina Historical and Genealogical Magazine* 58 (April 1957): 63 (hereafter abbreviated *SCHGM* and, when the title changes to *South Carolina Historical Magazine, SCHM*).

9. "The Elder Placide," *Spirit of the Times*, 18 March 1848, p. 44. For a detailed account of Placide's Charleston career, see Richard Phillip Sodders, "The Theatre Management of Alexandre Placide in Charleston, 1794-1812" (Ph.D. diss., Louisiana State Univ., 1983).

10. Charles Eugene Clagham, *Biographical Dictionary of American Music* (West Nyack, N.Y., 1973), p. 171; Hoole, *Ante-bellum Charleston Theatre*, p. 12.

11. "Dr. Irving's Reminiscences of the Charleston Stage," ed. Emmett Robinson, SCHGM 52 (July 1951): 177, 129. For William Gilmore Simms's impressions of Gilfert, see "The Humours of the Manager," in *Stories and Tales*, ed.

John C. Guilds, vol. 5 of *The Writings of William Gilmore Simms* (Columbia: Univ. of South Carolina Press, 1974).

12. Martin S. Shockley, "A History of the Theatre in Richmond, Virginia, 1819-1838" (Ph.D. diss., Univ. of North Carolina, 1938), p. 95.

13. Irving, "Reminiscences," p. 171.

14. The discussion of S.C. Carpenter is based on Charles S. Watson, "Stephen Cullen Carpenter: First Drama Critic of the Charleston *Courier*," *SCHM* 69 (Oct. 1968): 243-52.

15. Quoted in William Charvat, *The Origins of American Critical Thought, 1810-1835* (Philadelphia: Univ. of Pennsylvania Press, 1936), p. 125.

16. John Beete, *The Man of the Times* (Charleston, S.C.: W.P. Young, [1797]).

17. James Workman, *Liberty in Louisiana* (Charleston, S.C.: Query & Evans, 1804).

18. Quinn, *American Drama from the Beginning to the Civil War*, p. 135 n; J. Max Patrick, *Savannah's Pioneer Theatre from Its Origins to 1810* (Athens: Univ. of Georgia Press, 1953), p. 68.

19. Dorchester was twenty-six miles from Charleston on the north bank of the Ashley River. Biographical information on Ioor comes principally from the *Dictionary of American Biography*, his obituary in the *Courier* (Aug. 10, 1850), and a collection of family records provided by a descendant, Elizabeth McDavid of Pelzer, South Carolina.

20. William Ioor, *Independence* (Charleston, S.C.: G.M. Bounetheau, 1805). For further information, see Charles S. Watson, *Antebellum Charleston Dramatists* (Tuscaloosa: Univ. of Alabama Press, 1976).

21. Thomas Jefferson, *Notes on the State of Virginia* (1787), ed. William Peden (Chapel Hill: Univ. of North Carolina Press, 1955), p. 175.

22. Ibid., p. 165.

23. William Ioor, *The Battle of Eutaw Springs and Evacuation of Charleston; or, The Glorious 14th of December, 1782* (Charleston, S.C.: J. Hoff, 1807).

24. *Richmond Enquirer*, Sept. 27, 1811; Reese D. James, *Old Drury of Philadelphia* (Philadelphia: Univ. of Pennsylvania Press, 1932), p. 21; Quinn, *American Drama from the Beginning to the Civil War*, p. 155.

25. William Gilmore Simms, "Our Early Authors and Artists," *XIX Century* 1 (Sept. 1869): 279-80.

26. John Blake White, *The Mysteries of the Castle* (Charleston, S.C.: J. Hoff, 1807).

27. John Blake White, *Modern Honor* (Charleston, S.C.: J. Hoff, 1812).

28. Josef A. Elfenbein, "American Drama, 1782-1812, as an Index to Socio-Political Thought," (Ph.D. diss., New York Univ., 1952), pp. 243, 245.

29. "The Journal of John Blake White," ed. Paul R. Weidner, *SCHGM* 43 (July 1942): 167-68.

30. Ibid., *SCHGM* 43 (April 1942): 111-12.

31. Clement Eaton, *Freedom of Thought in the Old South* (Durham, N.C.: Duke Univ. Press, 1940), p. 323.

32. David Duncan Wallace, *South Carolina: A Short History, 1520-1948* (Chapel Hill: Univ. of North Carolina Press, 1951), pp. 490-91.

33. John Blake White, *The Forgers*, in *Southern Literary Journal* 1 (April-Aug. 1837).

34. Donald A. Koch, ed., *Ten Nights in a Bar-Room and What I Saw There by Timothy Shaw Arthur* (Cambridge, Mass.: Belknap Press, 1964), pp. xlix, li, liv.

35. The manuscript of this speech is in the possession of the South Carolina Historical Society.

36. From manuscript dated 1829, now in the possession of the South Carolina Historical Society.

37. White's letter is in the possession of the South Carolina Historical Society.

38. *Southern Literary Journal* 1 (April 1837): 190.

39. William Gilmore Simms, ed., *The Charleston Book: A Miscellany in Prose and Verse* (Charleston, S.C.: S. Hart, 1845), pp. 130-32.

40. John Blake White, *The Triumph of Liberty; or, Louisiana Preserved* (Charleston, S.C.: J. Hoff, 1819).

41. Much of the biographical information on Harby is taken from "A Memoir" by Abraham Moise, in *A Selection from the Miscellaneous Writings of the late Isaac Harby*, ed. Henry L. Pinckney and Abraham Moise (Charleston, S.C.: James S. Burges, 1829); and L.C. Moise, *Biography of Isaac Harby* (N.p., 1931).

42. L.C. Moise, *Biography*, p. 32.

43. Simms, "Our Early Authors," p. 280.

44. Harby, *Selection from the Miscellaneous Writings*, p. 15.

45. Ibid., pp. 256, 265-66.

46. Harby, *The Gordian Knot* (Charleston, S.C.: G.M. Bounetheau, 1810), p. v.

47. "Stefanoff" is identified as Harby in Gary Phillip Zola, *Isaac Harby of Charleston, 1788-1828* (Tuscaloosa: Univ. of Alabama Press, 1994), pp. 195-96 n. 20.

48. Charvat, *Origins of American Critical Thought*, p. 60.

49. Patrick, *Savannah's Pioneer Theatre*, pp. 79, 71.

50. Cited in Kahan's ed. of Maxwell, *The Mysterious Father*, app. 2, p. 49.

51. William P. Trent, *William Gilmore Simms* (Boston: Houghton Mifflin, 1892), pp. 26, 47.

52. Martin S. Shockley, "American Plays in the Richmond Theatre, 1819-1838," *Studies in Philology* 37 (1940): 119.

53. Maria Pinckney, *Essays, Religious, Moral, Dramatic and Poetical* (Charleston, S.C.: Archibald E. Miller, 1818). For information on Pinckney, see *The Library of Southern Literature*, ed. Edwin Anderson Alderman et al. (New Orleans: Martin and Hoyt, 1908-13), 15: 345.

3. The Dramatist as Humorist in New Orleans

1. For a thorough account of James H. Caldwell's activities, see James H. Dormon Jr., *Theater in the Ante Bellum South, 1815-1861* (Chapel Hill: Univ. of North Carolina Press, 1967), pp. 47-49, 76-101, 173-88. For theater in New Orleans, see John S. Kendall, *The Golden Age of the New Orleans Theatre* (Baton Rouge: Louisiana State Univ. Press, 1952); and Nelle Smither, *A History of the English Theatre in New Orleans* (1944; rpt. New York: Benjamin Blom, 1967).

2. Noah Ludlow, *Dramatic Life as I Found It* (1880; rpt. New York: Benjamin Blom, 1966); Sol Smith, *Theatrical Management in the West and South for Thirty Years* (1868; rpt. New York: Benjamin Blom, 1968).

3. This sketch is reprinted in Smith, *Theatrical Managements*, pp. xv-xx.

4. *Daily Reveille*, Oct. 2, 1845, rpt. in *Old Southwest Humor from the St. Louis Reveille, 1844-1850*, ed. Fritz Oelschlaeger (Columbia: University of Missouri Press, 1990), p. 151.

5. Quoted in Dormon, *Theater in the Ante Bellum South*, p. 179.

6. Letter from Field to Smith, in Ludlow-Maury-Field Collection, Missouri Historical Society, St. Louis.

7. For extensive information on the theatrical management of Ludlow and Smith, see, Dormon, *Theater in the Ante Bellum South*, chap. 8.

8. Smith, *Theatrical Management*, p. 138.

9. For information on Grice, Hennicott, and Hentz, see Quinn, *American Drama from the Beginning to the Civil War*, pp. 154, 263-64, 265.

10. Joseph Holt Ingraham, a popular romancer, had published *Lafitte; or, The Pirate of the Gulf* in 1836.

11. A.Q. Walton, *A History of the Detection . . . of John A. Murrell, the Great Western Land Pirate* (Athens, Tenn., 1835).

12. For other native plays presented in New Orleans, see Joseph P. Roppolo, "Local and Topical Plays in New Orleans, 1806-1865," and "American Themes, Heroes and History on the New Orleans Stage, 1806-65," *Tulane Studies in English* 4 (1954): 91-124, and 5 (1955): 151-81.

13. For information on Field's life and career, see Oelschlager, introduction to *Old Southwest Humor*, Meserve, *Heralds of Promise*, pp. 166-69; *America's Lost Plays*, vol. 14, ed. Eugene R. Page (Bloomington: Indiana Univ. Press, 1940, 1965), 237-40; Carle Brooks Spotts, "The Development of Fiction on the Missouri Frontier," *Missouri Historical Review* 2 (1935): 186-94; and the *Dictionary of American Biography*.

14. Bernard J. Reynolds, *Sketches of Mobile: From 1814 to the Present Times* (Mobile, Ala.: B.H. Richardson, 1868), pp. 54-55.

15. "Debts due by the late J.M. Field in Mobile—as far as yet ascertained—April 18, 1856," in Ludlow-Maury-Field Collection.

16. Joseph M. Field, *The Drama in Pokerville, the Bench and Bar of Jurytown, and Other Stories* (Philadelphia: T.B. Peterson, 1847). References in the text cite this edition.

17. Letter from Field to Ludlow, Sept. 1, 1840, in Ludlow-Maury-Field Col-

lection; Lilian Whiting, *Kate Field: A Record* (Boston: Little, Brown, 1899), pp. 11-12.

18. Letter from Field to Smith, Oct. 6, 1835, in Ludlow-Maury-Field Collection.

19. "A Lyncher's Own Story," *Daily Reveille,* July 6, 1845, rpt. in Oehlschlaeger, *Old Southwest Humor,* pp. 226-32.

20. Quoted in Dwight Thomas and David K. Jackson, *The Poe Log* (Boston: G.K. Hall, 1987), p. 651.

21. Letter from Field to Smith, March 25, 1835, Sol Smith Collection, Missouri Historical Society, St. Louis. Also in Oelschlaeger, *Old Southwest Humor,* pp. 13-14.

22. Ludlow, *Dramatic Life,* pp. xxv, 264.

23. Smith, *Theatrical Management,* pp. 180-81.

24. Ludlow, *Dramatic Life,* pp. 570-71.

25. This information is given in Kendall, *Golden Age,* p. 174.

26. Smith, *Theatrical Management,* p. 157.

27. Oelschlaeger, introduction to *Old Southwest Humor,* p. 13.

28. Ludlow, *Dramatic Life,* p. 570.

29. Reprinted in *Spirit of the Times* 15 (July 21, 1845): p. 200.

30. Ludlow, *Dramatic Life,* pp. 624-25.

31. For information on Bennett, see Oliver Carlson, *The Man Who Made News: James Gordon Bennett* (New York: Duell, Sloan & Pearce, 1942); and James L. Crouthamel, *Bennett's New York Herald and the Popular Press* (Syracuse, N.Y.: Syracuse Univ. Press, 1989).

32. Ludlow, *Dramatic Life,* pp. 507-8.

33. Joseph P. Roppolo, "Uncle Tom in New Orleans," *New England Quarterly* 27 (1954): 219.

34. Ibid., 220.

35. Francis Hodge, *Yankee Theatre* (Austin: Univ. of Texas Press, 1964), pp. 148-49.

36. Joseph M. Field, *Job and His Children,* in Page, *America's Lost Plays,* 14: 240.

37. Quoted in Whiting, *Kate Field,* p. 36.

38. Field, *Job and His Children,* 14: 258.

39. Reprinted in *Spirit of the Times* 22 (September 1, 1852): 360.

4. Drama Goes to War

1. See Thomas F. Gossett, *Uncle Tom's Cabin and American Culture* (Dallas: Southern Methodist Univ. Press, 1985), pp. 430-31; and Jeannette Reid Tandy, "Pro-Slavery Propaganda in American Fiction of the Fifties," *South Atlantic Quarterly* 21 (April 1922): 41-50.

2. Gossett, *Uncle Tom's Cabin,* p. 271; Robert C. Toll, *Blacking Up: The Minstrel Show in Nineteenth-Century America* (New York: Oxford Univ. Press, 1974), pp.

91, 94-95. For further information, see Harry Birdoff, *The World's Greatest Hit: Uncle Tom's Cabin* (New York: S.F. Vannie, 1947).

3. Gossett, *Uncle Tom's Cabin*, p. 281; Dormon, *Theater in the Ante Bellum South*, p. 279.

4. Roppolo, "Uncle Tom in New Orleans," pp. 221-22.

5. Maria Ward Brown, *The Life of Dan Rice* (Long Branch, N.J.: author, 1901), p. 438.

6. Roppolo, "Uncle Tom in New Orleans," p. 222.

7. Quoted in ibid., p. 222.

8. Ibid., pp. 222-23.

9. Ibid., p. 224.

10. Watson, *Antebellum Charleston Dramatists*, pp. 116, 117.

11. William Gilmore Simms, *Michael Bonham; or, The Fall of Bexar,* in *Southern Literary Messenger* 18 (Feb.-June 1852). References in the text cite this edition.

12. Simms, "Calhoun.—An Ode," printed at the end of "Charleston, The Palmetto City," *Harper's New Monthly Magazine* 15 (Jan. 1857): 22.

13. William Gilmore Simms, *Norman Maurice*, in *Poems: Descriptive, Dramatic, Legendary, and Contemplative*, 1 (New York: Redfield, 1853). References in the text cite this edition.

14. For Canonge and other French dramatists of New Orleans, see Charles S. Watson, "Early Drama in New Orleans: The French Tradition," *Journal of American Drama and Theatre* 2 (Winter 1990): 11-26.

15. L. Placide Canonge, *La Louisianaise* (New Orleans: Sourdes Chassaignac, n.d.).

16. L. Placide Canonge, *Nojoque: Une grave question pour un continent* (New Orleans: Imp. de la "Plume de Bronze," 1867).

17. *New Orleans Times Democrat,* Jan. 22, 1893; Edouard Fortier, *Les lettres française en Louisiane* (Quebec: Imp. l'Action Sociale Limitée, 1915), p. 8; Joseph Gabriel de Baroncelli, *Le théatre français* (New Orleans: Geo. Muller, 1906), p. 54.

18. E.g., T. Wharton Collens, who composed *The Martyr Patriots; or, Louisiana in 1769*, performed at the St. Charles Theatre, 1836. It is collected in *The Louisiana Book: Selections from the Literature of the State*, ed. Thomas McCaleb (New Orleans: R.F. Straughan, 1894).

19. *Dictionary of American Biography;* Amos Aschbach Ettinger, *The Mission to Spain of Pierre Soulé* (New Haven, Conn.: Yale University Press, 1932), pp. 115-16.

20. L. Placide Canonge, *France et Espagne; ou, La Louisiane en 1768 et 1769* (New Orleans, 1850), p. 17. References given in the text cite this edition.

21. Kendall, *Golden Age of the New Orleans Theatre*, p. 450ff.; Thomas Allston Brown, *History of the American Stage* (New York: Dick & Fitzgerald, 1870); Montrose J. Moses, *Representative Plays by American Dramatists*, 3 vols. (New York: Dutton, 1918-25), 2: 767-70.

22. Birdoff, *World's Greatest Hit*, p. 431.

23. Moses, *Representative Plays*, 2: 768.

24. William Gilmore Simms, *Katharine Walton; or, The Rebel of Dorchester* (New York: Redfield, 1954; Spartanburg, S.C.: Reprint, 1976).

25. C.W. Tayleure, *Horse-Shoe Robinson* (1858) in Moses, *Representative Plays*, 2: 808-9. References in the text cite this edition.

26. See John Pendleton Kennedy, *Horse-Shoe Robinson* (New York: American Book, 1937), p. 389.

27. Clifton W. Tayleure, *The Boy Martyrs of Sept. 12, 1814. A Local Historical Drama in Three Acts.* (New York: French, 1859). All references are given in the text.

28. Robert J. Brugger, *Maryland: A Middle Temperament, 1634-1980* (Baltimore, Md.: Johns Hopkins Univ. Press, 1988), pp. 269-79.

29. Information on the Confederate theater is taken primarily from Iline Fife, "The Theatre during the Confederacy" (Ph.D. diss., Louisiana State Univ., 1949), and the "Confederate Theatre," *Southern Speech Journal* 20 (1955): 224-31; O.G. Brockett and Lenyth Brockett, "Civil War Theater: Contemporary Treatments," *Civil War History* 1 (1955): 229-50; Richard B. Harwell, "Civil War Theater: The Richmond Stage," *Civil War History* 1 (1955): 295-304; and Kendall, *Golden Age of the New Orleans Theater.*

30. Harwell, "Civil War Theater," p. 302.

31. Quoted in Fife, "The Theatre during the Confederacy," p. 259.

32. Ibid., p. 232, citing comments by John Hill Hewitt's daughter.

33. *Dictionary of American Biography.* For more information see John W. Wagner, "James Hewitt: His Life and Works" (Ph.D. diss., Indiana University, 1969). For Hewitt and other Confederate dramatists, see Charles S. Watson, "Confederate Drama: The Plays of John Hill Hewitt and James Dabney McCabe," *Southern Literary Journal* 21 (Spring 1989): 100-12.

34. William Craig Winden, "The Life and Music Theatre Works of John Hill Hewitt" (Ph.D. diss., University of Illinois, 1972), p. 24.

35. John Hill Hewitt, introduction to *Shadows on the Wall; or, Glimpses of the Past* (Baltimore, Md.: Turnbull Brothers, 1877). All works by Hewitt are held in the John Hill Hewitt Collection of Emory University Library, Atlanta, Georgia. I am indebted for the opportunity to use this valuable archive. All holdings in the collection are carefully listed in Frank W. Hoogerwerf, *John Hill Hewitt: Sources and Bibliography* (Atlanta, Ga.: Emory University, 1981).

36. Richard B. Harwell, "A Reputation by Reflection: John Hill Hewitt and Edgar Allan Poe," *Emory University Quarterly* 3 (June 1947): 104-15; and John Hill Hewitt, *Recollections of Poe,* ed. Richard B. Harwell (Atlanta: Emory University Library, 1949).

37. John Hill Hewitt, "Aunt Harriet Becha Stowe" (Baltimore, Md.: Henry McCaffrey, 1853). This is the printed sheet music for this song.

38. Information included in an unpaged manuscript of Hewitt's pseudonymous autobiography, "Gilbert Crampton - Romance and Reality. Being the biography of a man of letters. Edited by a Cosmopolitan" (n.p.), in the Hewitt Collection.

39. Fife, "The Theatre during the Confederacy," pp. 146-47.

40. Hewitt, *The Scouts,* manuscript play is held in the Hewitt Collection. Quotations are from the unpaged copy.

41. Iline Fife, "The Confederate Theatre in Georgia," *Georgia Review* 9 (1955): 309.

42. According to Richard B. Harwell, "John Hill Hewitt Collection," *South Atlantic Bulletin* 13 (March 1948): 4, Hewitt lists 43 titles for the stage—some un-performed—composed before, during, and after the war. The figure is obviously incomplete, since there are 35 plays in the collection, and Hewitt lists 21 not at Emory.

43. Hewitt, *The Vivandiere*, unpaged manuscript in the Hewitt Collection.

44. Quoted in Fife, "The Theatre during the Confederacy," pp. 231-32.

45. Katharine M. Jones, *Heroines of Dixie* (New York: Bobbs-Merrill, 1955), pp. 33, 39.

46. Elizabeth Moss, *Domestic Novelists in the Old South* (Baton Rouge: Louisiana State Univ. Press, 1992), pp. 176-78.

47. Jones, introduction to *Heroines of Dixie*, p. v.

48. John Hill Hewitt, *King Linkum, The First*, ed. Richard B. Harwell (Atlanta, Ga.: Emory University Library, 1947). References in the text cite this edition. This is the only play of Hewitt's to be published. All quotations (cited in the text) are from this edition. See also David M. Potter, "Review of *King Linkum, The First*," *Emory University Quarterly* 3 (June 1947): 124.

49. Quinn, *American Drama from the Civil War to the Present*, 1: 6.

50. Hewitt, *The Veteran*, unpaged manuscript in the Hewitt Collection.

51. James D. McCabe, *The Guerillas* (Richmond, Va.: West & Johnson, 1863). A copy of this play is held in the Rare Book Collection, Virginia State Library, Richmond. References in the text cite this edition.

52. See "Editorial Introduction" to *The Guerillas;* and Carla Waal, "The First Original Confederate Drama: *The Guerillas*," *Virginia Magazine of History and Biography* 70 (1962): 459-67.

53. This biographical information is taken from James Wood Davidson, *The Living Writers of the South* (New York: Carleton, 1869), pp. 345-46.

54. Fife, "The Theatre during the Confederacy," pp. 417-19.

55. Quoted in ibid., p. 246a.

56. Quoted in Waal, "First Original Confederate Drama," p. 461.

57. Quoted in Fife, "The Theatre during the Confederacy," pp. 246-48.

58. Joseph Hodgson, *The Confederate Vivandiere* (Montgomery, Ala.: J.M. Floyd, 1862). See Harwell, "Civil War Theater," p. 297.

59. Brockett and Brockett, "Civil War Theater," p. 235.

5. The Modern Drama of Espy Williams

1. For lists of plays composed in the postbellum South, see Paul T. Nolan, "Alabama Drama, 1870-1916: A Checklist," *Alabama Review* (1965) in *Provincial Drama in America, 1870-1916: A Casebook of Primary Materials*, ed. Paul T. Nolan, pp. 21-28 (Metuchen, N.J.: Scarecrow, 1967); Nolan, "Georgia Drama between the Wars, 1870-1916: A Checklist," *Georgia Historical Quarterly* 51 (1967): 216-30; Katherine Finley and Paul T. Nolan, "Mississippi Dramas between Wars, 1870-

1916: A Checklist and an Argument, Part II," *Journal of Mississippi History* 26 (1964): 299-306.

2. Richard Moody, ed. *Dramas from the American Theatre* (Cleveland: World, 1966), p. 573.

3. This chapter is based on Charles S. Watson, "The First Modern Dramatist of the South: Espy Williams," *Southern Quarterly,* Winter 1989, pp. 77-91.

4. Biographical information for Espy Williams is taken from Patricia K. Rickels, "The Literary Career of Espy Williams: New Orleans Poet and Playwright (1852-1908)" (Ph.D. diss., Louisiana State Univ., 1961); *Who Was Who in America* (Chicago: Marquis, 1963); and the essays on Williams in Nolan, *Provincial Drama.* Both Rickels and Nolan make extensive use of the Espy Williams Collection at the University of Southwestern Louisiana, Lafayette, which holds manuscripts of his plays and other writings.

5. Paul T. Nolan, "An Edition of *The Atheist,*" in Nolan, *Provincial Drama,* p. 102n. For complete bibliographical information on this and other essays by Nolan, see *Provincial Drama.*

6. Paul T. Nolan, "Journal of a Young Southern Playwright: Espy Williams of New Orleans, 1874-75," *Louisiana Studies* 1, no. 3 (1962): 30-50.

7. Quoted in Paul T. Nolan, "A Shakespeare Idol in America," in *Provincial Drama,* pp. 198-210.

8. Quoted in preface to *The Selected Works of Espy Williams: Southern Playwright,* ed. Paul T. Nolan, Kentucky Microcards, ser. A, no. 45 (Lexington: University Press of Kentucky, 1960), p. iv.

9. Espy Williams, *The Dream of Art and Other Poems* (New York: Putnam, 1892), p. 20. References in the text cite this edition.

10. Quoted in preface to Williams, *Selected Works,* p. iv.

11. Rickels, "Literary Career," p. 152.

12. Paul T. Nolan, "Williams' *Dante:* The Death of Nineteenth Century Drama," in Nolan, *Provincial Drama,* pp. 127-28.

13. Williams, *Dream of Art,* p. 22.

14. Quoted in Paul T. Nolan, "Classical Tragedy in the Province Theater," in Nolan, *Provincial Drama,* p. 139.

15. Quoted in Rickel, "Literary Career," p. 43.

16. Espy Williams, *Parrhasius; or, Thriftless Ambition: A Dramatic Poem* (New Orleans, La.: Southern, 1879), p. 26.

17. Rickels, "Literary Career," pp. 33-34.

18. Nolan, "Journal," p. 30.

19. Quoted in Rickels, "Literary Career," p. 89.

20. Nolan, "Edition of *The Atheist,*" p. 109.

21. This play is included in Williams, *Selected Works,* pp. 80-145, and cited by reference in the text.

22. Williams, *Selected Works,* p. 127.

23. Williams, *The Husband: A Society Play* (New Orleans, La.: Theo A. Ray, 1898), hereafter cited in the text.

24. Quoted in Rickels, "Literary Career," pp. 140-41.

25. Rickels, "Literary Career," pp. 154-55.

26. Williams, *Selected Works,* p. 140.

27. Ibid.

28. Paul T. Nolan, "The Life and Death of a Louisiana Play: Espy Williams' 'Unorna,'" in Nolan, *Provincial Drama,* pp. 142-57.

29. *New Orleans Item,* June 21, 1902, quoted in Nolan, *Provincial Drama,* p. 149.

30. Nolan, "Life and Death," p. 152.

31. Nolan, *Provincial Drama,* p. 170.

32. Nolan, "Shakespeare Idol," p. 210n.

33. Rickels, "Literary Career," pp. 153-54.

34. Hamlin Garland, *Crumbling Idols: Twelve Essays on Art and Literature* (1894); rpt. Gainesville, Fla.: Scholars' Facsimiles, 1952), pp. 99-100.

35. *The Clairvoyant* is included in Williams, *Selected Works,* pp. 215-85, cited by page references in the text.

36. Nolan, "Life and Death," p. 145; Paul T. Nolan, ed. *Marlowe: The Buried Name,* Kentucky Microcards, ser. A, no. 31 (Lexington: Univ. Press of Kentucky, 1961), hereafter cited in the text.

37. Rickels, "Literary Career," pp. 155-57.

6. The Leadership of Paul Green

1. *The One Act Plays of Lee Arthur,* ed. and intro. Paul T. Nolan (Cody, Wyo.: Pioneer Drama Service, 1962). The playwright's original name was Lee Arthur Kahn. See also Paul T. Nolan, "A Southern Playwright: Lee Arthur Kahn," *Southern Speech Journal* 27 (Spring 1962): 202-12.

2. Nolan, *Provincial Drama,* p. 24.

3. Quoted in George Brown Tindall, *The Emergence of the New South,* 1913-45 (Baton Rouge: Louisiana State Univ. press, 1967), p. 104.

4. Quoted in ibid., p. 110.

5. Three sources that have been valuable to me are Vincent S. Kenny, *Paul Green* (New York: Twayne, 1971); Laurence G. Avery, "Paul Green," in *Fifty Southern Writers after 1900: A Bio-Bibliographical Sourcebook,* ed. Joseph M. Flora and Robert Bain (Westport, Conn.: Greenwood Press, 1987); and *A Southern Life: Letters of Paul Green, 1916-1981,* ed. Laurence G. Avery (Chapel Hill: Univ. of North Carolina Press, 1994).

6. *Reviewer,* Jan. 1925, pp. 71-76.

7. Quoted in Walter J. Meserve, "An American Drama, 1920-1941," in *The Revels: History of Drama in English,* vol. 3, *American Drama* (London: Methuen, 1977), p. 243.

8. Paul Green, *The Last of the Lowries* (New York: Samuel French, 1922), p. 264.

9. Green, *The Hawthorn Tree* (Chapel Hill: Univ. of North Carolina Press, 1943), p. 32.

10. Quoted in Kenny, *Paul Green,* p. 49.

11. Quoted in Barrett Clark, *Paul Green* (New York: Robert M. McBride, 1928), p. 14.

12. Green, *White Dresses,* in *Five Plays of the South* (New York: Hill & Wang, 1963), p. 307.

13. Green, *Hymn to the Rising Sun,* in ibid., p. 194.

14. Alan Downer, *Fifty Years of American Drama, 1900-1950* (Chicago: Regnery, 1951), p. 82.

15. Green, *In Abraham's Bosom,* in *Five Plays of the South,* p. 167.

16. Green, *Out of the South* (New York: Harper, 1939), pp. 207, 307.

17. Hallie Flanagan, *Arena: The History of the Federal Theatre* (New York: Benjamin Blom, 1965), pp. 84-85. Copies of the script of *Roll, Sweet Chariot* (labeled "Script No Date") are held in the Paul Green Collection, University of North Carolina, Chapel Hill. This version of the play was never printed, but in 1935 under the inaccurate title *Roll, Sweet Chariot* the first version, originally entitled *Potter's Field,* was republished with minor changes. It was mistakenly called "the complete acting version." See *Roll, Sweet Chariot: A Symphonic Play of the Negro People* (New York: Samuel French, 1935), second page unnumbered of the reprinted cast. Finally, returning to the title and first version Green included *Potter's Field* in his collection *Out of the South* (1939).

18. *New York Times,* Oct. 14, 1934, sec. X, p. 1; *New York Daily Mirror,* October 15, 1934.

19. *Theatre Arts Monthly* 18 (November 1934): 814; Paul Green, "Symphonic Drama," in *Dramatic Heritage* (New York: Samuel French, 1953), p. 22.

20. Green, *Dramatic Heritage,* pp. 21-22; Letter from Hewes to Green, n.d. [1934], Green Collection.

21. *Reviewer,* Jan. 1925, p. 109.

22. Script of *Roll, Sweet Chariot,* n.p., Green Collection.

23. Green, *Letters,* p. 537.

24. Green, *Potter's Field,* p. 360.

25. Ibid., p. 363.

26. *New York Times,* Oct. 14, 1934, sec. X, p. 1.

27. Quoted by Agatha Boyd Adams, *Paul Green of Chapel Hill* (Chapel Hill: Univ. of North Carolina Press, 1951), p. 38.

28. Green, *The Field God and In Abraham's Bosom* (New York: Robert McBride, 1927), p. 301.

29. Green, *Dramatic Heritage,* pp. 81-82.

30. Green, *Five Plays of the South,* p. 205.

31. Adams, *Paul Green,* p. 50.

32. Paul Green, "With the Group Theatre—A Remembrance," in *Plough and Furrow* (New York: Samuel French, 1963), p. 49.

33. Harold Clurman, *The Fervent Years* (New York: Knopf, 1945), p. 44.

34. Green, *Plough and Furrow,* p. 48; *Dramatic Heritage,* p. 82.

35. The last version of *The House of Connelly* appears in Green, *Five Plays of the South.*

36. Green, *Plough and Furrow,* pp. 43, 48.

37. Kenny, *Paul Green,* p. 32, errs in saying that these women are bastard offspring of the Connellys.

38. See N. Bryllion Fagin, "In Search of an American Cherry Orchard," *Texas Quarterly* 1 (Summer-Autumn 1958): 132-42.

39. Green, *Letters,* p. 569.

40. Green, "Symphonic Drama," and "The Lost Colony: A Dialogue at Evening," in *Dramatic Heritage,* pp. 25-26, 46-47.

41. Green, "Lost Colony," p. 47.

42. Ibid.; "Symphonic Drama," p. 26.

43. Green, *Dramatic Heritage,* pp. 49-51.

44. Green, "Some Notes on Art and Southern Attitudes," in *Plough and Furrow,* pp. 57-79.

45. Green, *The Lost Colony,* in *Out of the South,* p. 573.

46. Green, *The Common Glory* (Chapel Hill: Univ. of North Carolina Press, 1948), p. 117. References in the text cite this first edition. A revised edition was published in 1975.

47. Green, *Letters,* pp. 459-60.

48. Green, *Dramatic Heritage,* p. 68.

49. Green, *Letters,* p. 545.

50. Letter, April 29, 1954; Green Collection.

51. Letters, December 5, 1954; Green Collection.

52. Letters, May 14, 1953; August 5, 1954, Green Collection.

53. Letters, March 20, 1955; December 20, 1955, Green Collection.

54. Paul Green, *Wilderness Road* (New York: Samuel French, 1956), p. 156.

55. Ibid., pp. 70, 80.

56. Letter, July 18, 1955, Green Collection.

57. Letter, August 13, 1955, Green Collection.

58. Undated copy of Sanborne's sermon, Green Collection.

59. Letter, October 28, 1955, Green Collection.

60. Thomas L. Connelly, *The Marble Man: Robert E. Lee and His Image in American Society* (New York: Knopf, 1977), p. 97. Donald Davidson, "Lee in the Mountains" in Louis D. Rubin, Jr., ed., *The Literary South* (New York: Wiley, 1979), pp. 457-60.

61. Douglas Southall Freeman, *R.E. Lee,* 4 vols. (New York: Scribner, 1934-35).

62. Connelly, *Marble Man,* chap. 5 in Lewis Funke, "History Relived," *New York Times,* July 13, 1958, sec. II, p. 1.

63. Paul Green, "Dialogue by the Lakeside," in *Plough and Furrow,* pp. 19, 29.

64. Paul Green, *The Confederacy* (New York: Samuel French, 1959), p. 36. All references in the text cite this edition.

65. Gamaliel Bradford, *Lee the American* (1912; rpt., Boston: Houghton Mifflin, 1927), pp. 39-43. For Lee's sympathy with the South's position on slavery, however, see Freeman, *R.E. Lee,* 1: 271-73.

66. Telegram, April 9, 1958, Green Collection.

67. *Norfolk Virginian-Pilot,* May 27, 28, 1958.

68. Parry Edmund Stroud, *Stephen Vincent Benét* (New York: Twayne, 1963), p. 53.

69. Letter, February 13, 1958, Green Collection.

70. Letter, March 15, 1965, Green Collection.

71. Letter, March 25, 1965, Green Collection.

72. Green, Letters, p. 638.

73. Green, *Dramatic Heritage,* pp. 52-60.

74. Green, *Letters,* p. 629.

75. Green, *Louisiana Cavalier,* rehearsal script, 1976, North Carolina Collection, Wilson Library, University of North Carolina, Chapel Hill.

76. Green, *Letters,* pp. 685-87.

7. DuBose Heyward's Transmutation of Black Culture

1. Two helpful books on Heyward are Frank Durham, *DuBose Heyward: The Man Who Wrote Porgy* (Columbia: Univ. of South Carolina Press, 1955; Port Washington, N.Y.: Kennikat Press, 1965); and William H. Slavick, *DuBose Heyward* (Boston: Twayne, 1981).

2. Gerald Johnson, "The Congo, Mr. Mencken," *Reviewer,* July 1923; rpt. in *South-Watching: Selected Essays by Gerald W. Johnson,* ed. Fred Hobson (Chapel Hill: Univ. of North Carolina Press, 1983), p. 8.

3. Quoted in Fred Hobson, *Serpent in Eden: H.L. Mencken and the South* (Chapel Hill: Univ. of North Carolina Press, 1974), p. 70.

4. Gerald W. Johnson, "Call for a Custom Built Poet," *Southwest Review* 10 (April 1923): 30.

5. Alain Locke, "The Drama of Negro Life," *Theatre Arts Monthly* 10 (October 1926): 706.

6. Slavick, *DuBose Heyward,* p. 78.

7. Ibid., p. 80.

8. Thomas Wolfe, *Welcome to Our City,* ed. and intro. Richard S. Kennedy (Baton Rouge: Louisiana State Univ. Press, 1983); this was its first publication.

9. DuBose Heyward, "Contemporary Southern Poetry," *Bookman* 62 (Jan. and March 1926): 561-64, 52-56.

10. Quoted in Hobson, *Serpent in Eden,* p. 65.

11. Paul Green, "Diary Notes," June 10, 1928, p. 1, North Carolina Collection.

12. Quoted in Slavick, *DuBose Heyward,* p. 185, no. 9.

13. Hershel Brickell in *Saturday Review of Literature* 5 (Feb. 23, 1929): 703.

14. Donald Davidson, "An Author Divided against Himself," *Critical Almanac,* February 3, 1929; rpt. in *The Spyglass: Views and Reviews, 1920-1930,* ed. John Tyree Fain (Nashville: Vanderbilt Univ. Press, 1963), p. 33.

15. W.J. Cash, "The Mind of the South," *American Mercury* 18 (Oct. 1929): 185-92.

16. Gerald Johnson in *Virginia Quarterly Review,* January 1935; rpt. in Hobson, *South-Watching,* p. 35.

17. DuBose Heyward, *Brass Ankle* (New York: Farrar & Rinehart, 1931), p. 63.

18. Ibid., p. 100.

19. Quoted in Durham, *DuBose Heyward,* p. 133.

20. DuBose Heyward, *Mamba's Daughters* (New York: Farrar & Rinehart, 1939), p. 141. References in the text cite this edition.

21. Durham, *DuBose Heyward,* p. 134.

8. The Southern Marxism of Lillian Hellman

1. For Hellman's family background and biographical information, I have used Lillian Hellman, *An Unfinished Woman: A Memoir* (Boston: Little, Brown, 1969); Hellman, *Pentimento: A Book of Portraits* (Boston: Little, Brown, 1973); William Wright, *Lillian Hellman: The Image, the Woman* (New York: Simon & Schuster, 1986), esp. pp. 17-23; and Carl Rollyson, *Lillian Hellman: Her Legend and Legacy* (New York: St. Martin's Press, 1988). Two critical works are Doris V. Falk, *Lillian Hellman* (New York: Frederick Ungar, 1978); and Katherine Lederer, *Lillian Hellman* (Boston: Twayne, 1979).

2. Information obtained from Fall Pilgrimage brochure, 1995, the Marengo County Historical Society of Alabama.

3. Hellman, *Unfinished Woman,* pp. 3-5; *The Little Foxes,* in *Six Plays by Lillian Hellman* (New York: Vintage Books, 1979), p. 225.

4. Hellman, *Pentimento,* p. 70.

5. Ibid., p. 32.

6. Ibid., pp. 12-13.

7. Hellman, *Unfinished Woman,* p. 27.

8. Ibid., p. 14.

9. Ibid., p. 15.

10. Hellman, *Pentimento,* p. 94.

11. *Conversations with Lillian Hellman,* ed. Jackson R. Bryer (Jackson: Univ. Press of Mississippi, 1986), pp. 196-97.

12. Rollyson, *Lillian Hellman,* p. 2.

13. Thomas P. Adler, *American Drama, 1940-1960: A Critical History* (New York: Twayne, 1994), p. 53.

14. *Another Part of the Forest,* in *Six Plays by Lillian Hellman,* pp. 332, 379. References in the text to this play and *The Little Foxes* cite this edition.

15. Quoted in Lederer, *Lillian Hellman,* p. 71.

16. The apt title describes a scene in Shakespeare's gory *Titus Andronicus.* See Manfred Triesch, "Hellman's *Another Part of the Forest,*" *Explicator* 24 (Oct. 1965), item 20.

17. E. Merton Coulter, *The Confederate States of America* (Baton Rouge: Louisiana State Univ. Press, 1950), pp. 220, 226-29.

18. For a comparison of the Hubbards with another profiteering family of Alabama in T.S. Stribling's novel *The Store,* set in 1885, see William T. Going, "The Prestons of Talladega and the Hubbards of Bowden: A Dramatic Note," in *Essays in Alabama Literature* (Tuscaloosa: Univ. of Alabama Press, 1975), pp. 142-55.

19. E. Merton Coulter, *The South during Reconstruction, 1865-1877* (Baton Rouge: Louisiana State Univ. Press, 1947), pp. 202-3. For a more favorable description, see Thomas D. Clark, "The Post-Civil War Economy in the South," in *Jews in the South,* ed. Leonard Dinnerstein and Mary Dale Palsson (Baton Rouge: Louisiana State Univ. Press, 1973), pp. 159-69; and Arnold Shankman, "Friend or Foe? Southern Blacks View the Jew, 1880-1935," in *Turn to the South: Essays on Southern Jewry* (Charlottesville: Univ. Press of Virginia, 1979), pp. 105-23.

20. Lucius Beebe, "Stage Asides: Miss Hellman Talks of Her Latest Play, *The Little Foxes,*" *New York Herald Tribune,* March 12, 1939, sec. 6, pp. 1, 2; rpt. in Bryer, *Conversations with Lillian Hellman,* p. 8.

21. Rollyson, *Lillian Hellman,* pp. 123-25.

22. Ibid., p. 141.

23. For a discussion of these three dramas of business, see Robert Heilman, "Dramas of Money," *Shenandoah* 21 (Summer 1970): 20-33.

24. Lillian Hellman, *Toys in the Attic* (New York: Dramatists Play Service, 1960), p. 81, also echoes Scarlett's closing words when she says, "Tomorrow's another day."

25. Lederer, *Lillian Hellman,* p. 40.

9. Black Drama: Politics or Culture

1. For biographical information, see William Edward Farrison, *William Wells Brown* (Chicago: Univ. of Chicago Press, 1969); and William Wells Brown, M.D., *My Southern Home; or, The South and Its People* (1880; rpt. Upper Saddle River, N.J.: Gregg, 1968).

2. See Farrison, *William Wells Brown,* p. 279.

3. William Wells Brown, *The Escape; or, A Leap for Freedom: A Drama in Five Acts* (Boston: Robert F. Wallcut, 1858), in *Black Theater, U.S.A.: 45 Plays by Black Americans, 1847-1974,* ed. James V. Hatch (New York: Free Press, 1974).

4. For a bibliography including dramatists born after 1900, see Bernard L. Peterson Jr., *Early Black American Playwrights and Dramatic Writers* (Westport, Conn.: Greenwood Press, 1990).

5. For this biographical information, see Robert T. Kerlin, "A Poet from Bardstown," *South Atlantic Quarterly* 20 (1921): 213-21; and *Caroling Dusk,* ed. Countee Cullen (New York: Harper, 1927).

6. Kerlin, "A Poet from Bardstown," p. 220.

7. Sterling Brown, ed., *Negro Caravan* (New York: Dryden, 1941), p. 343.

8. Joseph S. Cotter, *Caleb, the Degenerate: A Study of the Types, Customs, and Needs of the American Negro* (Louisville, Ky.: Bradley & Gilbert, 1903), in Hatch, *Black Theater, U.S.A.*

9. For unfavorable opinions, see Hatch, introduction to *Caleb* in *Black Theater;* and Doris E. Abramson, *Negro Playwrights in the American Theatre, 1925-1959* (New York: Columbia Univ. Press, 1967), pp. 14-18.

10. John White, *Black Leadership in America, 1895-1968* (London: Longman, 1985), pp. 23-43.

11. Cotter, *Caleb, the Degenerate*, p. 43.

12. Ibid., pp. 44-46.

13. On this distinction, see Kathy A. Perkins, ed., introduction to *Black Female Playwrights: An Anthology of Plays before 1950* (Bloomington: Indiana University Press, 1989), p. 3.

14. Quoted in Warren G. Carson, "Hurston as Dramatist: The Florida Connection," in *Zora in Florida*, ed. Steve Glassman and Kathryn Lee Seidel (Orlando: Univ. of Central Florida Press, 1991), p. 122.

15. Quoted in *Columbia Literary History of the United States*, ed. Emory Elliott (New York: Columbia Univ. Press, 1988), pp. 838-39.

16. Green, *Letters*, p. 312.

17. Zora Heale Hurston, *Color Struck* and *The First One*, both in Perkins, *Black Female Playwrights*. References in the text cite this edition.

18. Langston Hughes and Zora Neale Hurston, *Mule Bone: A Comedy of Negro Life* (New York: Harper Perennial, 1991), ed. and intro. George Houston Bass and Henry Louis Gates Jr. (Unfortunately, the reproduced text of the play in this welcome volume is riddled with typographical errors.) References in the text cite this edition.

19. Quoted in Robert E. Hemenway, *Zora Neale Hurston: A Literary Biography;* excerpted in the Bass and Gates edition of *Mule Bone*, pp. 183-84.

20. Henry Louis Gates Jr., "A Tragedy of Negro Life," in *Mule Bone*, p. 21.

21. Ibid., p. 11.

22. On this kind of verbal interplay, see the excerpt from Hemenway, *Zora Neale Hurston*, in *Mule Bone*, pp. 182-83.

23. May Miller in *Journal of Association of College Women* (1936), quoted in Perkins, *Black Female Playwrights*, p. 143.

24. May Miller, *Riding the Goat* and *Stragglers in the Dust*, both in Perkins, *Black Female Playwrights*.

25. Georgia Douglas Johnson, *A Sunday Morning in the South*, in Hatch, *Black Theater*, and in Perkins, *Black Female Playwrights*.

26. Johnson, *Blue Blood*, in Perkins, *Black Female Playwrights*, p. 41.

27. Johnson, *Blue-Eyed Black Boy*, in *Black Female Playwrights*, pp. 47-51.

28. Mary P. Burrill, *Aftermath* and *They That Sit in Darkness*, both in Perkins, *Black Female Playwrights*, pp. 55-74 (with some biographical information).

29. For biographical information on Richardson, see Bernard L. Peterson Jr., "Willis Richardson: Pioneer Playwright," *Black World* (1975), in *The Theater of*

Black Americans, ed. Errol Hill (New York: Applause, 1987), pp. 113-25; and Leslie Catherine Sanders, *The Development of Black Theater in America* (Baton Rouge: Louisiana State Univ. Press, 1988), pp. 19-38.

30. Alain Locke and Montgomery Gregory, eds., *Plays of Negro Life* (New York: Harper, 1927).

31. Willis Richardson, *The Chip Woman's Fortune,* in *Black Drama in America,* ed. Darwin Turner.

32. Richardson, *The Broken Banjo,* in *Black Writers of America,* ed. Richard Barksdale and Kenneth Kennemon (New York: Macmillan, 1972).

33. Richardson, *The Idle Head,* in Hatch, *Black Theater,* p. 238.

34. *Contemporary Authors,* vol. 124, ed. Hal May and Susan M. Trosky (Detroit: Gale Research, 1988), p. 361.

35. Carter G. Woodson, introduction to *Negro History in Thirteen Plays,* ed. Willis Richardson and May Miller (Washington, D.C.: Associated Publishers, 1935).

36. Georgia Douglas Johnson, "The Negro in Art," *Crisis* 32 (1926): 193.

37. May Miller, *Sojourner Truth,* in Richardson and Miller, *Negro History in Thirteen Plays,* p. 328.

38. Statement by Theodore Ward, printed in the *Daily Worker,* March 9, 1950, quoted in Abramson, *Negro Playwrights,* p. 117.

39. Theodore Ward, *Our Lan',* in Kenneth Rowe, ed. *A Theater in Your Head* (New York: Funk & Wagnalls, 1960), p. 414. This play has also been collected in Turner, *Black Drama in America.*

10. Randolph Edmonds and Civil Rights

1. Randolph Edmonds, *Six Plays for a Negro Theatre* (Boston: Walter H . Baker, 1934), pp. 7-8. For biographical and bibliographical information on Edmonds, see *Contemporary Authors,* vol. 125, ed. Hal May and Susan M. Trosky (Detroit: Gale Research, 1989), pp. 110-12.

2. Foreword to Edmonds, *Six Plays,* p. 6.

3. Ibid., pp. 7-8.

4. Leslie Catherine Sanders, *The Development of Black Theater in America* (Baton Rouge: Louisiana State Univ. Press. 1988), p. 42.

5. Randolph Edmonds, "Negro Drama in the South," *Carolina Play-Book* 13 (June 1940): 74.

6. Ibid., pp. 75, 78.

7. Ibid., p. 78.

8. Edmonds, *Six Plays.* All further references are given in the text.

9. William Styron, *The Confessions of Nat Turner* (New York: Random House, 1967), pp. xiii-xv.

10. Frederick W. Bond, *The Negro and the Drama* (Washington, D.C.: Associated Publishers, 1940), p. 123.

11. Edmonds, *Bad Man,* is collected in Hatch, *Black Theater, U.S.A.,* as well as in *Six Plays.*

12. Edmonds, *Earth and Stars*, is collected in Turner, *Black Drama in America.* Page references in the text cite this edition.

13. Loften Mitchell, *A Land Beyond the River*, in *The Black Teacher and the Dramatic Arts: A Dialogue, Bibliography, and Anthology*, ed. William R. Reardon and Thomas D. Pauley (Westport, Conn.: Negro Universities Press, 1970).

14. Mitchell, *Tell Pharaoh*, in *The Black Teacher.*

15. Quoted in James A. Page, ed., *Selected Black American Authors* (Boston: G.K. Hall, 1977). For an account of the Free Southern Theater, see Thomas C. Dent, Richard Schechner, and Gilbert Moses, *The Free Southern Theater* (Indianapolis: Bobbs-Merrill, 1969).

16. Ossie Davis, *Purlie Victorious*, in *Contemporary Black Drama*, ed. Clinton F. Oliver and Stephanie Sills (New York: Scribner, 1971), p. 134. Further references are given in the text.

17. Green, *Letters*, p. 662.

18. Douglas Taylor Ward, *Day of Absence*, in Oliver and Sills, *Contemporary Black Drama*, p. 340.

19. Lyle Leverich, *Tom: The Unknown Tennessee Williams* (New York: Crown, 1995), p. 236.

20. Reardon and Pawley, *The Black Teacher.*

21. Thomas D. Pawley, *The Tumult and the Shouting*, in Hatch, *Black Theater, U.S.A.*

22. Quoted in Theresa Gunnels Rush et al., eds., *Black American Writers Past and Present* (Metuchen, N.J.: Scarecrow, 1975), p. 663.

23. Ted Shine, *Morning, Noon, and Night*, in Reardon and Pawley, *The Black Teacher*, p. 455.

24. Ted Shine, *Contributions* (New York: Dramatists Play Service, 1970).

25. For these and other reviews of Shine's one-acts, see *New York Theatre Critics Reviews* 31, no. 26 (1970): 282-84; and Winona L. Fletcher, "Ted Shine," in *Dictionary of Literary Biography* (Detroit: Gale Research, 1985), 38: 250-59.

11. The Cultural Imagination of Tennessee Williams

1. *The Night of the Iguana*, in Tennessee Williams, *Three by Tennessee* (New York: New American Library, 1976), p. 105. References in the text cite this edition.

2. *Orpheus Descending*, in Tennessee Williams, *Four Plays* (New York: New American Library, 1976), p. 142. References in the text cite this edition.

3. Eliot, *Notes towards the Definition of Culture*, p. 39.

4. See Ruth D. Weston, *Gothic Traditions and Narrative Techniques in the Fiction of Eudora Welty* (Baton Rouge: Louisiana State Univ. Press, 1994).

5. Jacob H. Adler, "Tennessee Williams' South: The Culture and the Power," in *Tennessee Williams: A Tribute*, ed. Jac Tharpe (Jackson: Univ. Press of Mississippi, 1977), pp. 30-52. For other studies of Williams's view of the South, see Jacob H. Adler, "The Rose and the Fox: Notes on Southern Drama," in *South: Modern*

Southern Literature in Its Cultural Setting, ed. Louis D. Rubin Jr. and Robert D. Jacobs (Garden City, N.Y.: Doubleday, 1961); and Signi Falk, *Tennessee Williams* (New York: Twayne, 1978).

6. Leverich, *Tom: The Unknown Tennessee Williams,* p. 328.

7. Quoted in ibid., p. 434.

8. Nancy M. Tischler, *Tennessee Williams: Rebellious Puritan* (New York: Citadel, 1962), p. 28.

9. Tennessee Williams, *Memoirs* (Garden City, N.Y.: Doubleday, 1975), p. 11, refers to his happy years in Clarksdale.

10. Albert J. Devlin, ed., *Conversations with Tennessee Williams* (Jackson: Univ. Press of Mississippi, 1986), p. 257.

11. Tennessee Williams, *The Glass Menagerie,* in *Six Modern American Plays,* ed. Allan G. Halline (New York: Random House, 1951), p. 276. Page references in the text cite this edition.

12. Williams, *The Glass Menagerie,* acting edition (New York: Dramatists Play Service, 1948), pp. 51-52.

13. John Crowe Ransom, introduction to Twelve Southerners, *I'll Take My Stand,* p. xxv.

14. Charles S. Watson, "The Revision of *The Glass Menagerie:* The Passing of Good Manners," *Southern Literary Journal* 8 (Spring 1976), rpt. in Tennessee Williams's *"The Glass Menagerie": Modern Critical Interpretations* (New York: Chelsea House, 1987), pp. 75-78.

15. Williams, *A Streetcar Named Desire* (New York: New American Library, 1947), p. 49. References in the text cite this edition.

16. Williams, *Cat on a Hot Tin Roof* (New York: New American Library, 1955), p. 82. References in the text cite this edition.

17. George Washington Harris, "Rare Ripe Garden Seed," in Louis D. Rubin Jr., ed., *The Literary South* (New York: Wiley, 1979), p. 250.

18. For pertinent information on C.C. Williams, see "The Man in the Overstuffed Chair," preface to *Tennessee Williams: Collected Stories* (New York: New Directions, 1985).

19. Williams, *The Last of My Solid Gold Watches,* collected in *27 Wagons Full of Cotton and Other One-Act Plays* (New York: New Directions, 1966).

20. Donald Spoto, *The Kindness of Strangers: The Life of Tennessee Williams* (Boston: Little, Brown, 1985), p. 198.

21. For a discussion of the Agrarian myth in *Cat on a Hot Tin Roof,* see Roger Boxill, *Tennessee Williams* (New York: Macmillan, 1987), p. 120.

22. Leverich, *Tom: The Unknown Tennessee Williams,* p. 417.

23. Tischler, *Tennessee Williams,* p. 15.

24. See Norman J. Fedder, *The Influence of D.H. Lawrence on Tennessee Williams* (The Hague: Mouton, 1966).

25. Leverich, *Tom: The Unknown Tennessee Williams,* pp. 77-78, 132, 400.

26. See Gerald M. Berkowitz, *American Drama of the Twentieth Century* (New York: Longman, 1992), p. 87, for a perceptive discussion of this appeal in Williams's plays.

27. Permission to quote from this letter, which is deposited in the Horton Foote Collection, Southern Methodist University, Dallas, has been granted me by Horton Foote.

28. Quoted in Dakin Williams and Shepherd Mead, *Tennessee Williams: An Intimate Biography* (New York: Arbor House, 1983), p. 205.

29. See Gene D. Phillips, *The Films of Tennessee Williams* (London: Associated University Presses, 1980), p. 93-94.

30. See Robert Frederick Burk, *The Eisenhower Administration and Black Civil Rights* (Knoxville: Univ. of Tennessee Press, 1984), pp. 205-9.

31. Williams, *Baby Doll* (New York: New American Library, 1956), p. 105; Stephen J. Whitfield, *A Death in the Delta: The Story of Emmett Till* (New York: Free Press, 1981), p. 67.

32. Williams, *Orpheus Descending*, p. ix.

33. Whitfield, *A Death in the Delta*, p. 67.

34. Henry Hewes, "Tennessee's Easter Message," *Saturday Review* 46 (March 28, 1959): 26; Phillips, *Films of Tennessee Williams*, p. 154.

35. See "Florida Premiere for New Tennessee Williams Play," *Theatre Arts* 40 (Aug. 1956): 66-67.

36. Benjamin Nelson, *Tennessee Williams: The Man and His Work* (New York: Ivan Obolensky, 1961), p. 267, places Boss Finley in the Huey Long tradition. Warren wrote three dramatic versions of *All the King's Men*, the last of which was performed off-Broadway in 1959. See Charles Bohner, *Robert Penn Warren* (New York: Twayne, 1964), pp. 77-78.

37. For a good account of the highly charged atmosphere in Little Rock during the integration of Central High School, see Virgil T. Blossom, *It Has Happened Here* (New York: Harper, 1959), pp. 38-56.

38. *Sweet Bird of Youth*, p. 106, in Williams, *Three by Tennessee*. References in the text cite this edition.

39. Leverich, *Tom: The Unknown Tennessee Williams*, p. 37. The sermons are held in the Walter Dakin Collection of the Jessie Bell DuPont Library, University of the South, Sewanee, Tennessee.

40. *Suddenly Last Summer*, in Williams, *Four Plays*, p. 19.

12. Past and Present Cultures in Recent Drama

1. Samuel G. Freedman, introduction to *Cousins* and *The Death of Papa*, by Horton Foote (New York: Grove, 1989), p. xi.

2. *Who's Who;* for general treatments of Foote's life and writings, see also Marian Burkhart, "Horton Foote's Many Roads Home: An American Playwright and His Characters," *Commonweal*, February 26, 1988, p. 110; David Copelin, "Horton Foote," in *Contemporary Dramatists*, ed. D.L. Kirkpatrick (Chicago: St. James Press, 1988); and Samuel G. Freedman, "From the Heart of Texas," *New York Times Magazine*, February 9, 1986, pp. 61-62.

3. *The Habitation of Dragons*, in Horton Foote, *Four New Plays* (Newbury, Vt.: Smith & Kraus, 1993).

4. Quoted in Weldon B. Durham, *American Theatre Companies, 1931-1986* (Westport, Conn.: Greenwood Press, 1987), p. 61.

5. Ronald L. Davis, "Roots in a Parched Ground: An Interview with Horton Foote," *Southwest Review* 73 (Summer 1988): 298.

6. Ibid., p. 316; *New York Times*, April 21, 1985, sec. 2, p. 22.

7. Letter from Horton Foote to the author, May 19, 1992.

8. Davis, "Roots," pp. 316-17.

9. Ibid., p. 316.

10. Marjorie Smeltsor, "'The World's an Orphan's Home': Horton Foote's Social and Moral History," *Southern Quarterly* 29 (Winter 1991): 13.

11. Davis, "Roots," pp. 303-4.

12. Katherine Anne Porter, *Collected Essays*, pp. 468-69, quoted in Gerald C. Wood, introduction to *Selected One-Act Plays of Horton Foote* (Dallas: Southern Methodist Univ. Press, 1989), p. xiii.

13. Wood, pp. xix-xx.

14. Davis, "Roots," p. 303.

15. Robert Drake, *Survivors and Others* (Macon, Ga.: Mercer Univ. Press, 1987); Lee Smith, *Cakewalk* (New York: Ballantine, 1983).

16. Horton Foote, *The Trip to Bountiful* (New York: Dramatists Play Service, 1954). References in the text cite this edition. The television version is collected in Horton Foote, *Harrison, Texas: Eight Television Plays* (New York: Harcourt, Brace, 1956).

17. Quoted in Horton Foote, "The Trip to Paradise," *Texas Monthly*, December 1987, p. 140.

18. See Charles S. Watson, "Beyond the Commercial Media: Horton Foote's Procession of Defeated Men," *Studies in American Drama, 1945-Present*, 8, No. 2 (1993).

19. Davis, "Roots," p. 308.

20. Nina Darnton, "Horton Foote Celebrates a Bygone Era in *1918*," *New York Times*, April 21, 1985, sec. 2, p. 17. Smeltsor, "The World's an Orphan's Home," p. 9, errs in saying that Horace is modeled after Foote's grandfather.

21. Foote, *Lily Dale*, p. 231 in *The First Four Plays of the Orphans' Home Cycle* (New York: Grove, 1988).

22. Foote, *Courtship, Valentine's Day, 1918: Three Plays from the Orphans' Home Cycle* (New York: Grove, 1987), p. 123.

23. Preface to *Selected One-Act Plays of Horton Foote*, ed. Gerald C. Wood (Dallas: Southern Methodist Univ. Press, 1989), p. xi.

24. *New York Times*, April 12, 1982, and July 14, 1988.

25. Ibid., May 27, 1985.

26. Ibid., December 29, 1985.

27. *The Land of the Astronauts*, in Foote, *Selected One-Act Plays*, p. 497.

28. For information on Henley's life and treatments of her plays, see Walter Meserve, "Beth Henley," in *Contemporary Dramatists* (Chicago: St. James Press, 1988), pp. 245-46; Nancy D. Hargrove, "The Tragicomic Vision of Beth Henley's

Drama," *Southern Quarterly* 22 (Summer 1984): 54-70; Billy J. Harbin, "Familial Bonds in the Plays of Beth Henley," *Southern Quarterly* 25 (Spring 1987): 81-94; Lisa J. McDonnell, "Diverse Similitude: Beth Henley and Marsha Norman," *Southern Quarterly* 25 (Spring 1987): 95-104; Mark Morrow, *Images of the Southern Writer* (Athens: Univ. of Georgia Press, 1985), p. 42; *Who's Who*.

29. John Griffin Jones, ed., *Mississippi Writers Talking* (Jackson: Univ. Press of Mississippi, 1982), p. 181.

30. Kathleen Betsko and Rachel Koenig, *Interviews with Contemporary Women Playwrights* (New York: Beech Tree Books, 1987), p. 216.

31. Jones, *Mississippi Writers Talking*, pp. 181-83.

32. Betsko and Koenig, *Interviews*, pp. 215-16.

33. Ibid., p. 219. Henley's "Southern Gothic" writing is also referred to in Jones, *Mississippi Writers Talking*, p. 182.

34. Beth Henley, *The Wake of Jamey Foster* (New York: Dramatists Play Service, 1983); *The Miss Firecracker Contest* (New York: Dramatists Play Service, 1985); *The Lucky Spot* (Dramatists Play Service, 1987). All references in the text cite these editions. The University Press of Mississippi published Henley's early play *The Debutante Ball* in 1991. Henley's latest play, *Abundance* (New York: Dramatists Play Service, 1991), is set in nineteenth-century frontier Wyoming; for an interesting analysis, see Richard Wattenberg, "Challenging the Frontier Myth: Contemporary Women's Plays about Women Pioneers," *Journal of American Drama and Theatre* 4 (Fall 1992): 51-54.

35. Lisa J. McDonnell, "Diverse Similitude: Beth Henley and Marsha Norman," *Southern Quarterly* 25 (Spring 1987): 95.

36. Marsha Norman, *Loving Daniel Boone*, has since been published in *By Southern Playwrights: Plays from Actors Theatre of Louisville*, ed. Michael Bigelow Dixon and Michele Volansky (Lexington: University Press of Kentucky, 1996).

37. Norman, "Articles of Faith: A Conversation with Lillian Hellman" in *American Theatre* 1 (May 1984): 10-15.

38. Norman, *Getting Out* (New York: Avon, 1978).

39. Norman, *'Night, Mother*, in *Modern and Contemporary Drama*, ed. Miriam Gilbert et al. (New York: St. Martin's, 1994), p. 731.

40. Betsko and Koenig, *Interviews*, p. 337.

41. Douglas Watt, "Staging of *'Night, Mother*," in *Modern and Contemporary Drama*, ed. Miriam Gilbert, pp. 716, 736.

42. Irmgard H. Wolfe asks for such an approach in "Marsha Norman," *American Dramatists Since 1945: A Guide to Scholarship, Criticism, and Performance*, ed. Philip C. Kolin (Westport, Conn.: Greenwood Press, 1989), p. 356.

43. Norman, "Articles of Faith," p. 12.

44. Mark Busby, "Contemporary Western Drama," in *A Literary History of the American West* (Fort Worth: Texas Christian Univ. Press, 1987), p. 1232.

45. Preston Jones, *A Texas Trilogy* (New York: Hill & Wang, 1976), p. 248. References in the text cite this edition.

46. For biographical information, see *Southern Writers: A Biographical Dictio-*

nary, ed. Robert Bain, Joseph M. Flora, and Louis D. Rubin Jr. (Baton Rouge: Louisiana State Univ. Press, 1979). An excellent bibliographical essay is Don B. Wilmeth, "Romulus Linney," in *American Dramatists since 1945*, ed. Philip C. Kolin.

47. For an appraisal of Linney's standing as a dramatist, see Christian H. Moe, *Contemporary Dramatists* (Chicago: St. James Press, 1988), pp. 324-26.

48. Green, *Letters*, p. 663.

49. Don B. Wilmeth, "An Interview with Romulus Linney," *Studies in American Drama, 1945-Present* 2 (1987): 75, 70.

50. Ibid., p. 78.

51. Ibid., pp. 77-78.

52. Ibid., p. 77.

53. Romulus Linney, *The Sorrows of Frederick and Holy Ghosts* (New York: Harcourt, Brace, Jovanovich, 1977), pp. 156, 185.

54. *Contemporary Literary Criticism* (Detroit: Gale Research, 1986) 51: 245.

55. Linney, *Heathen Valley* (New York: Dramatists Play Service, 1988), p. 17.

56. Linney, *Tennessee*, in *The Best Short Plays, 1980*, ed. Stanley Richards (Radnor, Pa.: Chilton, 1980), p. 43.

57. Linney, *Laughing Stock* (New York: Dramatists Play Service, 1984).

58. *New York Times*, February 3, 1981.

59. Linney, *The Captivity of Pixie Shedman* (New York: Dramatists Play Service, 1981), p. 68.

Bibliography

This list does not include everything cited in the notes, but it will direct readers to sources of the plays discussed in the text and to the relevant scholarly and critical work. Anthologies are included under primary sources; plays that appear in these collections are cross-referenced to them. (Anthologies may also be consulted for related plays and information on the dramatists.) For early plays of which only a manuscript or rare copy is available, a library location is provided. "RM" in brackets designates titles included in the valuable Readex Microprint collection *Three Centuries of Drama: American*, ed. Henry W. Wells.

Primary Sources

Arthur, Lee. *The One Act Plays of Lee Arthur.* Ed. Paul T. Nolan. Cody, Wyo.: Pioneer Drama Service, 1962.

Betsko, Kathleen, and Rachel Koenig. "Marsha Norman." In *Interviews with Contemporary Women Playwrights.* New York: Beech Tree Books, 1987.

Brown, William Wells. *The Escape; or, A Leap for Freedom: A Drama in Five Acts.* Boston: Robert F. Wallcut, 1858, collected in Hatch, *Black Theater, U.S.A.*

___. *My Southern Home; or, The South and Its People.* (1880). Rpt. Upper Saddle River, N.J.: Gregg, 1968.

Bryer, Jackson R., ed. *Conversations with Lillian Hellman.* Jackson: Univ. Press of Mississippi, 1986.

Burk, John Daly. *Bethlem Gabor.* Petersburg: John Dickson, 1807. [RM]

___. *Bunker Hill; or, The Death of General Warren.* New York: T. Greenleaf, 1798. [RM]

Canonge, L. Placide. *Le Comte de Carmagnola.* New Orleans: Imprimerie du Courrier de la Louisiane, 1856. [Copy in W.S. Hoole Special Collections, University of Alabama Library]

___. *France et Espagne; ou, La Louisiane en 1768 et 1769.* New Orleans, 1850. [Copy in the Louisiana Collection, Tulane University]

Collens, T. Wharton. *The Martyr Patriots; or, Louisiana in 1769.* In *The Louisiana Book,* ed. Thomas M'Caleb. New Orleans: R.F. Straughan, 1894.

Cotter, Joseph S. *Caleb, the Degenerate: A Study of the Types, Customs, and Needs of the American Negro* (1930). In Hatch, *Black Theater, U.S.A.*

Custis, George Washington Parke. *The Indian Prophecy.* Georgetown, D.C.: James Thomas, 1828. [RM]

___. *Montgomerie; or, The Orphan of a Wreck.* [Manuscript copy in Huntington Library, San Marino, Calif.]

____. *Pocahontas; or, The Settlers of Virginia* (1830). In Quinn, *Representative American Plays.*

Davis, Ossie. *Purlie Victorious* (1961). In Oliver and Sills, *Contemporary Black Drama.*

Dixon, Michael Bigelow, and Michele Volansky, eds. *By Southern Playwrights: Plays from Actors Theatre of Louisville.* Lexington: Univ. Press of Kentucky, 1996.

Edmonds, Randolph. *Earth and Stars* (1961). In Turner, *Black Drama in America.*

____. "Negro Drama in the South." *Carolina Play-Book* 13 (June 1940): 73-78.

____. *Six Plays for a Negro Theatre* [*Nat Turner, Breeders, Bleeding Hearts, Bad Man, The New Window,* and *Old Man Pete*]. Boston: Walter H. Baker, 1934.

Field, Joseph M. *Job and His Children.* In *America's Lost Plays,* vol. 14, ed. Eugene R. Page. Bloomington: Indiana University Press, 1940, 1965.

Foote, Horton. *The Chase.* New York: Dramatists Play Service, 1952.

____. *Courtship, Valentine's Day, 1918: Three Plays from the Orphan's Home Cycle.* New York: Grove, 1987.

____. *Cousins* and *The Death of Papa.* New York: Grove, 1989.

____. *Four New Plays.* Newbury, Vt.: Smith & Kraus, 1993.

____. *Horton Foote's Three Trips to Bountiful,* ed. Barbara Moore and David G. Yellin. Dallas: Southern Methodist University Press, 1993.

____. *Roots in a Parched Ground, Convicts, Lily Dale, The Widow Claire: Four Plays from the Orphans' Home Cycle.* New York: Grove, 1988.

____. *Selected One-Act Plays of Horton Foote,* ed. Gerald C. Wood. Dallas: Southern Methodist Univ. Press, 1989.

____. *To Kill a Mockingbird, Tender Mercies,* and *The Trip to Bountiful: Three Screen Plays.* New York: Grove, 1989.

____. *The Traveling Lady.* New York: Dramatists Play Service, 1955.

____. *The Trip to Bountiful.* New York: Dramatists Play Service, 1954.

____. "The Trip to Paradise." *Texas Monthly,* Dec. 1987. p. 140.

Green, Paul. *The Common Glory.* Chapel Hill: Univ. of North Carolina Press, 1948.

____. *The Confederacy.* New York: Samuel French, 1959.

____. *Cross and Sword: A Symphonic Drama of the Spanish Settlement of Florida.* New York: Samuel French, 1966.

____. *Dramatic Heritage.* New York: Samuel French, 1953.

____. *The Field God and In Abraham's Bosom.* New York: Robert M. McBride, 1927.

____. *Five Plays of the South* [including *In Abraham's Bosom* and final version of *The House of Connelly*]. New York: Hill & Wang, 1963.

____. *The Founders: A Symphonic Outdoor Drama.* New York: Samuel French, 1957.

____. *The Hawthorn Tree.* Chapel Hill: Univ. of North Carolina Press, 1943.

____. *The House of Connelly and Other Plays.* New York: Samuel French, 1931.

____. *In the Valley and Other Carolina Plays.* New York: Samuel French, 1928.

____. *The Last of the Lowries.* New York: Samuel French, 1922.

____. *Lonesome Road: Six Plays for the Negro Theater.* New York: Robert M. McBride, 1926.

____. *The Lord's Will and Other Carolina Plays.* New York: Henry Holt, 1925.

____. *Louisiana Cavalier: A Symphonic Drama Based on the Life and Times of Louis Juchereau de St. Denis.* Rehearsal script, 1976. North Carolina Collection,

Wilson Library, University of North Carolina-Chapel Hill.

___. *Out of the South* [Contains *The Lost Colony, The House of Connelly,* and *Potters' Field*]. New York: Harper, 1939.

___. *Plough and Furrow.* New York: Samuel French, 1963.

___. *Roll, Sweet Chariot: A Symphonic Play of the Negro People.* New York: Samuel French, 1935.

___. *A Southern Life: Letters of Paul Green, 1916-1981.* Ed. Lawrence G. Avery. Chapel Hill: Univ. of North Carolina Press, 1994.

___. *Wilderness Road.* New York: Samuel French, 1956.

Hellman, Lillian. *Six Plays* [including *Another Part of the Forest, The Little Foxes,* and *The Autumn Garden*]. New York: Vintage Books, 1979.

___. *An Unfinished Woman: A Memoir.* Boston: Little, Brown, 1969.

Henley, Beth. *Crimes of the Heart.* New York: Dramatists Play Service, 1982.

___. *The Lucky Spot.* Dramatists Play Service, 1987.

___. *The Miss Firecracker Contest.* New York: Dramatists Play Service, 1985.

___. *The Wake of Jamey Foster.* New York: Dramatists Play Service, 1983.

Hewitt, John Hill. *King Linkum the First: A Musical Burletta.* Ed. Richard Barksdale Harwell. Atlanta: Emory University Library, 1947.

___. *The Scouts; or, The Plains of Manassas* (1861). [Manuscript copy in the Hewitt Collection, Emory University Library]

___. *The Veteran of '76 and '62* (1863). [Manuscript copy in the Hewitt Collection, Emory University Library]

___. *The Vivandiere* (1863). [Manuscript copy is held in the Hewitt Collection, Emory University Library]

Heyward, Dorothy, and DuBose Heyward. *Mamba's Daughters.* New York: Farrar and Rinehart, 1939.

___. *Porgy.* In *Twenty-Five Best Plays of the Modern American Theatre,* ed. John Gassner. New York: Crown, 1949.

Heyward, DuBose. *Brass Ankle.* New York: Farrar & Rinehart, 1931.

___. *Porgy* (the novel). New York: Grossett & Dunlap, 1925.

Hughes, Langston. *Mulatto.* In *Five Plays of Langston Hughes,* ed. and intro. Webster Smalley. Bloomington: Indiana Univ. Press, 1963.

Hughes, Langston, and Zora Neale Hurston. *Mule Bone: A Comedy of Negro Life.* Ed. and intro. George Houston Bass and Henry Louis Gates Jr. New York: Harper Perennial, 1991.

Hurston, Zora Neale. *Color Struck* (1925). In Perkins, *Black Female Playwrights.*

___. *The First One* (1927). In Perkins, *Black Female Playwrights.*

Ioor, William. *The Battle of Eutaw Springs.* Charleston: Hoff, 1807. [RM]

___. *Independence.* Charleston: G.M. Bounetheau, 1805.

Johnson, Georgia. *Blue Blood* (1926). In Perkins, *Black Female Playwrights.*

___. *Plumes* (1927). In Perkins, *Black Female Playwrights.*

___. *A Sunday Morning in the South* (c. 1925). In Hatch, *Black Theater, U.S.A.*

Jones, Preston. *A Texas Trilogy.* New York: Hill & Wang, 1976.

Linney, Romulus. *The Captivity of Pixie Shedman.* New York: Dramatists Play Service, 1981.

___. *Heathen Valley*. New York: Dramatists Play Service, 1988.

___. *Jesus Tales*. San Francisco: North Point, 1987.

___. *Laughing Stock* [*Goodbye, Howard, Tennessee,* and *F.M.*] New York: Dramatists Play Service, 1984.

___. *Sand Mountain*. New York: Dramatists Play Service, 1985.

___. *Seventeen Short Plays*. Newbury, Vt.: Smith and Kraus, 1992.

___. *The Sorrows of Frederick and Holy Ghosts*. New York: Harcourt, Brace, Jovanovich, 1977.

___. *Tennessee*. In *The Best Short Plays 1980*, ed. Stanley Richards. Radnor, Pa.: Chilton, 1980.

Matheus, John Frederick. *'Cruiter*. In *Plays of Negro Life*, ed. Alain Locke and Montgomery Gregory. New York: Harper, 1927.

McCabe, James D. *The Guerillas*. Richmond, Va.: West & Johnson, 1863. [Copy in Virginia State Library, Richmond]

Miller, May. *Harriet Tubman* and *Sojourner Truth*. In *Negro History in Thirteen plays*, ed. Willis Richardson and May Miller. Washington, D.C.: Associated Publishers, 1935.

Mitchell, Loften. *A Land beyond the River* (1957). In Reardon and Pawley, *The Black Teacher*.

___. *Tell Pharaoh* (1967). In Reardon and Pawley, *The Black Teacher*.

Moody, Richard, ed. *Dramas from the American Theatre, 1762-1909*. Cleveland: World, 1966.

Moses, Montrose J., ed. *Representative Plays by American Dramatists*. 3 vols. New York: Dutton, 1925.

Munford, Robert. *The Candidates; or, the Humours of a Virginia Election* (1798). In Moody, *Dramas from the American Theatre*.

___. *A Collection of Plays and Poems*. Petersburg, Va.: William Prentis, 1798.

___. *The Patriots* (1798). *William and Mary Quarterly* 6 (1949): 437-502.

Norman, Marsha. "Articles of Faith: A Conversation with Lillian Hellman." *American Theatre* (May 1984): 10-15.

___. *Getting Out*. New York: Avon, 1978.

___. *'Night, Mother*. In *Modern and Contemporary Drama*, ed. Miriam Gilbert et al. New York: St. Martin's, 1994.

___. *Traveler in the Dark*. New York: Dramatists Play Service, 1988.

Oliver, Clinton F., and Stephanie Sills, eds. *Contemporary Black Drama*. New York: Scribner, 1971.

Paterson, Lindsay, ed. *Anthology of the American Negro in the Theatre*. New York: Publishers Co., 1968.

Pawley, Thomas D. *The Tumult and the Shouting* (1969). In Hatch, *Black Theater, U.S.A.*

Perkins, Kathy A., ed. *Black Female Playwrights: An Anthology of Plays before 1950*. Bloomington: Indiana Univ. Press, 1989.

Quinn, Arthur Hobson, ed. *Representative American Plays*. New York: Appleton-Century-Crofts, 1953.

Reardon, William R., and Thomas D. Pawley, eds. *The Black Teacher and the Dra-*

matic Arts: A Dialogue, Bibliography, and Anthology. Westport, Conn.: Negro Universities Press, 1970.

Richardson, Willis. *The Broken Banjo*. In *Black Writers of America*, ed. Richard Barksdale and Kenneth Kennemon. New York: Macmillan, 1972.

___. *The Chip Woman's Fortune* (1923). In Turner, *Black Drama in America*.

___. *The Idle Head* (1929). In Hatch, *Black Theater, U.S.A.*

___, ed. *Plays and Pageants from the Life of the Negro*. Washington, D.C.: Associated Publishers, 1930.

Richardson, Willis and May Miller, eds. *Negro History in Thirteen Plays*. Washington, D.C.: Associated Publishers, 1935.

Simms, William Gilmore. *Michael Bonham; or, The Fall of Bexar. Southern Literary Messenger* 18 (February-June 1858).

___. *Norman Maurice; or, The Man of the People*. In William Gilmore Simms, *Poems: Descriptive, Dramatic, Legendary, and Contemplative*, vol. 1. New York: Redfield, 1853.

Shine, Ted. *Contributions*. New York: Dramatists Play Service, 1970.

___. *Herbert III* (1974). In Hatch, *Black Theater, U.S.A.*

___. *Morning, Noon, and Night*. In Reardon and Pawley, *Black Teacher* (1970).

Tayleure, Clifton W. *The Boy Martyrs of Sept. 12, 1814*. New York: French, 1859.

___. *Horse-Shoe Robinson* (1856). In Moses, *Representative Plays by American Dramatists*, vol. 2.

Tucker, St. George. *The Patriot Cool'd* (1815). [Manuscript copy in Greg Swem Library, William and Mary College]

___. *The Wheel of Fortune: A Comedy* (1796-97). [Manuscript copy in Greg Swem Library, William and Mary College]

Turner, Darwin T., ed. *Black Drama in America*. Greenwich, Conn.: Fawcett, 1971.

Ward, Douglas Taylor. *Day of Absence*. In *Oliver and Sills, Contemporary Black Drama* (1971).

Ward, Theodore. *Our Lan'*. In Kenneth Rowe, ed., *A Theater in Your Head*. New York: Funk & Wagnalls, 1960.

White, John Blake. *The Forgers. Southern Literary Journal* 1 (April-August, 1837).

___. *Foscari*. Charleston: J. Hoff, 1806. [RM]

___. *Modern Honor*. Charleston: J. Hoff, 1812. [RM]

___. *The Mysteries of the Castle*. Charleston: J. Hoff, 1807. [RM]

___. *The Triumph of Liberty; or, Louisiana Preserved*. Charleston: J. Hoff, 1819. [Copy held by The Library Company, Philadelphia, Pa.]

Williams, Espy. *The Atheist* (1892). In *Provincial Drama in America, 1870-1916: A Casebook of Primary Materials*, ed. Paul T. Nolan. Metuchen, N.J.: Scarecrow, 1967.

___. *The Clairvoyant* (1899). In *The Selected Works of Espy Williams: Southern Playwright*, ed. Paul T. Nolan. Lexington: Univ. Press of Kentucky, 1960. [microcards]

___. *The Husband: A Society Play*. New Orleans: Theo A. Ray, 1898. [Copy in W.S. Hoole Special Collections, University of Alabama Library]

___. *Ollamus, King of Utopiana: A Musical Comedy* (1894). In *The Selected Works of*

Espy Williams: Southern Playwright, ed. Paul T. Nolan. Lexington: Univ. Press of Kentucky, 1960. [Kentucky Microcards, ser. A, no. 45]

___. *Parrhasius; or Thriftless Ambition. A Dramatic Poem.* New Orleans: Southern 1879. [Copy in W.S. Hoole Special Collections, University of Alabama Library]

Williams, Tennessee. *Baby Doll* (the film script). New York: New American Library, 1956.

___. *Cat on a Hot Tin Roof.* New York: New American Library, 1955.

___. *Collected Stories.* New York: New Directions, 1985.

___. *Four Plays* [including *Summer and Smoke, Orpheus Descending, Suddenly Last Summer,* and *Period of Adjustment*]. New York: New American Library, 1976.

___. *The Glass Menagerie.* In *Six Modern American Plays,* ed. Allan G. Halline. New York: Random House, 1951.

___. *The Glass Menagerie.* Acting edition. New York: Dramatists Play Service, 1948.

___. *Memoirs.* Garden City, N.Y.: Doubleday, 1975.

___. *The Night of the Iguana.* In Tennessee Williams, *Three by Tennessee.* New York: New American Library, 1976.

___. *Orpheus Descending.* In Tennessee Williams, *Four Plays.* New York: New American Library, 1976.

___. *Orpheus Descending with Battle of Angels.* New York: New Directions, 1958.

___. *A Streetcar Named Desire.* New York: New American Library, 1947.

___. *Sweet Bird of Youth.* In Tennessee Williams, *Three by Tennessee.* New York: New American Library, 1976.

___. *Suddenly Last Summer.* In Tennessee Williams, *Four Plays.* New York: New American Library, 1976.

___. *Summer and Smoke.* In Tennessee Williams, *Four Plays.* New York: New American Library, 1976.

___. *The Theatre of Tennessee Williams.* 8 vols. New York: New Directions, 1971-92.

___. *Three by Tennessee* [including *Sweet Bird of Youth, The Rose Tattoo,* and *The Night of the Iguana*]. New York: New American Library, 1976.

___. *27 Wagons Full of Cotton and Other One-Act Plays.* New York: New Directions, 1966.

Secondary Sources

Abramson, Doris E. *Negro Playwrights in the American Theatre, 1925-1959.* New York: Columbia Univ. Press. 1967.

Adams, Agatha Boyd. *Paul Green of Chapel Hill.* Chapel Hill: Univ. of North Carolina Press, 1951.

Adler, Thomas P. *American Drama, 1940-1960: A Critical History.* New York: Twayne, 1994.

Adler, Jacob H. "The Rose and the Fox: Notes on Southern Drama." In *South: Modern Southern Literature in Its Cultural Setting,* ed. Louis D. Rubin Jr. and Robert D. Jacobs. Garden City, N.Y.: Doubleday. 1961.

___. "Tennessee Williams' South: The Culture and the Power." In *Tennessee Williams: A Tribute*, ed. Jac Tharpe pp. 30-52. Jackson: Univ. Press of Mississippi, 1977.

Arata, Esther Spring. *More Black American Playwrights: A Bibliography.* Metuchen, N.J.: Scarecrow, 1978.

Arata, Esther Spring, and Nicholas John Rotoli. *Black American Playwrights, 1800 to the Present: A Bibliography.* Metuchen, N.J.: Scarecrow, 1976.

Avery, Laurence G. "Paul Green." In *Fifty Southern Writers after 1900: A Bio-Bibliographical Sourcebook*, ed. Joseph M. Flora and Robert Bain. Westport, Conn.: Greenwood, 1987.

Bain, Robert, Joseph M. Flora, and Lois D. Rubin Jr. *Southern Writers: A Biographical Dictionary.* Baton Rouge: Louisiana State Univ. Press, 1979.

Bain, Rodney M. *Robert Munford: America's First Comic Dramatist.* Athens: Univ. of Georgia Press, 1967.

Belman, Richard R. "Robert Munford and the Political Culture of Frontier Virginia." *Journal of American Studies* (Aug. 1978): 68-83.

Bigsby, C.W.E. *A Critical Introduction to Twentieth-Century Drama: Tennessee Williams, Arthur Miller, Edward Albee.* Cambridge: Cambridge Univ. Press, 1984.

___. "Three Black Playwrights: Loften Mitchell, Ossie Davis, and Douglas Turner Ward." In *The Theater of Black Americans: A Collection of Critical Essays*, ed. Errol Hill. New York: Applause, 1987.

Bills, Steven H. *Lillian Hellman: An Annotated Bibliography.* New York: Garland, 1979.

Boxill, Roger. *Tennessee Williams.* New York: Macmillan, 1987.

Bradbury, John M. *Renaissance in the South.* Chapel Hill: Univ. of North Carolina Press, 1963. (Contains section on Green.)

Braymer, Meta Robinson. "Trying to Walk: An Introduction to the Plays of St. George Tucker." In *No Fairer Land: Studies in Southern Literature before 1900*, ed. J. Lasley Dameron and James W. Mathews. Troy, N.Y.: Whitson, 1986.

Briley, Rebecca Luttrell. *You Can Go Home Again: The Focus on Family in the Works of Horton Foote.* New York: Peter Lang, 1993.

Brockett, O.G., and Lenyth Brockett. "Civil War Theater: Contemporary Treatments." *Civil War History* 1 (1955): 229-50.

Brown, Sterling, ed. *Negro Caravan.* New York: Dryden, 1941.

Brown, T. Allston. "Clifton W. Tayleure." In *History of the American Stage.* New York: Dick & Fitzgerald, 1870.

Burkhart, Marian. "Horton Foote's Many Roads Home: An American Playwright and His Characters." *Commonweal*, Feb. 26, 1988, p. 110.

Busby, Mark. "Contemporary Western Drama." In *A Literary History of the American West.* Fort Worth: Texas Christian Univ. Press, 1987.

___. *Preston Jones.* Boise, Idaho: Boise State Univ. Western Writers Series, 1983.

___. "Christianity Today Talks to Horton Foote." *Christianity Today*, April 4, 1986, p. 30.

Clark, Barrett. *Paul Green.* New York: Robert M. McBride, 1928.

Coffman, George R. "The Carolina Playmakers: Retrospect and Prospect." *Carolina Playbook* 13 (June, 1940), 38-39.

Cohn, Ruby. *Dialogue in American Drama.* Bloomington: Indiana Univ. Press, 1971.

Contemporary Literary Criticism. Vol. 51. Detroit: Gale Research, 1986.

Copelin, David. "Horton Foote." In *Contemporary Dramatists,* D.L. Kirkpatrick. Chicago: St. James Press, 1988.

Davidson, James Wood. *Living Writers of the South.* New York: Carleton, 1869.

Davis, Ronald L. "Roots in a Parched Ground: An Interview with Horton Foote." *Southwest Review* 73 (Summer 1988): 298-318.

Devlin, Albert J., ed. *Conversations with Tennessee Williams.* Jackson: Univ. Press of Mississippi, 1986.

Dent, Thomas C., et al. *The Free Southern Theater.* Indianapolis: Bobbs-Merrill, 1969.

Dormon, James H., Jr. *Theater in the Ante Bellum South, 1815-1861.* Chapel Hill: Univ. of North Carolina Press, 1967.

Downer, Alan S. *Fifty Years of American Drama, 1900-1950.* Chicago: Henry Regnery, 1951.

Durham, Frank. *DuBose Heyward: The Man Who Wrote Porgy.* Columbia: Univ. of South Carolina Press, 1955; rpt. Port Washington, N.Y.: Kennikat Press, 1965.

Durham, Weldon B. *American Theatre Companies, 1749-1887.* Westport, Conn.: Greenwood, 1986.

___. *American Theatre Companies, 1931-1986.* Westport, Conn.: Greenwood, 1989.

Dusenburg, Winifred. *The Theme of Loneliness in Modern American Literature.* Gainesville: Univ. of Florida Press, 1960.

Edgerton, Gary. "A Visit to the Imaginary Landscape of Harrison, Texas." *Literature/Film Quarterly* 17 (1989): 3-12.

Fabre, Genevieve E. *Afro-American Poetry and Drama, 1760-1975.* Detroit: Gale Research, 1979.

___. *Drumbeats, Masks, and Metaphor: Contemporary Afro-American Theatre.* Cambridge, Mass.: Harvard Univ. Press, 1983.

Falk, Doris V. *Lillian Hellman.* New York: Frederick Ungar, 1978.

Falk, Signi. *Tennessee Williams.* New York: Twayne, 1978.

Farrison, William Edward. *William Wells Brown.* Chicago: Univ. of Chicago Press, 1969.

Fife, Iline. "The Confederate Theatre." *Southern Speech Journal* 20 (1955): 224-31.

___. "The Confederate Theatre in Georgia." *Georgia Review* 9 (1955): 305-15.

___. "The Theatre during the Confederacy." Ph.D. diss., Louisiana State University, 1949.

Fortier, Alcée. *Louisiana Studies.* New Orleans: F.F. Hansell, 1894.

Freedman, Samuel G. "From the Heart of Texas." *New York Times Magazine,* Feb. 9, 1986, pp. 61-62.

Gagey, Edmund M. *Revolution in American Drama.* New York: Columbia Univ. Press, 1947.

Going, William T. "The Prestons of Talladega and the Hubbards of Bowden: A Dramatic Note." In *Essays in Alabama Literature,* pp. 142-55. Tuscaloosa: Univ. of Alabama Press, 1975.

Gunn, Drewey Wayne. *Tennessee Williams: A Bibliography*. Metuchen, N.J.: Scarecrow, 1980.

Harbin, Billy J. "Familial Bonds in the Plays of Beth Henley." *Southern Quarterly* 25 (Spring 1987): 81-94.

Hargrove, Nancy D. "The Tragicomic Vision of Beth Henley's Drama." *Southern Quarterly* 22 (Summer 1984): 54-70.

Harrigan, Anthony. "DuBose Heyward: Memorialist and Realist." *Georgia Review* 5 (1951): 335-44.

Harwell, Richard Barksdale. "Civil War Theater: The Richmond Stage." *Civil War History* 1 (1955): 295-304.

___. "John Hill Hewitt Collection." *South Atlantic Bulletin* 13 (March 1948): 3-5.

Hatch, James V., ed. *Black Theater, U.S.A.: 45 Plays by Black Americans*. New York: Free Press, 1974.

Hatch, James V., and Omarii Abdullah. *Black Playwrights, 1823-1977: An Annotated Bibliography of Plays*. New York: Bowker, 1977.

Heilman, Robert. "Dramas of Money." *Shenandoah* 21 (Summer 1970): 20-33.

Hobson, Fred. *Serpent in Eden: H.L. Mencken and the South*. Chapel Hill: Univ. of North Carolina Press, 1974.

Hoogerwerf, Frank W. *John Hill Hewitt: Sources and Bibliography*. Atlanta, Ga.: Emory Univ., 1981.

Hoole, W. Stanley. *The Ante-bellum Charleston Theatre*. Tuscaloosa: Univ. of Alabama Press, 1946.

Hubbell, Jay B. *The South in American Literature*. Durham, N.C.: Duke University Press, 1954.

Hurley, Daniel F. "Down in the Valley, the Valley So Low." *Appalachian Journal* 16 (1988): 52-55.

Ilacqua, Alma A. "Paul Green—In Memoriam: A Bibliography and Profile." *Southern Quarterly* 20 (Spring 1982): 76-87.

Kendall, John S. *The Golden Age of the New Orleans Theatre*. Baton Rouge: Louisiana State Univ. Press, 1952.

Kenny, Vincent S. *Paul Green*. New York: Twayne, 1971.

Kerlin, Robert T. "A Poet from Bardstown [Joseph Seamon Cotter]." *South Atlantic Quarterly* 20 (1921): 213-21.

Kullman, Colby H., and Miriam Neuringer. "Beth Henley." In *American Playwrights since 1945: A Guide to Scholarship, Criticism, and Performance*, ed. Philip C. Kolin. Westport, Conn.: Greenwood, 1989.

Lederer, Katherine. *Lillian Hellman*. Boston: Twayne, 1979.

Leverich, Lyle. *Tom: The Unknown Tennessee Williams*. New York: Crown, 1995.

Long, E. Hudson. *American Drama from Its Beginnings to the Present*. New York: Appleton-Century-Crofts, 1970.

Ludlow, Noah. *Dramatic Life as I Found It* (1880). Rpt. New York: Benjamin Blom, 1966.

May, Hal, and Susan M. Trosky. *Contemporary Authors* [Willis Richardson; Randolph Edmonds]. Vols. 124-25. Detroit: Gale Research, 1988-89.

McClure, Charlotte S. "Preston Jones." In *American Playwrights since 1945*, ed. Philip C. Kolin. Westport, Conn.: Greenwood, 1988.

McDonnell, Lisa J. "Diverse Similitude: Beth Henley and Marsha Norman." *Southern Quarterly* 25 (Spring 1987): 95-104.

———. "Beth Henley." In *Contemporary Dramatists*. Chicago: St. James, 1988.

Meserve, Walter. *American Drama to 1900: A Guide to Information Sources*. Detroit: Gale Research, 1980.

___. *An Emerging Entertainment: The Drama of the American People to 1828*. Bloomington: Indiana Univ. Press. 1977.

___. *Heralds of Promise: The Drama of the American People during the Age of Jackson, 1829-1849*. Westport, Conn.: Greenwood, 1986.

Moe, Christian H. *Contemporary Dramatists*. Chicago: St. James Press, 1988.

Nelligan, Murray. "American Nationalism on the Stage: The Plays of George Washington Parke Custis (1781-1857)." *Virginia Magazine of History and Biography* 58 (1950): 299-324.

Nelson, Benjamin. *Tennessee Williams: The Man and His Work*. New York: Ivan Obolensky, 1961.

Nolan, Paul T., ed. *Provincial Drama in America, 1870-1916: A Casebook of Primary Materials*. Metuchen, N.J.: Scarecrow, 1967.

O'Daniel, Therman B. *Langston Hughes, Black Genius: A Critical Evaluation*. New York: William Morrow, 1971.

Page, James A. *Selected Black American Authors*. Boston: G.K. Hall, 1977.

Peterson, Bernard L., Jr. *Contemporary Black American Playwrights and Their Plays: A Biographical Directory and Dramatic Index*. Westport, Conn.: Greenwood, 1988.

___. *Early Black American Playwrights and Dramatic Writers*. Westport, Conn.: Greenwood Press, 1990.

___. "Willis Richardson: Pioneer Playwright." *Black World*, 1975. Rpt. in *The Theater of Black Americans*, ed. Errol Hill. New York: Applause, 1987.

Phillips, Gene D. *The Films of Tennessee Williams*. London: Associated University Presses, 1980.

Quinn, Arthur Hobson. *A History of the American Drama from the Beginning to the Civil War*. 1923; rpt. New York: Appleton-Century-Crofts, 1943.

___. *A History of the American Drama from the Civil War to the Present*. New York: Harper, 1927.

Rankin, Hugh S. *The Theater in Colonial America*. Chapel Hill: Univ. of North Carolina Press, 1965.

Richardson, Gary A. *American Drama from the Colonial Period through World War I: A Critical History*. New York: Twayne, 1993.

Rollyson, Carl. *Lillian Hellman: Her Legend and Her Legacy*. New York: St. Martin's, 1988.

Roppolo, Joseph Patrick. "Uncle Tom in New Orleans: Three Lost Plays." *New England Quarterly* 27 (1954): 213-26.

Rubin, Louis D., Jr., et al. *The History of Southern Literature*. Baton Rouge: Louisiana State Univ. Press, 1985.

Rush, Theresa Gunnels, et al., eds. *Black American Writers Past and Present.* Metuchen, N.J.: Scarecrow, 1975.

Sanders, Leslie Catherine. *The Development of Black Theater in America.* Baton Rouge: Louisiana State Univ. Press, 1988.

Sherman, Susanne K. "Thomas Wade West, Theatrical Impresario, 1790-1799." *William and Mary Quarterly,* 3d ser. 9 (Jan. 1952): 10-28.

Shockley, Martin Staples. *The Richmond Stage, 1784-1812.* Charlottesville: Univ. Press of Virginia, 1977.

Shulim, Joseph I. "John Daly Burk: Irish Revolutionist and American Patriot." *Transactions of the American Philosophical Society,* n.s. 54, pt. 6 (1964): 1-60.

Slavick, William H. *DuBose Heyward.* Boston: Twayne, 1981.

Smeltsor, Marjorie. "'The World's an Orphan's Home': Horton Foote's Social and Moral History." *Southern Quarterly* 29 (Winter 1991): 7-16.

Smith, Sol. *Theatrical Management in the West and South for Thirty Years* (1868). Rpt. New York: Benjamin Blom, 1968.

Smither, Nelle. *A History of the English Theatre in New Orleans* (1944). Rpt. New York: Benjamin Blom, 1967.

Spoto, Donald. *The Kindness of Strangers: The Life of Tennessee Williams.* Boston: Little, Brown, 1985.

Stephenson, Shelly. "Folk Imagination and Music in Paul Green's Early Drama." *North Carolina Historical Review* 60 (April 1983): 193-204.

Tharpe, Jac, ed. *Tennessee Williams: A Tribute.* Jackson: Univ. Press of Mississippi, 1977.

Tischler, Nancy M. *Tennessee Williams: Rebellious Puritan.* New York: Citadel, 1961.

Thompson, Judith J. *Tennessee Williams' Plays: Memory, Myth, and Symbol.* New York: Peter Lang, 1989.

Turner, Darwin. "Loften Mitchell." In *Contemporary Dramatists,* ed. James Vinson. London: Macmillan, 1982.

Waal, Carla. "The First Original Confederate Drama: *The Guerillas.*" *Virginia Magazine of History and Biography* 70 (1962): 459-67.

Watson, Charles S. *Antebellum Charleston Dramatists.* Tuscaloosa: Univ. of Alabama Press, 1976.

___. "Beyond the Commercial Media: Horton Foote's Procession of Defeated Men." *Studies in American Drama, 1945-Present* 8, no. 2 (1993): 175-87.

___. "Confederate Drama: The Plays of John Hill Hewitt and James Dabney McCabe." *Southern Literary Journal* 21 (Spring 1989): 100-12.

___. "Early Drama in New Orleans: The French Tradition." *Journal of American Drama and Theatre* 2 (Spring 1990): 11-26.

___. "Early Southern Dramatists: An Introduction and a Checklist of Their Plays." *Mississippi Quarterly* 43 (Winter 1989-90): 45-58.

___. "Early Theater." In *Encyclopedia of Southern Culture,* ed. Charles Reagan Wilson and William Ferris, pp. 871-72. Chapel Hill: Univ. of North Carolina Press, 1989.

___. "Eighteenth and Nineteenth Century Drama." In *A Bibliographical Guide to the Study of Southern Literature,* ed. Louis D. Rubin Jr., pp. 92-99. Baton Rouge: Louisiana State Univ. Press, 1969.

___. "The First Modern Dramatist of the South: Espy Williams." *Southern Quarterly* 27 (Winter 1989): 77-92.

___. "The Revision of *The Glass Menagerie:* The Passing of Good Manners." In *Tennessee Williams's The Glass Menagerie: Modern Critical Interpretations,* ed. Harold Bloom. New York: Chelsea House, 1987.

Weales, Gerald. *American Drama since World War I.* New York: Harcourt, Brace & World, 1962.

___. "American Theatre Watch, 1980-1981." *Georgia Review* 35 (Fall 1981): 598-99.

Willis, Eola. *The Charleston Stage in the XVIII Century.* Columbia: State Co., 1924.

Wilmeth, Don B. "An Interview with Romulus Linney." *Studies in American Drama, 1945-Present* 2 (1987): 71-84.

___. "Romulus Linney." In *American Dramatists since 1945: A Guide to Scholarship, Criticism, and Performance,* ed. Philip C. Kolin. Westport, Conn.: Greenwood, 1989.

Wilson, Charles Reagan, and William Ferris, eds. *Encyclopedia of Southern Culture.* Chapel Hill: Univ. of North Carolina Press, 1989.

Wood, Gerald C., and Terry Barr. "'A Certain Kind of Writer': An Interview with Horton Foote." *Literature/Film Quarterly* 14, no. 4 (1986): 226-37.

Wright, William. *Lillian Hellman: The Image, the Woman.* New York: Simon & Schuster, 1986.

Zola, Gary Phillip. *Isaac Harby of Charleston, 1788-1828: Jewish Reformer and Intellectual.* Tuscaloosa: Univ. of Alabama Press, 1994.

Index